Lisa Appignanesi was born in Poland, grew up in France and Canada, and lives in London. A novelist and writer, she is Visiting Professor of Literature and the Medical Humanities at King's College London, Chair of the Freud Museum, and former President of English PEN. She was awarded an OBE for services to literature in 2013. She is the author of *Mad, Bad and Sad*, *All About Love* and *Losing the Dead*.

TRIALS OF PASSION

Crimes in the Name of Love and Madness

LISA APPIGNANESI

virago

VIRAGO

First published in Great Britain in 2014 by Virago Press

Copyright © Lisa Appignanesi 2014

The moral right of the author has been asserted.

Image credits:
Endpapers: The Vitriol Thrower, 1894 (colour litho), Grasset, Eugene (1841–1917)/
The Higgins Art Gallery & Museum, Bedford, UK/The Bridgeman Art Library
Part One: The Female Airing Court, Broadmoor Asylum
Part Two: Getty Images
Part Three: Evelyn Nesbit – Mary Evans/Library of Congress;
Harry Thaw – Mary Evans/Everett Collection

A CIP catalogue record for this book
is available from the British Library.

Hardback ISBN 978-1-84408-874-4
C-format ISBN 978-0-3490-0481-5

Typeset in Spectrum by M Rules
Printed and bound in Great Britain by
Clays Ltd, St Ives plc

Papers used by Virago are from well-managed forests
and other responsible sources.

MIX
Paper from
responsible sources
FSC
www.fsc.org   FSC® C104740

Virago Press
An imprint of
Little, Brown Book Group
100 Victoria Embankment
London EC4Y 0DY

An Hachette UK Company
www.hachette.co.uk

www.virago.co.uk

For
Suzette Macedo
Adam Phillips
Marina Warner
(friends who always inspire)

Every love story is a potential grief story.

Julian Barnes

I must draw an analogy between the criminal and the hysteric. In both we are concerned with a secret, with something hidden ... In the case of the criminal it is a secret which he knows and hides from you, whereas in the case of the hysteric it is a secret which he himself does not know either, which is hidden even from himself ... The task of the therapist, however, is the same as that of the examining magistrate.

Sigmund Freud

Contents

PART TWO: FRANCE
Virtue on Trial

II. A HYSTERIA OF THE HEART:
THE CASE OF MARIE BIÈRE

III. HYSTERIA, HYPNOSIS AND
CRIMINAL RESPONSIBILITY

IV. NATURALIZING THE
IMPULSIVE FEMININE

PART THREE: THE UNITED STATES
The Paranoia of a Millionaire

V. BRAIN STORM OVER MANHATTAN

Acknowledgements

This book would not have been possible without the individual scholars who have come before me in the many fields this volume dips into: Joel Eigen, Gerald N. Grob, Ruth Harris, Allen Norrie, Roger Smith, Nikolas Rose, Tony Ward, Martin J. Wiener, to name but a few. For the case material and help provided, I thank the National Archives at Kew; Mark Stevens of the Berkshire Record Office which hosts the Broadmoor Archives and whose *Broadmoor Revealed* appeared while I was working on the latter parts of this book; the archivists who guided me through the dossiers of the Préfecture de Paris now held at the Archives de Paris; and the invaluable Kate Elms at the Brighton and Hove Archive. I also owe a debt of gratitude to the many psychiatrists, psychoanalysts and lawyers who have answered my questions along the way, amongst them Estela V. Welldon, Cleo Van Velsen, Frank Farnham, Michael Kopelman, Lisa Conlan, Faisil Sethi, Helena Kennedy and Martha Spurrier.

I am grateful to my editor, Lennie Goodings, and my agent, Clare Alexander, two formidable women, who between them steered me in the direction that eventually became this book. My thanks also to Victoria Pepe, to Zoe Gullen at Virago, and to my fine copy-editor, Sue Phillpott.

As ever, I am also indebted to my now husband John Forrester, who has more facts in his daily repertoire than I can dream of, and my wonderful children Katrina Forrester, Josh Appignanesi and now also Devorah Baum and Jamie Martin, with whom discussion is a constant inspiration.

Passion Goes to Court

This is the story of crimes that grew out of passion, their perpetrators, and the courtroom dramas in which they were enmeshed. It is also the story of how medics who became experts in extreme emotion came to probe and assess the state of mind of these passionate transgressors. The cases in question as well as the experts' views affected justice and left their mark on history. The views were no more gender-blind than justice itself.

When thirty-one-year-old Mary Lamb, not yet co-author of the long-loved *Tales from Shakespeare*, murdered her mother in 1796, her brother Charles told the Coroner's Court she was mad. This resulted in her being sent home into his care and absolved of all responsibility for her crime. Murder was considered to be an act, not an essence marking her out as a naturally born criminal, an aberrant being tainted by degeneracy from birth – as various crime and mind experts might insist a century later. No psychiatric witnesses were called on to investigate Mary's state or to give an opinion in court. The determination of her 'lunacy' was – everyone agreed – visible to a common-sense appraisal by coroner and jury. Sifting what and who was bad from what and who was mad took no expert training. Roman Law enshrined a principle of mitigation for those who were *non compos mentis* – of unsound mind and not in control of their mental faculties. English common law followed suit: law-breakers with a defect of understanding, such as children, or a deficiency of will, such as 'lunatics', could not be held accountable for their acts. Madness was its own worst punishment; Mary Lamb needed no additional one.

In the course of the nineteenth century and into the beginning of the twentieth, such rulings took on the growing complexity we recognize as the norm today. The line between who was mad, who bad, grew more opaque and began to waver. If justice was to be done, an untrained eye could not be trusted to make the judgement. This required the expert opinion of mad-doctors and 'alienists' (the keepers of people whose reason has been 'alienated'), nerve medics and those who by the turn of the century as the profession proliferated had started to become known as 'psychiatrists'. Theirs was an expertise founded on the very passions that sweep reason away, on vagrant emotions and erratic cognitive powers, on manias, delusions, delirium and automatisms. Their knowledge could serve the courts and inform justice, as well as protect society. Disseminated from debates in the courtroom through an ever more popular press, their thinking also subtly changed our view of the human.

A Pandora's box flew open as psychiatric experts and a sensationalizing media probed motivation in a variety of murder and attempted-murder trials. Transgressive sexuality, savage jealousies, rampant forbidden desires, passions gone askew, vulnerable, suggestible, hysterical minds, were revealed to be aspects not only of those 'others' we label mad, but potentially of us all. When humanity dreamt collectively – as Robert Musil noted in *The Man Without Qualities*, his novel about the year that led into the Great War – it dreamt a Moosbrugger, a sadistic pervert, a psychotic murderer who wore an everyday aspect of mild good citizenry, a face 'blessed by God with every sign of goodness'.

Musil had his characters respond to the murderer Moosbrugger in ways that have become common: their gaze idealizes him into an exceptional individual – a sublime beast, a genius, a criminal revolutionary; or it pathologizes him – as a deviant, degenerate, the very 'lust murderer' the Austrian forensic psychiatrist Richard von Krafft-Ebing examined in his *Psychopathia Sexualis* of 1886. But Moosbrugger is also an ordinary man who inhabits a historical moment and a particular set of circumstances that propel him into the murder of prostitutes. If he had been a woman – as many of the passionate criminals in what follows are – not only his choice of murderee but also the diagnosis he received and society's response would have been quite different. So too might the court's verdict. It may aspire to be, but justice is rarely blind to its time's expectations of gender.

This book journeys into the heart of dark passions, feminine and masculine, the crimes they impel, and their trial by daylight and doctors in the courts of justice and in the larger public arena of the press between 1870, the date of my first case, and 1914, when war changed so much. It also charts a power struggle that continues today between the law's definitions of insanity and the more complex understandings of the human that the mind specialists promulgate. Where does justice lie?

The criminal law envisions a human who is an emphatically rational (male) being, capable of knowing his own motives and intentions, of recognizing his freely willed acts and the difference between right and wrong. The humans, often enough female, who stand in the dock rarely live up to this enlightened ideal. They may be of partially 'unsound mind', derailed by passion, in states of disarray or numbed coldness. Trapped in what may be their own delusional system, their criminal act seems to them a (heroic) way of attaining justice, of righting a fundamental wrong, of warding off a greater evil, or of achieving a reparation for some unnameable suffering. Sometimes the expert psychiatric witnesses who speak in their defence seem to understand them as little as the judges. Their form of control or 'therapeutic confinement' is not necessarily any less punitive than the prison.

Though the line between madness and badness becomes increasingly difficult to draw, the authorities all agree that the line is fundamental to any legal system. This was already clear to the English Solicitor General, Charles Yorke, back in 1760 at the height of the Enlightenment when the modern law was being established. The 4th Earl Ferrers was on trial for murder. Known for his heavy drinking, womanizing and violence, this major landowner had killed his estate

steward after the latter had sided with Ferrers' wife during the divorce
proceedings she had instigated on grounds of cruelty. Ferrers' friends
had made him put up a plea of occasional insanity. John Monro, physician to Bethlem Hospital, served as an expert witness, one of the first
to be recorded. In everyday language and based on his observation of
inmates at Bedlam, Monro stated that uncommon fury, jealousy and
suspicion without grounds were common symptoms of insanity. The
Solicitor General summed up astutely:

> My Lords, in some sense every crime proceeds from Insanity. All
> cruelty, all brutality, all revenge, all injustice is Insanity. There were
> philosophers in ancient times who held this opinion as a strict
> maxim of their sect; and my Lords, the opinion is right in philoso-
> phy, but dangerous in judicature. It may have a useful and a noble
> influence to regulate the conduct of men, to control their impotent
> passions, to teach them that virtue is the perfection of reason, as
> reason itself is the perfection of human nature; but not to extenu-
> ate crimes, nor to excuse those punishments which the law
> adjudges to be their due.

Passions out of control, Yorke states, do not equal *legal* insanity. The
bad are bad. Ferrers was hanged, despite his rank. But the uncertainty
about crimes of passion and their relation to madness was hardly
resolved by this early case.

When it was a woman whose passions had led her to crime, the
uncertainty mounted. After all, a woman's hold on reason had long
been thought to be weak: passions, ever dangerous to her mental balance, could so easily topple it. Infanticide, the most prevalent form of
murder by women in the nineteenth century, brought into being an
early and legally accepted link with madness in what continues to be
understood as a post-partum psychosis. This was treated leniently by
the courts and rarely punished by the hanging that other capital
offences incurred. Even today, women's malign passions are often
turned against those helpless infants and children whom they fail to

see as separate from their own bodies and whom they attack in the ways they may attack themselves.

If a woman was being tried for murder and there was no insanity plea, then she could only be either innocent or a monster of depravity. There was little terrain in between. By the mid-nineteenth century, women of the upper classes had become the symbolic keepers of society's virtue, embodiments of a greater, nurturing goodness, of purity and morality. Their crimes of passion – particularly if they were independent women, wives who strayed, or spinsters – thus challenged all received wisdom about femininity. They had transgressed the very boundaries of nature. Press and public peered anxiously and voyeuristically at these objects of shuddering fascination and tried to understand secrets, motives and desires that before our own time rarely faced public exposure. The questioning and reporting of these private passions and inchoate emotions elaborated the ways in which women and their sexuality could be conceived.

The law's tug of war with the psychiatrists on the question of a defendant's 'insanity' intensified with the ambitions of the mind-doctoring professions. The latter expanded the span of their diagnoses and took on the legitimating mantle of scientific medicine. This gradually resulted in a shrinking of what could be considered the area of 'sanity' or 'normality': bad could often be (re)labelled mad, and partial madness could act as mitigation. From early on, the mind doctors had questioned the very basics of criminal responsibility, the meaning and underpinning of '*mens rea*', or a fully conceived conscious intention. They argued about what constituted delusion and volition, about when an impulse could not be resisted and might overwhelm (free) will to become that kind of modern, 'irresistible impulse' that Lorena Bobbit's attorney claimed in 1994 had impelled her to cut off her husband's penis, though she wasn't insane in any long-term cognitive sense.

The mind doctors talked of erotomania, in which passion tipped into madness; or moral insanity in which the person could not recognize wrong, certainly not the wrong that society indicated. In the 1880s they talked of the weak individual being unable to resist hypnotic influences and suggestions towards crime. They cited 'automatisms', or altered states in which the Jekyll and Hyde individual had no awareness of him or herself. At the beginning of the twentieth century they grew more sophisticated and complicated, describing personality disorders, schizophrenia, manic depression, perversions, paranoia and much more. They sometimes thought they could predict danger and calculate the risk of an eruption of violence. Their diagnoses were often gendered, though not absolutely so: erotomania started as largely a woman's diagnosis; more recently, with the rising incidence of stalking, it often crosses the gender divide.

With the Freudian era and a set of mind doctors who moved beyond classificatory descriptions and explanations rooted in heredity onto a terrain where a welter of hidden desires, repressed forces from childhood and murderous impulses propelled the individual, establishing the exact truth in court about guilt and innocence, free will and determinisms, became even more difficult.

Meanwhile, debate in the symbolically charged arena of the court educated the public in new ways of being human.

Trials of Passion is a complement to my last two books. In certain ways, it's the final part of a loose trilogy which began with *Mad, Bad and Sad* — a book that traced the rise of the mind-doctoring professions over the last two hundred years in their interplay with women. In that history, I found that love gone wrong emerged as one of the earliest causes of madness to be cited by the mind doctors. Love appeared high on William Black's table of 1810 listing the factors that had precipitated people into Bethlem. As erotomania it featured prominently in the madness classifications of one of the founding fathers of psychiatry, the French alienist J.-E. D. Esquirol. Contorted desire also wove its way into many of history's female maladies, from hysteria to nymphomania and beyond. For Freud, this was the propulsive force for any number of so-called functional disorders.

In *All About Love*, my anatomy of the unruly emotion that love is, I tried to tease out some of love's malignant as well as what I guess we could call its beneficent trajectories. Over these last decades, we have become singularly aware of the complexities of the emotion inside the family: from sexual abuse to emotional neglect, the too much or too little of 'love', and its attendant consoling or disruptive fantasies, shape the kind of human the child will become. The child's history within the family and its attachments, scientists now generally agree, affects the neurology of the mind, as well as any later so-called personality disorders the adult may suffer from.

Excess lies in the very nature of passion. In love, we become obsessional: only what relates to the beloved and our emotions preoccupies us. Fantasies and daydreams pile in. Thoughts that are inappropriate to a given situation or don't even feel like our own flood our minds. We grow akin to stalkers and pursue the object of our passions. Inflated by love, the pursuer feels grandiose, omnipotent, larger than him/herself. There is an assumption that the other is responsive to our passion. Love (and sex) has made us permeable, so that we can no longer feel our own borders, determine where we end and the other begins — just like when we were babes at breast. If rejected, we grow smaller than Alice through her looking-glass. Jealousy can then leap up and derail. So can hatred, passion's frequent shadow — particularly if the beloved then leaves us for good and we are cast into despair, become less than ourselves. Accepting the reality of loss can be a slow, painful and dismantling experience. Grief lies in wait for many loves, and the mourning over separation — just like that for the ultimate separation that death is — can tumble into melancholy.

Exactly where all of this too common experience shades into madness — or a score of more recent, itemized, psychiatric diagnoses — is a moveable feast. Romantic love, with its underlying carnal core in the notion that two beings will fuse and *merge* into one, can be a dangerous pursuit, even if for centuries it was backed up by the domestic fact of Christian marriage which annihilated a wife's independent legal identity. When two fuse into one, any later attempt at separation can entail a perilous tearing-away from the merged identity: the 'betrayed' lover feels dismantled, literally torn apart. She or he may be filled with disbelief and refuse the separating-out, or feel attacked and seek revenge. Murder of the other can sometimes, to the perpetrator, feel like a killing-off of a hated part of oneself, so closely have two become one.

Where the tipping or breaking point comes that precipitates a crime or triggers an existing psychosis (or set of delusions) into violence is hardly an exact and generalizable science. Individuals, including those that break and go mad and bad, are all different. So are definitions of crime: the horror of domestic violence has only become a crime late in the last century in the West. We have made the oddly named paedophilia – or love of children – a crime, while extending the legal period of childhood well beyond the moment when most young people have experiences they themselves call sexual.

Romantic love with its passionate core, its excess of longing, its necessary illusions, its idolization of the beloved, also slips easily into versions of erotomania: in the 1920s Gaëtan Gatian de Clérambault's erotomaniacs dreamt of distant, high-status affairs paralleling all phases of a 'real' romance, until illusion tumbled into delusion and a delirium of violence. Others, like intimate stalkers, misread cues, fell in love, imagined betrayal and sought revenge. Where the 'madness' of love erupts into crime and whether medico-legal definitions of insanity can then prevail are what this book investigates.

Because comparisons between societies, their legal and medical systems and understandings of justice help to illuminate what goes on in each, the following pages take us first to Britain, then to France and America. In each I have chosen a widely reported trial of passion – not in any way simply to do with sexual predation or perversion – to focus on, though other trials important to the doctors and for the cultural shifts they helped to provoke, cluster round. The first two major trials are of women who murdered, or attempted to. The third is that of a man. It seemed to me that since men and women are not deranged by love in altogether parallel ways, it would be interesting to chart some of the different paths each have taken.

The principal histories I've chosen are not the all too common domestic crimes in which violent husbands murder long-abused and allegedly straying wives, or even the more occasional crimes in which the downtrodden wife strikes out and back: violence of this sort was as sadly prevalent in the early history of the mind-doctoring professions as it is now. I have concentrated instead on the less usual crimes: the ones that captured the imagination of their time, provoked a social furore and necessitated the presence of the psychiatrists at some stage. They produced trials through which the mind doctors extended their influence. These were public events that elaborated and broadcast understandings of passion and 'insanity' in its many forms both in and outside the law.

Such uncommon and sensational trials had a marked impact on social debates and arguably on relations between the sexes. In them, women left conventional middle-class passivity behind to become actors: their crimes were calls to freedom in which they became agents of their own fate. In turn, the trials both reflected and generated anxieties about gender. They instigated greater scrutiny of women's condition and interrogated where social restrictions, sexual attitudes, unequal status and sheer injustice propelled crime. One could say these were trials that educated: they probed buried emotions, hidden sexual relations, and sometimes a larger, more generalized injustice that had erupted into crime.

At the time this book begins, in 1870, the divisions between the public and the private, to say nothing of the secret sphere, were far more rigid than they are today. Outside fiction and poetry, the emotions and the inner life of the individual, let alone sex, were rarely discussed. Criminal trials – in which lawyers pleaded on behalf of deranged lovers, while mind doctors gave an opinion on insanity and extreme emotion and journalists engaged in commentary and elaboration – dared people to think the unthinkable. They marked one of the new public arenas where the passions, the perversions, the sexually permissible and the attributes of the feminine were examined.

Between my first case and my last, the mind doctors had grown their influence and understanding and had become regular assessors of mental states, as well as expert witnesses. In many countries, the earliest being Germany, Austria and France, they worked as forensic psychiatrists within the apparatus of the law. A modern era of collaboration had been ushered in.

PART ONE: BRITAIN

THE UNSPOKEN

'A free woman in an unfree society will be a monster.'

Angela Carter

BROADMOOR ASYLUM.

I

Christiana Edmunds and the Chocolate Cream Murders

1. *The Borgia of Brighton*

On Wednesday 16 August 1871, a notice was posted by order of the Chief Constable of the Brighton police:

BOROUGH OF BRIGHTON
£20 REWARD
Whereas some evil-disposed person has lately sent
to different families in Brighton, parcels of fruit cakes and sweets,
which have been found to contain poison, the particulars of two
of which cases are stated at the foot hereof, notice is hereby given
that whoever will give such information to the undersigned as
shall lead to the apprehension and conviction of the
offender will be paid a reward of twenty pounds.

The bottom of the notice, printed in full in the *Brighton and Hove Gazette* the following Thursday, gave detailed descriptions of the boxes of 'white deal' (pine) in which the poisoned delicacies had been sent, carriage fully paid from London Victoria rail station to 'different persons in Brighton'. Each of the boxes contained a variety of preserved fruits, nuts, sweetmeats and cakes, some of which were separately wrapped. The outer wrapping paper carried a message: 'A few home-made cakes for the children, those done up are flavoured on purpose for yourself to enjoy. You will guess who this is from, I can't mystify you I fear. I hope this will arrive in time for you to-night while the eatables are fresh.' Another note, the police stated, was much the same, except it was signed 'G.M.'.

The message-wrapped delicacies contained the poison.

As rumour spread, something akin to panic gripped the city. Just two months back, on 12 June, a small boy, Sidney Albert Barker, aged four and two months, had died after eating a poisoned chocolate purchased from the well-known confectioner, Maynard of West Street. Everyone, it seemed, knew someone who knew someone who in those spring and summer months had been affected by chocolate creams and sweets. Left in bags in sundry places or purchased direct from Maynard's, these chocolates had produced stinging throats, nausea, diarrhoea and high temperature – all signs of 'irritant poison'.

Food scares were hardly rare in Victorian Britain. In 1862, the Privy Council had estimated that one-fifth of all butcher's meat came from diseased animals. Ice cream, or 'hokey-pokey', might contain anything from lice to bedbugs and any number of bacilli. Copper was used to heighten the colour of butter, bread and gin. Other treacherous additives adulterated everything from milk to mustard, wine and preserves, while arsenic dyes saturated wallpapers, curtains, upholstery and carpets. Indeed, arsenic use was widespread, and until the 1851 Arsenic Act, which required purchasers to sign a poison register, it was also freely available. Women used it in cosmetic preparations, to clean their bonnets or treat the 'itch' – STDs. Tobacco and food might well come wrapped in arsenic-tinted paper. Men, like the twenty-seven-year-old American Mrs Maybrick's fifty-year-old husband, used it as an aphrodisiac, a fact that didn't prevent her being convicted of his murder by poison in 1889, largely because she had all but confessed to adultery.

Hard chocolate, a novelty at the time, was still something of an upmarket and coveted delicacy. To find it becoming the bearer of poison gave it an emphatically sinister edge. Who could be responsible for the creation of these toxic sweets and their malicious diffusion?

The June inquest on little Sidney Barker had found against neither the chocolate-maker nor Maynard's the purveyor, despite clear testimony that his sweets were on occasion poisonous. Sidney had died from the effects of strychnine. Several letter-writing Brightonians – one of them signing himself a 'seeker after justice', while expressing condolences – had urged the boy's father to pursue legal proceedings against Mr Maynard. This hadn't happened.

Now came a new orchestrated wave of poisonings. It transpired that all the toxic sweet boxes referred to in the police notice had found their way to the homes of prominent Brighton citizens: Mrs Emily Beard, wife of Dr Charles Izard Beard of 64 Grand Parade; their neighbours Mr and Mrs Boys – who lived just a few numbers down on this elegant tree-lined avenue, a mere canter from the India-inspired exoticism of the domed Royal Pavilion where George IV, while Prince of Wales, had cavorted with his beloved Mrs Fitzherbert; Mr William Curtis, proprietor of the *Brighton Gazette*, the city's self-proclaimed 'fashionable and conservative chronicle'; Mr G. Tatham, a borough justice; and the chemist, Isaac Garrett of Queen's Road.

Chief Constable George White asked Inspector Gibbs to investigate. He had been in charge of the Sidney Barker case. Inspector Gibbs was alerted by the doctor treating Mrs Beard's servant, taken severely ill after eating some of the wrapped teacup-shaped plum cake her mistress had abstained from, that he had also been called to the side of one Christiana Edmunds. She too had received a poisoned gift box and was unwell. Inspector Gibbs was already acquainted with Miss Edmunds. She had come forward to testify at the inquest into little Sidney Barker's death, since she had been affected early on, it seemed, by the plague of poisonings. She had told the coroner then that on two separate occasions the chocolate creams she had purchased from Maynard's had produced a burning in her throat and made her ill. She had sent the chocolates to a chemist for examination: a report had come back saying they were 'strongly impregnated with zinc in combination with a vegetable or organic acid'.

Christiana Edmunds lodged with her mother at 16 Gloucester Place, just a few steps north and across the wide avenue from Grand Parade. Like its neighbours, this was a lofty, elegant residence, though their rented rooms were perhaps not quite what the women had been used to while Christiana's father, one of Margate's leading architects, had been alive. Giving her age as thirty-five, Christiana was single, self-possessed, fair, above average height and well dressed – as the press later commented. When Inspector Gibbs arrived at Gloucester Place on the afternoon of Sunday 13 August, Miss Edmunds was reclining on a sofa.

'Here I am again, Mr Gibbs, nearly poisoned.' She addressed him without rising from the couch. 'You have heard that I have had a box sent to me with some fruit in it.' The Inspector presumably nodded and pressed her a little, for Miss Edmunds went on: 'It came on Thursday evening, about half-past 7 by post; it is evidently from some one in the town, for it bears only the Brighton postmark, and it is evident that it is no one acquainted with me, or they would have known my address and known how to spell my name properly.'

In response to Gibbs's further questioning, Miss Edmunds told him the green box she had received contained some strawberries, two apricots and a pair of new gloves. Her mother had eaten the strawberries and was fine. 'I ate one apricot and that was all right, but the next was very bitter and I spat it all out, and have been ill ever since.' Evidently worrying about another burst of poisonings, she asked Gibbs whether it was true that other boxes had been received. She had heard that Mrs Beard had had one. Gibbs told her of the other parcels. 'How very strange!' Christiana Edmunds mused, 'I feel certain that you'll never find it out.'

But Inspector Gibbs was a shrewd and experienced detective. He also had a stroke of luck. Dr Charles Beard came to see him with a host of suspicions of his own. Beard was fairly certain that this was not the first time his wife had been subject to poisoning or attempted poisoning. He had let it pass before, since he had had no proof. But now, he could no longer contain his worries, whatever the personal risk to his reputation.

Charles Beard, an active and enterprising doctor, was one of three sons (one of whom now lived in Italy) of a propertied Brighton family. He had gone up to Trinity College, Cambridge, at the age of nineteen in 1846, taken a BA and then embarked on a medical degree at St Bartholomew's Hospital in London. A respected member of the Royal College of Physicians, Beard also had a more adventurous side. In 1860 he had joined the British volunteers who went to the aid of the Italian revolutionary Garibaldi and his *Mille*, or One Thousand, in the great and greatly romantic campaign – covertly supported by Britain – to liberate Sicily from Neapolitan rule and eventually unify Italy. The same year, Beard married Emily Izard, probably a cousin, the wife who was to bear him four children. A year later, they were living at 64 Grand Parade and Charles was building up a practice amongst the affluent of Brighton, as well as serving on the staff of the Sussex County Hospital. He would rise to the post of Government Inspector of Vaccination in the West Midlands and Yorkshire.

The story Charles Beard told Inspector Gibbs was not one that was easy for a Victorian gentleman to recount. This was an intimate tale and one that might impugn his respectability. For lack of definitive evidence and probably for fear of the implications it might have on his status, he had put off the telling of it, perhaps for too long. But now, he would brave the courtroom and the inevitable publicity.

Charles Beard was right to worry about his reputation. During this period, and increasingly since the new Court for Divorce and Matrimonial Causes had come into being in 1858, trials had become fodder for the national and local press. The intimacies revealed on the witness stand were often more shocking than what appeared in the pages of novels. The courts, as reported in the legal columns, had become one of the few spaces in Victorian Britain where the private sphere openly met the public. Under the interrogation of magistrates, the secret passions of both ladies and gentlemen stood to be exposed – often enough, verbatim – in the pages of the next day's newspapers. Veils were lifted on desires and types of relationships that had formerly remained unspoken and unscrutinized.

Christiana Edmunds had for about five years been both a patient of Dr Beard's and a friend – of his wife's as well, he stressed. Since 1869, she had also been writing him long and amorous letters, as often as two or three times a week. Sometimes more. She was, in short, in love with him. Whether he had encouraged a romantic liaison or whether any physical intimacy had taken place remains unclear. He denied the latter, but her letters – some twenty of which he had felt it necessary to destroy, lodging the rest with the court recorder – certainly point to an intimate 'friendship'. It would not be the first time the word had been used to cover over other kinds of intimacy. Whatever its precise nature, it is clear that in Christiana Edmunds's mind this was a uniquely passionate friendship.

In the summer of 1870, Beard had tried to cool the relationship and put a stop to her letters: these came to him at his home address, were forwarded to him, or even handed to him in the course of a medical visit. 'This correspondence must cease, it is no good for either of us,' he purportedly told her. Christiana didn't or couldn't see it that way. Meanwhile Beard's unsuspecting wife continued to welcome Christiana and her mother into the family home, often when Charles was away travelling.

Then in September 1870 everything changed. Christiana was making an evening visit to Emily Beard, who was with an old, deaf and ailing house guest, a Mrs Richardson. On the point of leaving, Christiana brought out some chocolates which she said were intended for the Beards' sleeping children. Abruptly, and with a gesture impelled by an uncustomary violence, she forced one of these sweets into Emily's mouth, then rushed off.

In the accounts, the suddenness of this gesture – as if it were propelled by an explosion from within – is reminiscent of other reports of unexpected violence by individuals living out a delusional fantasy.

Christiana may have been in the grip of a familiar erotic scenario. Charles had said her letters to him must stop, inevitably suggesting or using the existence of his wife as an excuse. In Christiana's mind, getting rid of the obstacle that was Emily thus became the logical solution to what Charles too wanted: he was as much in love with her, she imagined, as she with him. Her sudden violence, with no prior identifiable provocation from Emily herself, suggests that a propulsive inner narrative directed her action: she was acting, possibly in a state of delirium, for the couple-in-love that she and Charles were in her fantasy.

Christiana's chocolate cream, Emily told Charles when he returned home from one of his work trips, had had a cold metallic taste. She had spat out what she could of it. All night long, saliva had run from her mouth. She had felt very unwell and suffered from diarrhoea.

Late in September, Charles paid a visit to Christiana at her house. In a veiled and joking manner he alluded to his wife's illness after eating the chocolate Christiana had given her. He also mentioned the very precise use to which the new instrument, the spectroscope, could now be put in detecting poison in animal tissue. Christiana's response to his insinuation that she had poisoned Emily was emphatic. She denied any mischievous intent. She herself, she insisted, had been ill after eating chocolates from Maynard's.

It was shortly after this that Charles Beard told his wife about the many letters Christiana had sent him. Whether he told her anything more about the nature of their relationship remains unclear in the court record. He was not, after all, on trial, and despite the prodding of advocates, Victorians were still notoriously reticent about spelling out in public what went on in private. The question had even arisen of whether the new Court for Divorce and Matrimonial Causes should bar its often immodest proceedings from the press, since some maintained that, printed in full, the reports damaged public morality and could be thought to contravene the Obscene Publications Act. In any event, Beard didn't see Christiana again until after the New Year. He was preoccupied, he said, with work and travel – and perhaps with contemplating a move away from Brighton. When they finally met in January 1871, Christiana made it clear that she wanted to return to their old intimacy. He told her that was impossible: he just couldn't shed the suspicion that she had made some kind of attempt to poison his wife. At the direct accusation, Christiana waxed indignant. Hadn't she been poisoned too? she declared again.

She may well have believed it. Disavowal, a splitting-off of what one doesn't want to know about the self, is not an unusual psychic manoeuvre.

The following day Christiana went to Dr Beard's house with her mother. Mrs Edmunds later testified that her daughter had absolutely insisted on the visit. Both women expostulated with Dr Beard and reprimanded him strongly. His insinuations were slanderous. There may have been no absolute threat, but Beard was left with the certainty that if he didn't want to face a slander suit, one which he could ill counter given that there was no positive evidence to hand, he would have to retract his accusation of poisoning. He ended his meeting with the Edmunds women by laughing the matter off and putting his suspicions to one side.

Beard's attempt to cool relations with Christiana showed little sign of working. She felt his coldness all too 'keenly'. Over spring and summer, as reports of chocolate poisonings around Brighton gathered pace, so too, it seemed, did Beard's anxiety. In a letter postmarked 3 July, Christiana wrote to him of her appearance at young Barker's inquest. The letter is eager to stress that poisoning in Brighton is rampant, that she herself is a victim amongst many others, and that Emily Beard's poisoned chocolate cream all those months back had nothing at all to do with her – he of all people must understand that. Her long letter to this effect would eventually be read out in court.

It is a lover's letter, full of endearments, some, a little mysteriously, in Italian: Christiana may be making common cause with Charles's romantic interest in that country, as well as showing off her sophistication. She makes rather jaunty use of Italian, too, when talking of his wife and her mother, abstracting them into generic roles, 'La Sposa', 'La Madre', as if in private they shared this jocular foreign designation. The tone of the letter is thoroughly flirtatious and intensely familiar. It begins with a suggestion that a lovers' tiff has taken place, that Christiana's own last letter insisting on rupture was an overreaction, and now she is simply too weak to bear what she herself has set in train:

> Caro Mio, – I have been so miserable since my last letter to you. I can't go on without ever speaking to you. What made me write so? I thought perhaps it would be better for both of us, but I have not the strength of mind to bear it.

She goes on to say that she and her mother bumped into Emily, back from travel, in the street. She didn't like to talk about the poisoning case in a public place, so she called on Emily to tell her that she was obliged to appear at the Barker inquest. Christiana wanted her to tell Charles, but his wife had said she didn't want to unsettle him.

> However, dear, I mean you to know about this dreadful poisoning case, especially since I had to give evidence; and I know how interested you would be in it as you told me you would give anything to know what La Sposa swallowed. I sent you the analysis and have no means of knowing whether it was sent you ...

For Christiana, it is crucial that Charles recognize that the town is in the grip of a wave of poisonings of which she is wholly innocent and is herself a victim. The expert chemical report she has called for testifies to that. Only thus can she hope that their relations will be resumed.

After the inquest and what seems to have been for the Beard family a holiday period, Charles saw Christiana at his home for tea on 12 July: he and his wife had agreed that to see her in person would be the kindest way to proceed. He told Christiana that Emily had known about her letters since September last. He stressed again that they really had to stop. 'It wasn't good for either of them.' Christiana expressed great surprise that he should have shown his wife her intimate letters, and so long ago. Writing is a crucial, utterly private expression of her link with 'Caro Mio'.

The second attempt on Mrs Beard's life – by means of one of the several parcels of poisoned sweetmeats – follows in August, not long after Christiana learns that Emily has been made privy to her letters. Betrayal and resistance on the part of the beloved trigger violence in the lover. The violence seems to be carried out in a state of denial, by a part of Christiana that is separated off from her everyday self. Meanwhile, Christiana herself identifies with Emily, the wife she might want to be, the victim of her poisoning act, and can say quite honestly to the police, fully believing what she says, that she, too, has again been a victim of poisoning.

Having given the sweetmeats to her servants, Mrs Beard has had a lucky escape, but only just. One servant has been violently ill, and a second affected as well. All this has at last compelled Charles Beard to take his doubly incriminating, though somewhat expurgated, hoard of letters to the police and air his suspicions about Christiana.

Inspector Gibbs now knows that the parcels received on 10 August have all resulted in poisonings: people have been affected at the Beards', the Boyses', the chemist Mr Garrett's, and the home of the editor of the *Brighton Gazette*. The letters Dr Beard has shown to Gibbs also confirm that Christiana Edmunds's handwriting matches that of the person who had written anonymously complaining to Sidney Barker's father after the inquest into his son's death by chocolate. On Thursday 17 August, Inspector Gibbs apprehends Christiana and remands her in custody. Her response to the charge of the attempted murder of Mrs Beard and attempting to administer poisons with intent to do grievous bodily harm to the other addressees is this: 'Me poison Mrs Beard? Who can say that? I have been nearly poisoned myself.'

Christiana's earlier challenge to Gibbs – whether teasing, taunting or simply sincere – that he would 'never find it out' had underestimated the detective. Then again, after her long and formidably complicated odyssey to win over and win back Dr Beard, she may well unwittingly have wanted to be caught. Her poisoning ploys certainly involved her in sailing very close to the police. It would be for the magistrates and then the criminal court – with a little help from the mind doctors – to determine whether Christiana was an innocent wrongly accused; or a promiscuous, evil and jilted femme fatale inspired by the heroines of the sensational novels of her day such as Lady Audley or Lydia Gwilt – women willing to go to any lengths to get their man; or a poor benighted spinster whose mind was irretrievably addled, and had been so from birth. None imagined – or not openly and publicly, at least – that she might be all three: a woman in love whose passion had edged her into madness – an erotomania that insisted her love was returned – and attempted to create, however deviously and arrogantly, the conditions that would enable fantasy to become real.

2. The Hearing

Although it was only a middle-sized town, Brighton at that time had a cosmopolitan flavour. By choosing it as his 'health-giving' seaside retreat in the mid-1780s and buying a farm there, gradually to be transformed into the mammoth Royal Pavilion, the Prince of Wales and his entourage had helped to turn a small fishing village into a resplendent resort – one graced with well-designed squares built by leading architects. Artisans of all descriptions flocked there through the late eighteenth century and the nineteenth. So too did the new professionals, a chic bohemia and high society. During the various wars they were joined by continental aristocrats and other refugees. The Chain Pier, painted by both Constable and Turner, then the West Pier and high-wheeled, canvas-covered bathing machines lined the long beach. These latter, complete with steps and shielding umbrellas, permitted ladies to be discreetly dunked into the waters.

When the railway came in 1841, closing the distance between Brighton and the capital, it grew into a favoured pleasure resort for the new tourists. Queen Victoria may have found the town, and particularly the Pavilion, a little extravagant and over-indulgent for her tastes – and sold the latter back to the city in 1851 – but Brighton continued to grow. In 1871 the *Brighton Gazette*, a sophisticated paper interested in foreign news, the condition of women and John Stuart Mill as well as the comings and goings of lords, ladies and notables, remarked that the Franco-Prussian war and the terrors of the Commune had brought more visitors than ever to the 'hospitable refuge of Old England': 'many of the wealthier have made the watering places, Brighton in particular, their abode, engaging first class residences until Christmas'.

But neither events abroad, for all their tragic dimensions, nor John

Stuart Mill's thoughts on the subjection of women could command as many column inches or special editions of the *Gazette* as the proceedings against the alleged Borgia of Brighton. She herself certainly read the paper. Whatever her thoughts on Mill or on the sexual politics of her own situation, Christiana seemed to disapprove of some of the paper's coverage: she had, after all, targeted its publisher with one of her poison parcels.

Poisoning, particularly when the poisoner was a woman, was a crime beloved of the Victorian press. As one judge commented in mid-century, it was a crime of 'strange and horrible frequency'. He was referring in particular to its use by wives against husbands. Since poison could easily be cloaked in food and drink, and since its impact could be slow and steady, it was a means of murder amenable to use by women. Indeed, in the course of the century, poisoning acquired a particularly feminine stamp, certainly in the press. Fifty-five per cent of women who went to trial for killing their husbands, as opposed to five per cent of men who killed their wives, employed poison. Although the absolute numbers were far smaller than murders by men, the fear was about that many silent, secretive killings had in fact been carried out by vengeful wives, with no one any the wiser. A sinister threat to the marital and sexual order, poisoning was deemed a particularly unnatural form of murder: the dangerous, witch-like women who turned to it for their desperate crimes were considered singularly monstrous.

On 18 August 1871, Christiana Edmunds faced a hearing presided over by several magistrates, led by Deputy Stipendiary Magistrate F. Merrifield, as well as Brighton's mayor. Her defence attorney was Mr Charles Lamb. The prosecution was conducted by a Mr Stuckey. Depositions were made by Emily Beard, who recounted the two attempts on her life; Dr Charles Beard, who spoke of his and his wife's relations with Christiana and read out the letter she had sent him about the inquest; their servants, who corroborated the effects on them of the poison cake; and the surgeon who had examined the servants. He stated that he fully believed arsenic would produce the

violent stomach pains and retching that had been suffered. There
were other witnesses as well, all of whom built up an evidential trail
that led only to Christiana.

The chemist Isaac Garrett of Queen's Road made a crucial deposition. He had been one of the recipients of a parcel from London – in
his case one that contained two toxic peaches, and half a sovereign
wrapped in a note stating: 'The last of my debt and the first of the
peaches from my garden'. The brief letters Garrett read out in court
helped to explain this unsigned message. These letters had been delivered to him by three different lads, the first on 8 June, four days before
the child Sidney Barker's death by chocolate creams; the second
around 14 July, and the final one on the 19th – a few days after Charles
Beard and Christiana Edmunds had met and the occasion on which he
had attempted to sever all relations with her for the second time.

Two of the letters purported to be from a neighbouring North
Street chemists, Messrs Glaisyer and Kemp. The first asked for half an
ounce, or less if that quantity wasn't available, of 'strychnia', sealed up
in a bottle. Garrett sent the messenger back with a note saying he
could only supply a 'drahm'. A letter containing half-a-crown duly
came back saying that that would do for the time being until their
own supply arrived – 'their signature always being sufficient before in
their business transactions. Should Mr Garrett feel the least hesitation
in supplying them, they must apply elsewhere.' Evidently the signatory, even if not Messrs Glaisyer and Kemp of North Street, knew
that an act of 1865 had made obtaining poison a transaction that
demanded an authenticated signature. Garrett supplied the strychnia.

Around the 14th another messenger brought a note purportedly
from the borough coroner, one D. Black, saying he would be obliged
if Garrett could lend him the book in which he registered the poison
drugs he sold. It wasn't that he suspected any irregularity, but only to
help him in his investigation. Garrett complied and within half an
hour the book was returned, though as he noticed only later, several
of its pages relating to a period six months earlier were missing. The
final missive to Garrett came once more purportedly from Glaisyer

and Kemp, this time containing a shilling and asking for two or three ounces of arsenic. He was now suspicious and didn't send it. Instead he contacted the chemists directly, who told him they knew nothing of this or the prior transaction. It was then that Garrett informed the police that something was awry.

The deposition of the second chemist, Mr Glaisyer, confirmed Garrett's account.

Called once more by the prosecutor, Inspector Gibbs said that after hearing from Garrett he had on 26 July, and on a hunch, written to the woman known to him from the inquest as Christiana Edmunds. She had responded saying that she had bought her last chocolate creams from Maynard's on 10 March and she had immediately sent them to be analysed. It was this letter that provided a sample of Christiana's writing under her own name for the police. The writing matched the anonymous notes sent to Albert Barker, Sidney's father, urging him to pursue Maynard and have him held responsible for his son's death.

Christiana's advocate, Mr Lamb, protested. A handwriting expert needed to be called. The magistrate agreed. The long first day in court drew to a close and despite Lamb's best efforts, bail was denied. Christiana Edmunds was remanded in custody until Thursday 24 August. In the meantime, vomit was sent for analysis to the presiding expert, Dr Letherby. A second police notice was posted offering a reward of £6 to each of the three messenger boys who had carried notes to Garrett's.

On Thursday, 24 August a large and unusually feminine and affluent public crammed into Brighton's new courthouse well before pro-ceedings started. Completed in 1869, this ample red-brick structure trimmed with stone and wearing a royal coat of arms over its west entrance on the corner of Church Street, conveniently close to Grand Parade, proved too small for the excitement the case had generated. Many were turned away and had to settle for the numerous press accounts that appeared in papers across the nation.

The hearing began shortly after eleven. According to the *Daily*

News's account, 'The accused sat in a corner of the ordinary prisoner's dock, being attired in a black silk dress, black lace shawl and black bonnet with veil.' Christiana's demeanour was throughout 'quiet and self-possessed; but she occasionally glanced round the court with evident interest in the scene'. Other papers describe her with a pencil in her hand, methodically making notes; or looking about her like a diva and acknowledging acquaintances. *The Times* has her fair, well dressed and self-possessed and 'smiling as descriptions were given of the pains taken to trace the band administering the poisons'.

Like some observer of her own fate, Christiana seems to be enjoying the excitement she has generated around her. At least on the surface, she seems indifferent to the hearing's possible outcome. Her dramatic black may be a signal of modesty or of mourning: she was a woman who cared about clothes and the significances of appearance. It is tempting to see in her choice of dress an echo of Wilkie Collins's fatally seductive heroine in *Armadale*, the poisoning and poisonous Lydia Gwilt, who hides her powers behind the ladylike garb of 'a thick black veil, a black bonnet, and a black silk dress'. Christiana's assiduous note-taking is also much reported: she is evidently an educated woman and one for whom writing counts. The fact that Charles Beard held on to her letters for so long before destroying some and handing others over to the police may also suggest that these letters carried some kind of resonance for him – as they patently did for her. It is interesting to note that unstoppable writing seems to play a crucial part in many of these excessive and dangerous love stories – from Christiana's to our own contemporary 'stalkers'.

The proceedings begin with Mr Stuckey for the prosecution stating that he has a great mass of evidence to lay before the court and he will then ask for a further remand.

Mr Lamb objects, saying the court must confine itself strictly to the charge: the alleged attempt to poison Mrs Beard by means of arsenic. The chief magistrate agrees, but adds that attempts to obtain strychnine may also be relevant to the charge.

Witnesses appear: the Beards' cook testifies that the cake that came in a parcel from London had made her very sick; Mrs Cole, a greengrocer's wife, states she saw Christiana with Adam May, the eleven-year-old who then identifies Christiana as the woman who asked him to take a message to Garrett's the chemist. Having read it, Mr Garrett gave him a book which he took to Christiana. She paid him fourpence-halfpenny. Mrs Cole is called again, despite Defence Attorney Lamb's objection that the prosecutor is on a fishing expedition. The magistrate reminds him that this is a preliminary hearing and that any evidence obtained might have an important bearing on the ultimate case. So Mrs Cole returns to the stand and states that about a week before the inquest on Sidney Barker, the prisoner came into her shop, bought a few things, and at the same time left behind a paper bag from Maynard's which contained chocolate creams large and small and three lemon bullseyes. The sweets were fine, but when her daughter bit into the chocolate cream, it tasted foul and she spat it out. When Mrs Cole came across Christiana at the inquest, she denied doing any such thing.

A ten-year-old testifies that he had taken chocolate creams, given to him by Mrs Cole and left by Christiana, to his mother, who ate a small piece and felt as if her eyes were coming out of her head. She was shaken by convulsions, felt a great heaviness in her limbs, couldn't move and was ill for some four days. Another eleven-year-old states that the lady in the dock had sent him to Mr Garrett's on Queen's Road with a note, telling him that if he was asked where he had come from, he was to say Messrs Glaisyer and Co. He was given a packet, like a letter, and met the lady again on North Street. She gave him sixpence.

The evidence against Christiana was piling up and it seemed to implicate her in a far more ambitious poisoning spree than that directed at the wife of the man she was infatuated with. As the day unfolds, Isaac Garrett the chemist testifies that he knew the prisoner. She had made occasional visits to his shop over some four years, always paying in ready money, always mentioning a train she had to catch. At the start of the current year, she had begun to come more frequently; then on 28 March, after buying some toilet articles, she had asked if he could supply her with a small quantity of strychnine in order to kill some cats. She and her husband had been much annoyed by them of late and wanted to get rid of them.

Garrett refused. She coaxed him, said there were no children in the house and she would take care that it only passed through her own and her husband's hands. Garrett told her he could only supply it if there were a witness, and that witness well known to herself. She said the only person she knew in the vicinity was the milliner, Mrs Stone, three doors down from his own shop. Christiana fetched Mrs Stone, gave Garrett her own name as Mrs Wood, Hillside, Kingstown. He filled out the details in his book, which was duly signed by both women. The court's clerk read out the transaction from Garrett's 'Sale of Poisons, Registry Book': 'March 28, 1871. – Mrs. Wood, Hillside, Kingstown; strychnia, 10 grains; destroying cats'.

Masquerading as Mrs Wood, the prisoner had come to his shop several more times over the next two months, Garrett further testifies. She talked of her garden and brought him asparagus from it and complained that the strychnia had had no effect on the destructive cats, and she needed more. Garrett was persuaded, and on 15 April supplied her with ten more grains, following the same procedure as before. After several more visits on which she began to mention that she and her husband were moving to the country, on 11 May she asked Garrett for more strychnine, this time to kill an old and diseased dog whom they couldn't take with them. He finally granted her wish. He never saw the prisoner again until her appearance in court. The pages that had been torn out of his register under the ploy of the coroner having sent for it corresponded to the dates on which Christiana had purchased poison as Mrs Wood

Milliner Mrs Stone, the witnessing signatory in the poison register, corroborates Garrett's evidence. She testifies that the prisoner, heavily veiled, had been to her shop to purchase another veil, giving as her reason for the need of a second that she 'suffered from neuralgia'.

She had then returned to ask her the favour of signing Garrett's poison register. Mrs Stone went reluctantly. Mrs Wood came back a second time saying she had lost her veil: she bought another and asked for the same favour again. She needed the poison, she had said, to stuff some birds.

After Inspector Gibbs's narrative about visiting a reclining and supposedly unwell Christiana on Sunday 13 August, there comes a clinching statement from one of those 'downstairs' witnesses who haunt the sinners of 'upstairs' Victorian life. Adelaide Ann Friend, housemaid to a woman who let rooms in her Margate house, testified that a room had been rented for half-a-crown to the prisoner on 8 August. She had stayed for two nights. In Christiana's room the maid had seen several deal boxes, like the ones deposed. Opening them, she had found two peaches inside one – peaches had been sent to Mr Garrett. In another there were crystallized fruit. Another was empty. But after the lady left on the eight o'clock morning train to London the next day, the maid had found a small round cake, like that in the exhibits. She had eaten it and was none the worse for it.

Another servant, this time from Christiana's Brighton address, testifies that Miss Edmunds and her mother at seven o'clock on the morning of 8 August had left to get the train for Margate. Only Christiana had a case with her. She was going to visit her sister's grave and to look over a house. Her mother returned half an hour later, Christiana the next evening at six-thirty. The servant further tells the court that on the Friday before, 4 August, Miss Edmunds had asked her to throw away some powder packets, which were partly undone. She had kept one, thinking it might be myrrh, and had given that to Inspector Gibbs.

In response to the prosecutor's query, the servant says that, no, the house was not bothered by cats. However, another resident's perfectly healthy dog did suddenly die, twisting about and suffocating on 27 May, having an hour before spent a little time being patted by Miss Edmunds.

It is more or less on this morbid note that the hearing, having lasted for nearly six hours, is adjourned until the following week. When it is reconvened amidst even greater excitement, the prosecutor formally announces that he wishes to extend the charges against Christiana Edmunds to include not only attempts against all the individuals who had received parcels by post on 10 August, but also earlier attempts to administer poison to a number of people, one of whom has been seriously ill in hospital.

By the end of these preliminary hearings, the charge against Christiana will rise to murder, a rare charge against a middle-class woman. As witnesses detailing her activities – to obtain poison, infuse it into chocolate, return poisoned chocolates to Maynard's, leave bags of poisoned sweets in sundry shops – and their effects grow in number, 'deeply veiled' Christiana, *The Times* comments, remained 'perfectly calm and self possessed' and employed 'her time in writing notes to her sister [Mary] who sat below the dock, for her solicitor'. The prisoner's countenance, the reporter goes on to observe, 'is one likely to be remembered if once seen, and this will account for the readiness with which she was identified'. Christiana is indeed identified by a range of boys and young men who had acted as her messengers, as well as the various shopkeepers who had served her.

The excitement around the case is now such that the courtroom is completely filled an hour before start time. Lawyers overseeing the case for other implicated parties – Maynard's, Garrett's – and soon one representing the family of the dead boy, Sidney Barker, join the principal prosecution and defence counsels. Each poisoning charge is heard in turn and the inevitable repetition makes the evidence against Christiana rise with damning momentum. A bird-stuffer testifies to collecting, and another to examining, a dead dog picked up from 16 Gloucester Place: when opened up the dog was found to be full of poison. A handwriting expert from London deposes that the writing on the deal gift boxes and their notes corresponded to Christiana's, while that on the notes to the chemist didn't correspond to anyone at the neighbouring establishment, Glaisyer's, or to the coroner's. Christiana, in other words, has written all the notes herself.

Various expert witnesses, doctors and a professor testify to finding dangerous quantities of arsenic in the cake sent to Mrs Beard and lesser amounts in the sweetmeats in other parcels, as well as to treating those who had eaten fruit and cakes for symptoms corresponding to the effects of 'irritant poisoning'. More young messengers depose that over the summer they had bought chocolates from Maynard's at Christiana's request and then brought them back to the shop after showing them to her. Shopkeepers claim that she had left bags from Maynard's in their shops from as early as last March. When asked by one shopkeeper if she had forgotten a bag of Maynard sweets in her store, she denied it. Their contents eaten, serious illness followed. The chemist Professor Letherby reiterates the evidence he had given at the Barker inquest as to the strychnine contained in little Sidney's stomach. The difference now is that it is clear that Christiana Edmunds not only had access to strychnine some days before the child's death, but had also, through her messengers, had chocolates purchased from and then returned to Maynard's, where they were put back on display shelves. These chocolates contained poison.

On 7 September, Christiana Edmunds is charged with the murder of Sidney Barker. Like a woman in a trance, she seems oblivious to the seriousness of this new charge. Nor do the newspapers indicate any particular response from her as Sidney's uncle, Charles David Miller, a superintendent to a coach builder, describes how he asked for the 'best' chocolates from Maynard's on 12 June, then took them home for his nephew who was holidaying with his parents in Brighton. The chocolate the child ate at around eight in the morning had no effect. But the one he consumed in the afternoon he complained had a 'nasty' taste: after about ten minutes, he started crying, his limbs became stiff and within twenty minutes he was dead. The uncle's evidence is corroborated by his brother, the landlady and the doctor who arrived just as little Sidney was suffering his last convulsions. The post-mortem had shown a healthy child killed by poison. The doctor cut out his stomach whole, sent it in a sealed bag to Inspector Gibbs, who sent it to the expert Professor Letherby for analysis. It was found to contain a quarter of a grain of strychnine – enough to 'produce the death of a child of the age of this little boy'.

Christiana's 'self-possession', the term the papers repeat in describing her, has an ambivalent weight. In part it is a compliment to her lady-likeness. But it is also an attack, a condemnation of her imperturbability in response to the death of a child. This hard-heartedness utterly undermines Victorian notions of femininity. It turns Christiana into a monster, a threatening femme fatale, whose sexuality is so rampant in its pursuit of her male prey that she can only, in the eyes of some, be mad.

3. *A Wilful Killing?*

In charging Christiana Edmunds with murder, the prosecutor underlined that he had

> the most painful duty to discharge of proceeding against the pris-
> oner for wilfully killing Sidney Albert Barker . . . Her object . . .was
> that she had conceived a passion for Dr Beard, and having endeav-
> oured to remove Mrs Beard out of the way so long ago as
> September last, by placing in that lady's mouth a poisoned cream,
> she had endeavoured, by spreading poisoned sweets about, to give
> the idea that the poisoned cream she had thus tried to give to Mrs
> Beard was only one which she might have innocently received. The
> prisoner had this passion for Dr Beard, and in the desire to renew
> the intimacy broken off by her attempt of September last must be
> seen her reason for tampering with sweets.

The next day Christiana's letter to Charles Beard which included
material about the inquest was again read out in court. Against the
background of the new murder charge it had a far more ominous
ring. *The Times* reprinted it in full and noted, at the end of its ever-dry
account of Friday's proceedings, that 'the friends of the prisoner frequently wept'. Prosecutor Stuckey spelt out that he had now found a
motive for Christiana's murderous actions following her first attempt
to poison Emily Beard. Christiana 'was influenced to poison the sweetmeats' in order 'to draw off Dr Beard's suspicions, and lead to a
renewal of the friendship formerly subsisting between them'.

The details of Christiana's letter against this background of mounting incriminatory evidence took on a newly dramatic significance.
They gave reasons as to why she had sent chocolates from Maynard's

for chemical analysis; why she had made a point of appearing at the Barker child's inquest; why she had written anonymously to his father afterwards to protest that Mr Maynard hadn't been held responsible. Everything had been done so that Charles Beard would exonerate her from his accusation of attempting to poison Emily:

> My dear boy, do esteem me now. I am sure you must. What trial it was to go through, that inquest. La Madre was angry I ever had the analysis; but you know why I had it – to clear myself in my dear friend's eyes. She always said nothing was meant by you. No, darling; you wanted an excuse for my being so slighted.

The immensely complicated plot of buying arsenic and strychnine, of testing out quantities on animals, of masquerading and hiding her tracks, of initiating random poisonings in Brighton, of travelling as a lone woman to Margate and London, of lying to all and sundry, had all been undertaken in order to deflect the suspicions of the man she loved. She needed to have Charles allow their intimacy, and perhaps crucially also allow her letter-writing to begin again. The French would have called it a *crime passionnel*: her favoured Italians, a *delitto passionale*. Both countries might have been lenient with her and rather more understanding than the Victorian English about that temporary madness – that delirium – that love and jealousy could provoke. In the English courtroom, where Christiana was tried, no legal precedent was cited. Her relationship with Charles Beard was probed only once, in the initial court proceedings.

Pressed by Christiana's lawyer, Charles Beard stated emphatically that he had never written any letters to Christiana. He hadn't known immediately about the first attempted poisoning of his wife because he had been out of town. Nor had he seen Christiana for some months after that time because he was travelling:

> *Mr Lamb* – Why did you not tell her [Christiana] then that you had told your wife [about the letters]?

Witness – I had never answered her correspondence, and when I saw her I told her that I must decline to have a continuation of our friendship which had existed hitherto. I thought that was sufficient.

Mr Lamb – Say 'intimacy' instead of 'friendship'.

Witness – You can put it as you like; I saw her twice about Christmas, once with her mother and once alone.

Mr Lamb – Did you take any means to prevent letters being sent to you?

Witness – I took no action in the matter to prevent letters being sent.

Whatever Christiana might have hoped, there would be no defence for her from Dr Charles Beard, nor any greater indication that the man she addressed as 'Caro' or 'dear boy' acknowledged any substantial part in what for her was a patently obsessive, but also a reciprocal, passion. Upright Victorian family man that he was or pretended to be, respectability and reputation came first for Beard, who certainly wouldn't put his name to potentially incriminating letters. Yet that aura of respectability is one that Christiana also apparently honours. She may finish her letter to Charles '. . . make a poor little thing happy, and fancy a long, long bacio [kiss] from . . . ', but she then signs in another and secret name, 'DOROTHEA'. In recounting her appearance at little Barker's inquest in her letter to him, she repeatedly stresses that she never mentioned 'your name or La Sposa's'. 'No, the rack shouldn't have torn your name from me, and the only reason I said September [as the time the first poison chocolates circulated] was, that you might see I had concealed nothing.'

Unconsciously (or consciously) tempting fate, she presses her honesty home, writing that when at the inquest the reporters' pens rushed to take down everything she uttered, these lines flew into her memory: 'The chiel's amang them taking notes/ and faith he'll prent it.' They come from Robert Burns's 'On the late Captain Grose's Peregrinations Thro' Scotland'; translated, the full stanza reads:

If there is a hole in all your coats,
I advise you care for it:
A fellow is among you taking notes,
And faith he will print it.

The sentiment is one Burns often repeated: If you have anything to be ashamed of, beware: there's a scribbler in your midst who's taking notes. The truth will out and he'll make sure of it. Power should expect no free pass from the Muse.

Christiana, like so many reading Victorians, evidently knew her Burns; but in quoting him here to Charles Beard, was she expressing not only a worry that the interrogators at the inquest would find her out, but also a veiled threat to the man she patently considered her lover?

Their secret would out, and she might be the scribbler who – at once knowingly and unwittingly – revealed it.

4. *The Rumbles of History*

Who was this woman who is evidently well read, who clearly enjoys writing and does so in a style not all that different from the sensation novels of her day? A woman who in her attempt to rid the world of the wife of the man she was in love with unleashed an elaborate plot of wholesale poisoning on a town in order to cover her tracks – a plot worthy of Wilkie Collins or Mary Braddon, who were themselves inevitably, like Christiana, also inspired by the press reports of their day?

In early July 1857, when she was in her twenties, Christiana would have been aware of one of the most sensational of the period's court cases, one mingling sex and poison, and eagerly followed by all the newspapers. Twenty-one-year-old Glaswegian Madeleine Smith, like Christiana the daughter of a well-known architect, was accused of poisoning a young Frenchman, Pierre Émile L'Angelier, who, as Madeleine's letters scandalously proved, had been her lover. 'Our intimacy has not been criminal,' Madeleine wrote to Émile, in a letter of 30 April 1856 quoted in court, 'as I am your wife before God, so it has been no sin our loving each other. No darling, I am your wife.' But Émile was only a struggling foreign clerk, one her father couldn't approve. When a better match presented itself and Émile made himself difficult to shed and wouldn't return her many telltale letters, it is likely that Madeleine administered a deadly dose of poison, having tried lesser doses unsuccessfully in the past.

In any event, on the night of 23 March 1857 L'Angelier was found dead and large amounts of arsenic were discovered in his stomach. He had a letter from Madeleine on him, bidding him to come to her side – though she claimed it was from the day before. In court, neither judge nor jury wanted to believe in her guilt, and since the evidence was largely circumstantial, and hanging a terrible fate for a pretty, effervescent middle-class young lady, she was declared not guilty. 'There is something so touching in the age, the sex and the social position of the accused,' the judge stated, summing up a widespread wish that Madeleine be innocent and womanhood saved.

During the trial, detailed scientific evidence was given by a professor of chemistry, Frederick Perry, that Christiana might have been impressed by. Dr Perry was only one of several chemical experts who in the course of the latter half of the century took the stand in court and whose evidence was widely quoted in newspaper reports. Indeed ever since 1836, when James Marsh had developed the first test for detecting arsenic in the stomach, science had grown increasingly prominent in the witness box. In his evidence Dr Perry talked, like one of the many readily available domestic handbooks on medicine and drugs, of the quantities of arsenic needed to kill a man, the number of grains in a drahm, the most efficient forms of administering the poison. The fact that cocoa or chocolate were substances in which a considerable dose might be conveyed without the taste being instantly detected was mentioned several times. The evidence also seemed to suggest that a solid medium would be more effective than a liquid one. Some of these sensational facts may well have lodged themselves in Christiana's mind, together with the 'innocence' of the attractive young middle-class woman in the dock.

Christiana Edmunds was not quite the thirty-five-year-old initially described at the Brighton hearings. She was in fact forty-three, but the appearance of relative youth was important to the Dorothea she was posing as. Her true age would become significant at her trial.

She was born on 29 August 1829 in the growing Kentish coastal town of Margate to William Edmunds and his wife, Ann(e) Christiana Burn. Her mother was the daughter of a major; her father, the son of a carpenter, Thomas Edmunds, who had risen in society in the early 1800s to become the proprietor of the White Hart Hotel on Margate's up-and-coming Marine Parade. Thomas Edmunds was also the surveyor who after the gales of 1808 oversaw the rebuilding of Margate Pier, foreseeing that it might become a promenade for fashionable visitors. William Edmunds, born about 1801, followed in his father's footsteps. For a brief period after his father's death in 1824, William looked after the family hotel with his elder sister Mary, who in 1815 had been subject to a libel suit for having rather brilliantly lampooned a man ominously called Boys – though there is no clear indication that this Boys bore any relation to the one Christiana later targeted with her poisoning. (This aunt of Christiana's, perhaps not altogether unlike her niece, 'had a habit of writing offensive and annoying letters, not only to her friends but to persons to whom she was totally unacquainted'.)

William Edmunds became a surveyor and a principal architect in Margate's nineteenth-century efflorescence. In 1825, when the town's parishes had outgrown their churches, he won the Church Building Commissioners' competition to build Margate a new 'Gothic Church at the time of Henry the Third – to contain two thousand sittings'. From the remaining evidence, Edmunds was not only a fine draftsman but an imaginative architect. The church may have ended up costing more than the Commissioners had bargained for, but it was grand in conception and 'visible at a considerable distance from shore'. At the time of its consecration in 1829, which coincided with Christiana's birth, William Edmunds was at the height of his powers. His public buildings included the new Margate lighthouse, the offices of the important Pier and Harbour Company, known as the Droit House, and a lavish shopping precinct in the High Street called The Boulevard, locally known as 'Levey's Bazaar'. The *Kentish Chronicle* of 18 August that year noted that Edmunds's Boulevard commanded 'universal admiration ... It now takes the lead as a promenade.'

His flurry of activity spread, together with his reputation. Over the next few years, he completed Trinity Church in Dover, a new workhouse at Herne, extensions to the Kent and Canterbury Hospital – an establishment his youngest son would sadly have some connection with after his father's death – and a grand ornamental pavilion where the city of Dover gave a resplendent dinner for the ageing Duke of Wellington.

In 1828, William Edmunds married Ann Christiana Burn, and the couple came to live in Margate's elegant Hawley Square with its handsome, tall Georgian brick edifices. Christiana was their first child, followed by a boy, called William after his father. Mary Burn followed in 1832 and a year later Louisa Agnes. Finally, in 1841, came Arthur Burn.

As Christiana grew, so her father's fortunes declined. Official surveyor to two of Margate's major civic enterprises – the Margate Pier and Harbour Company and the Margate Commissioners for Paving and Lighting – Edmunds was targeted during 1836–7, a moment of public discontent with the Companies, for mismanagement of funds. The deputy chairman of the Pier and Harbour Company committed suicide in 1836, augmenting the sense that general embezzlement was taking place. Though Edmunds himself was just about cleared in the furore of accusation, his salary was reduced first by one and then by the other company. The family grew poorer, and after 1839 he built no new edifices and disappeared from public view.

In 1842, when Christiana was entering her teens, the family house was sold. Soon after, William Edmunds's state of mind must have become a trial for his family and affected them in deep, if differing, ways. 'He was very strange in his manner . . . He raved about having millions of money, and attempted to knock down his medical man with a ruler.' So stated an aged Ann Christiana Edmunds at her daughter's trial, as she revealed the story of William Edmunds's shadowy afterlife in the most cursory, if sensational, terms. Her deposition formed the only defence that could be offered for Christiana – a defence of hereditary insanity. But madness in the family has many more ways of affecting its members than the Victorian understanding of heredity gives room for. William's wild behaviour, the content of his ravings, his wife and children's ways of coping with it, the shame of his confinement to an institution, the poverty this in turn brought on the family – all of this affected its members as much as any loose notion of heredity.

'In 1843 my husband became insane and was sent to a private lunatic asylum at Southall, where he was confined till August 1844 ... He had to be confined in a strait jacket before going to the asylum. He had two attendants before he was sent there.' So stated Mrs Edmunds. Sydney Cornish Harrington of Datchworth, her son's brother-in-law, amplified this in the 'memorial' or affidavit he produced to plead Christiana's pardon after her trial: William Edmunds in his manic state had talked of his 'immense wealth and the vast number of cities that he had built' to his two listening attendants, before trying to overpower them. Only his wife, when called, could finally settle and command him.

Violent, William was described as a 'dangerous lunatic' by the proprietor of the Southall Park Asylum to which he was sent. This was a small private establishment, family-run and, like many of its kind, once a handsome residence now converted to new use. It had been opened in 1838 by the reputed Sir William Charles Ellis (1780–1839), whose humane methods of caring for the mad had been inspired by the Quaker William Tuke's famous York Retreat.

Like many of the early-nineteenth-century mind doctors, Ellis believed that work and the discipline it provided were crucial to providing possible cures for those who suffered madness. He had brought these principles to his work as superintendent of the large Wakefield Asylum, from where he had been recruited to the giant Hanwell Asylum in Middlesex. Here he put in place what were then considered progressive 'moral', by which were meant psychological treatment techniques. After political disagreements with the Middlesex magistrates, Ellis and his wife – ever a partner in his asylum management – left Hanwell and established the private Southall Park asylum in the vicinity. Advertised as a retreat suitable 'for any Lady or Gentleman whose mental state may require a separation from their immediate friends and connexions', the asylum offered gardens and grounds for outdoor exercise and relaxation as well as horses, billiards, music, cheerful views and the sense of a home away from home.

By the time William Edmunds arrived at Southall Park, Ellis had

been dead for some four years and the premises were licensed to a Dr
J. B. Steward, who testified at Christiana's trial. He described her father
as being fond of good living, but not a hard drinker. The spur to his
malady was, perhaps appropriately for an architect, 'the loss of the sale
of a house'. Acute mania characterized him on admission. He was
'violent and restless', and 'talked nonsense', insisting he was worth
millions. William Edmunds, it was clear, had his idée fixe: he felt he
had been cheated out of an elevated public position, one he couldn't
live without. Eventually he became 'paralyzed'. The 'paralysis' Dr
Steward mentions in his deposition is the catch-all classification of
the later 1800s: 'general paralysis of the insane'. Only in 1913 were its
symptoms definitively linked to the ravages of tertiary syphilis. If
William Edmunds did indeed have syphilis, this may also account for
the 'epilepsy' and 'idiocy', or learning difficulties, that the youngest
Edmunds, Arthur Burn, was said to suffer from, though there is no
indication that Mrs Edmunds was affected.

Southall contained only some nine 'lunatics'. A stay there did not
come cheap: two guineas a week for the better rooms. In today's
terms, depending on the measure used, this translates as around £200
(using the retail price index) or £1470 (when compared to average
earnings) per week. A lengthy confinement in such asylum style was
not something a mother with four children still to raise and little
income could afford. Unsurprisingly, William had to be brought home
from Southall in August 1844 'from considerations of expense'.

Christiana was then fifteen. As the eldest daughter, it is likely that
she had to help care for her father. Together with her siblings, she
would have heard his manic outbursts and the overblown fantasies
of grandeur, loss and resentment they contained, all with their
emotional and in part material core of truth. William had indeed
fallen from greater heights than he now occupied. We could speculate
that contained in his insistence on millions acquired and cities built,
there is a family narrative of a decline unjustly propelled by others –
his accusers at the Margate companies. This could well at some level
have infected Christiana's adolescent sense of herself. There are traces

of her father's malady in her own hypersensitivity about her status and her prickly arrogance: her complaints about her jailers, her insistence on being treated like a lady; the straining for equality that her letter to Dr Beard emits – with its Burns quotes and its fashionable smatterings of Italian. Class, after all, is central to Victorian life and its demarcations. Hanging on to gentility as well as reputation is crucial.

The financial plight of the Edmundses is clear from the fact that a mere six months or so after William's return from the private asylum, he is sent off in March 1845 to the far shabbier Peckham House, an institution with a less than sterling reputation. Often overcrowded, Peckham House by 1846 contained 402 inmates, the largest proportion of them pauper lunatics, sometimes as many as four to a small room, and with very few keepers. The food was insufficient and met with criticism from the Commissioners on Lunacy, who had begun investigative work in 1844 just before the 1845 Lunacy Act, which enshrined them as a centralized overseeing government body. Indeed the Commissioners had entertained thoughts of closing Peckham down, but given the lack of public asylum places, 'if licences were withdrawn from houses containing large numbers of paupers, there would be no alternative, but to send the patients to workhouses, or to board with other paupers, where they would not have the care which they now receive under regular visitation and supervision'. Apparently, by 1847 the situation at Peckham House had improved, but by 15 March that year, as Dr Henry Armstrong of Peckham House explained at Christiana's trial, Williams was dead, after suffering three years of 'general paralysis'.

There is no written record of how William's years of madness and ultimate death in confinement affected the family. But it is clear that his madness rumbled through their lives – whether we understand this in psychological ways or along the biological hereditarian lines the Victorian doctors then preferred. In that hothouse that a family is, his excessive and eccentric behaviour seems to have affected several of the Edmunds children and become something of a family trait.

Christiana's teenage years were coloured by her father's illness, the

family's decline and financial difficulties. She was nearing her twentieth birthday when her father died. Her youngest brother was eight
and would soon begin to have the epileptic fits that would have him
permanently committed to Earlswood Asylum, a vast institution at
Reigate, principally for those with learning disabilities, whose patron
was the Queen. According to his mother, Arthur had been an 'idiot'
from an early age, a condition which the family, but not the doctors,
attributed to 'a blow to the head'. A little while after or perhaps even
before the father's death, the family rented a house in Canterbury at
3 Watling Street – perhaps so as to avoid too many questions from
Margate acquaintances. Help for Arthur was sought from two doctors
here, both of whom were attached to the Kent and Canterbury
Hospital. Dr Hallowes and Dr Andrews signed the 1860 medical certificate that committed the young man to Earlswood, where he lived
until his death in 1866. Christiana and her mother may then have
moved back to Margate before moving again to those fatal lodgings in
Brighton.

After the death of her father, Christiana herself went through some
kind of episode. Around 1853, she was sent to London for treatment.
Like a case of hysteria from the annals of Jean-Martin Charcot or the
young Freud, she was then paralysed down one side and her feet were
so affected that she was unable to walk. In her deposition, her mother
emphasizes that Christiana 'suffered for many years from Hysteria
and when a child used to walk in her sleep'. It seems the challenges of
becoming a Victorian woman would stop her walking in her twenties
when wide awake.

Whether Christiana's 'hysteria' was in part the effect of an early
unrequited love or a way of escaping an unwanted marriage, whether
it was due to a lack of opportunities for intelligent women, genteel but
poor, or occasioned by a lack of suitable suitors, it is a fact that at one
point she chose what would later become known as a 'flight into illness', and remained unattached. She became one of those one in four
Victorian women classified as 'spinster'. Meanwhile her younger sisters, though not unaffected by the family's decline, did marry. The

dynamics of sibling relations, the way their mother may have characterized their successes and failures, the frustrations of the family situation, all inevitably played their role in shaping the rather girlish woman Christiana would become.

All the Edmunds girls were educated – Christiana at a private school, her later records show – and reached a 'superior' level of attainment. Louisa Agnes, four years younger than Christiana, worked for some time as a governess in London. It may have been here that she met the widower and naval surgeon Julian Watson Bradshaw: it was certainly in London that she married him in December 1862, when she was twenty-nine. It's tempting to speculate that the marriage didn't go well for her, since in a moment of 'violent hysteria' she tried to throw herself out of a window and was only saved by her mother and a servant holding her down. Or it may be that Louisa's 'violent hysteria' happened at a time closer to Christiana's, before she left home for London. Either way, by 1867, at the age of only thirty-three, four years into her marriage, Louisa was dead, buried in Margate. There was no inquest, so a second suicide attempt can't be inferred.

Christiana's and Louisa's labile and excessive states seem to have found an echo in their brother William. There are few traces of him in the historical record, but according to the memorial sent to the Home Secretary after Christiana's trial by Sydney Cornish Harrington of Datchworth, William as a young man had dramatically threatened suicide when he was refused permission to marry Sydney's sister. So great were the family fears on both sides, that William's wish was granted. His own family seems to have provided a fertile training ground for his later profession. At the time of Christiana's trial he was head of the asylum on Robben Island, which also served as a leper colony and a political prison, much later to house Nelson Mandela for eighteen years.

The only Edmunds child whose behaviour seems to have been unaffected by the early family drama was Mary Burn, the middle sister. At the age of twenty-four, on 18 September 1856 in Henley on

Thames, she married the Reverend Edward Foreman of Amberley in Sussex. Sister Mary seems to have lived an ordinary middle-class Victorian life, giving birth to five children, the youngest of whom went up to Cambridge. But Mary's elder sister's acts plunged her into a different world. She attended Christiana's trial, helped where she could and also cared for her tireless mother, who died only in April 1893, five years before Mary herself. There is no record of what Mary thought of Christiana's passionate delusion.

5. *Sex and the Victorian Hysteric*

As a young woman classified as a hysteric in the 1850s, Christiana would have been understood as suffering from an illness that engaged both her nerves and almost certainly her uterine system. This latter incorporated what we would now name 'sexual', a word whose meaning shifted rapidly from that time on. J. Crichton-Browne, the influential medical director of the West Riding Asylum, lecturing to students at the Leeds Medical School, points out:

> ... mental phenomena in health and disease ... are influenced in no slight degree by the sexual functions, and they exercise a reciprocal control ... The period of the rut in animals is accompanied by mental activity, which borders upon morbid excitement, while the gravid state of the uterus in females of our own species may lead not merely to change of temper, morbid appetites, and capricious eccentricity, but to chorea [tics, or involuntary movement], somnambulism, amaurosis [darkening or loss of vision], convulsions, or mental derangement. On the other hand, a condition of mental agitation may derange the menstrual discharge, and ideas may modifiy the nutrition of the sexual apparatus.

Crichton-Browne goes on to give an example of a hysterical pregnancy in which the power of the delusion induced changes in the 'vascularity of the uterus and the ovaries'. In this lecture he wants to distinguish between what he calls ordinary hysteria – which involves 'incontinence of the emotions', 'moral obliquity', 'towering egotism' and 'positive delusions' – and the even more serious 'hysterical mania'. While 'the mental affection is the more prominent feature' in common hysteria, in hysterical mania both the uterus and the brain are definitely in play. Crichton-Browne is a believer in the physiological base of mental illness, and although he states that there is no necessary continuum between his first and second kind of hysteria, it only takes a small increase in 'intensity and persistency' for recognized 'mental derangement' of the second sort to come into effect.

It's clear that, for Crichton-Browne, the very condition of being female and possessing a uterus is a dangerous business, prone to tumble one into insanity at the merest provocation. The very biological factors that differentiate women from men – menstruation, pregnancy, lactation and menopause – are seen as trigger points for madness. The whole reproductive system enchains women to uterine, and thus nervous, disease. Meanwhile female desire, itself, as the leading Victorian gynaecologist William Acton underlined, giving scientific back-up to the period's ideological presumptions, is an aberration. In his *Functions and Disorders of the Reproductive Organs* (1857), which deals mainly with male sexuality and the danger to vital energy that masturbation constitutes, he notes that 'happily for society', the majority of women 'are not very much troubled by sexual feeling of any kind'. After the opening of the new divorce courts in 1858 and its examples of sexually desiring women, he revised his views slightly:

What men are habitually, women are only exceptionally. It is too true, I admit, as the divorce courts show, that there are some few women who have sexual desires so strong that they surpass those of men, and shock public feeling by their consequences. I admit, of course, the existence of sexual excitement terminating even in nymphomania, a form of insanity that those accustomed to visit lunatic asylums must be fully conversant with; but, with these sad exceptions there can be no doubt that sexual feeling in the female is in the majority of cases in abeyance, and that it requires positive and considerable excitement to be roused at all . . .

In his footnote on nymphomania, Acton discusses the excision of the clitoris, which has been recommended as a cure, only to say that he doesn't consider it effective, since there is also 'special sensibility' in several portions of the vaginal canal.

Not all the mid-nineteenth-century mind doctors in Britain bought into the uterine or ovarian theory of hysteria and presumed it had a physiological base. Argument was rife, and continued at least until the end of the century. Nor did all of them agree with the guiding Victorian notion that the existence of female desire was itself an indication of a classifiable condition, such as nymphomania, calling for confinement in an asylum. But many shared a sense of the precarious nature of being woman. Women are both endangered and dangerous.

Julius Althaus (1833–1900), a cultivated German-born and -trained neurologist, prolific writer and eventual founder of the Maida Vale Hospital for Nervous Diseases in London, for instance, is keen to leave the uterus to one side and focus on hysteria's emotional character alone. Althaus had briefly worked with the young Jean-Martin Charcot in Paris, and at times sounds more radical than that French Napoleon of the Neuroses himself – certainly in his conception of hysteria. All symptoms of hysteria, Althaus writes in 1866, 'have their prototype in those vital actions by which grief, terror, disappointment and other painful emotions and affections are manifested under ordinary circumstances, and which become signs of hysteria as soon as they attain a certain degree of intensity'. Women whose 'sensibility is blunt', Althaus argues, 'never become hysterical; while those who are readily accessible to impressions coming from without, who feel acutely and are liable to strong emotions, are certain to become hysterical and made to suffer mental agony or prolonged pain'.

The Protean range of symptoms they may then manifest can include any or several of the following: convulsive attacks, fainting fits, pain, cough, difficulty in swallowing, vomiting, asthma, hiccups, palpitations of the heart, general and partial loss of power, paralysis, anaesthesia and hyperaesthesia. These are extreme symptoms, and yet this is an ordinary enough condition, one that 'impressionable' women who are not particularly 'strong-minded' are prone to suffer from in an age that requires a 'long and laborious training' in 'self-control'.

George Drysdale, in his *Physical, Sexual and Natural Religion, by a graduate of Medicine* (1857), a book that was soon renamed *The Elements of Social Science* (1861), was more outspoken in his analysis of hysteria. He had a reformer's zeal and it was clear to him that hysteria was a mentally and emotionally occasioned condition linked to the sexual abstinence the age demanded, particularly of women. 'A morbid sexual state both physical and mental lies at the root of hysteria,' he writes. He emphasizes that the disease is particularly prevalent amongst women of the upper classes, 'among whom the sexual feelings are much more prominently developed, from the want of a necessary employment to occupy the mind, as well as from the various causes – such as novel reading, poetry, romance, dancing, theatricals, and so many other excitements which elevate to the highest pitch the sexual desires, and paint the delights of love in the most glowing colors'.

Hysteria begins, in his view, with puberty when the young girl is filled with tempestuous desires and surrounded by endless temptations and excitements that are necessarily ungratified. She is forced to hide her feelings and desires. 'That which should have been the young girl's pride and delight, becomes her shame and her torture; she must conceal, the unhappy one! And studiously repress her eager and beautiful emotions, and can we wonder that bewilderment, timidity, and impotence result?' The inability 'to select her marital mate' for herself compounds the difficulty of her condition: '. . . nature cannot bear this constant state of slavery; and ever and anon she shows in the hysterical convulsions, in the wild tumultuous hysterical emotions, or in the delirious excitement of nymphomania (love-madness) that she will not be repressed. The passions of youth are a volcanic fire, which in the end will burst through all obstacles.'

Drysdale, though not a woman, had experience of this 'volcanic fire'. Son of a prominent Edinburgh family, he had had a deeply troubled adolescence which resulted in a breakdown brought about by guilt over his uncontrollable desire to masturbate. Fleeing to the continent, he had disappeared so totally that his family thought him dead. When he finally returned, it was as a free-thinking social and sexual radical. Unrepressed sex had cured him. After studying medicine, Drysdale published his book anonymously: voicing his ideas as himself would have brought shame on his family.

Drysdale is an early feminist. He links hysteria to the fact that a girl is never allowed 'to go about alone, like a young man'. Subjected to a 'constant espionage', she is frequently forced to do things in an underhand manner, to the destruction of her sense of dignity and rectitude. Nor do things necessarily get much better with age. Hysteria, that disease which can take all shapes and any, also attacks the 'single or widows, or barren women, or such as are indifferent to, or dislike their husbands (which last class in this country of indissoluble marriage is unhappily so large a one)'.

The intolerable Victorian restrictions on women's movement and desires are in the name of that supposedly great female virtue of chastity. As long as the ideas regarding this so-called virtue remain, it is impossible for woman to obtain greater freedom. 'Until the difference in "sexual privilige" between man and woman is attended to,' Drysdale emphasizes, nothing will make much impact on hysteria. 'If we do not remove the main cause of hysteria, namely, insufficient sexual gratifications', it is totally impossible to prevent the disease.

Nor is cure by a physician to be anticipated. Like some early Freud recommending a dose of *penis normalis*, 'love is the only physician, who can cure this peculiar disease; and it is vain for a medical man to expect to supply his place. The passions, which have been repressed and thrown into disorder, must be gratified, and the proper healthy stimulus given to the sexual organs, so as to restore their nervous balance, before we can have any rational expectation of a cure.'

Reading Drysdale, one begins to think, as Freud might later have done, that Christiana Edmunds's 'love-madness' was an unconscious attempt to initiate a self-cure.

It is not altogether impossible that an educated woman like

Christiana, whose life was criss-crossed by members of the medical profession, would have read the revolutionary primer on sexuality that *The Elements* was. A doctor like Charles Beard, who had travelled abroad and had an experience of other cultures, would probably have read it and might silently have shared its stress on the importance of unrestricted sex for the physical health and mental balance of both men and women, who were more usually idealized in Victorian England as desire-free. *The Elements*, after all, sold some ninety thousand copies and was translated into eleven languages.

The Victorians, increasing work on the period has made clear, were not uniformly the dutiful, sexually repressed and rampantly moral exemplars they often aspired to be and preferred to portray themselves as. There would have been no treatises against masturbation if self-pleasuring didn't exist. Many men, from chief justices such as Alexander Cockburn to prime ministers such as Palmerston, kept mistresses, often perfectly respectable ones. These were women worldly enough to ascribe sexuality a place, which wives, worn out by repeated pregnancies, may not have been. What is not publicly spoken about may still be privately lived. Christiana Edmunds, grappling with the tensions and inner conflicts in which her social place enmeshed her as a young woman destined to become one of Victorian England's redundant spinsters, was evidently tempted by other possibilities, one of which was the mantle of mistress – which might even be a stopping point on the way to wife, if only the existing *sposa* could be made to vanish.

6. *Fashions in Treatment*

Short of the extreme recourse to a uterine operation, which could include a form of clitoridectomy, the treatment Christiana Edmunds would have undergone for hysteria would not have differed all that much, whatever understanding of hysteria the doctors she saw held. Althaus speaks of three different categories of treatment. The first is emotional and consists of removing the causes of the hysteria, 'viz., painful emotions'. This, he notes altogether reasonably, is the most difficult feat of all and often fails to work despite the doctor's best efforts, since it entails rousing the will of the patient 'to reconcile her to her position in life, and obtain for her the best possible conditions from those who surround her'. Returning lost fathers or lost suitors is not within the doctor's usual range. Tact and perspicuity are necessary in treating the patient; and sometimes the recommendation of a total change of air and scene – 'a voyage to the Cape or Australia does wonders'.

The uterine theorists would not have bothered with the first of Althaus's headings for treatment, but would instead have replaced it with a physical intervention, such as pressure on the uterine area, a dose of nitrate of silver to the cervix, the use of a vaginal pump syringe or douche, perhaps even the sedative potassium bromide, so much of which was used later in the century at the Salpêtrière asylum in Paris for both hysterics and epileptics. Or they might have leapt straight to the second and third of Althaus's facets of treatment: modifying the constitution and relieving the symptoms. Modifying the constitution is basic to much Victorian medicine and indeed our own, though we would probably replace the term 'constitution' with 'lifestyle'. This usually entailed a type-specific regime which included diet (bland or nutritious), baths (hot or cold), and taking the waters in a variety of recommended spas from Malvern to 'St Moritz in the Engadin where the highly rarified Alpine air, the carbonated baths, and the chalybeate mineral springs combined often produce marvelous results'.

As for the direct relief of hysterical symptoms, faradization – the conveying of a powerful current to the affected area – was as the century moved on the most common treatment, alongside its galvanic kin. Althaus was a great champion of the electrotherapies (not shock therapies, like the later ECT). The popularity of such treatments – not altogether unlike those used by beauticians and physiotherapists today – can be gauged from the numerous press advertisements that vaunt their efficacy and ever growing variations.

'Pulvermacher's improved patent Galvanic chain bands, belts and pocket self-restorable chain batteries' promise that 'Galvanism – nature's chief restorer of impaired vital energy' – provides 'effective rational treatment [of] nervous and rheumatic pains, debility, indigestion, nervousness, sleeplessness, paralysis, neuralgia, epilepsy, cramp, and the functional disorders' (of which hysteria is one). By listing a host of professional supporters for the therapy, including the Paris Medical School and the Royal Society, the ad tries to circumvent the worry that these faradic and galvanic treatments may edge a little too close to quackery or mesmerism, which was touted by some as treatment and considered by others a popular spectacle, like hypnotism just a little later. Some have suggested that these electric treatments were equivalent, or at least akin to, the medical masturbation that doctors also occasionally practised on hysterical patients, bringing them to paroxysm or what we would call orgasm.

Whoever the doctor that she saw in London might have been, it is likely that Christiana chatted a little about herself, was recommended a diet and baths, and was given a course of faradization, thought to be particularly useful for partial paralyses. Talking, touching, tapping, examining, stimulating, alongside the care that a stipulated regime evoked, all helped. It certainly helped more than the punishing and detrimental surgeries that were also undertaken. A side effect of this first course of treatment, however, could be that the doctor all too easily became a love object for the patient, with or without any reciprocity on his side. (Desire being ever a riddle, this sometimes happened even with the more punitive second form of treatment.)

We don't know whether Christiana developed an attachment to the doctor or doctors who treated her for the hysteria she suffered from in her twenties. Her later passionate obsession with Charles Beard may have been one he, at least initially, reciprocated. They may have kissed, as her letter to him suggests, or even gone further during one of his home visits – the usual way doctors were then seen. It may be that he used and emphasized his married state as an excuse for putting a stop to emotions that on Christiana's side were growing rampant; and this excuse in turn became her internal justification for attempting to get rid of his wife. Alternatively, Christiana may have aggrandized an ordinary caring doctorly concern, which may or may not on occasion have slipped into physical contact, and transformed it into something other and bigger, something that became delusional – fantasizing that eliminating Emily Beard would bring the doctor to her alone.

There is no record of what kind of ailments Christiana brought to Beard's attention. Apart from what she chose to convey, it is unlikely that he knew much of her medical history. We can only guess at what he treated her for or whether he had much knowledge of hysteria, though as a medic practising in the affluent quarters of Brighton, he probably had some: hysteria was widely diagnosed for any woman who was visibly chafing at the feminine status quo – as evidenced in her words or her mysterious physical symptoms. During the subsequent trial at London's Old Bailey, Christiana's mother mentions in her evidence that 'even now at times' Christiana would come to her room and say she 'had had a fit of hysteria and could not breathe'. Lack of breath and the sensation of a globus, or ball, in the throat, blocking it or causing nausea, were common hysterical symptoms. So perhaps Charles Beard had been called on to treat Christiana's nerves, amongst other ills, and had in the process generated his own form of electricity.

Hysteria, as Julius Althaus states, is not an easily curable condition, and though it may disappear, its progress 'is powerfully influenced by the events of life'. Christiana certainly remained in Althaus's terms 'impressionable' and her relationship to 'self-control' had gone sensationally askew, as the sequence of poisonings shows. But her hysteria had by then toppled into something the condition did not, by all historical accounts, entail. Hysterics may have converted their unhappy and unconscious thoughts into symptoms, but classically these affected their own bodies, not the bodies of others: actions directed outwards, acts of violence, whether overt, masked or delayed, belonged to some other, graver classification. Whether it was a moral or a medical one was something Christiana's jurors were to determine.

7. Loving Doctors

Christiana comes into the public record with her love for Dr Beard and the criminal activities it set in train. The passion itself was already criminal enough. After all, Dr Beard was a married man and secret liaisons were hardly condoned in Victorian England. Yet doctors – like their mesmerian kin who provided treatments of an unlegitimated kind – feature regularly in this period as targets for women's illict, often enough unnamed, desires. These are sometimes reciprocal. It is as if Freud's understanding of transference love – the love that underpins and makes possible the whole therapeutic relationship and is a slippage from earlier and other loves – should be extended to all medical practice and not just its psychoanalytic variety, that 'dangerous' method which had Carl Gustav Jung entangled with his patient Sabina Spielrein.

In a way, Victorian England itself encouraged the potential amorousness of the medical encounter. The emphasis on female purity, which underpinned Victorian morality, meant that middleclass women rarely had any experience of (unclothed) men or of the body's sexual vagaries, at least until marriage, and sometimes not even very fully after that. There was no language except a euphemistic romantic one in which to speak of desire. Meanwhile, marriage didn't come until around twenty-seven – and could, of course, prove unsatisfactory.

Contact with doctors would for some women have been the only time when talk of body and sensation was permissable. The consulting room provided a space of intimacy and confidentiality, akin to a confessional but without the separating grille. For the young woman, the doctor may have been the only male ever to touch her – either with his eyes, that searching clinical gaze, or with his hands. Or with

that ancient and in the Victorian era newly rediscovered and contro-
versial gynaecological instrument, the speculum. There was a fear
that the speculum, which took on several innovatory shapes at this
time and provided the male with a glimpse of what the woman herself
would never see, might, with frequent insertion, provoke her desire –
or indeed, like the doctor's 'examination' itself, satisfy it. So the doctor
could easily become the site of fantasy; or use his privileged access to
the advantage of seduction.

Christiana Edmunds was scarcely the first or last Victorian woman
to fall in love with her doctor. Nor was she the only one to ignite scandal and public trial as a result. In 1858 Isabella Robinson, an unhappy
wife with something of a Madame Bovary about her, found herself and
her illicit passions dragged all too publicly through the Court for
Divorce and Matrimonial Causes – as Kate Summerscale narrates so
well. Her husband had discovered a diary filled with intemperate prose
relating her sensual desires and describing some charged, seemingly
adulterous, scenes with a certain Dr Edward Lane. Isabella's husband
used the evidence of her diary to sue for divorce, but in court and in
the press the relationship of journal entries to truth claims proved
open to a great deal of argument.

Lane was a decade younger than Mrs Robinson: lawyers and doctors
advanced her age to fifty in order to be able to term her 'menopausal',
a period received wisdom allied to erratic, lascivious behaviour, and
sometimes madness. Lane was married to Mary Drysdale, the sister of
the sexual reformer. Mrs Robinson and he had first met in
Edinburgh's progressive intellectual circles. Over the years, Lane saw
her with some regularity at the popular spa he opened in Moor Park,
an ideal location not only for a healthy regime of water, walks and the
nineteenth-century version of detox, but also for amorous friendship,
certainly for amorous imaginings.

At the first divorce trial of Robinson vs Robinson and Lane, Dr
Lane staunchly refuted any sexual doings and was cleared of adultery.
In the second trial, thanks to the fine-tuned literary intelligence and
worldly wisdom of the great Sir Alexander Cockburn, so was Mrs

Robinson. In his summing up, Cockburn emphasized the unreliability of diaries, and the wavering line between fantasy and realism that such writing could fall prey to. He described Mrs Robinson, on the evidence of her writing, as 'a woman of more than ordinary intelligence and of no inconsiderable attainments' whose imagination was too vivid and whose passions were too strong.

By then, Isabella Robinson's reputation had already been thoroughly muddied by press and by prosecution, as well as defence. The last pleaded madness. Medical witnesses testified that Mrs Robinson's rampant sexuality, itself abnormal though not unusual during menopause, was fostering delusions. She was suffering from 'a disease peculiar to woman', from 'hysteria' or 'erotomania' or 'nymphomania', produced by an addiction to 'self-pollution', abetted by the imaginings in her journal, which were 'the hallucinations or the rhapsodical expressions of an over-excited mind', as *Lloyd's Weekly Newspaper* had it.

The wealthy heiress Florence Bravo, suspected of poisoning her second husband Charles in 1876, also engaged in an illicit love affair with a doctor under whose sway, some thought, she had committed murder. Dr James Manby Gully was the doctor in question, and he was mid-century England's premier hydropath. Sophisticated, well travelled, a recognized authority with several books to his name, Gully was the inventor of the famous Malvern water cure, a holistic therapy of exercise, diet, detoxification and healing mineral waters. His hydro, opened in 1842, was frequented by a host of notables from Darwin to Disraeli. Florence Nightingale, who as a young woman suffered from an 'immobilizing' despair, from trances and rampant daydreams, came to Malvern for Gully's water cure. Versed in the ways of the continental spas, Gully had a way with nervous or hysterical women: he recognized that the pressures of chastity and the lack of meaningful occupation could contribute to illness.

In Gully's view the many nervous symptoms his patients brought to him had their source in both mental and physical causes. Improper diet, forced sexual relations, insomnia, masturbation, the use of opiates, drink, together with prolonged study, disappointed passions and boredom all produced nervous symptoms which the water cure could help alleviate. Gully's views about the difficulties unhappy marriage could cause were echoed in the 1870s in the correspondence columns of women's magazines.

It was in April 1870 that Florence Bravo's mother sent her nineteen-year-old daughter and her then husband, twenty-one-year-old Alexander Ricardo, to Dr Gully's Malvern spa, so that they could reorder their unhappy and dissolute lives. Ricardo was violent when drunk. He was often drunk. Brutal sexual relations may have blighted the young Florence's romantic views on marriage. In any event, Gully recommended the couple separate. A year later, Ricardo was dead after a spree in Cologne. A prostitute was at his side.

Gully's ministrations saw the now very rich Florence through shock, mourning and all the attendant travails. Soon the married Gully, who was estranged from his seventeen-years-older second wife, gave up much of his work at Malvern, in part to devote himself to his young widowed patient. Her parents disowned her as a result.

Gully travelled to the continent with her. If they didn't formally share rooms, they were certainly intimate. He was sixty-three to her twenty-one. Perhaps his older man's sexuality proved less violent than the rampant Ricardo's. In any case, sex there certainly was, since veiled comments abound about a female malady that probably veiled an abortion. This, together with Gully's very success as a doctor, is perhaps what led to Florence breaking off relations with him. Cured, newly capable of independence, the wealthy young widow wanted the marriage her parents approved and the married Gully couldn't provide. One came with the reportedly tempestuous lawyer, Charles Bravo. When Bravo died of poisoning in April 1876, only four months after the wedding, it seemed for a while that the inquest would find Florence guilty. Her immoral past with Gully, the suggestion that they had been complicit in abortion, were already for the Victorians signs of criminal propensities. Then too, Dr Gully had moved into the mansion next door to hers, and Charles Bravo loathed this predecessor in his wife's affections.

Florence's relations with Dr Gully formed the scandalous centrepiece of the second inquest, and it looked likely that the doctor – whom *The Times* called a man 'in violation of the heavy duties of his profession and with no excuse from the passions of youth or even of middle life' – would be implicated in murder. But in fact the inquest ended with an indeterminate verdict: there was insufficient evidence to lay Charles Bravo's death at any door, even his own. Shamed in court and in the press, Dr Gully and Florence never made it up. She died two years after the inquest, not yet quite thirty-three, and 'suffering from the effects of an undue amount of stimulants'. He was not around to tend to her, and he duly followed her five years later, in 1883 – a year after his wife: it was her unexpectedly long life that had prevented him from marrying the young Florence, whom he evidently loved.

Like Christiana, these women simply didn't seem to fit the sought-after Victorian mould. Yet the very avidity with which the press reported on their trials suggests that, as monstrous or excessive as they might be seen to be, they reflected a malaise that was hardly unique. Certainly by the late 1850s, newspapers regularly used such terms as 'hysteria', and even the newer diagnoses of erotomania and nymphomania, to describe a host of female maladies that the women before the divorce or criminal courts purportedly suffered from. The last two diagnoses had come into the current lexicon when J.-E. D. Esquirol published his *Mental Maladies* in 1838, a treatise on insanity that was translated into English in 1845.

Nymphomaniacs were considered to be victims of a physical disorder that could express itself in the most 'shameful and humiliating acts'. Erotomaniacs, on the other hand, suffered from a chronic mental illness characterized by a 'mad tenderness', an excessive love, sometimes for an imaginary other. In erotomania, love is in the mind and the imagination and solipsistic sex alone is in play. Esquirol describes his erotomaniacs as obsessively, deludedly in love with an

admired man of higher or idealized status. They devote their love to
the secret cult of this object with an ecstasy that blinds them to any of
his reality. They are 'restless, thoughtful, gently depressed in mind,
agitated, irritable and passionate. Their moods shift rapidly from gay
laughter to weeping melancholy.' They behave, in other words, like
classic romantic lovers. Christiana Edmunds would be called both a
nymphomaniac and an erotomaniac. In the twentieth century, de
Clérambault and then Jacques Lacan would explore erotomania's
forms, underlining components of arrogance, a belief on the part of
the sufferer in her own high and special status, a hypersensitivity to
slight, and a tendency towards paranoid thoughts – characteristics
Christiana exhibited.

A surprisingly long definition of erotomania, citing Esquirol in
French, appears in the commentary on Mrs Robinson's case in the
Morning Post of 8 July 1858. Perhaps to use English about such delicate
matters would have been considered a step too far. Interestingly, the
commentary begins with a line approving the work of the psychologists (a word that was only beginning to take on its medical meaning
at that time). The writer tells us these psychologists 'have accurately
described the mental disease of Mrs Robinson'. The proof of Dr Lane's
innocence, he argues, is also the proof of Mrs Robinson's insanity.
'The sliding scale of cases which lead from the domain of sanity to
those of insanity is so gently graduated as to render it difficult to say
where the dividing line between the two ought to be drawn.' But Mrs
Robinson's diary would, according to the best experts, mark her out
as an erotomaniac, 'possessed of highly imaginative powers morbidly
excited, of an immense copiousness in passionate eloquence, and of
an ungovernable *cacoetez* [*cacoethes*] *scribendi*'. The Latin term comes
from Juvenal and is best translated here as an 'itch' or irresistible
desire to write.

Christiana Edmunds in her torrent of letters to Charles Beard –
the traitorous showing of which to his wife occasioned Christiana's
poisoning spree – gave evidence of the itch and of the same imaginative loquacity as Mrs Robinson. So, too, did Edith Thompson in the

outpourings of her romantic passion for Frederick Bywaters, her lover: it was on the grounds of these 'immoral' letters and her own histrionic performance in court, in December 1922, that judge and jury deemed poor Edith to have made 'common purpose' with her lover in murdering her husband. Female stalkers today, the psychiatrists tell us, have a propensity to stalk by email or text.

The *Morning Post* commentator, who sounds as if he might well himself be a 'suffering' doctor, having quoted approvingly from Esquirol, finishes with a flourish that would place Isabella Robinson and Christiana Edmunds, as well as a host of unnamed others, in the erotomanic category. 'Many physicians,' he tells us, 'have suffered from baseless imputations, the result of the insane imaginings of monomaniacs of Mrs Robinson's class. Groups of cases often occur together ... '

Loving doctors, it seems, is something of a female habit at a time when they are seen to be part of a privileged cohort armed with expert knowledge of women's bodies and minds.

Meanwhile, the trials that ensued publicized the existence of women's sexual nature, its dangers and satisfactions, outside reproduction and marriage.

8. *At the Old Bailey*

At the end of her hearing at Brighton Crown Court, Christiana Edmunds was remanded to Lewes County Prison to await trial on the charge of murder. Of what went through her mind during her four months of waiting, only one matter is clear: Christiana wanted to see her beloved Dr Beard. This didn't happen. On 28 December 1871, under the Central Criminal Court Act of 1856, also known as Palmer's Act, she was taken up to London to be tried at the Old Bailey: it was thought the furore around her case would jeopardize the possibility of an unbiased trial in Brighton. There is an irony here that Christiana might have been alert to. William Palmer, after whom the Act was named, was a doctor who, in 1856 having poisoned a close friend with strychnine – and probably also his wife, mother-in-law, brother and children – and collected large sums in insurance, was moved to London for trial on the grounds that his native Staffordshire could not provide him with a fair one.

The press duly noted the Brighton Poisoner's arrival at Newgate and her dismay at the conditions there. Being housed in a double cell on the women's side of the prison in company with 'an educated woman in custody on a charge of bigamy' is simply not good enough for Christiana. Throughout her ordeal, she manifests a prickly sense of her own status and a marked attention to the signs that demonstrate it. She makes it clear that she is a lady and this is not the kind of treatment she is used to: she has to have her own clothes and her own cutlery.

Christiana immediately asked for an interview with the visiting magistrates, and then the governor of the prison. She remonstrated 'with great volubility'. At the Lewes prison, she claimed, she had occupied the same apartment as the matron, had 'been permitted to change her dress as often as she liked' and to wear her bonnet to chapel. Here, the 'velvet dresses and furs suitable for the present season which she had brought with her from Lewes to Newgate had been denied her'. When the prison chaplain came to see her, she explained that the chaplain at the Sussex County Prison at Lewes had been very kind to her, and it would make more sense for her to continue seeing him. He would not have forced her to submit to a regime that sent her to chapel without a bonnet, not to mention without her sealskin jacket – two items of which Newgate had deprived her. Even a visit from an alderman, sent by the governor, who patiently explained that it was desirable that Christiana exhibit 'a somewhat more conciliatory manner, and conform to rules which could not possibly be framed to suit every person', did nothing to mollify her. His arguments made not the 'smallest impression': she supposed she would now have to appeal to the sheriff. It was explained to her that he had nothing to do with the daily running of the prison.

So intensive was the reporting of the fuss that Christiana made, that the governor at Lewes felt forced the next day to point out that Christiana Edmunds had been treated in all respects according to the regulations of that jail and had had no special indulgences. She hadn't lodged with the matron. Her rail transport from prison to prison had been with a second-class ticket in an ordinary railway carriage in the company of the chief warder. However, since Christiana was not a convicted prisoner and with all due regard for prison security, the 'regulations do not require, neither does justice appear to demand the imposition of vexatious restraints or indignities upon persons who are committed to prison for safe custody only, but not for the infliction of penal correction'.

This was a gentle reminder that for all her time behind bars, Christiana had not yet been convicted. Her insistence on what we would now call her 'rights', or at least her dignities, are in that sense remarkable and point to the thought that, at least in her own mind, she was innocent of the charge of murder. Papers like the

Pall Mall Gazette mocked, while others reprimanded this uppity prisoner.

The trial of the Brighton Poisoner began on 15 January 1872. As ever, there was much else in the news to concern the public and the press. In the month around the trial there had been a total solar eclipse. Parents who neglected to send their children to elementary school – in accordance with the 1870 Education Act – were being fined. Differences had surfaced amongst the promoters of women's suffrage. Over in France there was a monetary crisis in the new Third Republic, while in Britain agitation was under way for a reform of the hereditary House, which was seen to be inconsistent with liberalism. In the United States, in the wake of the Civil War and continuing malaise between North and South, Federal and State authority, President Grant decided not to introduce martial law in Louisiana; while on 17 January a second African-American Congressman was sworn in.

But reporters and public poured into the Old Bailey. First of all, that January, they came to watch the unfurling of another rare middle-class trial, that of the so-called Stockwell murderer. The ageing and now feeble Reverend John Watson, having lost his post as master of Stockwell Grammar School in south London, had murdered his wife on 8 October the previous year in an act of brutal and uncharacter-istic violence. Watson shared a defence counsel with Christiana Edmunds. In the cleric's case, Serjeant Parry argued that the Reverend was of 'unsound mind' and had had no knowledge of the 'difference between right and wrong' at the time he had carried out his act of 'maniacal passion'. English law, Parry contended, had never attempted fully to define 'what insanity was', but it was as much of a disease as 'typhus, paralysis, or epilepsy'. Under ordinary circumstances, Watson was 'a kind and humane man', 'a man of learning and high character', who 'led an ordinary and blameless life'. But at the time of the murder, his mind had been 'perverted and overthrown' by his hope-less circumstances and he had committed a furious act utterly 'inconsistent with the whole of his former life'.

The Reverend Watson and Christiana Edmunds, these two unusually bourgeois murderers, would over the next weeks often be considered together by the press. It will perhaps come as no surprise that the elderly Reverend was treated far more sympathetically, despite the brutality of his murder of a loyal wife, than the Borgia of Brighton.

Well dressed women made up a large number of those crowding into the galleries of the Old Bailey's New Court on 15 January. From their numbers it would seem that Christiana interested women in particular. Her unrequited, excessive and illicit love had allegedly led her to attempt something monstrous. But how many other women may not have secretly wished a legitimate partner dead so that the man of their dreams might be free for them? Her plight, as she attempted to exonerate herself from Dr Beard's accusation of attempting to poison his wife by distributing ever more poison chocolates, elicited both horror and pity. By acting on her desires, Christiana had entered the zone of the impermissible. In attempting to make wish enter the domain of the real, she was sailing into the terrain of madness. Whatever echoes of their own lives, emotions and fears the gathered women may have found in her drama, it was clear that there was something about Christiana, their 'accused sister', that mesmerized.

As for the men who attended Christiana's trial or read about it in the press, their fascination may well have been edged with terror. Men, after all, were the most frequent victims of female poisoners, particularly if they happened to be married to them. Back in 1852, Charles Dickens's journal *Household Words* had run an article on poisoning which underscored its female nature, attesting that murder by poison 'admits more readily of fiendish sophistication in the mind of the perpetrator than any other form by which murder is committed'.

The *Daily News* reporter at the Old Bailey presents an unsettling and ambivalent picture of Christiana. It is redolent both of the conflicts she lived and of the contradictions with which she confronted her viewers. On the one hand she is a delicate and poised innocent, dainty in her gestures, a composed Everywoman. 'Attired in sombre velvet, bare headed, with a certain self-possessed demureness in her bearing – at the first glance she seems as common-place a woman as the world might well contain.' There is 'no perceptible blush or tremor' – which could suggest guilt or indeed a greater modesty than Christiana possesses – as she stands 'in her solitude' in the dock and looks 'straight to the front', or inspects the courtroom, 'dwelling specially in her gaze' on the benches where the 'lady spectators' sit and occasionally raising her brows with 'a sudden quick flash of the dark eyes' as she perhaps recognizes someone she knows. Once more, Christiana, an ardent writer, 'takes copious notes': 'her daintily gloved hand pushed a quill pen again and again up to the inkholder bedded in the flat top of the front of the dock'. Smiling occasionally, perhaps at what she is writing, she listens with 'attentive composure, watching every word' the prosecutor utters, occasionally darting a sharp glance at him.

On the other hand, Christiana is also a much more troubling creature than this would suggest. The reporter delves into animal imagery to conjure up a portrait reminiscent of the mad and prowling Bertha in Mr Rochester's attic, a creature of dangerous instinctual and criminal force all set to burn down the respectable edifice of bourgeois life. Marking the transition between the innocent and the madly bad is the figure of the governess. Aside from the teacher, the governess is the only other respectable working woman Victorian England permits. But this respectability itself is open to challenge. Not only does the governess have to work as something of a servant. She is also the outsider in the sanctuary of the home, the 'other' woman. Christiana, this 'rather careworn, hard-featured woman of 35', might have been a 'day governess for years – might have acquired the patience and chilled self-control that prolonged teaching under precarious conditions is calculated to impart, and that half sullen resignation – with an only occasional flash of self assertion – which successive batches of children and successive exigeant lady mothers are apt to engender'.

And now the reporter, having pitied, is freed to move into the terrain of bestial ugliness:

> The face is plain, decidedly plain; the complexion rather dark
> with some colour underlying the swarthiness. The forehead, and
> whole forefront of the head is large, and projects with somewhat
> exceptional prominence ... But the character of the face lies in
> the lower feature. The profile is irregular, but not unpleasing;
> the upper lip is long, and convex; mouth slightly projecting; chin
> straight, long and cruel; the lower jaw heavy, massive and animal
> in its development. The lips are loose – almost pendulous – the
> lower one being fullest and projecting, and the mouth is exceptionally large.

Like a good Victorian characterologist influenced by the ever popular 'science' of phrenology – an invention of the Viennese Franz-Joseph Gall, who had begun his work with criminals and the insane and in his hypotheses on brain localization had linked particular skull areas and their exaggerated bumps with murder and destructiveness – the *Daily News* reporter sees physiognomy as speaking a person's essence. Just four years later, in 1876, he would have had the Italian criminologist Cesare Lombroso to hand to argue that criminality could be read from physiognomy and inherited facial features, and to confirm him in finding something sinister, a mark of the inborn female criminal, in the unsightly sensuality of Christiana's pendulous lips and the force of that large, primitive, animal jaw.

Whether or not this description of Christiana is accurate we have no way of knowing. But the unsettling clash of features the reporter gives her falls into the period's typology of potentially dangerous women: those whose intelligence or sexuality shows, arousing anxieties about their gender. According to popular phrenological lore, the lower part of the face – lips, chin, jaw – gave evidence of 'appetite', the larger the first, the greater the second. Like Wilkie Collins when he first conjures up an uncannily double-gendered Marian Halcombe in

The Woman in White, the reporter attributes both masculine intelligence
and feminine weakness to Christiana:

> From the configuration of the lips the mouth might be thought
> weak, but a glance at the chin removes any such impression; and
> Christiana Edmunds has a way of compressing the lips occasionally,
> when the left side of the mouth twists up with a sardonic, defiant
> determination, in which there is something of a weird comeliness,
> that gradually hardens, and passes into absolute grimness. Of per-
> ception and intelligence the prisoner has no lack.

Through most of the first day's proceedings Christiana is utterly
composed, bar a certain weary lassitude which creeps in with the
afternoon. But everything changes when her beloved Dr Beard comes
to the witness stand at the end of the day. Then, 'her bosom heaved
convulsively, and her face flushed scarlet. But a moment after it had
faded to a leaden pallor, and she had regained her composure.' The
only other time that she manifests spontaneous feeling is when the
last witness of the day is being examined, a woman who has lived in
the same Brighton house as Christiana and her mother: the woman
testifies to her 'uniform kindliness and womanly demeanour'.
Christiana yields for a moment and appears to be moved to tears.
Reputation and passion are ever at war in her.

Christiana Edmunds folded into herself the tensions that characterized what it meant to be woman in her time: the desire for virtue
and reputation collide with wayward desire; the need for feminine
passivity abuts on the wish – perhaps inevitably unconscious or at
least repressed through time – for freedom of movement and action.
All this cohabits with a restless dissatisfaction with the dividing lines
between the secret and the licit.

John Ruskin, one of the period's leading moralists and critics – a
man who, from the evidence of his own unconsummated and
annulled marriage to Effie Gray, was terrified of women's 'living' as
opposed to idealized bodies – underlines the forces that prey on

women and the taxing demands they must strive to meet. From 1 January 1871, just before Christiana's trial, Ruskin began to publish the widely quoted and argued pamphlets that became his multi-volumed *Fors Clavigera*. Addressed to 'the workmen and labourers of Britain', these 'letters' both analytic and didactic on how to be and behave so as to attain the good life, mark out Ruskin's social and moral mission. Britain had, he was convinced, become too materialistic, a land governed by the trains he so loathed and everything that came with them. Instead of food, England now produced only 'infernal' goods: 'iron guns, gunpowder, infernal machines, infernal fortresses floating about, infernal fortresses standing still, infernal means of mischievous locomotion, infernal law-suits, infernal parliamentary elocution, infernal beer, and infernal gazettes, magazines, statues, and pictures'.

Ruskin's catalogue makes an equivalence between infernal guns, lawsuits, magazines, statues and pictures, the products of material production and media. All these latter seem to be particularly hazardous to women. He pictures a mother who may not be able to feed her children but who can 'get to London cheap', though she has no business to be there. Even though she has no concern for any of it, she can 'buy all the morning's news for a half-penny'. For a shilling, she can see that risqué Frenchman Gustave Doré's lowlife pictures – 'and she had better see the devil'. 'She can be carried through any quantity of filthy streets on a tramway for threepence; but it is as much as her life's worth to walk in them, or as her modesty's worth to look into a print shop in them.'

In Ruskin's vision women's very ability to walk around freely constitutes a danger to virtue: tempted by the depravity of the streets and led astray by cheap and seductive commodities, women are really only safe at home. Letter 33 in *Fors Clavigera* asserts:

> The end of all right education for a woman is to make her love her home better than any other place; that she should as seldom leave it as a queen her queendom; nor ever feel entirely at rest but within its threshold.

Christiana Edmunds had sinned against this ideal of womanhood in multifarious ways. She had dared to travel on her own: she had taken that smoky railway from Brighton to Margate and from there into the depravity of London; then came the two-hour journey back to Brighton on the same train as her poisoned sweetmeats. She had walked the streets on her own, an act that seems already to stand in for sexual activity, the euphemistic 'street-walking' that it is feared it may lead to; and she had taken a room at a 'hotel' on her own. This was transgression on a major scale, though to elicit Ruskin's heated warning it must have been shared by sufficient women.

On top of all this, in an attempt to win back her married lover together with her reputation (that term that carries the all-important Victorian slippage between status and virtue), she had planned and plotted and behaved in such a way as to divert suspicion from herself as the poisoner of Emily Beard. With no man's help, she had allegedly purchased her sweetmeats, injected them with the strychnine and arsenic obtained through a variety of ruses, distributed her chocolate creams and publicly testified at an inquest. She had even confronted police Inspector Gibbs with the taunt that he would 'never find it out'. The risk in all this was enormous, and at the end it had landed her here, at the Old Bailey. Christiana was definitely bad. Where that badness might shade into madness now became a matter for general conjecture.

There were several models available, in both press reports and popular literature, for Christiana and the public to draw on and elaborate.

Uncanny echoes of her trajectory exist in the 'sensational' novels of her own day. The femmes fatales here are often represented as seductively fatal to men, but in the end seem to be fatal mostly to themselves. In Mary Elizabeth Braddon's bestselling novel *Lady Audley's Secret* (1862), Lady Audley uses her outstanding beauty and her native cunning to escape poverty. Her path from first love to bigamy, and finally to a 'murder' which isn't quite one, is certainly bad. Yet her noble husband and nephew prefer to think such badness, when it resides in so lovely a receptacle of femininity, must be madness:

otherwise, the social order would be destroyed. As the mad doctor called in to diagnose Lady Audley states: 'You would wish to prove that this lady is mad, and therefore irresponsible for her actions.' Our hero Robert Audley, who can find no other way to comprehend such extreme behaviour, responds: 'Yes . . . I would rather, if possible, think her mad.'

Wilkie Collins's Lydia Gwilt in his novel *Armadale* of 1866 – like Christiana and Lady Audley, a woman who can barely afford the middle-class trappings she both wants and feels she is owed – is brazen both in her desires and in her class rage. Beautiful, she takes her freedom and strides the streets of London and foreign capitals, only to end her days a suicide at the quack Dr Downward's clinic for the mad. Fascinating it may be, but sexualized female badness slides into madness in the blink of a male eye that would prefer such excess to be utterly aberrant. Like these fictional creations, Christiana Edmunds, in that daring that had tragic repercussions, both attracted and repelled; and her much reported trial – headlined a 'sensation' trial by some papers – filled the unoccupied hours and the imaginations of a leisured class.

The 'Mean Places' of the Law

'Verily we administer justice in mean places,' the *Daily News* reporter opined as he navigated his way into the Old Bailey through a 'hurry of ladies' and robed men, through aldermen and sheriffs wearing unwieldy court swords, then through a Scylla and Charybdis of policemen. At last reached, the courtroom was a space so dingy that a surgeon would be ashamed to cut off a leg in it or a reputable professor deliver a lecture. 'It is a square well with a lid on the top.' To the west, the jury sits beneath a row of dirty windows. To the north is the bench, a long elevated platform, thinly upholstered. A wooden canopy and an antique sword, presumably of justice, mark the centre of the room; and next to these on either side sit the judge and the officials of the court. The room's east side is for the privileged spectators and the press. To the south, a large wooden pen makes up the dock, glass-panelled on both sides but open in the front. The gallery is above it, and here the public are squashed in. Finally, in the well of the court sit the barristers.

As the clock strikes two, the jury file into their box and the usher calls for silence. Ermine, gold chains and frills fill the empty bench. The judge Mr Baron Martin takes his seat, followed by the sheriffs, aldermen and under-sheriffs. This gaudy entrance almost blots out the arrival of a demure, quiet-eyed woman in black velvet trimmed with fur, who is followed by a hard-faced female warder and a male jailer. The indictment is read out. Christiana Edmunds is accused of 'wilful murder' in having caused the death by poisoning of the boy Sidney Albert Barker.

'Not guilty,' she says in a firm, low voice. This pronouncement was 'followed by a momentary aversion of the face'. The jury are sworn in and she challenges none of them. Then Serjeant Ballantine, presenting the case for the prosecution, begins his address in a 'studiously modulated voice of low pitch, and with a total absence of gesticulation'.

William Ballantine (1812–87), Christiana's prosecutor, was a leading criminal barrister, reputed to be a subtle and searching cross-examiner. Born into the legal profession, he had long served at the Central Criminal Court; but he loved theatre and literature above all else, and on retiring wrote *Some Experiences of a Barrister's Life* (1882). As a youth he had frequented literary taverns and met Dickens and Trollope. In *Orley Farm*, the novel that was his personal favourite, Trollope had based his wily barrister Chaffanbrass on his old friend, whose reputation had grown with his performance for both defence and prosecution. In this genial satire Ballantine becomes that 'great guardian of the innocence or rather not-guiltiness of the public', a lawyer who devotes himself 'to the manumission of murderers or the security of the swindling world in general'.

Ballantine was elevated in 1856 to the distinguished position of Serjeant at Law. The rank, which entailed the wearing of a special coif or wig, was abolished in the judicial reforms of 1873. He had tried some famous and also delicate cases, one of which was the notorious Mordaunt divorce trial of 1870 in which Sir Charles Mordaunt, a Conservative MP, sued his young and erring wife, who had just given birth, for divorce, threatening to name the Prince of Wales as co-respondent. The public scandal echoed the earlier Robinson divorce case. Harriet Mordaunt's father, a noble and conservative Scotsman, determined madness was more reputable than divorce and had his daughter confined. Ballantine's examination of the Prince on the witness stand was said to have been a model of tactful, prosecutorial behaviour.

Christiana's defence barrister, briefed by her Brighton lawyer Charles Lamb, was the eminent Serjeant John Humffreys Parry (1816–80). Parry, too, had literary leanings and had worked in the printed books department of the British Museum while studying law. He was called to the Bar in 1843 and developed a courtroom style that was notable for its clarity and simplicity, though it could also rise to melodramatic heights. Known for his criminal work, Parry also handled many compensation cases. His politics were those of an advanced liberal: he was one of the founders of the Complete Suffrage Association. Twice he contested a parliamentary seat and twice he lost. He and Ballantine were frequent sparring partners.

Parry had defended and Ballantine had prosecuted in the first British railway murder trial, in 1864, in which a city banker, Thomas Briggs, was beaten, robbed and then thrown out of the train compartment between London's Fenchurch and Hackney Wick, only to die after he was pulled from the tracks and taken to a Hackney pub. Public panic ensued: was this new high-speed technology of the railway not only bad for nerves and landscape, but unsafe for the respectable classes? The trail that led police to the German tailor Franz Müller began nine days later when a London cabbie came to them with suspicions. The police traced Müller to a ship bound for America and contacted police in New York. This piece of transatlantic cooperation eventually saw a small Armada awaiting Müller, together with shouts of 'Welcome to America, murderer!' as his vessel neared New York.

Shipped back to London, Müller stood trial at the Old Bailey that November. He maintained his innocence, and Parry battled for him against Ballantine's wealth of evidence. Though much of this was circumstantial and Parry contested that the incriminating witness had only come forward because of the promise of reward, Müller was found guilty. The fact that he had left what witnesses said was his unusual hat on the train, and exchanged it for Briggs's, was perhaps what did for him, though his foreignness didn't help. Nor did his statement that he had been in a brothel at the time of the murder. Müller was sentenced to hang and even King Wilhelm of Prussia's plea for a stay of execution couldn't save him. He was executed on 18 November that year before a rowdy crowd numbering some fifty thousand, four years before public executions were banned. The Newgate chaplain attested that Müller had confessed – 'Ich habe es getan' – just before his death. Public outcry would eventually lead to trains being built with a connecting aisle between the separate compartments, together with alarms: the earlier remedy of a peep-hole between compartments had brought an outcry from lovers . . .

Parry would go on to act for the artist James McNeill Whistler, who sued the very same Ruskin who preferred his women at home, for libel: in Fors Clavigera, commenting on an exhibition of his in 1876, Ruskin had written, 'I have seen, and heard, much of Cockney impudence before now; but never expected to hear a coxcomb ask two hundred guineas for flinging a pot of paint in the public's face.' Combative but poor, Whistler was unwise to sue: he never got damages. But Parry did win the case for the talented American-born painter, whose 'art for art's sake' Ruskin deplored.

On 15 January 1872 at the Old Bailey, Mr Serjeant Ballantine laid out the case against Christiana Edmunds with a damning logic and an understated aplomb. He had long passed the age, he told the jury, when the conviction of a prisoner brought him a sense of victory. He simply wanted to elicit the truth and administer justice. The prisoner, he said, had formed an acquaintance with Dr Beard which 'seems to have ripened into an intimacy scarcely consistent with the strict relations that ought to exist between a medical adviser and one of his female patients'. There could be no doubt that the lady herself entertained 'the strongest feelings towards Dr Beard, and expressed them in very strong language which indicated on her part a considerable amount of affection towards him'. All of which led her to pursue a course of conduct Ballantine described as 'so extraordinary as to be totally unparalleled in the records of any criminal court of justice'.

Ballantine's exposition of the case against Christiana was masterly. In setting out her relations with Beard he mentions the many letters that 'had been sent between the parties', and states that he will have no objection to them being read out in court in order to further the ends of justice, if 'there is a desire expressed that they should be read'. In the event, the letters are not read. Having shown the passionate motive behind Christiana's extraordinary actions, neither the judge, nor the prosecution, nor the defence seem keen to enter into these murky intimate waters. This, after all, is not a trial for the attempted murder of Emily Beard, but for the wilful murder of Sidney Barker.

At the end of the proceedings, it is clear that Christiana feels her own story has hardly been touched. An unstated gentlemen's agreement, perhaps, too, a moral worry about inflaming the imaginations of the ladies present in the courtroom and the wider readership of the press, means that her 'reality' is never heard. The ins and outs of Christiana's love affair, how much of it was in her mind, how much of it induced or even initially reciprocated by Dr Beard, would never be tested in open court. Wisely for himself, Dr Beard and his wife did not press charges, and so only Christiana's inadvertent murder of little Sidney Barker strictly concerned the court. The passion that had occasioned the crime – those matters that would have kept a French court busy and a French public enthralled – barely surfaced above the barricades of Victorian propriety.

The witnesses for the prosecution were those who had already been examined in the Brighton hearings: Garrett the chemist, the milliner,

the various boys who had served as Christiana's chocolate and strychnine messengers, Maynard the chocolatier, Sidney's father Albert
Barker, the handwriting experts and Inspector Gibbs, who had grown
suspicious of Christiana during the inquest. Christiana's eloquent
anonymous letters to Mr Barker, urging him, as a fellow parent, to
pursue Maynard after the inquest had termed little Sidney's death
'accidental' and had failed to find Maynard guilty of purveying poison
creams, were read out. Towards the very end of the day, Ballantine
called Dr Beard. It was then that Christiana was jarred out of her
composure, 'her bosom heaved convulsively and her face flushed scarlet'. But Parry objected to Ballantine's line of questioning, which
would have taken the court onto the terrain of Christiana's first
attempted poisoning of Emily Beard. Perhaps he was worried that too
much attention to these intimate matters would do his client more
harm than good. Neither did judge nor prosecutor seem eager to go
there. And so Dr Beard's moment on the witness stand extended only
to his saying that he knew the prisoner and had seen Christiana both
in her own home and his. The 'remoteness' of that night on which
Christiana had allegedly attempted to poison Mrs Beard made it
unsuitable to be called as evidence, the judge determined.

The next day Serjeant Parry led Christiana's defence. His tactic, in the
first instance, was to point out just how circumstantial the evidence
tying the chocolate cream that four-year-old Sidney Barker had eaten
to Christiana was. It was all fine and well, he argued in his opening
statement, to have witnesses lined up to say that Christiana might
have impregnated with poison the chocolate that had some weeks
later found its way into Sidney's mouth, but there was nothing to put
her at the scene of the crime or to indicate direct intent. Before con-
victing the prisoner, the jury must be satisfied beyond all doubt that the
'chocolate which caused the little boy's death came to be given to him,
directly or indirectly, through the agency of the prisoner'.

There was a gap in the evidential trail, and Parry wanted the jury to
be aware of his contention that Christiana was not 'wilfully', mali-
ciously or directly guilty of Sidney's murder.

His second line of defence was that Christiana was not guilty on grounds of insanity. The nature of that insanity was in her case 'the entire destruction of her moral sense'. He believed that she could not fully distinguish the difference between right and wrong, or recognize the quality of the act she was committing – the two grounds for legal insanity.

Playing to the jury, Parry 'thanked God that he had not to decide the question for it would baffle him altogether'. It was they who would have to determine whether Christiana's falsehoods in obtaining poison, distributing it in broad daylight among children – 'all for the alleged purpose of disabusing the mind of one man of a strongly formed conviction' – spoke of imbecility or of a strong and vigorous mind. Parry recognized the inconsistency of the argument he was making. At one and the same time, he was arguing, the prisoner was not guilty of the deed, and was not guilty on the ground of insanity, which virtually admitted it. He felt certain the jury would give their verdict under a full appreciation of the evidence adduced on both sides.

Parry then set out to prove that Christiana was of 'impaired intellect', not altogether easy given the intelligence of her letters. Heredity was his strongest suit. Most Victorian doctors believed that madness was inherited, and Christiana's family on both the maternal and paternal sides, as well as her siblings, had suffered from insanity and were of 'unsound mind'. Then, too, she herself had been treated for hysteria and her 'conduct for some time past had excited attention among her friends'. About twelve or fifteen months ago, Parry stated, a great change had come over her, and even now, 'she has the idiotic vanity to deny her real age'.

Christiana's mother was first up for the defence with her long trail of family woes, which the relevant asylum medics – Steward, Armstrong and George W. Grabbam of the Earlswood Asylum – corroborated. Mrs Edmunds finished by saying she had long dreaded that when Christiana reached the age of forty-two – the age at which her father had gone mad – the paternal lunacy would take her over. 'She is so very like her father.' For women the age also indicated the onset of menopause – as mentioned earlier, a time popular lore together with the medics linked to female madness and erotic flights.

Next on the witness stand was the Revd Thomas Henry Cole, the chaplain of Lewes Prison, about whom Christiana had spoken warmly in her first days at Newgate. She had been under his watch until Christmas Day 1871. Rules in the jail had it that if any insanity was noticed in a prisoner, a report should immediately be made to the governor, the surgeon and the visiting justices. Cole had noticed 'a peculiar formation and expression' in Christiana's eyes. At times, she looked vacant. While many conversations might be perfectly coherent, they struck him as extraordinary, given her situation. Where he expected 'great excitement and dejection', he found only 'calmness and exceeding levity'. When he tried to talk to her about the gravity of her situation, she would burst into 'an extraordinary laugh'. She had no power to focus and she would pass in an instant from sudden tears to equally sudden laughter. He believed her to be of 'unsound mind'.

Two Brighton neighbours, the Overs, who had shared the Edmundses' accommodation for two years, now gave witness to how much Christiana had changed over that time. Two years before, she had been ladylike, quiet and good in every way. Then in March or April of the previous year, everything about her had altered. Her eyes had grown very large, and rolled: her entire appearance made Mrs Over uncomfortable. Mr Over corroborated his wife's words, and also drew attention to Christiana's eyes and the 'wildness in her look'. Meanwhile her manner had grown much more excited than before. Christiana had even told Alice Over that she 'felt she was going mad'.

Borderlands: Between Crime and Insanity

It was now time for the medico-legal expert witnesses to take the stand.

Parry had obtained some of the most eminent alienists in the land to furnish opinions on Christiana's mental state at the time of the murder. Dr William Wood, the most junior of them, had served for some ten years as physician to St Luke's Hospital for Lunatics in London and was currently the resident at the oldest asylum in the land, Bethlem. Dr Charles Lockhart Robertson, educated at Edinburgh and Cambridge, had been the first medical superintendent of the Sussex County Asylum, universally recognized, according to his obituary in the *Lancet*, as a 'model institution'. He had very successfully, it seems, introduced calming Turkish baths for the women inmates. He had retired as the asylum's head in 1870 to become an eminent Visitor of Chancery Lunatics – a regular overseer to those individuals judged insane by public trial whose property was administered by the Treasury during the period of their confinement. He was one of the doctors to expose the campaigning alienist L. Forbes Winslow's alleged profiteering. He was also president of the Medico-Psychological Association, and with Christiana's third expert, Dr Henry Maudsley, co-editor of the *Journal of Mental Science*.

Robertson, known as a genial and sociable man, was also one of the alienist profession's early number crunchers. Addressing the delegates to an international congress in London in 1881, he detailed the rise of the lunatic population in England, which by then had reached seventy-one thousand, or one in every 350 of the population. Like his more internationally famous colleague, Dr Maudsley, Lockhart Robertson was hardly likely to find Christiana in full possession of her reason.

The popular and prolific Maudsley was the most publicly prestigious of Christiana's examiners. Victorian England's leading alienist and medico-legal expert, he had by 1872 already published two of his eleven widely read and much translated books: *The Physiology and Pathology of the Mind* (1867) and *Body and Mind* (1870). Maudsley adapted Charles Darwin's and Herbert Spencer's evolutionary ideas to his views on mental illness. He understood this to be a heritable disease with a physical basis and its own visible physiognomy.

Something of a misanthrope, Maudsley was most certainly a misogynist: women were for him inferior and possessed of little intellectual power or judgement. Like many Victorians, he was a believer in the wide-ranging and fluid concept of 'moral insanity', a mixture of ethical idiocy, asocial conduct and vicious, irresponsible character – a category given a medical imprimatur but born of a fear that the urban badlands with their fug of squalor and 'inherited' vice were breeding national degeneracy. Later, when he came to write about hysterics, a classification that could easily stretch, for Maudsley, to most women, he would see them as 'perfect examples of the subtlest deceit, the most ingenious lying, the most diabolic cunning, in the service of vicious impulses'. In 1874, Maudsley would publish *Responsibility in Mental Disease*, which became a touchstone text in formulating understanding of insanity in relation to the law and prodding the latter towards change.

Even if Christiana had had the moral intelligence and reasoning ability of George Eliot, these would have been difficult doctors, in the circumstances, to impress with one's sanity. That said, the insanity plea was Christiana's single defence against a verdict that would bring the gallows centre stage. Only if she could pass the legal definition of insanity was there hope for her life.

The trio of alienists, together with Mr Gibson, the surgeon to Newgate Prison, had seen Christiana some two weeks before the trial for approximately ninety minutes. Dr Wood had been struck by her utter indifference to her position and had failed to make her see its seriousness. He estimated that her mind was 'so weak that she was really incapable of judging between right and wrong in the same sense that other people would'. There was no doubt, he testified, that insanity was hereditary and that the children of the insane were predisposed to commit insane acts, all the more so when the insanity was on both sides of the family.

Cross-examined by Serjeant Ballantine, Dr Wood stated that Christiana had indeed been told the doctors had come to ascertain her state of mind. She seemed to take that in. He had asked her if she understood the consequences of a conviction. Miss Edmunds had replied that she would rather be convicted than 'brought in insane'. He interpreted what, under different circumstances, might be considered a proud woman's response, as her failure to understand the seriousness of the charge against her. Since the legal bar for sanity was the prisoner's ability to distinguish between right and wrong, not only in the general sense but more importantly in relation to her own case, he then asked her whether 'she thought it wrong for a person to destroy the life of another because she believed the husband of that person wished to get rid of her'. Apparently, Christiana took a moment to answer this query about Emily and Charles Beard. Finally she replied that she thought yes, it would be wrong. Yet her manner of saying it didn't convince Dr Wood that she really believed her own words.

It was at this juncture that Christiana abruptly rose from her place in the dock and addressed the court for the first time since her plea. She could remember the doctor's questions, she asserted. But her attempt to demonstrate her sanity – in this case her grasp of memory – was allowed to go no futher. The judge hushed her and ordered her to resume her seat. She could not be heard, he stressed.

Dr Wood was asked to continue. He stated that he couldn't recollect Christiana's response to his comment that sometimes innocent people were convicted. Four of them, after all, were asking questions, so he could only offer a general résumé of what had transpired at the examination.

Serjeant Parry, who despite his client's wish to be considered sane, needed her mad, then pressed Dr Wood on his overall assessment of Christiana. The doctor pointed out that he was judging Miss Edmunds by her 'demeanour and appearance', not by the answers she gave. This is an interesting resort to the physiological register, that textbook for the trained medical gaze. To conclude his expert opinion, Dr Wood repeated that he believed Christiana was not in a state to tell the difference between right and wrong as other people were.

Dr Lockhart Robertson, a specialist in 'insanity as a disease', was next in the box. He had seen the prisoner early in October in Sussex and then again in December when she was at Newgate, in order to ascertain her state of mind before the trial. He confessed that he had great difficulty in coming to a conclusion about her. He considered her case on the borderland between criminality and insanity. Her intellect was clear and free from delusion. But her moral sense was deficient. This was often the case in the offspring of insane parents. He had failed to impress the prisoner with the gravity of her situation. Given the history of the case, he finally determined that she was morally insane – in other words, could not determine right from wrong.

Cross-examined by Ballantine, Robertson repeated that he believed Miss Edmunds had the intellectual knowledge that it was wrong to administer poison to kill a person. But she had an absence of, or deficiency in, moral sense. Translated into current idiom, Robertson is saying that she may have the cognitive wherewithal to distinguish between right and wrong, but the hold of her rational faculties over her emotions or psychological make-up is so weak as to be deficient. The way in which Robertson situates Christiana on the 'borderland' foreshadows psychiatrists' use of the term 'borderline' today, as in borderline personality disorder.

In *Responsibility in Mental Disease* Maudsley would devote a whole chapter to the 'borderland', that shadowy zone where sanity 'shades imperceptibly into insanity', since there is no single 'hard and fast line' to divide one from the other:

> . . . it is a fact of experience that there are many persons who, without being insane, exhibit peculiarities of thought, feeling and character which render them unlike ordinary beings and make them objects of remark among their fellows. They may or may not ever become actually insane, but they spring from families in which insanity or other nervous disease exists, and they bear in their temperament the marks of their peculiar heritage: they have in fact a distinct neurotic temperament – a certain neurosis, and some of them a more specially insane temperament – an insane neurosis.

In his testimony to the court, Dr Maudsley stated he had made the disease of insanity his special study and had written a book on the subject. He largely agreed with Dr Robertson, insofar as he had understood him. Christiana suffered from an extreme deficiency of moral feeling as to the crime with which she was charged. Nor did she realize the position she was in. As to her moral sense, he believed her mind to be impaired: she had a 'want of moral feeling as to events or acts regarding which a perfectly sane person might be expected to exhibit feeling'. This was general amongst the mad who committed crimes. (He had, he added, signed a certificate to the Home Secretary in the case of Reverend Mr Watson, to plead his insanity, too. Watson had demonstrated the same lack of feeling as Miss Edmunds).

Unsurprisingly, the doctors summoned by the defence were united in their opinion of Christiana's insanity. Neither her actions nor her behaviour in prison as she awaited trial were those of a woman whose perceptions of right and wrong were in accordance with the time's morality. She was deviant. Nor did she have any recognizable 'moral feeling' for the little boy she had inadvertently killed. This moral insanity was understood as a disease, propelled into being by inherited facts, and it predisposed the patient to commit criminal acts.

9. *Insanity and the Law*

During the latter half of the nineteenth century, medicine as a whole was becoming more specialized and taking on the imprimatur of scientific ideas. Even in the psychiatric and neurological spheres, recent specializations, there was an aspiration to the exactitude of science and a search for physiological causes for mental disorder. Description and explanation grew a new density and complexity. A host of specialist books and journals appeared. Congresses brought together alienists from all over Europe and America to debate ideas and share research and methods of care. The size of asylums and the numbers considered insane kept pace with this growth, and indeed by the end of the century had outstripped even the profession's ambitions.

Christiana's case was one of several to bring a particular problem to the forefront: the legal understanding of insanity, the whole quagmire of what constituted 'responsibility', now rarely tallied with what was a more sophisticated and certainly more textured medical perception of mental and emotional states. Judging from responses in the press, many in Victorian England felt the doctors had humaneness on their side. The criminal law could be a blunt instrument in trials where madness was at issue. It was at once brutal and unforgiving. True, there was a tradition embedded in the common law that made executing an insane person palpably immoral. But how was a criminal court, with its jury of ordinary citizens who were no experts on the subject, to decide who was and who wasn't insane?

The legal thinking on insanity, rehearsed by barristers and judge in Christiana Edmunds's case, dates back to the great Lord Justice Hale (1609–76), who laid down the basis of English common law as it distinguished itself from the ecclesiastical courts. Hale was unequivocal in banning executions of the insane and is much cited, even in

American courts today, for his precision in delineating all the separate times at which madness might set in during the lengthy trial process:

> If a man in his sound memory commits a capital offence, and before his arraignment he becomes absolutely mad, he ought not by law to be arraigned during such his phrenzy, but be remitted to prison until that incapacity be removed ... If such person after his plea, and before his trial, become of non sane memory, he shall not be tried; or, if after his trial he become of non sane memory, he shall not receive judgment; or if after judgment he become of non sane memory, his execution shall be spared ...

A century later, Sir William Blackstone in his *Commentaries on the Laws of England* (1765–9) repeated the prohibition on the execution of the insane, calling it 'of extreme inhumanity and cruelty'. Insanity made a person 'unfit to plead'. If 'fit to plead', but deemed insane at the time the criminal act was committed, the person was then acquitted on grounds of insanity.

The trouble the courts had was in arriving at an actual definition of insanity, and that ever-wavering dividing line between reason and madness. Blackstone noted that those who suffered from 'a defect of understanding' such as children, or a 'deficiency of will' such as lunatics, could not be held accountable for their own acts, not even for treason.

But how, except in the most obvious cases, were defects of understanding or deficiencies of will to be ascertained? Lord Justice Hale had made a distinction between absolute insanity and partial insanity. The latter described a person who had lucid periods during which understanding reigned: such people, say a 'melancolic', could be considered responsible for a shooting in a criminal court, but yet be stripped of responsibility over property in a civil case. As Henry Maudsley argued in his *Responsibility in Mental Disease*, a disparity had long existed between the criminal and civil law in the definition of insanity, and the bar needed to prove it in court. Partial insanity could in the civil courts deem a person incapable of having full management of himself, his property and his affairs. It would see him confined. But the same partial insanity in the criminal courts was not enough to shield him from full responsibility for any criminal act. Under this aegis, 'it was right to hang for murder one who was not thought fit to take care of himself and his affairs'.

In that slow accrual of precedent that makes up English law, several key cases are repeatedly cited as crucial in defining insanity in the criminal courts. The first of these, given as precedent by Blackstone, is the 1723 trial of Edward Arnold who had shot at Lord Onslow in a country lane when the latter was returning from a hunting expedition. Arnold had never met Onslow, but felt he had been bewitched by him and believed him to be an enemy of the country, author of 'tumults, disturbances, and confusions, and wicked devices'. In court, those who knew him attested that he was mad, but not mad enough to need confinement; that he was sometimes in, sometimes out of, his senses.

Mr Justice Tracy instructed the jurors that in order to acquit they had to decide whether the accused was *totally* insane. 'It is not every kind of frantic humour, or something unaccountable in a man's actions, that points him out to be such a madman as is exempted from punishment: it must be a man that is totally deprived of his understanding and memory, and doth not know what he is doing, no more than an infant, than a brute or a wild beast; such a one is never the object of punishment.'

This landmark trial gave the courts the so-called wild-beast test as the standard of insanity. Arnold, his delusion about Onslow apart, was not completely raving, and was convicted. He had not met the absolute insanity criteria. A death sentence awaited him, but Lord Onslow successfully urged his reprieve, and Arnold became a prisoner at Southwark jail where he lived on for another thirty years. Mercy, even for the partially mad, was gradually enshrined as a tradition.

Justice Tracy's instruction to his jury clarified the law. Not guilty by reason of insanity was a possible verdict. But if insanity was only deemed partial – in other words the accused did not pass the wild-beast test and was not wholly deprived of understanding and memory – he would hang. Only at the turn of the century would a new understanding of what constituted criminal insanity come into play. This time the crime targeted the King himself.

On 15 May 1800, James Hadfield (or Hatfield), a soldier who had suffered severe head wounds, attempted to assassinate George III. His motive formed part of a delusion. He was convinced that only if he assassinated the King would he undergo judicial execution and be killed by the government of England, a fate that he was adamant would bring the second coming closer. While the national anthem played after a performance of *Figaro* at the Theatre Royal, Drury Lane, Hadfield took aim, fired two shots, and missed. Brought to trial for high treason, he was defended by the talented barrister Thomas Erskine, who put a new and subtler definition of madness into the casebooks.

Hadfield wasn't insane in the terms of the wild-beast test: he was neither a dumb animal – that is, mentally disabled – nor a wild one, in a state of perpetual savage raving. This, Erskine argued, was far too simple a description of insanity: total deprivation of memory and understanding was very rare. 'No such madness ever existed in the world.' In the many cases that had filled Westminster Hall with complicated considerations, it was delusion on a particular subject which was the marker of insanity.

> Insane persons ... have not only had the most perfect knowledge and recollection of all the relations they stood in towards others, and of the acts and circumstances of their lives, but had in general been remarkable for subtlety and acuteness; ... But the premises from which they reason, when within the range of the malady, are uniformly false: not false from any defect of knowledge or judgment, but because a delusive image, the inseparable companion of real insanity, is thrust upon the subjugated understanding, incapable of resistance, because unconscious of attack.

Hadfield, Erskine argued, not only knew right from wrong, but was conscious of the act he was committing and had manifested design and cunning in executing it. He fully expected to be punished, since that was his primary motive. Still, it was quite clear to everyone that he was mad. Delusion 'unaccompanied by frenzy or raving madness', Erskine argued, was the 'true character of insanity'.

Erskine won his case. With his victory, a subtler definition of madness, one that allowed for 'partial' insanity and did not necessarily lead to a guilty verdict, came into the law. Since the prisoner had both to be treated humanely and have his condition recognized, but had also to be kept off the streets so that society could be kept secure, a new Criminal Lunatics Act (1800) was speedily passed through Parliament. Hitherto, the criminally mad were often sent into the 'care' of their families – as Mary Lamb had been by the coroner after killing her mother – rather than institutionalized by law. With the 1800 Act in place, Hadfield could be detained indefinitely 'at His Majesty's pleasure' – a period which usually constituted a life sentence, though it could, if a reviewing body saw fit, mean eventual release. Eight years later, the County Asylums Act 1808 established institutions for the criminally insane, of which the first opened in Northampton in 1811.

Maudsley, in his *Responsibility in Mental Disease*, argues that the Hadfield trial – though it marked, thanks to Erskine's eloquent pleading, a victory of 'common sense over legal dogma' – did not definitively succeed in bringing forward 'a judicial adoption of delusion in place of the old criterion of responsibility'. He cites the Bellingham case of 1812 as an example.

In this complex case, Prime Minister Spencer Perceval was shot as he was making his way through the lobby of the House of Commons to the Chamber by John Bellingham, a man who had worked for a merchant in Russia, had been imprisoned there for five years, in both Archangel and St Petersburg, though he continually protested his innocence of the charge of fraud and of non-payment of a debt. Finally released through ambassadorial intervention, Bellingham sought compensation when he returned to Britain in 1809. It wasn't forth-coming, and he took his grievance ever higher, finally arriving at the Treasury. He wrote to the Treasury stating that 'I consider His Majesty's Government to have completely endeavoured to close the door of justice, in declining to have, or even permit, my grievances to be brought before Parliament for redress, which privilege is the birthright of every individual'. If his reasonable request were denied, Bellingham went on, 'I shall then feel justified in executing justice myself...'

On 11 May 1812, he did so. He was tried for murder four days later before Lord Mansfield, Lord Chief Justice of Common Pleas. Bellingham justified his action; his counsel, entering an insanity plea, asked for a postponement so that evidence of Bellingham's insanity from people who knew him in Liverpool could be put before the court. It was refused, a fact which pleased Bellingham who, like many of those con-fronted with an insanity defence, did not think himself insane. Indeed, he had proceeded with great logic, procuring two guns and ammuni-tion and making a prior visit to the Commons. The judicial reasoning that postponement was refused was that Bellingham had been living in London for some time before the assassination with no visible signs of insanity, and any family testimony produced would not relate to his current condition. A verdict of guilty was brought in and on Monday 18 May, only a week after the assassination, he was hanged.

In his statement to the jury, Lord Chief Justice Mansfield described the state of the law on insanity until that time. He drew attention to the distinction between partial and total insanity but, significantly, he never once referred to Erskine's stunning argument about 'delusion'. There were no specialist medical alienists to refute him to hand.

There are various species of insanity. Some human creatures are void of all power of reasoning from their birth, such could not be guilty of any crime. There is another species of madness in which persons were subject to temporary paroxysms, in which they were guilty of acts of extravagance – this was called Lunacy. If these persons committed a crime when they were not affected with the malady, they were to all intents and purposes amenable to justice. So long as they can distinguish good from evil, so long are they answerable for their conduct. There is a third species of insanity, in which the patient fancied the existence of injury, and sought an opportunity of gratifying revenge, by some hostile act; if such a person was capable, in other respects, of distinguishing right from wrong, there is no excuse for any act of atrocity which he might commit under this description of derangement ... The single question is, whether at the time this act was committed, he [Bellingham] possessed a sufficient degree of understanding to distinguish good from evil, right from wrong.

In the heated atmosphere of a prime-ministerial assassination, it is perhaps unsurprising that Bellingham was convicted. But some, notably Henry Brougham, an advocate of legal reform, were deeply critical. Bellingham had been tried with undue haste and in a climate that was inimical to justice, he argued: not enough time or attention had been paid to the insanity plea.

In Dr Henry Maudsley's analysis, some sixty-two years and a great deal of mind-doctoring activity later, what had happened was that the old wild-beast test of insanity and criminal responsibility had mutated, with Bellingham, into a test of whether the accused had the power of distinguishing right from wrong in a general way, even if not where his own crime was concerned. In Maudsley's view, many of the 'insane' had little trouble with abstract principles of right and wrong, but they were blind when it came to their own mad delusions.

Indeed, the logic of retributive justice that Bellingham himself presented to the court was impeccable, though it had led to murder. Underlying many of the murderous crimes committed by otherwise seemingly reasonable people is the sense that they are impelled to act in order to restore justice. The fact that others find their analysis of the 'real' bizarre, or are incapable of sharing their reality, is in fact what constitutes their madness. Bellingham's own address to the court could stand in for what many other accused feel: 'Gentlemen, a refusal of justice was the sole cause of this fatal catastrophe ... I was driven to despair and under those agonised feelings I was impelled to that desperate alternative which I unfortunately adopted.'

Bellingham concludes his defence like some political radical driven to direct action: '... what is my crime to the crime of government itself? It is no more than a mite to a mountain, unless it was proved that I had malice propense towards the unfortunate gentleman for whose death I am now upon trial. I disclaim all personal or intentional malice against Mr Perceval.'

In this vein it could be said of Christiana Edmunds that she found herself impelled to lift a hand with a poisoned chocolate in it to the mouth of the woman who stood in the way of her obtaining 'justice' in the form of Charles Beard's 'promised' love; when it didn't come, she was driven to the 'desperate alternative' of broadcasting her poison, but with no 'intentional malice' of killing Sidney Barker.

The M'Naghten case of 1843 introduced a new degree of subtlety into the understanding of legal insanity and became the model for all cases of criminal responsibility in Anglo-American and commonwealth law, including India.

Daniel M'Naghten (1813–65) was the illegitimate son of a Scottish woodturner. According to the great advocate who defended him, Alexander Cockburn, later to be the leading jurist in the Isabella Robinson case, M'Naghten was a man of sober habits and 'of singularly sensitive mind [who] spent his days in incessant labour and toil, and at night gave himself up to the study of difficult and abstruse matters'. After a period as a journeyman when his father would not accept him as a partner, he went on to run his own business in Glasgow, using his free time to attend the Glasgow Mechanics' Institute and a debating society. Late in 1840, already prey to a sense 'that persons persecuted him' and suffering from torturing headaches, he sold this lucrative enterprise. Why? – because 'the fearful phantasms of his own imagination rendered his existence miserable' and 'these terrifying delusions had become associated with the place of his abode haunting him at all hours of day and night'.

M'Naghten travelled to England and France, but he couldn't escape his persecutors, and late in 1841 he returned to Glasgow. He acted, according to Cockburn, as a sane man would act: he went to the authorities of his native place, to those who could afford him protection, and 'with clamours, entreats and implores them to defend him from the conspiracy' that was affecting his happiness and his whole life. But when M'Naghten told his father and the Glasgow police commissioner that he was being persecuted by the Tories and followed by their spies, they only tried to dissuade, and provided no help. So on the afternoon of 20 January 1843, M'Naghten approached Prime Minister Robert Peel's private secretary, Edward Drummond, who had just emerged from the Prime Minister's house, and shot him from behind at point-blank range. It is probable that he thought he was aiming at the Prime Minister. He was quickly apprehended and didn't resist arrest. Sadly, Drummond died five days later, having been bled by incompetent doctors.

At London's Bow Street magistrates' court the following morning, M'Naghten's statement repeated what he had earlier told his father:

> The Tories in my native city have compelled me to do this. They follow me and persecute me wherever I go and have entirely destroyed my peace of mind. They followed me to France, into Scotland and all over England; in fact, they follow me wherever I go. I can get no rest from them night or day. I cannot sleep at night in consequence of the course they pursue towards me. I believe they have driven me into a consumption. I am sure I shall never be the man I formerly was. I used to have good health and strength, but I have not now. They have accused me of crimes of which I am not guilty; they do everything in their power to harass and persecute me; in fact they wish to murder me. It can be proved by evidence; that's all I have to say.

The trial began on 3 March 1843, since the defence had been granted time to call in evidence from Scotland and perhaps France. The prosecution tried to place the attempt on the Prime Minister's life in the context of the ongoing furore around the protectionist Corn Laws which kept food prices high. The Solicitor General, Sir William Webb Follett, argued in a restrained opening that despite what might be M'Naghten's 'partial insanity', his morbid delusion of mind upon some subjects, it was not enough to deflect responsibility 'if he had that degree of intellect which enabled him to know and distinguish between right and wrong; if he knew what would be the effects of his crime and consciously committed it, and if with that consciousness he wilfully committed it'.

Cockburn's opening statement set a standard of debate and knowledge about mental illness and the insanity defence that had never before been seen in an English court. Amongst much else, it showed the growing sophistication of the medical literature on madness that had come into the public arena over the last decade. Cockburn, a Scotsman and an intellectual, drew on the authorities: 'Science is ever on the advance; and, no doubt, science of this kind, like every other, is in the advance of the generality of mankind ... We who have the ordinary duties of our several stations and the business of our respective avocations to occupy our full attention, cannot be so well informed upon it as those who have scientifically pursued the study and treatment of the disease [of madness].'

Cockburn then turned to the 'doctrines of matured science' and quoted from Dr James Pritchard's *On the Different Forms of Insanity in Relation to Jurisprudence*, published the preceding year. He drew on the American expert in the field Dr Isaac Ray, and his *Treatise on the Medical Jurisprudence of Insanity* (1838). Both criticized the verdicts in the Arnold and Bellingham trials, while Ray also took issue with Justice Hale, who had been blind to the power of 'those nice shades of the disease in which the mind, without being wholly driven from its propriety, pertinaciously clings to some absurd delusion ... Could Lord Hale have contemplated the scenes presented by the lunatic asylums of our own

times, we should undoubtedly have received from him a very different
doctrine for the regulations of the decisions of after generations.'
Cockburn even cited the French authority Charles Chrétien Henri
Marc, physician for twenty-three years to Louis-Philippe, who in 1840
had published *De la Folie dans ses rapports avec les questions médico-legales.*

Marc's main emphasis was that insanity was no simply understood
disorder of thought, or 'cognition' as we would say today; but a condition in which the will was perverted and the self couldn't be
mastered, functioning as it did not so much without reason, but
against the reasoning self. These distortions of passion and volition,
after Esquirol, would ever be a primary part of the language of the
French mind doctors, though the English legal system was loath to
allow into the courts any defence on the grounds of 'irresistible
impulse' or toppling of volition.

Cockburn even called on David Hume's *Commentaries on the Law of
Scotland* to dispute that, to be acknowledged by a court, madness must
needs expect of the accused that he 'must have lost all knowledge of
good and evil, right and wrong'. For Hume, this was a delicate question.
The accused might say it was wrong to kill a neighbour and 'yet is so
absolutely mad as to have lost all true observation of facts, all understanding of the good or bad intention of those who are around him, or
even the knowledge of their persons'. Every judgement in the matter
of right and wrong, Hume wrote, and Cockburn argued, 'supposes a
case, or state of facts, to which it applies'. And though the accused
may have the vestige of reason which enables him to answer in the general that murder is a crime, yet 'if he cannot distinguish his friend from
his enemy, or a benefit from an injury, but conceive everything about
him to be the reverse of what it really is, and mistake the illusions of his
fancy realities in respect of his own condition and that of others, those
remains of intellect are of no use to him towards the government of his
actions, nor in enabling him to form a judgment on any particular situation or conjunction of what is right or wrong with regard to it'.

If the great Hume didn't suffice to make the case, Cockburn then proceeded to call on medical experts to prove that M'Naghten's delusions

had left him in a state where he was no longer a 'reasonable and responsible being'. Dr Forbes Winslow was one of the medics to argue that
these delusions had robbed M'Naghten of all restraint over his actions.
Everyone was swayed by Cockburn's eloquence. Without leaving the
box, the jury gave a hurried verdict of 'not guilty on the ground of
insanity'. M'Naghten was discharged and moved to Bethlem Hospital
under an order from the Home Secretary. He remained there until 1864,
a quiet, methodical inmate but increasingly 'imbecilic', and was then
transferred to the newly opened Broadmoor Criminal Lunatic Asylum
where he died a year later.

But M'Naghten's name, in any variety of spellings, echoes through
the courts into our own day.

The public outcry over his not-guilty verdict was similar to the
explosions of moral outrage seen in our own time when an accused
deemed to be 'schizophrenic' or diagnosed with a 'dangerous personality disorder' seems literally to be getting away with murder. In 1843,
the unease amongst jurists and the profession about the status of
insanity in criminal trials, and the question of how to decide on
responsibility, prompted an immediate response from the House of
Lords. The Lord Chancellor, Lord Lyndhurst, convened a debate thus:

> The circumstances connected with that trial have created a deep
> sensation amongst your Lordships, and also in the public mind. I
> am not surprised at this. A gentleman in the prime of life, of a most
> amiable character, incapable of giving offence or of injuring any
> individual, was murdered in the streets of this metropolis in open
> day. The assassin was secured; he was committed for trial; that trial
> has taken place, and he has escaped with impunity. Your Lordships
> will not be surprised that these circumstances should have created
> a deep feeling in the public mind, and that many persons should,
> upon the first impression, be disposed to think that there is some
> great defect in the laws of the country with reference to this subject
> which calls for a revision of those laws, in order that a repetition of
> such outrages may be prevented.

Twelve judges of the Court of Common Pleas were duly convened and asked to consider five questions put to them by the Lords, many of them themselves lawyers. All the questions dealt in some way with the effect on law of alleging that a prisoner was suffering from delusion or partial madness. The Lords were not interested in the complexities of mental illness. Their concern was the proper working of the law and a firm definition of what constituted criminal responsibility in this area. On 19 June, the judges attended the Lords in order to provide their answers. Their one major clarification on previous law was to take on Hume's point and relate insanity not to any abstract or general knowledge of right and wrong, but to a knowledge of right and wrong with respect to their particular crime. The basic addition to the law that the much cited M'Naghten rules specify reads:

The jury ought to be told in all cases that every man is to be presumed to be sane, and to possess a sufficient degree of reason to be responsible for his crimes, until the contrary can be proved to their satisfaction; and that, to establish a defence on the ground of insanity, it must be clearly proved, that, at the time of the committing of the act, the party accused was labouring under such a defect of reason, from disease of the mind, as not to know the nature and quality of the act he was doing, or, if he did know it, that he did not know that what he was doing was wrong.

The judges also introduced a clarification that would lead to further decades of confusion and argument in Anglo-American and Commonwealth courtrooms. The Lords had asked them to consider the question: if a person under an insane delusion as to existing facts commits an offence in consequence thereof, is he thereby excused?

'Not altogether,' came the answer – itself a perfect model of misunderstanding, since it seemed to demand of the deluded person the same degree of 'reason, judgment and controlling mental power' as it did of one in sound mental health, an American judge later noted. The M'Naghten judges would have it that if the person labours under a partial delusion 'and is not in other respects insane', he should be considered in the same way as a sane person. 'For example, if under the influence of his delusion, he supposes another man to be in the act of attempting to take away his life, and he kills that man, as he supposes, in self-defence, he would be exempt from punishment. If his delusion was that the deceased had inflicted a serious injury to his character and fortune, and he killed him in revenge for such supposed injury, he would be liable to punishment.'

In the practice of everyday justice, all this led to muddle: insanity rulings had little consistency. Twenty-nine years after M'Naghten, when Christiana Edmunds came to trial, nothing much had changed, except that the numbers of mental specialists had grown. So had the population of asylum inhabitants.

10. 'Enceinte! She Says She Is, My Lord'

In the summary remarks of Sergeants at Law Ballantine and Parry and in Judge Baron Martin's final address to the jury in R. v Edmunds, the legal definition of insanity and its tangled history in English courts played a major part.

Parry began by arguing that the crime for which Christiana was being charged had no motive. She had no direct reason to murder the boy, Sidney Barker. Parry then moved on to the terrain of insanity, his main defence. He drew on the case of Hadfield, pointing out that even within his delusion he knew he had attempted murder, yet no one had questioned his insanity nor the propriety of a verdict that had named him mad. In Christiana's case the family record of insanity was greater than he, in his wide experience, had ever witnessed. All the experts as well as the Reverend at Lewes jail agreed that she was insane. Would this case end up being a contest between the law and medical science? The men who had made 'mental disease their particular study were benefactors of the human race' and were entitled to respect. They deemed Christiana to be of 'unsound mind' and incapable of knowing the difference between right and wrong, which was the ultimate test of insanity.

Ballantine responded with a rather different review of the case. His step-by-step description of Christiana's doings showed her to be 'a woman exhibiting powers of great contrivance and considerable cunning'. It was clear that Dr Beard's imputation of a crime against his wife had set her on the path of folly. The primary motive of the prisoner, he submitted, was to absolve herself from blame in a family with which she had been intimate and 'to fix on anybody else the culpability that would otherwise attach to herself'. This is what had resulted in the death of Sidney Barker.

In a shrewd piece of argument, Ballantine first praised the medical experts. Then, using a ploy still common today, he made light of and undermined their expertise, in particular its peculiar and obscure language. He did not deny, he stated, that the matter of 'hereditary taint' was one that might be fairly raised in matters of lunacy, but it could not on its own prove that an individual was insane. While 'a more noble profession than that of medicine, as it was constituted in this country never had existed', he couldn't help thinking that in this case the doctors had gone into the witness box confident in their own powers of verbiage but failing to convey any clear idea of Christiana's condition. In other words, the expert witnesses had dressed up opinion as science through the medium of obfuscating language.

Ballantine went on to finish with a flourish reminiscent of Erskine's defence of Hatfield (Hadfield), all the while out-doctoring the medics in his play on delusion's legal history. In the case of Hatfield, Ballantine argued, there had been an admitted delusion, as there had also been in the case of M'Naghten. Where there was an admitted delusion and where the act done was the necessary consequence of such delusion, then the person was not responsible for his actions. Lockhart Robertson had said the prisoner's intellect was clear and free from delusion. Insanity essentially consisted in delusions, and without delusions there might be mania, but there could be no insanity.

The fact that Christiana's doctors had opted for an insistence on hereditary madness, the time's fashionable medical theory about insanity, and had never attributed a fully delusional state to her, meant that they were out of sync with current legal emphases. But then, focusing on Christiana's 'delusion' would have meant teasing out the whole romantic and psychosexual ramifications of her passionate infatuation with Dr Charles Beard, and that would have been as morally slippery as putting erotic love on trial, not to mention their own profession. They had steered clear of that option, but had veered into a catch-22. The law tried individuals, not families, and though out of the courtroom, judges and lawyers may have bought into the period's hereditarian arguments about madness, inside the

Old Bailey individual knowledge of right and wrong at the time of the criminal act was what prevailed.

Baron (Samuel) Martin (1801–83) summed up the case for the jury. He was a senior judge and a respected member of his profession. He had been called to the Bar in 1830 at a time when the medical specialists in madness were only just beginning their explorations of the mind. He had served as a Liberal MP, worked for many years in the Court of Exchequer, had been knighted in 1850, and was known as a judge of 'unusual strength', one who didn't mind imposing heavy sentences. He was also kindly and often found mitigating circumstances. By the time of Christiana's trial, he was already very deaf, a fact that would lead him to retire just two years later.

There were two principal questions for the jury to consider, Baron Martin contended. The first was whether they believed the boy who had testified to buying chocolate creams at Mr Maynard's at the request of the prisoner; whether they also believed that Christiana had contrived to substitute these with poisoned chocolates that went back into the shop to be purchased by Sidney Albert Barker's uncle. The second question was whether the prisoner 'was in such a state of mind as to be responsible for her actions'. Baron Martin reviewed the evidence to do with Christiana's procurement of considerable quantities of strychnine, the manner in which she had given sweets to children in the street and left them in shops, and the illnesses those who had eaten them had suffered. He referred to her voluntary appearance before the coroner.

Next, he addressed the more difficult question of Miss Edmunds's insanity. It was evidently not a plea he found altogether satisfactory. In the courts, he pointed out, 'a poor person was rarely afflicted with insanity', though it was a common enough defence when people of means were charged with the commission of a crime. He had 'heard a doctor say that all mankind were mad more or less'. But this, he agreed, was an aside.

He then set out to review the law on madness. The state of mind that excused crime was well fixed in English law. There was the idiot who was born without any mind whatsoever; there was the man who was raging mad, and if he had what was called a 'homicidal tendency' he would have no more criminal responsibility than a tiger. The most numerous cases were persons said to be subject to delusions, who believed in a state of things which did not exist and acted on that state of things. To weigh the law dealing with 'delusion' as an insanity defence, Baron Martin read great chunks of the responses given to the Lords by the judges asked to clarify the state of the law after the M'Naghten ruling. In particular he read out the response of Justice Maule, the one judge to stand out against all the others and defiantly refuse any new medical knowledge or more lenient interpretation of criminal responsibility for the insane. Maule was a conservative for whom Hale was good enough. Those suffering from delusions, the partially insane, were responsible for their crimes. Only absolute unsoundness of mind provided an exemption, as far as he was concerned. Baron Martin submitted that on the high authority of these historic judges, every man must be responsible for his acts until it was shown to the contrary. Nonetheless, if the jury judged that the prisoner did not know right from wrong at the time she committed the crime, if she did commit it, they should acquit her on the grounds of insanity.

After that lecture, the jury didn't take long. They were back in exactly an hour and spoke their verdict to a court that was now densely crowded: Christiana Edmunds was pronounced 'Guilty'.

Now the drama of the day's proceedings leapt towards an unexpected climax. Asked by the clerk in the usual manner if she had anything to say as to why the court should not give her judgement to die, Christiana sprang up and replied that she 'wished she had been tried on the other charge which had been brought against her, namely her so-called improper intimacy with Dr Beard. That was the subject she wished to be examined on.'

A leap of the imagination into Christiana's position in the dock shows us a woman who has patiently waited, all the while making notes and following proceedings, for what to her is the crucial part of the trial. After all, if there is any delusion on her part, it is that passionate delusion of having done everything in the name of love, a love that she saw as returned. And now this passion, whatever its exaggerated or delusive aspect, is not to be weighed, explained, confessed, witnessed, acknowledged in court. There is to be no mutual ceremony, no public recognition of its potential two-sidedness. No letters are to be read. Her lover, real or imaginary, is not to be interrogated. And nor is she. But the one act of real violence she has committed was that sudden, impulsive and irresistible act of thrusting a poisoned chocolate cream into Emily Beard's mouth – an eruption out of love and hatred, out of an attempt to legitimize her relations (real or desired or utterly fantasized) with Charles.

This whole sexual-romantic-passionate matter has not been tried, and now won't be. Baron Martin has already donned the black cap which sits atop his long, wavy white wig. He looks down at her through his spectacles, his porcine face unsmiling yet gentle. He explains to her that it does not 'rest with him to have her tried on that charge, but with the prosecution who had not brought it'.

But, Miss Edmunds pleads – with what *The Times* calls 'modesty and propriety' – 'it is owing to my having been a patient of his, and the treatment I received in going to him, that I have been brought into this dreadful business. I wish the jury had known the intimacy, his affection for me, and the way I have been treated.'

Christiana was not to have the luxury of either public self-justification or revenge, or even of speaking her love out loud. This fact may only just have become clear to her. She had, it would seem, been waiting for far more. Baron Martin says hastily that he is inclined to believe her statement. The unhappy circumstances in which she placed herself towards the end of 1870 had indeed led to the position that she was now in; but the truth of that only confirmed the propriety of the verdict. In order to have her case fairly tried, he himself had wished to keep out the whole business with Beard. The more he thought of that matter, the clearer it was to him that to bring it in was only calculated to make her position worse.

Baron Martin is suggesting in publicly tactful terms that if Christiana's immorality, her sin against Victorian womanhood and the state of marriage, against all those respectable women now crowded in the courtroom, had been spelled out, it would so radically have affected her trial, so surely have turned the jury against her – as not only a criminal, but also as a sexually desiring and immoral, monstrous woman – that its fairness, from his point of view, would have been compromised. When you've been condemned to death, fairness hardly seems to be a problem, Christiana might well have thought. Her desire is to tell, to sing her passion, to prove that it hasn't been imaginary, but provoked. Her one prior utterance to the court, after all, was to protest that she wasn't mad!

But Baron Martin is still speaking. He is saying that he was quite satisfied that it was the unhappy circumstances under which she had become acquainted with Dr and Mrs Beard that had led to her bouts of poisoning. He, however, had only one duty to perform. He concurs with the jury's verdict in rejecting the defence of insanity: it was the right conclusion. The real question was not whether she was a person of weak mind, but whether her mind was in a state to distinguish right from wrong. Given her letters, it was clear that she could do that, and it was difficult for the jury to arrive at any other conclusion but that she was guilty.

From today's vantage point, it could seem Baron Martin is suggesting that distinguishing between right and wrong is not only a legal definition of sanity, but a moral distinction that brings female respectability in its train. Christiana knew that her love for Dr Beard was wrong, and while it isn't admissible to speak of it in the courtroom, it is better that she and they all recognize its 'wrongness'. Sorry as he is for her, she is guilty of a death, as well as of failing to recognize the immorality that led to it.

Baron Martin then embarked on the ritual form of words. The law imposed on him the duty to pass the sentence of death upon her. It would be carried out in the county of Sussex where the crime was committed. With much fervency, he prayed that the Lord would have mercy on her soul.

Standing in front of him at the supreme moment, Christiana's bearing was 'singularly firm', both 'respectful and becoming'. Her face
was slightly flushed, and her eyes beamed with an unwonted expression, yet she betrayed no visible emotion. She heard her sentence with
fortitude. But Christiana was not simply the noble heroine of
Victorian rectitude who accepted her many-faceted guilt with the
submission and stoicism *The Times* wished for and described. She was
inevitably more complicated than that.

In the 'mercy and justice of the English Law', as *Reynold's News*
pointed out coyly, using French to racy effect, 'a woman condemned
to death, who is *enceinte*, is respited until after the birth of her child. It
is usual, therefore, to interrogate the convict upon the point at the
time of the sentence and before the date is fixed for execution.' When
the clerk of arraigns put the customary question to Christiana, she
whispered to the female warder, who whispered to the jailer, who
said aloud, 'She says she is, my Lord.'

The court heaved with audible excitement. This was the very stuff
of sensational fiction. 'Let the sheriff empanel a jury of matrons forth-
with,' the judge ordered.

It had been over fifteen years since this ancient tradition had been
invoked in the Central Criminal Court. Christiana could not have
expressed more clearly her passion for Dr Beard and what had, according to her, transpired within it. And now 'under-sheriffs, with swords,
cocked hats, and frills', sallied into the body of the court and galleries
in quest of 'matrons' who would put Christiana's announcement of
pregnancy to the physical test.

In some twenty minutes, a dozen 'well-to-do and respectably
dressed women' were found, and directed to enter the witness box.
One of them, Mrs Adelaide Whittaw, was sworn separately as a forewoman, the others all together, and it was arranged that they would
examine the prisoner in the sheriff's parlour. Christiana joined them
there. Half an hour later a messenger came into the court and whispered to the judge, who passed his question on to the court. Was
there an 'accoucheur' in the room? – in other words an obstetrician-

gynaecologist. A doctor was duly found and directed to join the women. After another half-hour the messenger returned to the courtroom, this time in search of a stethoscope for the doctor. The rumour went round, injecting a little comedy into the tense drama, that a policeman had earlier been sent out and mistakenly brought back a telescope. After a further suspense-filled delay, the prisoner and the matrons took up their places in the courtroom once more. The forewoman pronounced a single word – 'Not.'

Reynold's News was highly contemptuous of this jury of upstanding, middle-aged women, this scandalous anachronism that reeks of witchcraft and ancient times and should 'be consigned to the limbo of historical curiosities' in favour of 'a proper scientific investigation by competent medical men'. The medical doctor recruited from the public in the courtroom felt the same way. Dr Beresford Ryley, surgeon of the Metropolitan Police, Woolwich District, described the experience to the *British Medical Journal*. *Reynold's News*, as well as *The Times*, reprinted it as a 'plea for Christiana Edmunds'. Here was sensation and science all in one.

Beresford Ryley was one of the doctors Christiana's solicitors had asked to visit her in Newgate, with the possibility of certifying her insane before her trial. He had been unable to obtain access when he had visited, but he subsequently attended her trial and had ended up on the matrons' panel which, he stated, treated their responsibility 'with feelings of no ordinary gravity and seriousness'. Ryley found that a very superficial examination of the 'unfortunate lady convinced me that the hope of reprieve from her dreadful doom that she had inspired within us all was utterly delusive. I aked her to save herself and me the distress of a more minute scrutiny by retracting the statement she had made, should it be false, but as she still persisted therein, I was obliged to make the usual stethoscopic examination.' Only after this did the 'full peril of her situation dawn upon her for the first time.'

The awful aspect of her despair was terrible to behold,' he writes. The poor ladies – 'of good social position and unusual intelligence' –

who were her unwilling judges wept around her, while she, unhappy creature, 'looked from one to the other in mute, unspeakable woe'. Sadly, Ryley doesn't reveal the full conversation that he and Christiana had, since it would not be becoming. He does say that she asked 'with a weary agony in her voice, "Oh how shall I sleep tonight?"' He recommends that she ask the prison surgeon for a draught of chloral hydrate, which may serve as a 'tender and compassionate physician to her poor aching mind'. It was, he says, one of the most solemn and pitiful scenes in which he has ever been an actor.

Ryley then moves on to science and law. He specifies that the panel's duty was not merely to find out whether Miss Edmunds was pregnant, but whether she was 'quick with child', and the 'absurd and obsolete custom of empanelling twelve matrons to try' such an issue was ridiculous, since they could have no reliable ground on which to come to a decision. Given that Christiana had been in custody for five months before her trial, and hadn't quickened, that conclusively proved she wasn't pregnant. It also proved that there had been no reasonable ground for her statement. Ryley is clear that Christiana's claim to pregnancy in conjunction with her 'heedless aspect throughout the trial', plus the facts about heredity there presented, constitute prima facie evidence of insanity. There is now a strong case on which 'to memorialize', in other words to petition the Home Secretary for a reprieve.

It may well be that for Christiana, the public announcement of her pregnancy was not unlike the gesture of forcing a poisoned chocolate into Emily Beard's mouth. It was an eruption of her inner delusional scenario (which may or may not have been triggered by actions performed by Beard on that cusp where the medical and the seductive meet, perhaps even by some form of vaginal penetration, real or mechanical). It was a way of telling the world that her secret love existed and could no longer be secretly contained. Having acted in a masculine fashion in her first poisoning attempt, Christiana is now asserting herself feminine. Her pregnancy is the expression of an inner anxiety about gender and an unconscious wish. And if she wasn't pregnant in the flesh, Dr Beard had certainly impregnated her mind and her imagination. In a French court, there is no question but that her crime would have been understood as a derailment by erotic passion.

Though the justice system in Britain didn't recognize crimes of passion (or any form of madness that had no primary cognitive base), or openly tolerate any leniency towards them, it's quite clear that Christiana's final act in court affected Baron Martin as well as the public and the doctor who examined her. Perhaps for all her seeming sanity, according to the legal weighing of evidence, Christiana did suffer from a delusion that had robbed her of her reason.

On 18 January, the trial barely over, and having just had time to consult some fellow judges, Samuel Baron Martin wrote to the Home Secretary, Henry Austin Bruce, to draw his attention to the case of Christiana Edmunds, convicted of murder before him. Although the 'defence of insanity failed in evidence' during the trial and the verdict was correct in point of law, Baron Martin does not think Miss Edmunds a proper subject for execution. He then details the family's insanity and her own history of early derangement, as well as her mother's fear that Christiana would be once again affected at menopause and at the same age as her father. The Home Secretary can see the medical men's evidence as well as the report of the trial in the press, he adds.

'My belief is that she is insane to a considerable extent,' Baron Martin writes; and although she is capable of 'knowing right from wrong she is affected by an hereditary taint of insanity'. Furthermore, the 'improper attachment' she formed for Dr Beard (he spells it Baird) 'caused or increased a morbid state of mind which led to the poisoning of the chocolate creams and also to an endeavour to cast the blame' upon others. He, as well as a majority of the judges he has consulted, think it would be a 'public scandal' if a person 'commonly deemed mad or insane should be put to violent death'. He suggests that her state of mind should be investigated by some competent and disinterested medical men and then it will be up to the Secretary of State to determine whether she is a proper subject for execution.

Baron Martin was not the only judge to have second thoughts about crimes where passion had arguably toppled over into madness, or something very like. It is said that just after Ruth Ellis, who had murdered her lover David Blakely (and who was examined by two psychiatrists and pronounced sane), was condemned to death in 1955, her judge Mr Justice Havers wrote to the then Home Secretary, asserting that this was a *crime passionnel* and recommending a reprieve. The Conservative Home Secretary refused, despite petitions numbering some fifty thousand. But Ellis was the last woman to be executed in England.

11. *Murder, Gender and Shifting Public Attitudes*

Judicial murder – particularly of women and other middle-class criminals like Reverend Watson, whose trial and sentencing just preceded
Christiana's – had begun to weigh heavily on Victorian liberals.
Already back in 1836 an Act had been passed allowing fourteen to
twenty-seven days between a murder conviction and execution,
thereby giving the Home Office time for consideration of often
numerous appeals.

Since the start of the century the number of capital offences in
England had been sharply reduced: from 222 at its turn to sixteen by
1837. This was in part due to a rebalancing of the law and of society's
emphasis from protection of property to protection of the person. In
the eighteenth century, a petty theft was crime enough to get the
perpetrator hanged. Robert Peel's period as Home Secretary and the
resulting 1828 Offences Against the Person Act marked a turning
point. Violence against individuals now became an enforceable crime,
and in the course of the century tolerance for violent acts, whether as
crime or punishment, diminished radically.

After 1837, when the death penalty was eliminated for most property offences and the second Offences Against the Person Act was
passed, only five people had been executed for a crime other than
murder. By 1861 only three crimes outside murder were punishable by
death; in the 1957 Homicide Act, murder itself was subdivided, so that
manslaughter became a non-capital offence and a plea of 'diminished
responsibility' was allowed – in effect, at last permitting an 'irresistible
impulse' element to enter the legal definition of madness. In
November 1965 the death penalty was suspended, finally to be abolished in 1969. Public hanging – that morbid display of judicial murder
that had for centuries drawn riotous crowds – had been stopped back

in 1868; though the last execution by hanging within the walls of a prison only occurred almost a hundred years later, on 13 August 1964.

As for women, the sex the century increasingly idealized – though largely in its middle-class version – as tender, susceptible and responsible for the time's moral and spiritual well-being, juries and judges were loath to pass the death sentence on them, even when they had committed murder – though poisoning had a higher conviction rate than other means. Between 1800 and 1899 in England and Wales 172 women were executed as against 3365 men. (The disparity in numbers is, of course, in part due to the fact that women traditionally commit fewer capital offences than men, though until prostitution in the late 1860s ceased to be a crime, women's crime was 40 per cent of men's, a much greater proportion than today. Now women make up only 5 per cent of the prison population.)

The number of women sent for execution – after having murdered brutal husbands or cheating partners who seduced and abandoned – diminished as the century went on. The Victorians did not approve of violent husbands, impulsive jealous lovers, or rakish, immoral seducers: their preferred versions of masculinity had to do with self-discipline, restraint and duty. In 1835–6, just before Victoria came to the throne, six women were hanged for murdering their husbands. Victoria's sixty-four-year reign saw only seven more go to the gallows, of the eighteen who were found guilty of murder.

Domestic violence was frowned upon, but all was hardly happy in the Victorian family. The championing of property rights for women increased the existing tensions. The number of spousal murders committed by men went up significantly in the latter half of the century, while those by wives fell sharply: the figures shifted from eighty-two wife murders and twenty-one husband murders in the 1840s to 158 wife murders and seven husband murders in the 1890s. Some social and legal historians, such as Martin J. Wiener, have seen in these shifting figures not an absolute escalation in violence against women, but rather a signal of a hardening of attitudes towards male violence in what was the increasingly idealized space of the home, where there was a male duty to protect and support wives and children. Past epochs had given men wide discretion on the 'disciplining' of wives, even to the point of death. There was now a greater readiness to charge men with murders that earlier might have gone unprosecuted or had perpetrators charged only with manslaughter.

From the 1870s on, juries preferred to find a woman murderer insane rather than sentence her to execution. Women were twice as likely as men to be acquitted on grounds of insanity, even when the the crime committed was the same. After all, they were the 'weaker sex', prone to the female malady that could rob them of sound mind at any number of life's critical junctures. Indeed, if Christiana Edmunds had seemed more helplessly feminine and fainted in the dock rather than appearing coolly practical and thus frightening in her dissemination of poison; or if she had attempted to murder Charles Beard rather than that icon of family values, his wife, it may well be that her jury would have arrived at a far more lenient verdict.

12. *Saving (Mad) Christiana*

Baron Martin was not the only person to write to the Home Secretary on Christiana's behalf. Over the next days and weeks memorials and petitions in substantial number, from strangers and familiars alike, made their way to his office, all asking that the capital sentence be commuted. Christiana's mother wrote a heart-rending memorial detailing the mental illness in the family, a feat all the more poignant when the stigma attached to insanity is taken into consideration.

Sydney Cornish Harrington, Christiana's brother's brother-in-law, who had stepped in to help the two manless women out both financially and humanly – though he hadn't known them previously – submitted a lengthy memorial. Having put up security for the costs of the defence, he had had repeated interviews with Christiana both at Lewes and Newgate jails, each lasting nearly an hour. His testimonial corroborated Mrs Edmunds's and confirmed that there was madness in the family. He added a moving first-hand layperson's account of Christiana's state of mind before and after her trial.

Harrington remarks on the 'utter impossibility of confining her to any particular subject of conversation. She would always bring in Dr Beard.' The only time he found her at all affected by what he himself said was when he 'told her he had heard that Dr Beard had shown her letters'. Then she burst out, 'Now you have made me wretched indeed!!' Harrington also notes the extraordinary appearance of Christiana's eyes, the pupils dilated and 'a semblance of looking into space however interested she might be in the conversation'. On 17 January, just after the trial, he saw her in the presence of the prison governor and one of the warders. Again he was shocked at the appearance of her eyes – their glare and now unnatural contraction – as well as by her remarks. Repeatedly, she chanted: 'I am going to

Brighton to see Dr Beard!! They have promised to take me to Brighton to see Dr Beard!!' This was grimly interrupted sotto voce, 'The Police have sent a woman to break me and she has been following me all night' – then a new and delighted outburst of 'I am going to see Dr Beard. I am going to Brighton.'

Harrington found it all deeply distressing. When it was time to leave, he asked the governor if he could shake Christiana's hand. He was told he could. 'Chrissie, won't you shake hands with me?' he asked. 'Oh yes,' she murmured, but she barely touched his fingers before repeating her refrain about going to Brighton to see Dr Beard.

Harrington finishes his memorial by pointing out to the Home Secretary that he has conversed with many mad persons in various countries, but he has never met one he more firmly believes to be insane than Christiana.

From this document, it would seem that the trial and imprisonment have thrust Christiana further into her delusional state.

The press and the medics now pleaded for Christiana's 'respite'. As the *Daily Telegraph* of Monday 22 January put it, 'The whole issue which the Home Secretary has to decide is whether an observation of the letter [of the law] is not an infraction of the spirit . . . Strict adherence to the law is often an outrage or injustice.'

On the 23rd, the eminent Sir William Gull (1816–90) of Guy's Hospital and Dr William Orange, Medical Superintendent of the new Broadmoor Criminal Lunatic Asylum, were dispatched by the Home Secretary to Lewes Prison to make an unbiased medical appraisal of Christiana. The earlier assessments had been done for defence counsel and so had a less objective status.

Gull – the son of a Colchester barge owner and his industrious wife, who had been left early on to bring up her eight children single-handedly – had come up the hard way through university and the medical ranks to become one of Victorian England's great society doctors. He was a man of vast energy, highly respected for what was reputed to be an outstanding clinical talent. In 1843, as a young man, he had briefly been in charge of the ward for lunatics at Guy's, but he was a generalist and by the 1850s he was attached to Guy's as a 'full physician'. He left in the 1860s to run a lucrative high-society practice, always retaining his consultancy at Guy's. Eventually, he became the hospital's governor.

The year before he came to examine Christiana, Gull had attended the Prince of Wales during his battle with typhoid. He was knighted in January 1872, just in time for his visit to Lewes Prison. This may account for the exorbitant fee of fifty guineas that he charged, which despite assiduous and repeated billing, travelled from Treasury to Home Office and back, queried by a variety of civil servants, until it was finally paid in June that year. Gull wrote amply for the medical journals and had made contributions to the understanding of melancholia, or 'hypochondriasis'. He was also one of the first clinicians to name and study anorexia, differentiating it from the tuberculosis so prevalent amongst young women of the time, and accurately describing its symptoms. He was known to be good with women patients, and also, by furnishing special scholarships, encouraged women into the medical profession.

Dr William Orange, junior to Gull in the Edmunds affair and Christiana's second examiner, had been deputy superintendent at England's first asylum dedicated especially to criminals, Broadmoor, since its opening in May 1863. Then it was a facility for women. Male 'criminal lunatics' arrived only the following year when the complement of special buildings had been added. In 1870 Dr Orange, then thirty-three, became the chief medical superintendent of the hospital and introduced a more humane, rehabilitative system. Though once attacked by an inmate, he was held in great affection by the patients, who briefly included M'Naghten and also the artist Richard Dadd. Dadd left a portrait of Orange and painted murals in his house.

That same day, 23 January, Sir William penned the eight-sided letter to the Home Secretary detailing their visit of over four hours to Christiana Edmunds. Gull points out that they would have gone on longer, made a repeat visit or asked for additional evidence, had they thought it necessary. But four hours of 'personal communication' and 'examination' had proved 'sufficient for a conclusion'. Christiana Edmunds was in their view most definitely 'a person of unsound mind'.

The doctors report that Christiana appears to have had 'a tranquil, easy and indifferent childhood and womanhood up to a period of about three years ago . . . since which time there is evidence of mental perversion and defective memory'. Though she suffered no special crisis beforehand, 'there is proof of an indifferent intellectual state which led up to the present state'. Citing the madness of her father and the hysteria of her sister, the doctors note that her 'physical organisation presents marks of low cerebral and feeble cerebral organisation which characterises this class of criminals'. Miss Edmunds's narrative to them of her life and feelings since September 1870 they consider to have been given 'in good faith', and 'truthful so far as her perverted feelings admitted'. The crime of murder 'she seems incapable of realizing as having been committed by her, though she fully admits the purchasing and distributing the poisons as put forth in the several counts against her'. Maddest of all, she 'even justifies her conduct and in an insane way tries still to give a justification of it'.

Gull and Orange don't mention their fellow professional Dr Beard, but it may not be too great a leap to imagine that Christiana did, as part of the justification for her own actions. Such feminine perceptions or even misperceptions of cause, when they are shared, can easily feed into a professional designation of insanity. Passionate love is, after all, ever a form of mental derangement from the norm. The doctors emerge certain that the 'acts referred to and acted by her were the fruit of a weak and disordered intellect with confused and perverted feelings of a most marked insane character'. Christiana Edmunds ought to be treated accordingly.

The Secretary of State acted instantly on the medical report. The very next day, the 24th, Christiana's death penalty was respited. This does not mean her sentence as a whole was yet permanently commuted: 'perhaps it will be better to do nothing in that respect, at all events at present,' the letter to Sussex County Prison, also carrying the doctors' report, stated. This was in no way a pardon, or a reconsideration of what Christiana's sentence might be. It was simply a removal of the death penalty for the present. The letter also noted that Christiana could be moved at once to Broadmoor. A return letter from the governor of the Sussex County Prison on 25 June confirms that Christiana is now 'respited until further signification of Her Majesty's Pleasure'. Christiana has not been absolved of her crime because of her medically certified insanity: she is guilty but insane, and under the provisions of the 1800 Criminal Lunatics Act subject to 'safe custody' rather than to judicial murder.

The Home Secretary's action was not universally applauded, particularly since it was the second such decision in a matter of weeks. The *Spectator* and the *Pall Mall Gazette*, quoting it on 27 January, argued: 'The plain meaning of the respite of Christiana Edmunds is that a weak Secretary has allowed himself to be bullied by the *Daily Telegraph* into an act of cruelty (confinement) towards an unhappy but most wicked convict, to destroy respect for the law by placing the mad-doctors above it, and to liberate an immensely numerous class (those insane by descent) from all fear of legal retribution for crime.' Moreover, Home Secretary Bruce had reversed a verdict on the 'private unexplained report of two doctors', and thereby overturned a judgement made by judge and jury. This was tantamount to undermining the law.

Much has changed, but the battle between the so-called mad-doctors, who, some felt, were gaining too much influence, and those who wanted punishment for crime unmediated by psychological considerations, still goes on. The year 1872 marked an early moment in an argument in which the public, given the rise and rise of the popular press, had an increasingly vocal say. In the specialist journals Christiana Edmunds's case, like that of the Reverend Ian Watson, would be fought out for months to come. Even those who were on the side of the doctors thought the case, with its swift reversal of a jury's verdict, had brought the law into disrepute. It was 'injurious to the welfare of society' for uncertainty to exist about 'whether a person shall be convicted as a criminal or acquitted as insane'.

The long-time champion of psychological medicine, Forbes Winslow, saw the battle as one between punishment and compassion, the two axes of Victorian morality. In an article on 'Insanity and Homicide' he cites the approbation of one critic of the first ilk for a judge who, in sentencing a prisoner to death for sheep-stealing, says, 'I do not sentence you to be hanged for stealing sheep, but ... that sheep may not be stolen.' This, Winslow states, shows a complete failure 'to grasp the real nature of insanity as a disease for which the sufferer is not responsible, and which renders him irresponsible for what he does. Were one half of the lunatic population of the country hanged the spectacle would have no effect upon the insane person who cannot help doing what he does.' He gives the example of a boy in school who wilfully pulls faces at the headmaster as against one who suffers from tics and chorea. 'The one is a proper object of punishment; the other is a sad object of compassion, whom it would be a barbarous and cruel thing to punish.' He points out that to execute a madman is no punishment to him and no warning to others, but simply an act of extreme inhumanity and cruelty.

Only if the notoriously imperfect test of insanity is changed can the current impasse be navigated, he argues. It is not a question of whether the accused can distinguish between right and wrong and whether she knows she is acting against the law of the land. This omits 'the form of insanity in which the power ... to choose the better and reject the worse – the power of self-control – is destroyed'. The homicidal impulse can be irresistible. Esquirol's continental language of madness here comes in to support the English doctors once more. People can and do suffer from an irresistible 'impulse – sudden, instantaneous, unreflecting, and uncontrollable'. Such concepts will be part of the mind doctors' argument against legal definitions of insanity and criminal responsibility, until these are finally changed halfway through the next century. An anonymous writer in the *BMJ* of February 1872 further and presciently notes, as if he had read writings on psychosis of a far later era, that the crime itself can be 'the first symptom of the lurking and latent disease' that has silently eaten away at the mind of the accused to produce, after a 'sudden strain', the 'brain disaster'. Madness is a subtle matter.

Indeed, one way to make sense of Christiana's crime is to think of her as someone in the grip of an inner psychotic structure. Masquerading (to herself) as the sophisticated, flirtatious but poised, letter-writing Dorothea, she has been able to control her erotic obsession with the idealized Charles Beard, or we might say keep it secret, split off from her everyday self, until it explodes in the violent poisoning attack on Emily. This is the first outward manifestation of her delusion. In this view, the force with which she thrusts the poisoned chocolate into Emily Beard's mouth is the wordless eruption of the illness she suffers – an obsessive erotic investment in Charles which in her inner scenario he returns.

'La Sposa', that abstracted, and made foreign, entity of the eternal wife, Emily, is someone the world and Charles need to be rid of. Then, magically, spinster Christiana, or at least Dorothea, will have Charles all to herself. After the murderous act, Christiana can protest her innocence to Charles because she *feels* innocent: to prove that innocence to him, she will carelessly broadcast poisoned chocolates, talk to the police and even stand in the witness box during the inquest on Sidney Barker, pointing the finger at Maynard. She is unmoved by the trial accounts of the death of little Barker, or the sufferings her poison has caused: all of this is split off from the narrative she lives inwardly. It happens in a separate world. Only the story of Charles, Dorothea and 'La Sposa' matters. So when her 'Caro Mio' doctor tells her he has blurted the secret of the Dorothea letters to La Sposa a long time back, the betrayal sets off another poisoning spree aimed at La Sposa and all those whom Christiana imagines as somehow ranked against herself.

Notable in the sexual politics of the case and the tensions it mirrors is the fact that Christiana parodies the image of girlish Victorian femininity – one attached to good behaviour and fetching looks. She attacks through that most feminine and nurturing of modes: poison robed in sweetness. Christiana would like to be a good and sweet woman, whatever the bitterness within. It may even be that in the symbolic universe she inhabits, her declaration of pregnancy after the lawyers conspire not to put her love story on the witness stand is a way of saying that Charles started the whole business. He 'injected' her first with his male poison. When she takes on an active male role, it is to carry on the process, injecting her chocolates and sweetmeats in the same way and, notably, forcing her poison into Emily's mouth.

But what of the man who, whatever his intents, could be considered a precipitating factor in Christiana's derailment? There is no record of Dr Charles Beard visiting Christiana, either in prison or during her lengthy stay in Broadmoor. But his name does figure in relation to hers once more, whether out of guilt or compassion or a mixture of both cannot be known. It appears on a petition, dated 7 February 1872, though put in train before the Home Secretary's speedy respite. The covering letter is from Charles Lamb, Christiana's Brighton attorney. He is lodging this petition with the Home Secretary, he says, because it stands as 'a way of proving, if necessary, that the Public were not indifferent to the evidence which was tendered at the trial in proof of the Prisoner's state of mind during the commission of the acts laid to her charge'. He underlines that Dr Beard and his wife Emily are both signatories.

The text of the petition repeats the two aspects of Christiana's defence: 'there is no ground for supposing the Prisoner to have been actuated by direct malice towards the child or any other person to have partaken of the poisonous chocolates'. Secondly, having regard to the insanity in her family, to 'her own partial paralysis and hysteria' and to 'the motiveless and irrational character of many of the acts committed by her', even though she may not have been proved legally insane 'her mind was in so diseased and unnatural a state as greatly to weaken ordinary moral restraints, to diminish her responsibility for her action and to render her a fitting object for the exercise of the Royal Clemencies'.

The petitioners include in first place the mayor, aldermen and town councillors of Brighton. Charles and Emily Beard come next, along with all the other Brightonians to whom Christiana's poisoned packages were addressed. Even Emily Beard's father signs, together with some four hundred 'intelligent and respectable inhabitants and visitors of Brighton'. It is tempting to think that some of the women signatories recognized the plight of this spinster, and with one part of themselves cheered her rebellion against passive acquiescence to convention. Certainly, the pathos of Christiana's situation – the way love, which ever bears the freight of imagination, can so easily slip into obsessive delusion, and overturn the mind – was something this seaside town of many pleasures could well understand, even if the law itself continued to reject aberrant passion as a mitigating circumstance.

It may seem a little far-fetched to draw any commonality between Christiana Edmunds and Oscar Wilde, yet it was the secret passions of both that brought them down, and Wilde's moving words in *De Profundis* have a bearing on Christiana and her fate:

Desire, at the end, was a malady, or a madness, or both. I grew careless of the lives of others … I forgot that every little action of the common day makes or unmakes character, and that therefore what one has done in the secret chamber one has some day to cry aloud on the housetop. I ceased to be lord over myself. I was no longer the captain of my soul, and did not know it.

13. *Broadmoor*

On 28 June 1872 Christiana Edmunds, in the company of a matron and a warder, is transported by train from Lewes County Prison to Broadmoor. It is one of the wettest summers on record and the two-hour trip to London followed by the trek between stations and the ongoing journey to Crowthorne in Berkshire must have taken most of the day.

Christiana's transfer sets in motion a round of administrative problems that point to just how unusual her situation is. No one wants the financial responsibility for her. From 6 July on, letters race between Lewes Prison's visiting justices and administrators to Whitehall and back, and from there to Brighton town hall and Canterbury and back, and again to the Home Office and Treasury – all of them trying to shift the burden of keeping Christiana jailed. The Prison Act comes into question in an attempt to define whether where the crime is committed, or where the prisoner is jailed, or where her home parish is, takes precedence for her maintenance. Even the high cost of her train ticket is queried, and the clerk of Lewes Prison has to explain that the railway authorities on the Broadmoor branch insist on a fee amounting to the whole train compartment, since no one, warders apart, is permitted to travel in a 'lunatic's' compartment.

Mrs Edmunds had originally agreed to pay Christiana's maintenance, but it seems she was no longer in a position to do so. In the event, the Broadmoor cost of fourteen shillings a week is disputed for years. The authorities are still arguing in January 1875, Lewes having taken the case to the Court of Queen's Bench to determine Christiana's place of settlement under the Prisons Act. Dr William Orange's letters from Broadmoor demanding payment from the Lewes authorities now begin to pile in. Finally, a 'writ of maintenance' is taken out by the

Home Office on the Guardians of the Poor in the city of Canterbury, Christiana's earlier home, together with an order that £56. 5s 7d be paid immediately (to include Sir William Gull's original invoice) together with a guarantee of all future maintenance.

On 2 November, payment seems at last agreed and a Treasury civil servant notes: 'This is a satisfactory resolution of this long vexed question.' Yet the amount owed to Broadmoor from Christiana's arrival there in July 1872 until November 1875 is still outstanding. Orange writes to A. J. O. Liddell, the new Secretary of State at the Home Office, emphatically stating that Broadmoor is owed £121.10. Solicitors to the Treasury give advice to the Home Office, pointing out that they have already advised on Christiana Edmunds and the matter of 'Criminal Pauper Lunatics' of which she is one: there is a loophole in the law here that needs to be tightened. In 1878 the whole question of arrears of maintenance goes to the Lords, and an amendment to the Criminal Lunatics Act to make recovery possible is urged. On 1 May that year the Treasury finally sanctions the Broadmoor authorities to abandon the claim against both the Lewes and Canterbury authorities.

Dr William Orange had been medical superintendent of Broadmoor for less than two years when Christiana arrived. The asylum now had its full complement of blocks, two for women, six for men; the men usually outnumbered the women four to one, with the more violent inhabitants being kept in a block furthest from the grounds and playing fields. A significant proportion of the 'criminally insane' women confined at any one time had committed infanticide, then the main form of female murder: this accounted for what, from time to time, was the higher percentage of female to male murderers. The class breakdown amongst the women was balanced even more than amongst the men towards a working and 'underclass'.

Treatment consisted largely of the discipline of asylum life. The total environment that was the asylum provided work, order and recreation. The hope was that this methodical discipline would 'cure' or at least regularize the lives of the inhabitants. Work could take place on the asylum farm and grounds, or indoors in the general running and maintaining of the facilities, or in sewing, etching or even painting, as the outstanding example of Richard Dadd shows. The more orderly inmates could go for walks, play team sports or attend the occasional musical evening or ball. For a long time there were only two medical doctors and a complement of about a hundred warders to look after some five hundred inmates. Many patients had their own rooms and visitors could be seen. Inhabitants might stay the length of their sentence or in some cases be moved into an ordinary prison. Under Orange's reforming and humanitarian aegis, some of those confined may have lived better lives at Broadmoor than in the terrible circumstances they had experienced before.

A series of brief hospital notes (mostly of the formulaic kind submitted in annual reports to the Lunacy Commissioners as demanded by the Criminal Lunatics Act 1884) and one letter make up the rest of Christiana Edmunds's documented life. The examination letter from Sir William Gull and Dr Orange, together with a report from Surgeon Richard Turner of Sussex County Prison, are lodged on her arrival at Broadmoor. Turner states: 'After 10 months daily Supervision, I fail to satisfy myself that Christiana Edmunds is insane, or irresponsible for her actions. She is of delicate constitution & disposed to be hysterical and is much weakened by her long detention in prison.' Responding to the query 'Whether Suicidal or Dangerous to others', Turner writes: 'She has never shown any symptoms of being suicidal or dangerous to others.' Under 'Chief Delusions or indication of insanity' he writes: 'Has manifested no delusion in my presence.' Nor had she had, or was she subject to, any fits. Removed from Dr Beard and, it would by now seem, from the hope of ever seeing him again – and perhaps, too, faced with the attention of other doctors – Christiana's monomania, or erotic obsession, seems to have dissolved.

The Broadmoor staff, particularly the matron in charge of her, however, find her decidedly peculiar, not to say irritating. Christiana manifestly lacks that ordinary human remorse, that sense of responsibility for her crimes, or indeed that fellow-feeling that signals 'normality'. She is just not a good girl: she has none of that quota of submissive goodness that the matron expects of sane women.

Referring back to William Gull's letter in a note made soon after Christiana's arrival, Dr Orange writes that the opinions expressed in the letter are confirmed by Christiana's 'conduct and conversation' since admission. At the news of her brother William's death on Robben Island she 'appears quite unable to experience any feeling of sorrow although she tried to look grieved'. Christiana, it seems, can only enact emotion for her family, not experience it. In the same note, Orange points out – as if the lack of feeling were somehow a consequence of her vanity – that when she was admitted Christiana was 'wearing a large amount of false hair and her cheeks were painted. She also has false teeth & she is very vain.'

Christiana's vanity is the subject of many subsequent notes. Her desire to have her own clothes or send them out for mending, her penchant for false hair and make-up, are never interpreted as a proud attempt to keep up appearances (and indeed status) in a distressing environment and not to succumb to its lack of aesthetic resources. It is seen as a mark of moral madness. It's clear that, like some unprincipled Becky Sharp in *Vanity Fair*, Christiana is both rebellious and driven by a need to behave seductively in male company. She seems to continue to believe, even with the passing years, that her ability to charm is intact. It is the only means open to her to be a woman.

When on 21 August 1873 her mother comes to visit – perhaps worrying that the doctors may release Christiana once more into the proximity of the hangman – she tells Dr Orange that her son William 'gave evidence of mental illness before his death'. She also tells him that Christiana never once expressed any sorrow for the trouble she caused her family. She would regard her want of feeling as shocking if she were not insane, Mrs Edmunds says, adding that Christiana was not truthful as a child.

As if given a key to the daughter by the mother's words, Christiana's hospital notes are now full of 'her desire to deceive' (2 November). Asylum discipline is not what Christiana does best. A letter she sends to her sister Mary, the record states, 'ingeniously con-tains a single scrap of paper covered with very small writing'. Christiana's writing is evidently fated to doom her. This time her letter asks her sister to bring her 'some articles of wearing apparel clandestinely at her next visit and also half a crown which was to be given to one of the attendants'. Found out, Christiana exhibits neither surprise nor shame and simply carries on in the same way. One begins to wonder whether this behaviour has been long in the making and learned at home. Another letter to her sister repeats a desire for 'arti-cles of dress different from other patients' and also reflects on 'modes of applying paint to the face'. Her sister, the matron thinks, colludes. She is irate. A letter needs to be sent stipulating that 'the patient is at all times well provided with comfortable and suitable clothing to her present position'.

Some kind of cushion or 'leather toy or loaf' arrives for Christiana and is found to contain false hair! Dr Orange is rounded up to write to Mary Foreman to tell her that not only has this stuffed cushion been confiscated, but that this kind of secret gift is in no one's interest. She says she will comply. The matron, Mrs Jackson, is asked to return the gift (which she can't because it has fallen apart) and to write saying that if Mary 'really wishes to assist in promoting her sister's happiness, she ought to try gently in all her letters to her to make her as con-tented as possible with her surroundings feeling assured that everyone has every wish to be kind to her'.

In July 1874, the Broadmoor authorities learn that Christiana has been 'endeavouring to set on foot a clandestine correspondence with the chaplain of Sussex County Prison'. Her sister has been asked to post the letters for her, but when a reply from him comes through ordinary channels the matter is found out. Christiana, it seems, is again playing with secrets and revelation. She is resistant to the controlling asylum authorities. 'There would have been no objection to her writing to the chaplain of the prison from which she came,' the notes primly state, 'had she asked to be allowed to do so, but it is in conformity with her state of mind to prefer mystery

& concealment.' But then, if Christiana is still subject to an under-
current of inexpressible sexuality, she can hardly cease her rebellion
and tell the authorities what she's up to, since she doesn't altogether know herself.

Almost a year later, in April 1875, when she moves from her present room to another and the first is searched, numerous hidden
articles are found and yet another letter – this time addressed to an
attendant. 'Her love of deception is quite a mania,' her record states.
On 30 July even more secreted articles are found. Her hospital notes
state that 'her mind becomes more impaired and she is more irrational in her conduct. She deceives for the pure love of deception and
with no sufficient motive.' We have no way of knowing, but perhaps
Christiana is caught up in the torrid world of her obsessions once
more, bringing into being an attendant-lover whom only she knows
about. Certainly this masquerade of femininity, with its accou-
trements of hair and clothes, shows a continuing anxiety about fitting
into the delimitations of being mid-nineteenth-century woman.

Christiana uses all the ladylike wiles she can muster in her impoverished surroundings – except when her mother comes to visit,
when, according to the record, she looks as pitiful as possible.
Matron, it is clear, doesn't approve. 'When visited by her mother she
omits the colour on her cheeks, sheds tears, and complains of the
injustice and cruelty with which she is treated, and of the searching
of her room. At the same time, the faculty of secretiveness is so
strong that she is probably quite unable to resist the desire to conceal,
even when there is no occasion for it.' Like one of Freud's patients,
Christiana is excited by secrecy, a stand-in for sexual excitement,
when not its accompaniment.

By the time of this update, 8 July 1876, Christiana has been moved
into Ward 2, close to the Broadmoor gardens where 'she has been
tolerably tranquil and orderly in her behaviour'. While she was in
Ward 3, her 'delight and amusement seemed to be in practising the art
of ingeniously tormenting several of the more irritable patients, so
that she could always complain of their language to her whilst it was

difficult to bring any overt act home to herself'. This may in part have been why she was moved, and in her new ward Christiana doesn't indulge in baiting other patients and then grumbling about them. Perhaps she doesn't feel the need in this better accommodation to set up her superiority, or at least her difference, a constant theme in her character armoury. From now on, she seems to be more or less resigned to her place in institutional life.

Somewhat 'more uniform & settled', state the hospital notes in January 1877, even though the regime hasn't managed to cure her of her superficial character faults. She is still 'very vain & affects a youthful appearance'. In September 1877, she 'continues to paint & "get herself up" – as far as she can', but 'she does not interfere so much with the other patients as formerly'. Nothing has changed on the seductive front, however: 'Bent of her mind, as evidenced by the tendency of her conversation & by her manner & expression, evidently lies towards sexual and amatory ideas.'

And so it continues over the next years. Christiana remains 'tractable and amenable to the ordinary rules of the place', 'quiet and orderly in her behaviour'; painting, etching, doing bits of embroidery. There is 'no prominent indication of insanity'; she is 'free from actively insane indications'. Yet immediately, as if this moral fault were a signal of insanity, comes the sting in the tale the hospital notes tell: she is still 'vain and frivolous' in her appearance and 'in the general tone of her conversation and behaviour'. Christiana can only repeat her parody of everyday Victorian girlishness: it is her only remaining act. But once inside the walls of the largely working-class asylum, these characteristics of femininity garner disapproval. She is also too old for such vanities. She is meant to be penitent.

Yet with the passing of her obsession with Dr Charles Beard, can Christiana still be considered insane?

On 30 October 1880, she writes a letter to the Home Office in a neat and regular script. It is the only piece of her handwriting that remains. The letter itself is a cogent and moving memento to a troubled woman who has left no other personal trace.

Sir,

I venture to petition for my release from the Broadmoor
Asylum. I have been eight years in confinement and am very
anxious to regain my liberty. I earnestly trust that my conduct
has been such as to gain for me the favourable regard of the
Superintendent and those over me. I shall feel very grateful if you
will kindly consider my petition and grant my release.

I remain Sir

Your humble Petitioner

Christiana Edmunds

The accompanying letter from Broadmoor notes that she 'is at present tranquil and orderly in her conduct, but her mind is unsound'. On
4 November, there is a note from the Secretary of State saying that he
'cannot comply with her appeal'. Christiana never appeals again, and
as the years go by, her asylum notes grow briefer and briefer, testifying
to her good health and 'the same vain indifferent irresponsible
manner'. An entry of 1886 finds her 'quiet and well behaved, cheerful
and pleasant in conversation, but [she] is very vain, courts and desires
attention and notoriety, pushes herself forward on all occasions, paints
and tricks herself up for inspection and in almost her every act shows
how little she appreciates the gravity of her crime or the position in
which it has placed her'. Vanity – in Christiana's circumstances – has
become a mark of insanity.

The hospital records do not reveal whether she responded in any
way to her mother's death in 1893. She is 'cheerful and contented'
that year, and in the following year 'employs herself in painting and
sketching'. Nor is there any note to mark a response to her sister
Mary's death in 1898. Perhaps, in the way of things, they had long
ceased to visit her. No change is noted in Christiana's condition until
1901, when signs of physical deterioration set in. Her sight is failing and
there are backaches and various pains. In 1902 her symptoms improve
as the annual ball approaches. After that, comes physical decline.
Perhaps fittingly for a woman so concerned with appearances, time is

kind to her: increasingly impaired sight accompanies the passage of the years. In one of those little ironies of history, the Brighton house in which Christiana spent her most passionate years as the Borgia of Brighton, became a site of spectacle; a cinema.

On 22 November 1906, when she is scarcely able to walk without assistance and has spent over a week in the infirmary, a note records a conversation that could provide a fitting epitaph for Christiana Edmunds, a woman whom the delusions of passion led into criminality and an unintended murder. She is overheard talking to a patient who has 'been in the habit of rendering her various little services':

E[dmunds] – How am I looking?
A[friend] – Fairly well.
E – I think I am improving. I hope I shall be better in a fortnight, if so, I shall astonish them; I shall get up and dance – I was a Venus before and I shall be a Venus again!

We don't know whether Christiana rose from her sickbed to be the Venus she at least wished she had once been. In the way of those who today might be considered to suffer from a psychotic mental structure, wishes and fears for Christiana seemed to have acted as facts might for others. The Venus of Broadmoor gradually grew weaker and died at half-past five on the morning of 19 September 1907 at the age of seventy-eight. Charles Beard, who had left Brighton with his family soon after the trial and moved to Southport in Lancashire, outlived her by nine years, to die at the age of eighty-nine in London. His will shows him leaving £1889 18s. 2d., not a vast sum compared to Sir William Gull's £344,022 19s. 7d.

It is unlikely that Charles Beard knew of or marked the passing of the woman who had nurtured a morbid passion for him, one he had somehow provoked into murderous rage.

Perhaps Christiana Edmunds would have thrived a little better if she had been born at a slightly later date and in belle époque France. Propriety may have reigned here as well, but the public discussion about the passions had a far greater openness to it, even in the courts, where the required 'confession', adapted from the Catholic inquisitorial system, could incorporate sexuality. Mind doctors, writers and that floating demi-monde – which might find itself part of the *beau monde*, the moneyed and respectable classes – even lawyers, all had a say about how love can drive you mad. Then, too, the earliest French alienists – who also had the excesses of the French Revolution in mind – had incorporated passion into the language of lunacy: there it would stay, through the course of subsequent upheavals, both social and individual.

PART TWO: FRANCE
VIRTUE ON TRIAL

'If you asked eighty years ago if feminine virtue was part of universal humanism, everyone would have answered yes.'

Michel Foucault

Le Petit Journal

Le Petit Journal
CHAQUE JOUR 5 CENTIMES
Le Supplément illustré
CHAQUE SEMAINE 5 CENTIMES

SUPPLÉMENT ILLUSTRÉ
Huit pages : CINQ centimes

ABONNEMENTS

	SIX MOIS	UN AN
SEINE ET SEINE-ET-OISE	2f.	3f. 50
DÉPARTEMENTS	2 f.	4 f.
ÉTRANGER	2 50	5 f.

Douzième année

DIMANCHE 11 AOUT 1901

Numéro 560

TRAGIQUE ÉPILOGUE D'UNE IDYLLE

II

A Hysteria of the Heart: The Case of Marie Bière

During the cold winter days and nights of the last month of 1879, thirty-one-year-old concert singer Marie Bière, partly disguised by a wide-brimmed hat and a lorgnon, stalked her lover through the streets of Paris. A revolver to hand, she followed him to dance halls and theatres. She hired a carriage and for hours staked out his apartment at 17 Rue Auber, a few steps from the newly completed Palais Garnier, home of the Paris Opera where Marie had once aspired to sing. Her despair was total. She could only wait, wait and watch. She was waiting for an opportunity to shoot.

Around nine o'clock on the evening of 7 January, her chance came. Robert Gentien, accompanied by his new mistress Lucie Colas, a twenty-two-year old actress from the Palais-Royal, stepped out of the building. When Colas got into a carriage some way from the entrance, Marie hurled herself onto the street from her waiting vehicle and fired three shots at close range. After the first two shots, it was clear that Robert had been severely wounded in back and leg. The third bullet, fired as she was being stopped by passers-by, missed its target. To the police who were quickly on the scene Marie manifested no remorse. She regretted Robert wasn't dead, she stated emphatically. As soon as she could she would try to murder him again. He owed her a life.

What circumstances had led Marie Bière, a gentle, sensitive young woman, to these straits? What concatenation of overwhelming emotion and social impediments had toppled her into carrying out a raging and murderous act? The mind doctors were called in to examine her state. But if Marie Bière was mad – then her madness was contagious. It was a condition that spread through the *belle époque* and affected more women than at any time before or since.

Marie Bière, wearing her stage name of Maria Biraldi, had met Robert Gentien in the elegant Atlantic resort of Biarritz over two years before. At twenty-eight, she was a lyric performer of some standing. Considered a child prodigy in her native Bordeaux, she had sung at a young age with the Philharmonic Circle, and had then trained at the Paris Conservatoire. Her voice had charm and clarity. But its power was not altogether sufficient for her to attain the heights she hoped for. She had aspired to sing Verdi and Meyerbeer at the famous Théâtre-Italien, one of Paris's two leading opera companies: they had taken her on, but her ambitions were never fulfilled. The one major production she was scheduled for was cancelled for lack of funds. Nonetheless, at a time when any career for a young woman who also wanted respectability was a considerable achievement, Marie Bière certainly had one. She had regular engagements throughout the provinces. She appeared in famous resorts and spa towns – on the Riviera, at Pau, at the glittering Biarritz. Programmes headlining her still exist.

Despite her distinct ambition and sense of her own talent, Marie was strangely enough also well liked by her peers. There is something childlike about her. 'She was a good and gentle soul' until Robert Gentien led her astray, her friend and fellow artiste Mathilde Delorme said of her at the trial. She was certainly 'no coquette', the kind of woman whose successes in the artistic sphere could only be measured by her success in the bedchamber.

In the police-archive files that detail the period of her investigation and trial, which also contain letters, her 'confession' and notebooks,

Marie Bière insistently repeats that she is no coquette, as if she is haunted by the very possibility. She is, she states, a respectable woman. She needs to distance herself both in the public eye and in her own mind from the courtesans, or *horizontales*, so prevalent at the time, particularly in the world of musical theatre and spectacle. One might even suspect that mixed up amongst the passionate motives that lead to her taking aim at Gentien is a sense that he stands for everything that she doesn't want herself to be: his gaze, his very existence, turn her into the woman of easy virtue she despises yet verges on being. If class and finances collude, the slippage for a woman between virtue and easy virtue is as quick as it is precipitous.

In *belle époque* France, attractive women of uncertain class could supplement their living, all the while making their way up the social hierarchy, by providing sexual favours for men of the middle and upper classes. It was a time when marriage for men came relatively late and was contracted on grounds of property and progeny, rather than love. Sex with unmarried women of their own class, whose chastity and innocence were essential attributes for marriage, was a near-impossibility. So from a young age, men often had recourse to prostitutes or their higher-status version, the courtesans. This was at one and the same time a clandestine and an acceptable form of behaviour. Repectable bourgeois mothers would far prefer their sons being initiated into sex by a woman of easy virtue to having them engage in the wrong kind of marriage. Keeping a courtesan had the added advantage that the woman might be 'cleaner' than a prostitute – that is, uninfected by one of the many sexually transmitted diseases from gonorrhoea to syphilis that made the period's sexual relations a risky business.

For the kept women of the demi-monde – so sumptuously portrayed by Alexandre Dumas *fils* in *La Dame aux Camélias*, the basis for Verdi's opera *La Traviata*, and in the novels of Balzac, Zola and Proust, whose Odette rises from murky origins to the height of Parisian aristocracy – there might be advantages of independence and financial ease to be had from their status, which was at once shadowy and showy. One of the many dangers, however, for both men and mistresses, was that while their arrangements were always most satisfactory if they provided a simulacrum of the passionate rituals and forms of romantic love, this could too often topple into the real thing. The unruly emotion then took over and played havoc with lives, since marriage, that sanctified 'for ever', was in most cases an impossibility. Families, inheritance, all of the bourgeois and indeed aristocratic world, stood in the way. Dumas's *La Dame aux Camélias* was based on his own enduring love affair with a courtesan whom he could neither give up nor marry.

Marie Bière clearly wanted to stress that she could never be mistaken for a woman of the demi-monde. She may also have wanted to distinguish herself from the notorious actress-courtesan charged as an accomplice to attempted murder by vitriol, Madame Gras, whose case less than three years before, in July 1877, had filled the pages of the press. Eugénie Gras, in her trajectory from rags to riches, shared something with Zola's infinitely desirable and rapacious blonde Venus of the demi-world, Nana. The novelist was working on his portrait of the artiste-courtesan at the time of the case. He gave his public a vision of a tarnished masculinity and an irresistible, but utterly uncaring, femininity – a sex goddess enamoured only of luxury and destruction. In his research notebooks he said he wanted to describe 'Abasement . . . of the naked man, throwing everything to the winds for cunt. Everybody led by the tail, and the women indifferent. A pack of dogs in pursuit of a bitch who's not in heat and who mocks the dogs that follow her.'

In her deposition, Marie Bière was at pains to differentiate herself both from bitches in heat and courtesans. She stressed that she came from a respectable Bordeaux family, though one of modest means. Her father Philippe worked for the railways, the Chemin de Fer du Midi. Marie had gone to a convent school, and apart from being seen as a good, well brought-up young girl, had been known only for her slightly excessive sensitivity. She loved nature and poetry. She had a gift for 'exalted' states, a propensity for being carried away. Teachers interviewed in the pre-trial inquiry, led by the investigating magistrate, remarked on her intellectual and emotional precocity.

They also commented on one particular episode from her school-days. Marie had become very closely attached to another girl: it was a friendship marked by vigilance, perpetual anxiety, and the pure passion of someone who had found a 'soul sister', a part of herself she couldn't let go. When the young Marie sensed her soul sister had grown indifferent, she fell into profound despair and contemplated suicide. She had what one witness called a propensity to a 'hysteria of the heart'.

Music back then had saved Marie from her despair: she was the star soloist at school. The best of Bordeaux's music teachers took her up and promoted her, before she left for the Conservatoire in Paris at the age of eighteen accompanied by her mother. Indeed, the entire family moved around this time, her father's job taking him to the railway office in Paris. Marie's mother, a cook before her marriage, dedicated her life to her daughter and her talent. Her only other child, a son slightly younger than Marie, had left home at the age of fifteen to pursue adventure in South America. Whether his mother's attention or inattention played into what commentators considered a radical departure is unclear. In any event, Madame Bière was her daughter's constant companion, at once agent and chaperone, in her professional itinerary across the country. The closeness between mother and daughter would echo through Marie's life. When Robert Gentien paid court to her, he probably didn't know he had her mother to contend with, as well as his own libertine lust and Marie's awakened interest.

A handsome, amiable, wealthy thirty-year-old man about town, who loved his pleasures and the delights of Paris rather more than life on his sizeable estates in the Gironde in southwest France, Robert paid court to Marie throughout his stay in Biarritz and then by letter from his family home, the Château de Tustal. For a sentimental and inexperienced young woman, courtship and letters may easily have taken on the semblance of a serious affair of the heart, perhaps even a prelude to eventual marriage, rather than a worldly and fugitive romp. Robert addresses Marie as 'ma chère Miss Fauvette', my little Miss Warbler.

The letters are sent to her not at home, but via a trusted friend. Her suitor may hardly be nineteenth-century France's most subtle stylist. Even so, it's not beyond belief that his letters could be read romantically by an unjaded imagination such as Marie's, one steeped in sentimental opera lyrics. She takes Robert's courtship and his declarations of love seriously — at his word, rather than in recognition of a seductive game: 'The more I think of the beautiful days we spent together, my dear friend, the more I think of how much gratitude I owe you for your charming welcome,' he writes. 'You are, without flattery, the most adorable woman I've ever met. Everything in you is honest, sympathetic and generous. I've known many young women in this world: none was as gifted as you are. I swear to you, you're a real little phenomenon.'

He urges Marie to meet him on 16 October, when he will be in Paris. Anticipating the long-awaited date of their tryst, he writes the lines that a high-minded Marie might well have been swayed by:

> Next to you, I feel myself better and raised in my own eyes. I've kept a delicious memory of our last day together: I felt I was impregnated by a heady perfume, which gave me exquisite dreams, like those of opium smokers.
>
> Do you ever think of that evening in Saint-Sébastien and our first kiss, so long desired, and so often refused? Courage, my little warbler, and have faith in me. The future belongs to us. No friend could be more sincere and grateful, and if I can give you a little pleasure I'll do it with an open heart.

In her comments to the investigating magistrate for whom these letters formed part of the trial dossier, it is clear that Marie thought such sentiments were evidence of Robert's early love for her. Certainly, they were evidence of her belief in it. As she stated at her trial in April 1880, she would never have sacrificed her purity, her honour, for a mere three-month frolic. Since she claimed, honestly or not, that she had never expected marriage from Robert (which does not preclude her having wished for it), what seems clear is that Marie anticipated at least a simulacrum of marriage, a tender, somewhat high-minded, lasting relationship.

The date of 16 October that the lovers had settled on for their first Paris tryst proves difficult to arrange. Marie is still living at home, and secrecy has to be maintained at all costs. This makes even going to the post office to pick up letters a challenge. At the last moment, Mathilde Delorme, the old friend Marie calls her 'sister', won't provide the cover she needs. Robert tells her that this is understandable and shouldn't be reproached. He knows that they must take care, but they'll find a means. The need for secrecy, which accentuates the forbidden, of course, also plays into their early passion, heightening excitement with obstacles and inaccessibility. 'I so need you all to myself,' Robert writes, 'and to prove myself worthy of you, that I'll go mad if I have to wait any longer.'

The tryst takes place. The lovers enter the summer of their relations. To facilitate their meetings (every second day and on Sunday), to keep their relations private from his own parents and sister, who come and go at the family home on the Rue de Vienne where their first meetings took place, Robert rents a small set of rooms in the Rue de Hanovre, not far from the Boulevard des Italiens. He is even more careful of appearances than Marie. He is, after all, a man of his world, that part of the French Republic that persists in aristocratic love arrangements: passion is extrafamilial, whether the 'family' consists of spouse or parents. The gentlemanly rules, the courtly code of the *homme galant*, or gentleman libertine – as he calls himself at the trial – put reputation, discretion and honour above much else. But that honour and reputation have nothing to do with seduction leading either to marriage or care of children. At best, the prize for Marie is pleasure and the security of being a kept woman. Robert's assumption is that Marie, artiste that she is, is both aware of and shares this code. That she palpably doesn't is evidence of the slowly changing nature of love arrangements and indeed class relations during France's Third Republic.

Secure in her rather haughty sense of her own worth and the justice of her petty-bourgeois values, Marie seems to be at least partly oblivious to the impossibility for Robert of a recognized match between them. Hardly a protofeminist, she is none the less a working woman and in that sense an independent one; and when work becomes impossible, she stands up for what she believes is her due. Leaving the frame of conventional femininity in her 'act', she has to re-emphasize how centrally she remains within its bounds during her trial.

The secret lovers have not quite three months before Marie's mother finds out about their liaison through an anonymous letter from a chattering concierge, urging her to go to the site of the lovers' illicit acts. Madame Bière had already warned Marie about Gentien's intentions in Biarritz. She had also told Gentien that she wanted to see her daughter married, and his frequent visits and attention would compromise her. According to gossip amongst the Bordeaux neighbours who were interviewed before the trial, Madame Bière had wanted to arrange a match between Marie and a wealthy forty- or fifty-year-old when her daughter was only fifteen. Marie had then refused, though perhaps the maternal value put on a wealthy marriage fed unconsciously into her relations with Gentien – as the prosecution would eventually argue.

Now, as she discovered the full extent of her daughter's relations with Gentien, Madame Bière was furious. She went to see Robert and roundly rebuked him. She and her husband threw Marie out of the family home. 'I reproached her severely when I learned she had strayed. I didn't want to forgive her,' Philippe Bière told the magistrate. 'It was too shameful for me to see her.'

Faced with this familial response, Robert Gentien took fright. In January, he embarked on travels that led him first to the Midi, then through Italy, to Algeria and Spain. He advised Marie to take up an engagement in Brussels to perform in a new comic opera, *La Fée des Bruyères* (The Briar Fairy). Being away from Paris would temper family rage. It's not difficult to imagine that he might have wanted to cool his own relations with Marie as well. He was not a man prepared for difficulties – as she claims again and again in her deposition. He wanted no worries at any cost.

Alone for the first time in her journeying life, Marie made her way to Brussels while Robert headed south. His letters to her are full of the excitement of his travels, the people, the hotels, the sights, the food, and with indications of the *poste restante* where she can reach him. Marie, however, is not at her best. She has prepared herself for her role, but now she is feeling ill. When she attends the first group rehearsal, her voice gives out. She takes herself to a doctor. He tells her she is pregnant.

Distraught, she writes to Robert, who counsels calm and tells her his thoughts are with her – though in fact he's heading off from Naples to Tunis. Voiceless, Marie can't fulfil her contract, and it is cancelled. Her employer writes to inform Madame Bière that her daughter can't take on the role of the fairy and is very distressed. Luckily, despite the fact that, feeling humiliated, she had originally refused his offer, Robert is sending her five hundred francs a month. In the confessional narrative the investigation in France always demands of the accused, it is clear that Marie is ever trying to distance herself from the shaming fact that she receives money from her lover. For her, their relations are always first and foremost love relations. As she points out, if she had really been interested in money, she would not have set out to kill the man who supplied it.

14. The Love Child

Not wanting to believe the doctor who tells her she's pregnant, though she knows he's right, Marie goes back to Paris and tries to make it up with her parents. A few days in Paris, and she's once more persuaded that her pregnancy is real. She doesn't want to shame her family, so she returns to Brussels. Here she is very ill and believes, retrospectively, that she only survived thanks to the care of a stranger. Back in Paris once more, she holes up in a small room in a hotel in the Rue du Château d'Eau. The only person who visits her there is her mother. She is very grateful to her mother for restoring her relationship with her.

Marie's letters don't survive. But she recaps her Brussels odyssey for the investigating magistrate in the margin of one of Robert's early letters about the pregnancy. The contrast between her account and his travel document is in itself an indictment of not only their relationship but also of the period's cavalier male–female relations. In the same breath as she charts her travails, he describes for her the formidable beauty of the Kabyl women. This, together with his repeated caution to 'be calm', acts as a reproach. Though her last letter was charming and affectionate, he writes, it was quite clear that she was allowing her *petite tête folle*, her mad little head, to dominate her. The proof lies in the folly of her journey to Paris.

A few weeks later, on 20 February 1878, he writes to express his sadness at all the trouble he has caused her. The trouble, Marie's marginalia attest, is that he assumes she has gone ahead with the abortion she mooted in her own last letter. She had indeed considered it. She wanted to keep Robert's worries to a minimum, and to do that, she had been prepared to sacrifice both her health and her position. But this thought of an abortion occurred while she was still uncertain that she was pregnant, and it had passed with the baby's reality.

Abortion was a criminal act in Third Republic France and could carry a heavy prison sentence, both for the woman and the abortionist. So Robert, though he thinks the abortion has taken place, never mentions the act by name. Marie confesses her thoughts of undergoing one to the judge because she is trying to make sense for him of Robert's innuendoes – and of course to point a vengeful finger at her one-time lover. When Robert's letter states that it really isn't up to him to make a judgement about what she has done, that 'her generous soul has perhaps led her to extremes' but there is nothing he can do to change matters because her letter arrived too late, he is referring to the abortion.

Marie is eager for the judge to know all this, since one of her strikes against Robert is that she has told the investigating magistrate – and will tell the court – that her one-time lover urged her to have an abortion on his return to France, even though it was now very late in her pregnancy. He even supplied a doctor's name. Gentien, of course, will refute this.

On 12 March 1878, in response to a letter in which it seems Marie evoked her lacerating situation in dramatic terms, Robert writes to his *pauvre amie* to tell her how he sympathizes with her suffering. He really hadn't expected all these complications. Bitter reflections of his guilt now pursue him: he came to trouble her gentle quiet and now he is unable to give her the compensation that she is within her rights to expect. Marie interprets this as his recognition that he owes her marriage!

Robert doesn't mention that word, but he does write, 'Decidedly your mother was perhaps right: I'm your evil genius and instead of facilitating your career as I had so much hoped to do, it's I who stop you on the first step of the ladder.' He goes on to ask her to burn all his correspondence since one never knows what worries can grow out of it – a sign, Marie notes, of his bad conscience. Since none of Marie's letters except for a few roughs find a place in her sizeable judicial dossier, it's clear that he burnt hers.

Back in Paris in early May, Robert at last arranges a rendez-vous, though not at his home. He has serious reasons not to want anyone in his entourage to see her or know anything about her state. According to Marie's later testimony, this is the moment when he bullies her into going to see a certain Dr Rouch for a late abortion: women, she claims he said to her, should do what their lovers ask. Marie protests and feels her child move at the very same time as Robert demands its life be terminated. Needless to say, both Robert and Dr Rouch deny Marie's unprovable imputation. Rouch says that it was she who wanted the abortion and he made it clear that it was too late and counselled patience. Whatever the exact truth, what is clear is that Robert, playboy that he is, is out of sorts and inconvenienced by Marie's pregnancy, while she states, 'I love you too much to kill your child.' He makes appointments and breaks them, frequently apologizes for lateness; sees her, but with little zest; then goes off on 20 July and delays returning to Paris until the autumn. He wants nothing to do with this baby and little to do with this maternal Marie.

It is around this time that Marie begins keeping the journal that she headlines 'Impressions, sufferings, tortures'. The erratic entries at first read like unsent letters to her lover. Like Christiana Edmunds, like Mrs Robinson, Marie had the writing urge, but Robert has warned her not to do so too frequently. Her notebook runs from 14 July 1878 to 10 November 1879, approximately the moment when her final obsession takes shape. There is a flurry of entries at the start when, pregnant and alone in her tiny rooms, she despairs of her love and her fate. A letter from Robert, and she weeps with joy, exclaims her faith in him to the blank page, says how much she values him as well as loves him. She should never have doubted his heart. Her own marginal notes here, written while she is in detention awaiting trial, tersely comment on the vagaries of illusion that love puts in train: 'I was wrong in thinking that I esteemed him. I only loved him.'

On Sundays she goes to church to ask God to inspire Robert with love for her and to beg him to bless their union – 'because you must, my adored one, be mine one day! Isn't it the case that the father of my child should be my husband? . . . God demands it.'

Her magical thinking in her abandonment is wholly understandable. An eight-day silence from Robert and she is in despair again, recognizing that she is just a burden and, worse, a regret for him. Her thoughts leap to suicide and retribution: if men don't condemn him, when she's gone, then God in his justice will know how to deal with him.

Marie swings to the pendulum of Robert's letters, adoring him when they arrive, deploring him and her fate when they don't. In her helplessness, the ups and downs and occasional illnesses of her pregnancy, she is every abandoned woman.

Meanwhile, his letters are increasingly filled with pleas for caution and circumspection: secrecy is even more important now. He responds to her despair by telling her she isn't the first woman to find herself in this situation and to make this 'big journey'. 'Time passes. Things get sorted – or else what would become of the world!' On 11 September he writes from his château saying that he would like to see her calm and certain of the future. Marie interprets this as a further demand to be guarded in her actions and a reminder of her promise to conform to his wishes. He wants her to go to a midwife in Montmartre and leave the child there, without telling her mother what has happened. Since Montmartre at this time was still an outlying village peopled by the poor and vagrant, alongside the *apaches* of the criminal classes, no one from Robert's circle would see her there. Artists were only just beginning to trickle into what through the 1880s would become the capital of Paris's Bohemia.

In mid-September Robert comes to Paris for a day or so. Marie states in her deposition that on meeting her, he continues to make scenes, 'ever and always reproaching my pregnancy. He leaves me just as my pains start. He hands me over to my concierge, giving her an envelope containing an address where she can reach him in case of accident. He had so tortured me that he hoped my death and the baby's would take place.'

Yet until June of the following year, Marie would still be holding out hopes of Robert.

On 4 October 1878, Marie Bière, after a thirty-six-hour labour, was delivered of a little girl she named Juliette Claire. The birth certificate (with a slippage of Marie's age) registers her as the natural daughter of Marie Madeleine Bière, *artiste musicienne*, twenty-five years old.

The day after the birth Marie writes to Robert covertly to say that their friend has been delivered of a little girl and they are despairing of trying to save her. Indeed, it had been a difficult birth and there may have been some question whether the enfeebled child would live, but as Marie notes in her marginalia to a letter of Robert's dated 9 October, she had deliberately masked the truth in order to save him from the worries he so hates. Believing what he wanted to believe, Robert thinks the child dead. He says, 'I learned with great joy that you had been relieved of a heavy weight and that all in all everything happened for the best. Now, no brainstorms, you must rest and rest.'

She finally admits to him that the child is alive and that her mother was with her for the birth. A tortuous tug of love and war then begins. Marie, as Robert has instructed, has put the child out to a wet-nurse – one in Saint-Denis, whom she found through an agency. She wants Robert to come and see her; she wants his love, so she succumbs to his wishes about the child. But Marie also wants him to meet and acknowledge his daughter, whom she adores and who, she says, is so beautiful and the very portrait of her father.

Robert won't do either. It takes him twenty-five days after the birth to visit Marie and he certainly doesn't want the baby there.

Marie begs. They have begun to sleep together again, though erratically. In her deposition she says she's doing this for her child. But she also loves him in a 'senseless' way. She prostrates herself before him. He withdraws in horror. He hates her talking endlessly about the child. In her journal she writes that he detests her and doesn't bother to hide it. 'He's thinking of getting married!!!' she notes with an army of exclamation marks. Robert spends long stretches of time away from Paris. In the trial documents she recounts how, having surreptitiously brought the child and her nurse home when Robert was due to visit, he erupted in fury and refused to enter the room where little Juliette lay. He tells her she lacks intelligence: 'I come here to distract myself and not to take part in scenes.'

In a letter of 5 December Marie threatens suicide:

Robert,

If you knew the tortures you make me undergo when you don't see me two days in a row, you would shed tears of shame and regret: you aren't as bad as you want to appear.

Hell's supplications are as nothing in comparison to those I have to endure: I must be very strong still to be alive.

It's five o'clock and you're not here, so I won't see you today. What are these many things you have to do?

Don't overstep the mark, Robert. I'm capable of everything, even of killing myself, in order to cause you remorse and trouble you in your pleasures. From what rock can your heart have been hewn? I blush to have a child of yours: it will have no feeling and will damn its mother.

Just tell me you'll never change and I'll get rid of both of us at the same time, mother and daughter; it will be better to finish things off immediately. It's cowardly to go on with the life you make me live.

Mercy, Robert! Take pity, let me live, because I swear to you, I feel myself dying; I'm at your knees, I cry, I implore! Come back. Love me. I love you enough to lose my reason or my life. M

This letter went unsent. But it allows us to imagine the tenor of the others. Marie veers frantically between passionate declarations and hate and recrimination. According to the marginalia in this letter, Robert appeared while she was writing it. A terrible scene took place. To Marie's reproaches, Robert responded that he would never see the child and would break off all relations if she carried on in this way. It's clear that Robert is appalled both by Marie's frantic state and the situation he has got himself into. He tries to behave correctly according to his own code: he must support Marie and the child, but that support certainly doesn't include legally recognizing the child's existence or loving both – a toxic bundle for a sybaritic gallant.

Furious after his departure, Marie decides to take her revenge by going to complain to his uncle of his conduct towards her. The uncle refuses her visit.

If Marie's letters and the notebook she subsequently kept seem both melodramatic and masochistic, they are reflections of the rhetoric of love of her times. The operatic material she was so familiar with could easily have supplied her with both. But her writings also reflect the true terror of her situation. Her reputation, already compromised, would be completely wrecked if she lived openly with her child. Yet she loved her little girl, perhaps excessively, as her investigating magistrate notes, and wanted her close. Short of prostituting herself, nor were there any ready means, Robert aside, of earning her keep and recovering her injured pride. Her voice has gone. Her father won't take her in. As he said in his deposition, 'It was too shameful for me to see her. I allowed my wife to, but I couldn't.'

In a letter of 26 January 1879 to an old friend, a lawyer in Auch in southwest France, we hear Marie in a less frantic state. She assesses her situation coolly, noting that above all she is tormented by the fact that she can no longer sing. She recognizes that she is now only a burden for Robert. 'My amour propre is disturbed by it, all the more so since he makes me feel it. How I regret not having remained faithful to my virginal vows! I would have kept your affection and esteem.'

To give Robert his due – as Marie tried by fits and starts to do, since she wanted to keep both his love and her self-respect – a man of his background could neither recognize the child nor marry Marie without alienating his all-important family. The thought of marriage, it seems, had never entered his mind – nor, if she's to be believed, Marie's either, at least initially. She allowed passion to carry her away. Now, as she explains to her lawyer friend, Robert makes only 'ceremonial visits', regular but 'very cold and monotonous'.

Soon, he explains, a new business venture will mean even less time for her.

Matters take a dramatic turn with little Juliette's sudden death on 9 April of bronchial complications. She goes 'like a little bird, in the night', Marie says. She had seen her daughter just the night before and she is now beside herself: bereft, guilty, tormented by her failed loves, both passionate and maternal. Robert has alienated her from her family and her work. And now her child is dead. Racked by guilt, she imagines if she hadn't given her over to a nurse, the baby would not have died. The night after she learns of the death, she writes a vow on a photograph of herself, and places it in a box next to one of the child: 'I give my life and that of her father to my little dead girl.'

Robert, when she tells him of the death, seems pleased.

15. *'Going Mad'*

Marie blames herself for her daughter's death. She also vehemently reproaches Robert, the man who has 'bewitched' her and coerced her into giving up her little one. Her suffering is terrible to bear. She asks him to give her another child to replace little Juliette. When he refuses, her despair is total. Vengeance enters her mind: a life for a life. Under May–June in her notebook there are only two entries. The first reads: 'He comes and makes use of me, but he doesn't love me. I'll kill him!' The second is a long poem about the baby, her beauty, the pride she took in her. She writes that like her daughter she is now going to leave this damned world, where death is the only truth. The last stanza asserts that before making her exit, however, she will take revenge on the father who damned the child and made a martyr of the mother: death will unite them in eternity.

Marie's love has turned to hate. After a violent scene with Robert, she buys a revolver, intent on killing herself or him, or both of them: hatred and self-hatred blur into each other with slippery ease. By her own later admission, she writes him a despairing letter full of provocative insults. She says it's over between them. He comes to see her, intent on complying with her wish for a final rupture, but when she hears him voicing it aloud, she goes to pieces.

In his 7 July description of the 'crisis' scene to Monsieur Oudinet, a former tutor of Robert's who serves as their 'business' go-between, Robert says Marie started by taunting him, then very calmly went to her mirrored wardrobe and opened the door while saying, 'It's all decided then? Fine, I'll show you how a woman who loves you behaves.'

With that, I see her with a revolver in her hand ready to kill herself. I only have time enough to throw myself on her and grab it from her hand. She then falls into a terrible nervous crisis. I call her maid and escape . . . She exhausts me because at times she goes mad, like Estelle [a former mistress]. I'm going to take precautions, because she's a woman who's capable of all the mad things one can imagine. She'll kill herself, or having now turned against me, what won't she do . . . ? I'm still shaken and ask myself whether it wouldn't be a good idea to go to the police . . . I'm going to wait two or three days to see if she calms down. After that, I'll meet her, though with a little trepidation, and this time in the street: I don't want to fall into a trap or be involved in a scandal. Ah! Women! My dear friend, they have their good side, but we pay for it dearly. Not a word of any of this at Tustal.

On 30 June, immediately after the threatened suicide scene, Robert, ever wary of his reputation, had written to Marie advising courage and above all no more impetuous mad acts or *coups de tête*. He was happy, he said, to have been at her side and prevented her folly and the eruption of a scandal. Rupture, as difficult as it might seem for the moment, would give her the tranquillity she needed. What has he been to her for such a long time now, but a good and devoted friend? He will remain so if she allows him to – that is, by not creating a furore and by giving him the right to conduct himself as a *galant-homme*, a gentleman.

We don't know Marie's response to him. An undated July entry in her notebook records that she had the opportunity to kill him, but didn't, God only knows why. He has humiliated her. Can it be, she asks, that despite herself she still holds out hope? In a calmer mood she writes to Monsieur Oudinet, who, as the subsequent trial would make apparent, was himself rather taken with Marie, and less than enamoured of Robert's ways with women. To Oudinet she announces the end of Robert's relations with her. She has been alerted by a letter from him saying she doesn't have to worry about the future, since he'll pay her a monthly sum. This has so humiliated her that she feels she no longer has to shield him from public disgrace. She's prepared to take back her full liberty; but she doesn't want to be at his mercy and dependent on the monthly sum he'll choose to give her. So she's going to ask him for a lump sum. She doesn't see this as an offering, but as a small restitution of what he owes her, since he has ruined her life and her future, rendering her incapable of doing anything.

Almost simultaneously Robert writes to Oudinet saying that the split having taken place, he is prepared to pay Marie a monthly sum for the foreseeable future, but he wants his freedom in return and he'll be rigorous about the rupture. He won't see her. 'I know a lot of men who wouldn't do as much: they wouldn't keep a woman for two years having been her lover for some two or three months.' He wants Marie to have a holiday: a rest will lessen her distress.

She finally goes to Royan, a resort on the Atlantic coast, with her mother. Here she sees a graphologist, those experts of the time who, not so unlike the neurolinguists of today, were said to be able to read personality – in their case, from handwriting. She is told she has an astonishing power of loving, or *amativité*. (Mrs Robinson's phreno-logical reading attributed a similar power to her.)

Over the course of the summer, Marie learns that Robert has replaced her with another woman. She had already spied on him a year ago, while she was heavily pregnant with Juliette. Now she does so more assiduously. Her need for revenge has grown into an obses-sion. She can't bear Robert's total abandonment: the desire for vengeance, the steps towards its implementation, are a continuation of the affair by different means.

Like a divorcing partner who, however reasonable her statements, can't yet let go, she turns to monetary demands as a form of com-munication – now that sex is over and the matter of children settled. In October she writes to Robert to ask for a lump sum of three thou-sand francs in addition to the three hundred a month he has been sending her, since favours presumably ceased, so that she can install herself as a music teacher. His contemptuous reply, telling her he is skint, infuriates her. She threatens to expose his conduct to his family, to write to Oudinet and to his brother-in-law and create a scandal if he doesn't comply. She visits his flat and bursts in on his new mistress.

He writes to say, 'Your visit this morning was wholly inconvenient. One doesn't force oneself into people's houses unexpectedly. The day I broke with you, I intended to take back my liberty wholly and I have begun a serious liaison since then.'

On 10 November she tells her notebooks that seven months have passed since her daughter's death and she hasn't seen Robert in four. He sends her a paltry pension, and imagines that she can live this life. But she can't. She has resolved to die because he doesn't love her and because all hope of being a mother again is lost to her. Yet she doesn't want another woman to be the mother of his children. Because of that, she has to kill him.

She also writes that she feels she is going mad.

'*Je sens que je deviens folle*' are the first words scribbled in pencil in a small day diary covering the period from 21 November till the eve of her murder attempt. (The police discovered the diary in her cupboard: she threw it into the fireplace during one of her interrogations, so its entries are somewhat singed.) Marie has just bought a revolver and has started stalking her former lover. The investigating magistrate's report says that she has also started practising how to use it. In her first diary entry she vows to kill Robert, but a note of two hours later, at six o'clock, declares he is still alive. Her strength betrayed her. Next time it won't, she tells the page and her daughter. Many of these entries are addressed to little Juliette, in whose name she wants this death.

On 13 December she tells the notebook that she wrote to Robert, but the insolent man didn't answer. 'He has forgotten me. And thinks because he sends me pennies to eat with, we're quits. I don't want your money, Robert. I want your life. I don't want to live on charity or prostitution! I can't work, because my health is destroyed and my courage has abandoned me ... I want to die, but I want him to die first.' Her use of the word 'prostitution' for the first time marks her self-abasement, as if she has finally allowed herself to acknowledge that her notions of romantic love with Robert were a veil thrown over her real status, that of the kept coquette she has always resisted.

On 19 December she goes to the Fête des Inondations de Maresie, knowing that he'll be at this major event in the Paris social calendar. She has her revolver with her. But although she sees Robert, he is too far away for her to take aim. The crowd, she writes, is his shield. But she'll get him in the end.

On Christmas Day she notes in her diary: 'My little Jesus is dead, rots in the earth while I'm still here . . . her mother. Mother . . . what a gentle word: it's so sad to have already lost it.' New Year's Day has her scrawling on the reverse side of a photo of Robert: 'RG – condemned to death by me, Marie.' That morning he had sent her five hundred francs, wanting to get rid of her, humiliating her further, or so she says in her deposition. She no longer sleeps, or goes out. She hardly eats, sees no one: she is altogether given over to her obsession.

At four o'clock on 3 January, Marie heads out once more with her revolver. Her diary entry salutes her own mother, the woman whose all-encompassing form of maternal love she has interiorized as an ideal. She asks her mother to forgive her: '. . . but you know the power of maternal love and you'll understand that I've gone off to find my child again.' At eight o'clock, she notes, 'he's still alive. Until tomorrow then.'

Periodically in her notes she calls Robert 'the monster': dehumanized, it is easier to shoot him. She hires a carriage and sits in front of his house in the Rue Auber, waiting for her moment. Now, as she says in her statement, her mind was 'in chaos'. Women come and go from the premises. She follows the starlet from the Palais-Royal, watches her carriage take a tumble, and sees the younger woman thrown. Marie evidently looks so pitiful that the driver, once he has dropped her at her mother's, says he'll stake out Robert's premises for her. It is he who tells her that her former lover's new inamorata is Mlle Colas.

On the evening of 7 January, Marie at last spies Robert. He comes out of the apartment with Mlle Colas and sees her off in a carriage. He then heads towards the Rue Scribe. Marie launches herself out of her vehicle, rushes after him and takes aim. At her first shot, he falls. She doesn't know whether vengeance is at last hers, or if he has merely taken fright and dropped down. She shoots again, and this time he gets up and starts to run. He's shouting and she realizes he doesn't recognize her beneath the large hat and lorgnon she has donned as a disguise. She fires a third shot which goes wide. Passers-by have gathered and a guardian of the peace has jumped on her from behind. He disarms her and she now can't turn the pistol on herself, as she had resolved to do.

Robert is staring at her, but he doesn't recognize her. She identifies herself, and publicly points a finger at him, accusing him of having murdered her daughter.

'She's mad,' he says, and turns away.

In her signed deposition, which describes the scene, Marie states that in those first moments she regretted not having managed to kill him. In her calmer state, without for an instant regretting what she has done – because this man merited a punishment for toying with her love and all the rest of her feelings – she no longer wishes him dead. She is indifferent: life will perhaps be a greater punishment for him. 'I've experienced both physical and moral pain and I don't know which is harder to bear,' she writes.

Marie Madeleine Bière, known as Maria Biraldi, is eventually charged with having voluntarily attempted to commit homicide on the person of Robert Gentien. The attempt failed only because of circumstances independent of her will. In other words, this is a murder attempt with premeditation. Under French penal law, Marie is remanded in custody in the women's prison of Saint-Lazare, while the investigating magistrate, Monsieur Adolphe Guillot, prepares the dossier of her case – and deliberates on the exact charge.

16. *The Investigation*

French judicial procedure, fundamentally laid down in the Napoleonic *Code d'instruction criminelle* of 1808, differs markedly from the English and American.

In France the trial itself is preceded by a long period of inquiry, or *instruction*, led by an investigating magistrate. This figure, a cross between chief detective and a judicial eminence – not altogether unlike the King's magistrates of the *ancien régime* who themselves had sombre links to a secular version of the Spanish inquisitors – prepares the case against the defendant until he is satisfied that it is ready to be prosecuted by the court. The investigating magistrate has wide-ranging powers in what is understood as a procedure that will establish the truth. He carries out seizures and searches, orders expert testimony and verifies evidence. He interrogates the defendant as well as a host of witnesses.

This instruction is scarcely limited to material evidence or witnesses to the crime. An entire life is under investigation here. Character and psychological make-up are of as much importance as material facts. It was this interest in the psychology of the defendant and of the crime that perhaps made the French judicial system in the nineteenth century so much more permeable to the rising profession of psychiatry – even though the terms they used might not be the same. Psychology, after all, includes rational, cognitive processes as well as emotional and perceptual ones.

In France, as in other continental jurisdictions influenced by the Napoleonic Code, the specific crime came to be understood as part of a larger context in which a criminal personality could be detected. Questions of material evidence and moral responsibility, so central to Anglo-Saxon jurists, would often come second to investigations into the dangerous personality of the defendant and the risk he or she posed to society. This – and the possibility of repeat offence that it implied – would also influence sentencing. When in 1876 the Italian criminologist Cesare Lombroso introduced his hereditarian theories of the 'born criminal', that reversion to an atavistic type supposedly common to those who offend, his work found a ready home in French medico-legal thinking, which had long been interested in the personality of the accused as much as in the particular crime committed.

Lombroso's view of the criminal woman – doubly exceptional and therefore a true monster – also influenced the courts. Already present in the characterizations of the female that Darwin and Maudsley offered, this criminal woman was a contradictory creature, both excessively 'feminine' in her deceitfulness – not seen to be at odds with her supposed limited intelligence – and somehow masculine in her eroticism, her increased sexuality. She shared in the epoch's understanding of woman as childlike, morally deficient, sexually cold, pious and maternal – all stereotypes that were in play but at the same time challenged by the passionate criminals of the *fin de siècle*.

To help build up a personality profile, the French investigating magistrate asks the defendant to submit an autobiographical account, a 'memoir' of her life and her acts, alongside letters, poems and writings. In this Rousseauian confessional, it is hoped the psychology of the crime will be laid bare and intention and motive made clear. Witnesses of the accused's early life, even if from far-flung jurisdictions, are called: her ways of loving, her friendships, her faith, her family relations, her forebears, are all interrogated in order to arrive at a full picture. Gossip and hearsay often enough find a place in the final dossier. This 'hearsay' evidence provides intriguing testimony about the nature of the period's received and accepted ideas. So, for example, when men – in the manifold instances of terrifying and drunken domestic abuse that then filled the courts – killed their wives, neighbours would often corroborate that, like the husband, they knew from the sounds of her many and therefore 'acceptable' beatings that the wife must be 'straying'. No hard evidence for her unfaithfulness might exist – simply prejudice, which elided brutal punishment into proof of a prior crime.

Meetings between the investigating magistrate (or his delegates) and witnesses are recorded in writing by a *greffier*, a clerk of the court. This is no true verbatim record, but the magistrate's version of the interview proceedings dictated after the event by him, and then read, signed and approved by the witness. The magistrate may inevitably, however accurate his notes, transpose these into better French and subliminally offer an interpretation. This is why archival memoirs in the defendant's own words can be so revealing: they haven't passed through the disciplined structures of the magistrate's style and language.

The defendant herself may be present at witness interviews and ask questions, or indeed supply them to the magistrate if she can't be part of the interrogation. She is also permitted to interrupt proceedings, even if it is her victim who is being interviewed. The magistrate, like some novelist, may then interpolate his sense of the scene and the tensions between the parties in his recorded account. (The defendant in the dock can interrupt witnesses on the stand in court, as well.) However, defendants did not – until reforms of 1897 – have access to representation by a lawyer during the instruction stage. Nor were charges against the defendant definitively stated or brought until the end of that stage. All the material gathered during the instruction, the so-called *pièces*, were then put together – and this continues today – into a large document, a dossier, and presented at court, where it forms the foundation of the trial. It is used and often referred to by the presiding trial judge, the *président* of the court, but rarely argued with.

The investigation period and the work of the magistrate within it can be a long and tangled process. The notorious Madame Steinheil, the former mistress of President Félix Faure, who died in her arms – some said while she was performing fellatio on him – was nine years later implicated in the murder of her husband and mother-in-law: she went through two investigating judges and a year-long instruction before finally being acquitted in 1909. The German title of Kafka's novel, *The Trial — Der Prozess* — as well as its arduous content and the mystified state of its accused hero who doesn't know the charges against him, gives a better sense of the whole 'process' of the instruction and continental judicial procedure than its English title or Anglo-Saxon legal fictions.

Marie Bière was fortunate in her *juge d'instruction*. Adolphe Guillot (1836–1906) was already in 1880 a highly respected judge, one of the crop of judges with socially liberal and Republican sympathies who had displaced the judicial stars of the earlier monarchy. Over the coming years his reputation, indeed celebrity, would grow because of his writing and campaigning work on behalf of the independence of the judiciary, as well as on jury and prison reform. Guillot called for the revision of the *Code d'instruction criminelle*, the rules governing investigatory procedure, and won the right for defendants to have a lawyer present during the interrogations of the instruction period. (Other changes included that any charge against the accused must be issued within two days.) He also campaigned on behalf of children's rights, and took pioneering steps to have both children and young girls protected in the judicial system. His two volumes of the 1880s on Paris prisons, *Paris qui Souffre*, won him election to the elite circle of the Académie Française: contemporary femininists, criminologists such as Cesare Lombroso and the world-famous analyst of the crowd, Gustave Le Bon, all cited Guillot's exemplary work.

Like many defendants held on remand, Marie Bière developed a close relationship with her *juge d'instruction*. Saint-Lazare, the women's prison where she was sent, was a vast place: in 1885 it housed some ten thousand women. Run by nuns, it was both a detention centre and a detaining hospital, and found its largest cohort of inmates among the so-called *insoumises*, the prostitutes who didn't or wouldn't register under the Paris vice squad clean-up plan and were sent to prison both as punishment and for deliberately demeaning hospital checks on their sexual health. In this atmosphere, Marie's warmest links were with her inquisitor. Her letters to him have an intimate ring. On 16

February 1880 she writes from her cell, '*Je suis horriblement triste*' – 'I'm horribly sad. I beg of you, save me.' Attending witness interviews, being interrogated by Guillot, constituted Marie's principal moments of human contact in jail.

Marie was, according to the judge's notes, too weak to attend the first interrogation session with Robert Gentien. He, too, couldn't or wouldn't respond to the investigating magistrate's first summons to an interview at which Marie would be present. The doctors had warned him such an encounter would be bad for his health, he said. He had been slow to recuperate from his wounds after the shooting. These were serious, if not fatal.

The documents seem to imply that through February and March, Marie Bière was impatient for this encounter to take place. She had written down five questions she wanted the judge to put to Robert, even if he refused to have her there. The questions already signal the substance of her character defence: she was an honest woman – no coquette, no prostitute – until Robert led her astray. He wanted her to have an abortion, and when that didn't happen he coerced her into giving up her child, which ineluctably led to the child's death.

Guillot did indeed put Marie's questions to Robert, who had acquiesced to the second request for interview against his doctors' orders. He limped badly: the doctors had not been able to extricate the bullet lodged in his right leg. But his speech, the deposition states, was clear and self-assured and he maintained his sang-froid throughout, even when Marie came in at the end for the signing of the statement.

To Marie's first question – 'On the night of 16 October 1878 when I came to see you for the first time, was I an honest woman and did you consider me such?' – Robert replied as the practical man of the world that he was: 'It was in 1877 and not in 1878 and the question is embarrassing . . . A young girl who accepts a rendez-vous with a young man and then comes to his house is really going too far if she expects to pass as an honest woman.'

Marie's second question focused on her 'honesty' once more: 'When I was pregnant, did you ever for a moment doubt that the child was yours?' Robert answered: 'I didn't doubt it at the time, but now I do.'

In response to her query as to whether he had wanted her to terminate the pregnancy when she was in Brussels, Robert answered: 'All I had were her letters. These were habitually written in an intense [*exalté* – the suggestion is theatrically melodramatic] style. I thought she was in despair over what she believed was a pregnancy, and was prepared to go to any lengths. I told her to do nothing. I was trying to boost her spirits.'

But had he not sent her to Dr Rouch to get an abortion? Marie pressed her point. 'That's an odious slur,' Robert protested. 'She wouldn't go and see her family doctor, and I couldn't for personal reasons send her to mine, so I got a recommendation from someone for her to see Dr Rouch. She told me he had simply confirmed that she was three to four months pregnant and advised various precautions.'

Finally Marie asked: 'Since you didn't get what you wanted of me, did you not then tell me to undergo the birth in Montmartre with a midwife and abandon my child there?' 'I only said,' Robert replied, 'that to avoid problems with your mother, it would be easier.'

When Marie was brought into the interview room for the read-through and signing of the deposition notes, she was extremely pale. She fixed her eyes on Robert without speaking. This strange judicial scene, translated into contemporary terms, has something of the feel of a professional mediation between divorcees who can't be brought to agree either on the facts or on a mutual language of negotiation, so opposed are their views on the etiquette and practices of love. After Robert's answers to her questions were read out to her, Marie simply stated: 'I maintain the truth of everything I said. If Monsieur contests it, that surprises me not at all.'

Robert 'absolutely' denied her imputation that he was lying. There was nothing he wanted to add to his deposition. 'Nor I,' Marie stated, then burst out: 'You're base, odious [*infame!*]! You're the cause of my daughter's death. If you'd left her at my side, she'd still be alive, and I wouldn't have tried to kill you.'

'I protest emphatically,' Robert retorted. 'I didn't stop you from keeping your daughter and I'm not responsible in any way for her death.'

The complex slippage between truths and lies inevitable to passion rarely translates easily into the harder certainties of the courts. That Marie was guilty of attempting to murder Robert Gentien was clear to everyone, let alone herself. Whether she was an 'honest' woman – a virtuous innocent from the provinces, despite her appearances on the stage – or had wanted money or marriage from Robert, from the first; whether the wish for an abortion was his or hers, or in the early days both of theirs; whether Robert's whole attitude to love and parenting was deeply reprehensible, or hers naive and unrealistic, or alternatively mercenary – these were not easily resolvable questions at any time, and particularly not at a historical moment when values were clearly in flux. Needless to say, when the *juge d'instruction*'s rendition of these interviews was read out in court, sensation ensued.

17. *Passion, Madness and Medics*

Love relations, understandings of passion and sexual etiquette, were under strain in *belle époque* France. Old habits and ways were colliding with the new with increasing speed, like the railway that now cut through the nation. High migration from the traditionally Catholic and conservative provinces to the increasingly secular capital, where a largely progressive Republican and scientifically oriented government was in power from 1879, resulted in a vertiginous clash of mores. Moving from provincial Bordeaux to Paris, as Marie Bière had, constituted a leap not only across kilometres but into a different modernity. According to the mind doctors, such migration, like the speed of the trains themselves, could also cause psychological shock. Vagabondage, alcoholism and prostitution were some of the consequences, alongside the growth in the asylum population.

Prostitution (together with the vice squads who battled against it) increased significantly in the course of the Third Republic as women, out of financial need, were forced or fell into or resorted to the oldest profession. In a world of double standards that separated them out, sometimes by class, into 'honest' and marriageable or fair game, punters were plentiful. A proportion of these were also single migrants from the country. Understanding of what behaviour was appropriately masculine, what respectably feminine, varied enormously from country to small town to capital city as well as, between the generations and the classes. The differences might be compared to some of our own confusions when old and young clash over the morality and appropriate etiquette for online and social networking sites; or when immigrant parents and their teenage children fall out over dating and sexual habits.

Against this kind of background, the trial of Marie Bière which began on 6 April 1880 seemed to be far less about the crime of attempted murder than about the vagaries of passion, changing sexual relations and the nature of the human mind. What roles, what behaviour in men and women, would the new Republic value? Were seduction and abandonment – a gentlemanly Don Juanism – to continue to be permissible? Did men owe a debt of paternity to their 'natural' children as well as official recognition to their mothers? Was marriage 'for ever'? Crucially, what could passion – sexual and maternal – do to the mind?

The eighteenth-century *philosophes* had vested all that was good in the 'triumph of reason'. Perhaps it was this absolutist emphasis that made passion and the irrational take on a competitive dynamic in the French thinking of the nineteenth century. In England, the Romantic movement had largely affected the arts and aspects of sentimental behaviour. In France, after the excesses of the Revolution, passion had also become an explanatory category, one used by the early alienists hand in hand with the diagnosis of monomania. They took it into the courtrooms as a mitigating factor. It was a category every citizen could understand. The mind, the mental faculties, could be overturned by an impulsive force that left rational will out of control, 'alienated' reason and diminished responsibility.

French mind doctors had made their way into the criminal courts as expert witnesses early in the century. They had done so noisily in the landmark case of the child murderer Henriette Cornier in 1825. The great alienist Esquirol's follower Étienne-Jean Georget had even argued for a classification of *monomanie instinctive*, or instinctive monomania, for five brutal criminals whose reason and moral sense were palpably intact. They could tell right from wrong, yet they were driven to monstrous crime. Homicidal monomania, Georget claimed, was a subspecies of Esquirol's classification of monomania. It was a lesion of the will, rather than of the intellect, a perversion of the affective passions and sentiments which propelled the individual to sudden violent acts.

In his pamphlets, Georget championed two roles for alienists: conducting a pre-examination of offenders; providing expert witnesses in court. Esquirol and other specialists testified in the case of Henriette Cornier, a young servant woman who had brutally killed a neighbour's toddler. They brought definitions of partial and not readily visible madness into the legal arena. Through them a diagnosis of monomania came to act as an extenuating factor in sentencing. Hidden madness, not readily visible to the lay observer, was now dissected by specialists in the criminal courtroom. Passion, love gone wrong, distorted or malignant love which bred violence rather than tenderness, perversion – all gradually became subjects both of forensic and of public discussion. Though, in the course of the century, a diagnosis of monomania went out of fashion and hereditarian explanations took on greater moment, French alienists continued to be interested in conditions that led to crime. In mid-century, the great clinician Charles Lasègue wrote detailed and evocative analyses of violence caused by persecutory delirium as well as studies of kleptomania and exhibitionism.

With the birth of the Third Republic after France's shaming defeat in the Franco-Prussian War and the violent uprising of the Paris Commune, there was increased scientific and wholly secular interest in 'unreason'. Whether it took the form of individual crime or mass explosion, it was clear that extreme emotion could overturn the rational mind. Emotion worked on the nerves. So could external hypnotic suggestions. The nervous impulses, it was thought, could set up their own autonomous activity and propel actions of which the conscious mind was not aware. Automatisms, automatons, alters (or alternating personalities), doubles, increasingly pervaded the *fin de siècle*, together with the accompanying medical theorizing. Such passionate or sleepwalking states engendered what English law, too, calls an 'alienation of reason'; and since the 'voluntary' acts that constitute the basis of crime can not be said to have taken place during such states, the individual perpetrator can not be held responsible.

By 1910, a doctoral dissertation by Hélie Courtis could assert that the passionate criminal suffered from 'psychic troubles that suppress all control by the intellectual faculties over the muscular reflex that constitutes the murderous deed'. The criminal acted under the influence of 'a succession of muscular jolts originating in a pure motor impulse'. Passions – frustrated love, jealousy, rage – 'distorted the functioning of the nervous system', and in that *état passionnel*, a transitory state in which the sane could be subject to insanity, 'a momentary modification of the cerebral circulation' took place.

As in other aspects of medicine, more needed to be learned here by the doctors so that preventive scientific measures could be taken by a state that had its citizens' best interests at heart – the interests of both those who suffered from 'disease' or disorder and those whose well-being needed to be safeguarded if they were endangered by the ill. The mind doctors could help to explain crime, and prevent it, by being put in charge of those who in their worst manic moments could imperil others as well as themselves. Thus, the medico-legal specialization grew in the Third Republic not only in such obvious areas as toxicology but also in psychiatry. It gradually acquired its own professorships and teaching sites; these were far more centralized than in the UK and readily became part of the state apparatus.

Public health and hygiene, prevention of disease and sanitation, had been important to the French state and its citizens since the 1789 Revolution. A decree of 18 June 1811 had instituted a role for the medico-legist in the criminal code, as well. Poisoning, infanticide, sudden death, would now mean the instant intervention of medical experts, who from 1829 also had their own journal, the *Annales d'hygiène publique et de médecine légale*. The law of 1838 made alienists – at least in part – servants of the state and administrators of a nationwide asylum system.

A related decree of 1845 demanded that a doctor countersign any police certificate committing a person to an asylum. As a result, the Paris police acquired a new and permanent medical post. This was first held by Ulysse Trélat, one of Esquirol's disciples. The Paris police préfecture now also had an infirmary attached. Here the wide range of offenders picked up by the police were examined and some then moved on to the famous Asile Sainte-Anne, where Clérambault and Jacques Lacan eventually worked. At the admissions department at Sainte-Anne, the resident alienist would determine whether the 'criminals' were to be held or moved on once more to the appropriate long-term or short-stay facility. Offenders might well be considered too devoid of mental faculties or too delirious to be tried: administrative justice rather than court hearings would then prevail.

It is worth noting that not only psychiatry but the medical profession as a whole reached new heights of status and influence during the Third Republic, and took on a wholly recognizable modern authority. Between 1871 and 1914, 358 medical doctors gained election as senators or deputies in the Assembly, the second-largest group after lawyers. Mostly left-wing and progressive, they had a shaping interest in both public health and family matters. They spoke out about the rising toll of alcoholism, which in their eyes had taken on epidemic proportions and was linked to suicide, crime, divorce, the declining birthrate and insanity. They also largely considered it to be a breach of the Hippocratic oath to pass on information about abortion – a crime in the eyes not only of a Catholic hierarchy but of the state as a whole, which until well into the twentieth century was strongly pro-natalist and ever worried about its population being smaller than that of neighbouring Germany. The doctors' presence in the courtrooms, as pathologists, as alienists, and as expert witnesses, took on a wholly modern configuration.

By the third quarter of the century, the *médecin légal des aliénés* was a figure who was often called by the *juge d'instruction* to assess the mental state of an accused. He also regularly appeared in court to give an impartial opinion on a defendant's mental state. Under a penal code which like the English was founded on a conception of the individual possessing a free and rational will as well as moral responsibility, the expert psychiatric determination of whether a person was in full possession of his mental powers, and could be deemed responsible for a crime, was a crucial issue. Passion of the morbid long-lasting kind or a sudden overwhelming impulse could topple such powers and induce madness. In women, whose hold on reason alienists and public largely agreed was weaker because of her biological make-up, her susceptibility to menstrual and other pressures, the rational will could more easily succumb either to passion or to suggestion.

18. The Trial of Marie Bière

One of the ways in which passion, madness and the understandings of the mind doctors moved into the public sphere was through the increased reporting of court cases in an ever growing number of newspapers, high- and low-brow, as well as in professional journals. Censorship died with the change of government in 1879. Between then and 1887, when the threat of a take-over by the populist hero General Georges Boulanger seemed imminent, almost every step the French government took worked to increase the sphere of democratic liberties, while curbing the power of the clerics. As in the United States, France had no law against pre-trial disclosure. In the press and the more specialist *Gazette des tribunaux*, crime columns now featured more prominently than ever, some providing near-verbatim records of trials. Newspapers popularized not only the 'exceptional' status of criminals, but also debates surrounding the psychology of crime and interrogations of madness.

The reported spectacle of crime, passion, potential lunacy and punishment was often echoed in the *feuilletons*, one-off fictions or serial novels, which filled the pages alongside court reports. Running into each other and occasionally penned by the same author, reportage and *feuilleton* thrived on each other's sensation and tropes: fact fed fiction and fiction fed life, in a looping effect that gathered in legal and medical practice on the way. Ideas, terminology, ways of classifying emotions and mental states, percolated through society invoking new ways of understanding the self while moulding the self into the categories of understanding. Courtroom players – defendants, lawyers, magistrates and even doctors – became stars whose names might be as well known as those of today's footballers. Like that of a match, the outcome of a case might not be uninfluenced by public will and the noise and heat with which it expressed itself.

Albert Bataille, the *Figaro* columnist who reported court cases with such panache that they found their way into bestselling bound volumes, calls Marie Bière's trial 'one of the strangest of our times'. Her case ranks for him amongst the most dramatic and most Parisian of novels. 'Criminal or victim, unworthy of indulgence or worthy of pity, Marie Bière isn't one of those vulgar accused who move from sad vice to crime and from crime to the central prison,' he writes, underlining that Marie doesn't belong to the *bas-fonds*, the dregs, of Paris. Her youth is a 'melancholy romance', her love a 'tragic novel'. Will the trial, Bataille asks rhetorically, prove her an ambitious woman in search of a lucrative marriage who played her passion to the hilt and couldn't forgive her lover for escaping her clutches, or a poor trusting romantic soul whom disillusion and the ruin of all her hopes of happiness drove to crime?

On the morning of 6 April 1880, the majestic Assizes courtroom in Paris's grand, though still not altogether reconstructed, Palais de Justice is packed with well dressed women and a panoply of writers, Conservatoire professors and theatre people. Amongst the latter is Alexandre Dumas *fils*, whose many popular boulevard dramas seem to have been made for Marie to star in. Tragically abandoned heroines and illegitimate children were Dumas's theme. He himself was one, and though his own father had recognized him, Dumas *fils* championed actual marriage between seducing men and the women who gave birth to their offspring, not merely the recognition of their children.

Marie Bière, when she appears in the courtroom at ten-thirty, evokes gasps of pity from the public: fragile, pale, her brown eyes vast and her face skeletal against the black of her severe dress, she is, according to the press, a shadow of her former beautiful self. She has to be held up as she is led to the bench of the accused, and then all but falls into it. Her face, according to the press, is ravaged with the marks of despair, her forehead white beneath the simple round hat poised on her auburn hair, which lets a few locks stray onto her brow – in the current style. She leans against the bar, her handkerchief to her eyes, and at eleven o'clock when the session is convened, listens to the clerk reading out the counts against her.

When she answers to the charge, her voice is soft and contained, with none of the melodrama the public has been led to anticipate, particularly since she is a woman of the stage. The trial is to be Marie Bière's most acclaimed performance and the one in which she has most at stake.

French trial procedure allows for the president of the court to act as a kind of chair of judges, jury and proceedings: with due ceremony he leads the interrogation of the accused, the *partie civile* – in this case the victim of the crime – and all witnesses. This can, in large part, be an oral replication of the *juge d'instruction*'s dossier, but the public stage and the presence of the jury often induce surprises. Le Président Bachelier, with his small well manicured hands and impeccable robes, was known as something of a pontiff amongst judges. He was a man with a soft-fluted voice who could make the most hideous crimes sing, and was a virtuoso of the summing-up statement that directed the jury.

Bachelier takes Marie through the facts of the crime. He describes the four days of stalking leading up to the shooting, her journal entries which show premeditation, the shooting itself, to all of which Marie acquiesces. If she no longer insists that she wants to see Robert dead, she is still adamant about the justice of her act. Bachelier then takes her through her life – her musical talent, her studies at the Conservatoire, her failure to attain the highest rank in her profession, her meeting with Robert . . . The latter two seem to elide in his mind. Despite his stress on her impeccable reputation, he implies that she might well have been ready for an affair with a wealthy man. Marie is instantly alert to his intention: when he states that she was introduced to Monsieur Gentien by a friend, she interrupts to stress – 'Yes, and he paid court to me straight away.'

'Didn't he say that you flirted with him, that you marked him out?'

'Me, flirt?' '*Moi, coquette?*' Marie smiles sadly.

'I don't want to say anything that will offend you,' Bachelier offers. 'I'm only pointing out that polite, familiar, sophisticated relations were established between you.' He goes on to evoke their excursion to Saint-Sébastien, the promise of a rendez-vous in Paris, the fact that she found Gentien handsome, elegant, amiable, well brought up, and a man in a hurry ... Marie agrees to this last, and emphatically to the fact that her mother knew nothing of the tryst.

Président Bachelier pushes her on this: 'See here, you were twenty-eight years old, no longer a child, an inexperienced girl. You'd spent ten years in the world of the theatre. You must have known very well what M. Gentien expected of you?'

Marie bows her head and says nothing.

Bachelier then leads her through to her discovery of her pregnancy during her time in Brussels. He interrogates her statement that Gentien urged an abortion first, there and then, with Dr Rouch in Paris. But even though Marie seems to be caught in an assertion that both Gentien and Dr Rouch deny, an accusation that the judge calls 'ill-founded', she insists in a firm voice, above the growing murmurs from an excited public, that her accusation is true.

'Monsieur Gentien finished by saying you were mad. Are you?'

'Not at all,' Marie answers drily.

The interrogation now moves towards the eve of the birth of her child, and Marie's responses take on an intensity that provokes out-bursts from the public. The president of the court has evidently nettled her by evoking how sick Gentien was of all the complications she 'created', how he didn't want to ruin his relations with his family by publicly admitting her as a lover, how all this led to his decision to terminate his relations with her.

Marie bursts out, 'Yes and on the eve of the birth of my child, he came to see me in a fury. He was full of reproaches. He left me in a ter-rible state. He clearly wanted to see both mother and child dead.'

'Calm yourself,' Bachelier orders. 'What is certain is that he didn't want to recognize the child as his. He didn't want you to recognize her either.'

'That's correct. Robert demanded that we be separated.'

As the story of her life moves towards the death of her daughter, Marie grows more and more visibly agitated. She quotes Robert saying, 'This child disgusts me!' when she tries to have him see the infant. She re-enacts her response, which is to look her lover straight in the face and say, 'Your life, Robert, is attached to that of this child! If she dies, you'll die, because I'll kill you.'

The court erupts in shock and excitement and Marie falls back on the bench, so distressed she can barely respond to the rest of the questioning.

Bachelier asks why, after the baby's death, she had continued to see Robert.

Marie replies in a murmur that she wanted another child. 'Mothers will understand me,' she says.

He takes her through the rest of their relations, including the scene in which she threatened to kill herself and after which she didn't see Robert again, though she sent him pleading letters asking him to come back.

'But he was bored with you: this man of the world's patience had reached its end . . . Then came your demands for money.'

Marie justifies her wish to be independent of the man who had made a martyr of her and doomed her child. She sits quietly through the reading of her journal and her vengeful notes, and finally affirms that she had planned to murder her former lover.

Robert Gentien is the first of sixty witnesses up on the stand. He limps markedly as he makes his way there. The papers note that despite his 'correct' attire, he looks far older than his years. In a monotone, he attests the points of his deposition. Apparently Marie's eyes never leave him, though her expression is sad and resigned. Drama erupts amongst the public and the key players over the question of whether he had wanted her to have an abortion.

When he denies this, Marie rises to intervene in the proceedings. 'You remember the evening when you first talked to me of Dr Rouch?

That was the night I first felt the child move inside me. I said to you, "Here's a sign from God!"'

There is a wave of noisy murmuring amongst the public, which Bachelier contains. He moves things on with a rapid question.

'You didn't want to come to the birth.'

'I was forced to be out of Paris at the time.'

'Did you demand that the child be sent to a wet-nurse at Saint-Denis?'

Robert's denial elicits a forceful intervention from Marie: 'He did demand it.'

'Everything she did, she did herself,' Robert contends.

'But did you ask her not to recognize her daughter?

'Indeed I did. It was for her mother's sake.'

Sniggers are heard amongst the public.

'She holds you responsible for the child's death: she failed to give the child sufficient maternal care because of you.'

Gentien replies in a bored voice, 'She's always upheld that thesis.'

And Marie bursts in once more, contempt in her voice. 'Everything he says is false.'

Now Maître Lachaud, Marie's defence counsel, rises to his feet.

At sixty-five, Charles Lachaud (1817–82) was the period's leading criminal defence lawyer. He had risen to fame under Napoleon III and had served as one of four defence counsels for the notorious twenty-four-year-old Marie Lafarge, accused in 1840 of the long-distance poisoning of her husband. Lachaud was renowned for his 'agile wit', 'his fiery eloquence' and his 'magical influence over juries'. He was also deemed to be 'a better psychologist than those that bear the name'. Certainly, his performance in Marie Bière's case showed him as a masterly advocate whose timing and way with the jury, singling each one out as an individual, were impeccable and turned the case into a precedent for posterity.

Maître Lachaud intervened to make more of Gentien's attitude to his child and his refusal to see it. Perhaps he realized that Alexandre Dumas was amongst the public. The latter had exclaimed loudly when Gentien repeated that not only was he unhappy about the child's birth, but that seeing it would have meant a tedious journey out of Paris, all the way to Saint-Denis. Lachaud pressed on: So when Marie had had the child brought to her flat one evening when Gentien was visiting and begged him to see the baby, why had he refused to do so then?

'There was a stranger present,' Gentien replies.

'What stranger?' Lachaud asks.

Gentien's response – 'The nurse' – draws more protests from the public. This perhaps gives Marie the added courage to stand up, lean on the bar and stare down her former lover.

'But you could have seen the child alone. I would have brought her to my room and told the wet-nurse to go. It was that night that I said to you, "Beware, Robert, your existence depends on this tiny being; if she dies, so will you."'

There are noisy gasps, then another outburst of murmurs from the public as Gentien withdraws.

The next sequence of witnesses is called by the prosecutor. Yet, according to Albert Bataille's columns, they all sound as if they have been called by the defence, so great is the esteem and regard they all express for Marie. The married conductor of the Opéra Comique, whom a gossiping rag had salaciously linked with Marie, utterly denies the mendacious slur. The famous Escudier from the Théâtre-Italien, the chief of the Brussels Opera, a lawyer from Auch and a flurry of others all testify to her gentleness, her charm, her uprightness, her honesty. It is as if Marie really is an utter stranger to the values of the Bohemian demi-monde that her profession would normally ally her to. Even her concierge – a category of witness known more for malice than sweetness – states how touched she was by the affection Marie showed for her child and elaborates on her evident and genuine pain at Gentien's treatment of her. Why, the woman had even once seen Marie throw down the money Gentien had sent her.

Président Bachelier raises an eyebrow at this. Himself a man of the world, he suggests that Marie, of course, then picked the money right up again. The concierge turns this straight round. When she sometimes encouraged Marie to hope that marriage might be the outcome of her and Gentien's relations, Marie would raise her eyes to heaven and cry, 'Alas, he's too rich!'

Dr Rouch, the purported abortionist, takes the stand and contests, even after Marie's direct questioning, that he ever had abortion on offer. What he had said was that he could arrange for the baby to be adopted after birth.

But Maître Lachaud is on his feet again. Reinforcing the idea that Robert sent Marie to an abortionist can only bring the jury onto her side. He interrogates Dr Rouch about a letter the *juge d'instruction* seized from the dossier. It is from an unknown woman who pleads in the most emotive terms that she can't bear the thought that she is pregnant, that doctors must have ways of dealing with this, that her husband knows nothing. And now Président Bachelier intervenes once more. He has for some time been pressing Gentien's case – as if he has a glimmering that what is unfolding before him is less about fact, or even psychology, than a contest in values: old and new, masculine and feminine, aristocratic and petty-bourgeois. He now firmly states that all doctors receive letters of this kind.

19. 'A Hyper-excitation of the Affective Faculties'

Next in line on the witness stand are the two medico-legal experts from the University of Paris faculty. Their faces may already be familiar to the court public. They certainly will be as the decade rolls on.

Docteur Émile Blanche (1820–93) is a celebrated alienist, well known in literary circles, and son of Docteur Esprit Blanche (1796–1852), who ran a private asylum in Montmartre and then in Passy. Émile worked with his father from a young age and inherited the second establishment. Though costs at the asylum were high, some three thousand francs per year, both father and son were known for their dedication to their patients.

The great Romantic poet and translator of Goethe, Gérard de Nerval, who so influenced the Surrealists with his vivid depictions of waking dream and who walked his pet lobster Thibault through the streets of Paris, was confined in Montmartre under the care of Esprit in 1841 when he first broke down. A later breakdown in 1853–4 saw him under the care of Émile Blanche. De Nerval suffered from 'lucid mania' – hallucinative delusions in which he was persecuted or thought the soul of Napoleon had migrated into him, or considered himself a god and blessed people in the streets. In these manic crises he could also sometimes become aggressive.

Nerval's writings on his experiences comprise some of the most evocative depictions of altered states in any language. He also described the treatment offered by the Doctors Blanche. This differed remarkably little from that available either in the English spas or in the better madhouses. It largely consisted of hydrotherapy, or hot and cold showers – to shock the subject out of fury – and baths, to calm the nerves. Sometimes there was an application of ice to the head while feet were plunged into very hot water. De Nerval conceived of this treatment as a mode of purification. There were walks too, and exercise, plus the presence of the doctors, by turn encouraging or intimidating as they engaged in the 'moral' – what we would now call 'psychological' – therapy that the best of the mid-century asylums provided.

Émile Blanche, in the manner that the pioneering doctor Philippe Pinel (1745–1826) had initiated of getting the disturbed to care for their fellows, had the good idea of interesting de Nerval in another young patient, a soldier returned from Africa who neither spoke nor seemed to see, had refused food for some six weeks and was being tube-fed. De Nerval's own state improved remarkably when he managed to get this young man to speak. Despite what were on the whole good relations with his doctor, however, de Nerval left the asylum well before Blanche thought he could manage in the world. Blanche turned out to be right. Increasingly ill and impoverished, de Nerval hanged himself from window railings on a narrow street near the Châtelet three months after he had left the asylum.

Émile Blanche's reputation didn't suffer as a result. He remained the literary world's alienist of choice: the writer Guy de Maupassant was confined in Passy during his last years, and died there (of tertiary syphilis, not then recognized as having a final stage of dementia). Blanche was apparently a charming man, who frequented France's famous chroniclers of the time, les frères Goncourt, and was on occasion a dining partner of both Pasteur and Turgenev. Indeed, in 1871 the people of Montmartre would have made a politician of Blanche if it hadn't been discovered that a cousin of his had also been successful in the election and the law prevented two members of one family taking office.

Auguste Motet (1832–1909), Marie Bière's second medico-legal expert, was another well-known courtroom alienist, who aside from his penal duties ran a private establishment in the Rue de Charonne, off the Boulevard Voltaire, a bit of Paris that had only been annexed to the city in the 1860s. Motet was a frequent contributor to the journal that helped shape the field of public medicine, the *Annales d'hygiène publique et de médecine légale.* He was a follower of the brilliant Charles Lasègue (1816–83), a clinician who always insisted on a thorough knowledge of a patient's extended medical history and whose work had defined areas of psychosomatic illness. Lasègue was also the first doctor to describe the condition of anorexia nervosa. Like others in his time, Lasègue and his disciples linked certain aspects of female derangement to the physiological processes associated with late or precocious menstruation, childbearing and lactation.

In trying to distinguish between criminal responsibility and states of derangement in an 'objective' manner for the courts, Motet was a compassionate doctor with an eye for human complexity, even for what the period saw as perversion. In 1881, for example, the year after Marie's trial, he was called in to assess a case against public decency in which a man in a public urinal had been arrested for masturbating. Drawing on the period's interest in automatisms and sleepwalking, 'altered' or hypnotized states, Motet had insisted that the poor man, who was of 'feminine' disposition, had been in a *condition seconde*, akin to trance, and was therefore not responsible for his actions. He had had bouts of nervous illness before his arrest and he remembered nothing of the urinal episode. Indeed his relatives had been looking for him that day, even in the morgue. During the trial, since the prosecutor didn't believe that what Motet was saying was possible, Motet hypnotized the man and had him relive the urinal moment, only snapping him out of his somnambulist state when he was about to repeat the offence.

Drs Blanche and Motet had assessed Marie Bière at Saint-Lazare several times during the period of instruction, and had submitted their report to the judge on 6 March. This stated – following the formal procedure of such reports – that although Marie Bière had a rational motive for the crime and had shown great lucidity during her various interrogations, there was nonetheless an obligation to check out whether in her past state of health, or in her family history, there were facts that needed to be taken into account in order to get an accurate measure of her criminal responsibility.

Heredity came first: Marie's mother, the report states, had never shown herself altogether balanced in her 'cerebral functioning'. She was subject to crises of agitation which alternated with crises of hypochondriacal melancholy. Marie's brother was of an adventurous spirit and intense imagination: as mentioned earlier, he had left his parents at the age of fifteen to go to America. A maternal great-uncle had died mad in the Pau asylum. Marie was thus born with a sorry predisposition and always gave evidence of extreme *sur-excitation* of the affective faculties. And although she never showed any symptoms of faulty reasoning or of disorders of the nervous system, the doctors concluded that she was evidently a woman of near-morbid intensity (*exaltation*), whose emotions and passions dominated and obliterated her judgement. These last were crucial statements for her case. But more followed, signalling that Marie's passion was of the maternal kind:

In her affective faculties, it is maternal love that seems to occupy the greatest place: she speaks of it in exaggerated terms which outstrip all measure. It was the violent pain she suffered with the death of her child that transformed the thought of vengeance into an unshakeable resolution. She nourished it for some time before it ended with the attempted murder of 7 January. She seemed sincere in her affirmations and also when she told us that if she had had a child a second time from the same father, she would have forgotten her grief and hatred in order to abandon herself altogether to the joy of maternity.

In the long conversations the doctors held with Marie, she exhibited no sign of mental trouble. She told them all the important circumstances of her life in these last years, recounted her hopes and her disillusionment, her despair, her hesitation and her struggles. This, they state, allowed them to 'chart the progress of the obsessional thoughts which overwhelmed her a little more each day as her ability to resist them diminished; and she was dragged along until she yielded to her obsession'.

The doctors' final opinion after their observations is that Mlle Bière acted 'under the influence of passions against which her constitution rendered her struggle extremely difficult. She did however know what she was doing and must by consequence be considered responsible.'

According to Albert Bataille's vivid account of the trial, when the 'celebrated' Dr Blanche was up on the witness stand in front of the large and attentive court public, his evocation of Marie's state of mind and motive was rather more dramatic than the relatively terse report lodged in her judicial dossier. Bataille comments on the doctor's 'clear, elegant and well-chosen' words, which begin, unlike the dossier, with a description of a past encounter with Marie's mother.

Three years before the trial, Dr Blanche states, he examined Madame Bière after she had been apprehended by the police on a minor charge. Since the period was one in which 'kleptomania' became a frequent diagnosis, it is just possible that Madame Bière was caught in the act in one of the city's tantalizing department stores, like Le Bon Marché, designed by the very same Eiffel as the tower that bears his name. Madame Bière seemed quite mad. She was in a state of 'mental hyper-excitation', and although she was soon released, Dr Blanche was reminded of her case when he read about Marie in the press, and he informed the police of it.

After Dr Blanche has run through the incidence of 'heritable' madness in this family of *aliénés*, he interestingly points to Marie's childhood environment as implicated amongst the causes of her condition – as if Pasteur's increasingly popular germ theory of contagion also had psychological applications. He describes Marie's rearing by an extravagant mother, who was at times depressed, and at other times manically nervous. One day Marie was threatened with a knife; on another, with being thrown from a window. And so she acquired her disposition to illness. From a very young age, her exalted intensity was in the making.

To the public's own ever-growing excitement, Dr Blanche then tells the story of how at the age of twelve at her convent school, Marie fell head and heart in love with one of her classmates. When her friend appeared indifferent, this 'violent affection' led to two suicide attempts.

Marie's state of excitation followed her into adulthood and she became a woman dominated by passion. She was always in the sway of her emotions. She told me, Dr Blanche states – adding that her sincerity was manifest – that the day her child died, she resolved to kill her lover.

Blanche's next statement provokes commotion in the courtroom, so rare is it to utter such thoughts in public: 'I know that she considered abortion early in her pregnancy. But once she felt her baby move, her maternal affection was awakened: it was profound and all powerful. I have no doubt that this exalted, exaggerated maternal sentiment was the motive for her murder attempt on 7 January.'

A seasoned court performer, Dr Blanche then iterates what it means to be an expert witness in France, where the psychiatrists are attached to the courts. He never appears, he says, either for the defence or for the prosecution. He is a man of conscience, as befits a member of a profession working in the service of the public.

Indeed, unlike their contemporaries in Britain's open market in alienism, the remuneration that French psychiatric experts officially received for their medico-legal work was small: ten francs for a consultation of three hours, a sum that some have argued remained largely unchanged since it had been set down in the Napoleonic *Code d'instruction criminelle* in 1808; (though in 1884 in the case of Hippolyte Forgerol, a trio of doctors including Blanche and Motet were receiving seventy francs each for visiting the patient and reporting, so perhaps payment hadn't remained altogether fixed). As a man of conscience, Blanche can testify that when Marie Bière aimed at Monsieur Gentien she knew very well what she was doing, but she was under the influence of such passions – of such morbid exaltation – that 'there was no resisting the forces that dominated her and obliterated her moral sense.' She was, in other words, at the mercy of what the US courts will call an 'irresistible impulse'.

It is this last formulation that will serve as the doctors', and often enough the jury's, explanation for crimes of passion: reason, responsibility, the moral sense are overcome by violent emotion. Irrational impulse holds sway, doing away with rational volition. It may seem that such a description could be given to any violent crime: rational judgement fails before strong emotions, passion topples reason and crimes are committed. In Anglo-Saxon courts such a plea for reduced responsibility or mitigation rarely passes muster. Nor does the French penal code ever altogether designate a crime of passion. But French courts did have something of a precedent to build on. The 1810 Code Napoléon contained one entry that provided a circumstance for a justifiable love crime. In the section dealing with 'Excusable Crimes and Delicts', Article 324-1 reads:

> Murder, committed by the husband, upon his wife, or by the wife, upon her husband, is not excusable, if the life of the husband or wife, who has committed such murder, has not been put in peril, at the very moment when the murder has taken place.

The mitigation here is self-defence, a principle that also holds in English courts and was extended by a 1992 precedent sometimes also to include psychologically damaged abused wives for whom long-term mistreatment could equal provocation. But the next line, 324-2, defines the famous in flagrante delicto exception:

> Nevertheless, in the case of adultery, provided for by article 336, murder committed upon the wife as well as upon her accomplice, at the moment when the husband shall have caught them in the act, in the house where the husband and wife dwell, is excusable.

Men, the code in its patriarchal wisdom allowed, could murder their wives if their wives were caught in the act of compromising their and the family's honour. An understandable passion of jealousy would then prevail, and provide mitigation. Women had no parallel exception in law: their husbands could only be fined for an adulterous offence, and then only if it had taken place in the family home. (The exception for wife murder was only repealed in 1975.)

During the *belle époque*, however, women occasionally behaved as if the law stretched to mitigate their passionate crimes as well as men's, particularly if their honour was at stake. Juries were more often than not on their side. The period's understanding of the feminine as less attached than the masculine to reason and moral judgement meant that in any event women were considered constitutionally more susceptible to passion and extreme, volatile emotion. Such a view slipped effortlessly into the ragbag diagnosis of hysteria, which could as easily implicate any woman, or apply to the very essence of femininity, as refer to what Freud later called 'conversion hysteria', with its more extreme set of symptoms from paralysis, to anaesthesia and muteness.

Whatever, if any, her precise diagnosis, Marie Bière's was one of the cases that set a precedent for other women afflicted with a severe case of moral outrage at the prevailing sexual etiquette.

Law may wear a blindfold, but its judges and juries are rarely blind to gender differences. At the turn of the last century, public feeling transmitted through press and juries seemed to want a different balance between the sexes: women's intimate crimes of passion as played out in the courtroom crystallized some of the dissatisfaction, and saw it judged. Those judgements sent out moral signals to society at large. Perhaps in the same spirit as our contemporary worries about sexual violence towards women, from the 1880s on, male attitudes to women, particularly the attitudes of the worldly male to the mothers of the future, were found severely wanting.

20. The Verdict

After Dr Motet echoed his eminent older colleague's testimony, Marie's trial moved towards its final moments. There were still witnesses to call and depositions, penned in Judge Guillot's fine prose, to be read. These include that of Robert Gentien's administrator and intermediary, Monsieur Oudinet, who during his deposition had stammered over Marie's questions – trapped, as Guillot's rendition made him seem to be, between his loyalty to his employer and his less than total approval of his relations with women and the Don Juanesque aspects of his behaviour. Oudinet also had an evident soft spot for Marie, though he didn't want it to be seen in open court.

To counterpoint, Mathilde Delorme, Marie's best friend since 1863, talked of her irreproachable character until Gentien had led her astray. The midwife who had delivered the baby in Montmartre described how difficult the birth had been, how sad Marie was, ever hoping that Gentien would fall in love with the child. Quizzed on whether Marie harboured plans of marrying Gentien, the midwife responded that Marie had hopes, of course: she had said, 'Why not? I'm well brought up, my family is honourable.' But the coldness of his demeanour was distressing: when he came to visit, he didn't even want her dress to touch his trousers.

Then it was the turn of Gentien's friends, who told the court how he had been frightened of Marie's character, how it was clear she was mad and could kill, and how his friends had advised him to alert the police. The guardian of the peace who had stopped Marie from firing her third shot recounted that when he had taken away her revolver, Marie had exclaimed that there was no point worrying that she would kill herself – but if he was dead, of course she would. She had also immediately blurted out that Robert was the cause of her daughter's death.

Here Marie interrupted, stating in a firm voice that she had no intention of starting all that again. She no longer considered Monsieur Gentien worthy of any passionate acts from her.

Finally, before the court rose on this penultimate day of the trial, which would be followed on the morrow by the *plaidoirie* – the summing-up statements from the prosecution, the defence and the trial's president – the audience heard a reading of Robert's interview with the *juge d'instruction*, based on Marie's questions to him; and the tense encounter of the former lovers in front of the judge.

Marie's questions are about her personal honesty and love; Robert's answers are about playboy rules, in other words about sex for money. His repeated insistence that Marie was never a 'disinterested' mistress, that she had always been calculating and dreamed of marrying him in order to get her hands on his fortune, won him no favours with the public. Nor did his recurrent emphasis on being *un parfait galant homme*, a perfect gentleman who had given Marie a monthly *pension*. After the public had heard Investigating Magistrate Guillot's finely honed description of Robert's cool assurance contrasted with Marie's extreme pallor, her fixed stare at her lover as she emphatically denied everything he said, came her dramatic final words to Guillot, uttered in exhausted despair: 'I was sure he would be forewarned of my questions to him. He could prepare his defence, while my strength utterly left me. I feel dead. He's a liar, a dishonest man! May God lend me the strength to confound him before the court; without that, I'd be better off dying right away!'

Sensation erupted in the courtroom.

The next day, 8 April, Maître Lachaud makes his summary statement for the defence. It lasts three-and-a-half hours. According to the participants, these are dramatically breath-taking hours in which Marie's entire life and great love are given expression. Reading out her letters, evoking her trajectory, Lachaud describes a feminine heart tossed between indignation at her lover and hope that he might recognize their child. The portrait that emerges is of an utterly honest woman, so innocent and decent, despite the theatrical world she moves in, that she doesn't recognize vice; a woman consumed by love for her child, a good woman who wanted only to love and instead found herself tormented, dishonoured and abandoned by a worldly seducer. Honour is key to Marie's final retributive act. There is more to life than mere life, Lachaud states: there is honour.

Lachaud's address is about far more than a justifiable *sur-excitation* on Marie's part: what is on trial here are the morals and sexual etiquette of an entire class. A war of values is under way. Why shouldn't an honest and good woman of heart, not a prostitute, a woman of rectitude and generous passion like Marie, sincerely believe a man like Gentien when he pays court to her, telling her she 'makes him a better man', and not think he's in search of nothing more than a roll in the hay, a passing affair. But no, Gentien belongs to a class of men who only want fleeting liaisons. The prosecutor had made reference to the estrangement of Marie's ambitions. For him a difference of wealth would seem to put an insurmountable obstacle in the way of union. But Lachaud has only contempt for this attitude. He doesn't understand why a young independent man of a fortune, valued at eighty thousand francs in annual rents, shouldn't have the right to give his name to a poor but estimable woman, if he loves her and has made her a mother.

The public erupt in cheers at Lachaud's moral fury. As if they were in a boulevard theatre, they applaud his peroration. Marie has given her word that she will never again target the man she now contemns. She has never lied.

'Will you condemn her, Gentlemen of the Jury?' Lachaud asks. 'No you won't: there is a limit to human endurance. You'll say that beyond the life of man there is something even more valuable: honour. You'll see beyond this regrettable act and you'll ask yourselves if this man shouldn't serve as an example to those sceptics who live life *à la* Gentien. That will be the great educative value of this trial.'

Turning to Marie, he offers her his closing remarks:

'Courage, my child. Life is hard because this man has taken everything from you – your honour, your future, your tranquillity of spirit.
You will suffer greatly; liberty won't give you happiness. The verdict of
acquittal which will soon be pronounced won't be a consolation. None
is possible. But at least it will give you some relief. Slowly through
work, calm and a regular life, you'll pull yourself together, and achieve
the rehabilitation you wish for.

'I place this unfortunate woman in your hands, members of the
jury. I have confidence in your justice.'

Apparently exhausted, Maître Lachaud then sat somnolent, head in
arms, while the president of the court summed up. In his attempt to
be even-handed and perhaps redress the feeling against Gentien,
Président Bachelier made the mistake of saying to the jury that they
needn't worry, in their deliberations, about the set sentence: 'It'll be as
you wish it.'

Quick as lightning Maître Lachaud was on his feet again, creating
the moment that appears in all his obituaries and which resulted in a
change in French legal procedure.

'You have no right to say this,' he tells the president. 'No right to
suggest that Marie Bière could serve a mere few months in prison,
when you clearly know the contrary. The jury needs to have it plainly
spelt out that if they condemn this woman without mitigating circumstances, it means death. With mitigation, the sentence still means
a minumum of five years of forced labour.'

Bachelier's monocle falls from his eye, he loses his place in his
notes. The public, meanwhile, have exploded in shouts of 'Bravo!'
For a full five minutes there is havoc in the courtroom. Everyone
protests at the ways in which presidents present their résumés to the
jury (in other words, 'direct' the jury). When Bachelier speaks again,
he is so befuddled that he calls Maître Lachaud 'Monsieur Bière' and
the accused 'Mademoiselle Lachaud' . . . Or so the papers like to
report.

The jury go out for a mere five minutes before returning with a
unanimous acquittal. It is clear that Marie Bière is guilty of having

attacked and maimed Robert Gentien. But these good men and true
are acting on that *conviction intime*, that intimate conviction, that the
revolutionaries of the 1790s had built into the jury system: they,
better than all the professionals, know where justice lies. This waif-
like suffering mother who has lost her child and mourned her with
a passion beyond reason is a Republican heroine. Her criminality is
only an excess of what is best in virtuous women – their nurturing,
maternal souls.

Given that French newspapers could cover all aspects of a case both
before and during the trial, and that juries had no restriction on what
they could read or whom they could discuss the case with, their own
'inner conviction' was inevitably also that most loudly sung in the
press.

When the verdict on Marie Bière is announced, jubilation breaks out
in the courtroom. According to Albert Bataille, no one wants to leave.
People stay to watch the smile illuminating Marie's face, the kiss she
gives Maître Lachaud, the hug she receives from her oldest friend . . .
Marie Bière has regained her liberty. She has also struck a new note of
freedom for women of all classes. The insouciant and oft-damaging
behaviour of careless cavalier seducers is no longer to be universally
tolerated as a norm. To be poor, to be a performer, is no longer a certain mark of exploitable availability for rich rakes.

But the jury's and clearly the attendant public's verdict on Marie
Bière sends out other unspoken signals to the ten-year-old Republic.
It now seems more permissible for women to act, and to act violently
if need be, to protect or avenge their honour. Passion that topples
reason can create a mitigating partial madness, unwritten in law but
understood by juries. This condition needn't affect the rest of one's
mental properties, nor is it socially dangerous, in that it is unlikely to
recur.

Over the next decades, love crimes committed by women become
a feature of the *belle époque* – a period enamoured of the drama of
public spectacle, whether on the boulevards, in the playhouses or in

the courts, in the press, in medical fora such as Jean-Martin Charcot's lectures where hysterics are paraded, or in Parliament. Through this multi-faceted theatre, the new Republican democracy is arguing out the values it wants to embrace: what it means to be a responsible citizen, what it means to be male or female, father or mother, mad or sane. Republican governments come and go, arguments about the secular and the religious state and the institutions that belong to each are as turbulent as those between the sexes, until in 1905 the separation of Church and state is enacted. Meanwhile, between 1871 and the turn of the century some 264 people pleading at the Central Criminal Court in Paris, the Cour d'Assises, claim their crimes are *crimes passionnels*.

As Ruth Harris has pointed out in her groundbreaking study, *Murders and Madness* (1989), the crime-of-passion defence rose faster in this period than the overall rate of murder, though this also went up. In 1880, out of a total of thirty crimes in the Paris area there were six crimes of passion. By 1905 the number had risen to thirty-five out of a hundred. The great majority of these love crimes – two hundred – were committed by men against wives or partners in incidents of alcohol-fuelled domestic violence, which archives show to be endemic and often too matter-of-factly accepted, particularly amongst the poor.

As a proportion of the total crime that women commit, the number of women's passionate crimes is much higher than men's. Male passionate crime never rises above a third of total murders or attempted murders. For women, it is the principal form: five out of six in 1881, nine out of eleven in 1905, fourteen out of fourteen in 1910. Juries tend to acquit 'passionate' women more than men, though they also acquit men when their wives or partners can be shown, often enough through gossip or by suggestion with little grounding in hard material evidence, to be straying. When female offenders are not acquitted, the sentences they receive are proportionately far lighter than men's. Class plays its part in this configuration: middle-class and therefore virtuous women – popular myth admixed with a degree of reality wants to show – will only engage in violent crime if catapulted into it by that passion which overturns reason and is akin to madness. And women's reason, as the mind doctors have long suggested, is more easily unseated than men's.

21. *Afterlife*

Despite acquittal, Marie Bière herself profited little from her crime. However great the attendant publicity in the spring of 1880, there was no tabloid paper to pay her for her story. Respectable young woman that she tried to be, nor did she relish the publicity: she tried ineffectively to stop the torrent of sensational reporting her acquittal received – damned by the conservatives, made into a monster or a heroine by others. On 13 April, just a few days after her trial ended, she wrote a pleading letter to a leading morning paper, reprinted in the popular *Le Petit Journal*:

> I beg the press to pay no more attention to me. Since I have been acquitted, any rancour, curiosity, or sympathy I may have excited is turned into articles. In these, I'm in turn praised, blamed, and ridiculed. I merit neither the honour nor the relentlessness of the pursuit . . . Might not just a little respect be due to a poor, unhappy woman?
>
> I know very well that it was wrong to take justice into my own hands: everyone has told me so, from the policeman who initially arrested me to the President of the Court of Assizes. I know I should have been more patient, more resigned and above all stronger. I also know the Jury didn't intend to glorify my crime. It was only touched by my sufferings and convinced of my sincerity. That is how I understand my verdict . . .
>
> I have many duties now to fulfil – my poor parents to console, the memory of my child to honour, as well as work to undertake to assure my independence. I would like to be left alone to accomplish these difficult tasks.

Marie sounds like a contemporary woman trying to reason with a hungry media that knows no bounds. Nor is maintaining a modicum of independence easy for a woman who has aspirations to respectability but no financial means. The papers have a few more stabs at her, bandying her name about every time a new crime of passion comes up. Finally they deliver an all but fatal blow.

On Monday, 7 February 1881, Marie Bière tried to relaunch her career by taking part in a concert in Nice. The fliers had gone out and critics were dispatched to cover her post-trial debut, which she had delayed and refrained from undertaking in Paris amidst the media frenzy of the last year. The *Figaro* reporter interviewed her prior to the concert. He found a woman who was more *bourgeoise* than he had anticipated and who seemed very worried about her undertaking. She told him she was appearing on stage once more because she didn't want to be dependent on her parents. But her strength didn't seem up to the task. In Nice with her mother, she was leading an isolated life and staying at a hotel frequented only by the English. She was nervous, and worried that the press would see her debut as a mere exhibition. Being a celebrity was taking its toll on her, but she had to earn her keep. She had heeded Alexandre Dumas's advice to lie low for as long as she could. Now, she resisted talking about anything other than her music. The reporter, Jules Prével, sees good sense, given her apparent frailty, in her choice to perform only three classic pieces in a concert that is neither follies nor full opera. But after the concert, Prével pens a brief and damning review.

The auditorium at Nice's Théâtre Français was bursting at the seams, he writes; the prices of seats had doubled for the occasion and the boxes were crammed with women in elegant attire and men in tails. But Marie Bière was stricken with stage fright at her entrance. She was badly made up and looked far less well than in Paris. Emotion seemed to paralyse her voice. Even the melody was off-key. The crowd grew agitated. People booed, hissed, whistled.

Marie Bière's attempt to return to the stage could hardly be deemed happy.

Poor Marie, with her frayed nerves and her damaged voice, her need to earn her keep – and, one imagines, both egged on by and needing to prove herself to her mother – attempted only one more public performance, this time in Aix on 1 March. But her stamina failed her, and despite the advance publicity the concert was cancelled.

After that, her main appearances in the press are only as a glamorous icon of crime, the *patronne de l'amour au revolver*, as *Le Figaro* dubs her in a piece from the spa resort of Royan near Bordeaux, where Marie is holidaying that August. Then on 13 January 1882 appears an advertisement laying naked her need to work and offering '*Cours et Leçons de Chant*'. Three months later, on 26 April, her mother dies. After this there seems to be nothing more in the newspapers about Marie Bière.

The record office, however, reveals an intriguing footnote to her trajectory. On 31 January 1883, just nine months after her mother's death – and three years after she took a shot at her one-time lover – Marie Bière marries thirty-nine-year-old Constantin Boudesco, a divorced engineer/rentier from Bucharest. The wedding takes place in Paris's 8th arrondissement, a wealthy and fashionable area in the 1880s with large new boulevards of impressive apartment blocks. Present at Marie's wedding are her father, Philippe, and the groom's friend, an industrialist. Then at last, on 21 August 1889, Marie gives birth to a little girl, Blanche Marie Claire, a replacement for the child she had so savagely grieved.

The contradictory position of women as mothers, the honour and respect due to them in a *belle époque* France that is adamantly pronatalist and idealizes motherhood while doing nothing to protect mothers, remains a key theme in a growing number of the period's crimes of passion.

22. Revolvers and Vitriol

In the wake of Marie Bière's much reported trial and acquittal, copycat crimes of passion break out across France, perpetrated by a rash of women the papers call the *émulo de Marie Bière*.

Women are suddenly liberated, or feel compelled by overpowering emotion, to take justice into their own hands. They have been given a new sense of agency. To protect their invigorated and now differently defined 'honour', they commit acts of vengeance against lovers who have abandoned them and their children, against betraying husbands and against the mistresses who are their rivals. Their preferred means are not the old-fashioned secret, slow and subterranean poisons, gendered feminine, but the emphatically public and masculine revolver and the burning horror of that sulphuric acid known as vitriol. The sheer quantity and novelistic force of crime reporting seems to feed their underlying sense of unhappiness at the lack of justice in the sphere of love, marriage and motherhood. Resentment explodes in violent expression. Despite the obsessive premeditation of their acts, they seem to expect acquittal or light sentences, not because they are deranged – the alienists called in will talk of hyper-excitation, or hysteria, but rarely attest to any failure of mental responsibility – but because they are in the right. The rules of society are askew and, without voicing it, they seem to feel they have natural justice on their side.

If this is not feminism, it is not altogether unrelated. There is an underlying similarity between the iconography the press use to illustrate feminists and *les vitrioleuses* – as the women become known. Both are portrayed as Amazonian, possessed and rabid.

At the end of an 1872 essay, *L'Homme–Femme*, exploring the psychosexual nature of man and woman and the socio-religious settlement they were currently enmeshed in, Alexandre Dumas *fils* had outrageously suggested, tongue only a little in cheek, that the way to deal with straying wives was – *Tue-la!* Kill her! He was in part referring to the famous Dubourg affair, in which a husband had with dagger and sword attacked his unfaithful wife in flagrante delicto – or at least in the apartment of her lover. She had died three days later. In love with this man well before she had been forced by her father to marry Dubourg, Madame Dubourg had found herself incarcerated for a time in an asylum, and when released she had taken up with her first love once more. Dubourg had received only a five-year sentence following his murderous, premeditated attack.

In his second most widely read novel, *L'Affaire Clemenceau* (1867), Dumas had already portrayed a virtuous husband killing a flagrantly deceitful wife and pleading his case in court. Having been criticized for his injunction to the male to kill his gallivanting wife, Dumas was also criticized for not allowing the betrayed wife in his play of 1872, *La Princesse Georges*, to carry out an equally passionate murder of her husband. The times were changing, and Dumas rode the shift in sexual relations: after the Marie Bière trial he wrote a provocative new essay, *Les Femmes qui tuent et les femmes qui votent* (Women who Kill and Women Who Vote (1880)). The two are closely related, Dumas contends, thereby outraging his vocal, moralizing, often Catholic opposition. Until the law – ever several steps behind shifting public mores – recognizes contemporary social reality and instates justice for women – mistreated by their own fathers, by seducers who abandon, by husband/fathers who stray – they will attempt to kill. And juries as well as the public will support natural justice over and above laws that are no longer just.

Dumas goes so far as to reproduce in the main body of his text a contemporary proclamation addressed to 'the women of France' and calling for women's rights. In its argument for the vote for women, for seats on juries and in the judiciary as well as in Parliament, the declaration includes a telling line linking the treatment of women with the treatment of the mad, as if being woman were equivalent to being mad: 'An Assembly of Men is about to legislate for women in the same way as it passes laws on and regulates the mad: are women then mad people to whom one can apply regulation from above?'

This sentence grounds a linkage often made by late-twentieth-century historians between suffragettes and hysterics, and shows that the slippage between madness and feminism was one of which feminists as early as 1880 were aware. Dumas and the writer of the proclamation he cites both make the connection. There were two ways, the suggestion is, in which women could respond to the inequities of the day: they could become campaigners for change or they could become hysterics – either poised to shoot the men who had done them wrong or to fall ill of the oft-unarticulated injustices and conflicts that the values of the time trapped them in. In some cases, like that of Breuer and Freud's famous Anna O (Bertha Pappenheim), the two paths were part of the same individual's life.

Dumas argues, following the most vocal French feminist of the time, Hubertine Auclerc, that since women are subject to taxes, they must also have the vote. They will then also have seats in the Assemblée, and will be able to change the laws – on divorce, on seduction, on the rights of mothers and children. Dumas and Auclerc's logic didn't see fruition until sixty-four years later, in 1944. Meanwhile, the rash of *vitriolage* and shootings spread.

Trying to get to the root of why the public idealized these women, Dumas wonders whether it was because existing laws protected the guilty, not the innocent. The murderesses were 'the incarnation of an idea suddenly rising up against stubborn and insufficient traditions. The idea comes through fire and blood. It poses its personal and necessary demand against laws which were once excellent, but now that customs have changed, appear unjust and barbaric.' Of course, the murderer hasn't reasoned all of this out. No. She blindly obeys her passion. But her passion is seen to reveal a natural, incontestable human right, which society should have considered, but failed to.

In the very month of Marie Bière's trial, a woman of thirty, one Hélène Dumaire, buys a revolver and shoots her former lover, Dr Picart – a man whose child she bore while he was a medical student. Dumaire was, according to the press, a woman of not quite the impeccable virtue of a Marie Bière. She was certainly no innocent virgin, but she had supported Picart through his studies, only to be told at their end that he was now going to marry a richer, younger woman. Asked at her trial whether she regretted her crime, Dumaire answered forthrightly: 'No, I'm happier that he's dead than married; I couldn't bear our daughter to have been an abandoned child.' Given this implacable honesty, the jury couldn't see their way to acquitting her. Nonetheless, given that she had killed a man – not merely wounded him, as in the case of Marie – her sentence was relatively light: ten years in prison.

On 18 May 1880, a month and nine days after Marie Bière's much discussed trial and verdict, the distinguished Comtesse de Tilly stepped out of her house in Saintes, a prosperous small town of some fifteen thousand inhabitants in the Charente-Maritime, went to her local chemists and purchased a canister of vitriol – commonly used in housework but which also burns, disfigures and blinds. Standing by the window of her home, she happened to spy the young *modiste* or milliner, with whom her cheating wastrel husband had long been having an affair that had set the whole of Saintes chattering. She flung the vitriol at the younger woman. 'I did it for the children,' the ailing thirty-year-old countess, a woman known for her piety and seriousness, tells the magistrate. Her husband was robbing his children to pay for his mistress, who would become the mother of Madame's children when she died.

In court, Madame de Tilly was defended by the brilliant Maître Lachaud, now the women's advocate of choice. He evoked the heroism of her maternal love, the brutality of her husband's insults, the shaming clamour in the small town. He called Madame de Tilly a saint, whom the jury could only acquit so that she could leave the courtroom with her honour restored and utterly intact.

Despite the seriousness of the crime, they did acquit. As in other crimes of passion, they were acting on that *conviction intime*, that inner

conviction that they understood natural justice. After all, hadn't they
learned in the course of the trial that the young mistress had had an
indemnity of twenty thousand francs settled on her by Monsieur de
Tilly, who never appeared in court and was presumed to have fled to
America.

It was cases like that of Madame de Tilly, together with the emotional polemic played out in the press, in essays and plays such as those
of Alexandre Dumas, that helped to modernize divorce laws in France.
On 27 July 1884, the radical socialist member of parliament from the
Vaucluse, *député* Alfred Naquet – a friend of the anarchist Bakunin and
a Jew who had written much on marriage and divorce and been cen-
sored under the Empire – saw divorce legislation through the Assembly
that effectively reinstated the revolutionary divorce law of 1792.

The new law, which would last until the 1970s with only small
modifications, instituted divorce with fault. Either party could sue.
For women like Madame de Tilly, who had hitherto had no recourse
against adulterous and often thieving husbands, it was a huge boon.
Divorce was now possible on grounds of adultery (with the caveat
that the adulterer could not marry the third party for three years),
injury, cruelty, addiction or long imprisonment. The 'innocent' –
wife or husband – was granted the children and a pension. Catholic
France, whose 115 deputies voted against the law, was up in arms. The
indissoluble union that made man and wife one was now dissoluble –
by other means than vitriol. In 1885, France saw four thousand
divorces.

It is unlikely that a working-class woman like twenty-three-year-old
Amélie Sanglé – who on 16 November 1883 threw vitriol at the man
she thought had taken her husband away from her, had led him to
drink and to other women while she and her children by him
starved – would have found her sense of justice appeased in the
divorce courts. But the Paris Assizes did acquit her, even though the
man she took aim at died of what was thought to be an associated
meningitis the next day.

Before her trial, Amélie was observed by the nuns and doctors at the prison infirmary of Saint-Lazare, where she was also delivered, when the time came, of a child. A very full 'mental state' report on Amélie from Dr Auguste Motet shows what by now are the regular categories according to which avenging women are examined and clinically described, even when they (and their victims) are working-class. Motet searches in Amélie's family and her past, where he finds reports of nervous crises, 'not epileptic in nature'. This, together with late onset of menstruation and a promiscuous ease in moving between partners, leads him to diagnose a *petite hystérie*. Such a minor hysteria is so common a female malady as to be attributable to almost any woman, and brings in its train no mental aberration that can excuse a violent act. Whatever compassion Motet may feel for this young woman in her rage, jealousy and despair as she attacks her target, he can find no delusional imaginings in her, or moral confusion.

Motet does, however, revealingly note the influence of 'contagion by example'. The notion of contagion comes from Pasteur's work with microbes. The crowd psychologists borrowed it, hypothesizing that ideas and extreme acts could spread from mind to mind in the same way as disease. Dr Motet states that just such a contagion has driven women to vitriolic acts. But since this contagion doesn't fall into any larger medical category of delirium, it cannot be an excuse for crime. A 'transitory mental trouble' that has no pathologic precursor in the patient's history is no evidence of mental alienation.

If in medico-legal eyes, despite her *petite hystérie*, Amélie is a responsible working-class woman who has committed a crime and should therefore be punished, the jury nonetheless acquits her. As Dumas might have said, they seem to think that Amélie, delivered of a baby while awaiting trial, has natural justice on her side. The epoch's juries are on the whole more radical than the psychiatrists, who line up firmly behind the state, which also pays their fees. They may take thorough histories of their patients, they probe for signs of 'insanity', but they refuse to allow their 'insights' into the individual mind to be used as an excuse for crime. They are agents of control.

Yet somehow their reports, perhaps by forefronting the passions and pathologies, emphasize the frailty of the individual mind. These may have signalled to more forgiving juries and the public a sense that the individual and her aberrations counted for more in the meting out of justice than any exemplary punishment. As for the protection of the social realm and any dangers these vengeful individuals presented, their hunch was that these acquitted women would not repeat their offence. The ones cited here never did.

III

Hysteria, Hypnosis and Criminal Responsibility

As the Third Republic steered its unsteady modernizing and democratic course through the 1880s, putting science and secularism in the foreground in its attempt to create upstanding Republican citizens, it met with the formidable populist challenge of the seemingly heroic monarchist General Boulanger and his reactionary politics of the three Rs – Revenge on Germany, Revision of the Constitution, and Restoration of the Monarchy. (Rhetoric played its part, too.)

Boulanger's popularity soared, until a putsch seemed imminent. The very way in which this happened made progressives – the new scientists and social scientists amongst them – worry that the suggestions of a sensationalist popular press could work their way into the minds of a gullible populace without the owners of those minds being aware of the process. A modern mass public, it seemed, could, just like any individual, be magnetized, mesmerized, hypnotized, and prey to suggestion. Consciousness was an unsteady entity: it could be led astray or even abolished under the sway of a more powerful individual. Emotive, half-grasped ideas could, like germs, spread with contagious fury through a badly educated and perhaps 'degenerate' crowd. All this, even before there was any such thing as the Twittersphere.

Worries about how the mind worked, and indeed how to counter-act popular notions that occult forces were at play when individuals felt possessed by gods or demons, fed the investigations of the neuro-logists, the alienists and the medico-legists. Their concepts, arguments and language, in turn, were translated by the press and distributed to a wide public, who assimilated and replayed their ideas in diverse ways. Keen to engender a 'scientific' study of the mind and its diseases, as well as treatments, the doctors were also eager to rid the public sphere of those they considered charlatans: a guileless populace might imag-ine that mesmerists and theatrical magnetizers or hypnotists shared a work sphere with doctors and scientists. They didn't. The doctors and psychologists were interested in the phenomenology of hypno-tism and altered states – the how, the why, and the what effect of the process. They were interested in how suggestion worked, whether it needed a 'weak' mind prone to dissociation to take effect, or in addi-tion some kind of physical triggering such as a sudden flash of light – as the German Hugo Münsterberg, who would later become the prop-agator of 'applied psychology' in the United States, speculated at the turn of the century.

For the period's best-known neurological researcher and clinician, Jean-Martin Charcot, and his team at the vast Salpêtrière hospital in Paris, priests and the occult were part of the same spectrum of sug-gestive charlatanry as the 'healing' animal magnetizers and popular amateur hypnotists, whose public spectacles, like those of 'Saint Bernadette' at Lourdes, drew vast crowds – not unlike today's mind-reading magicians or television pastors. Their influence needed to be kept at bay.

Charcot's scientific fame extended not only across the Channel to England, but also across the Atlantic to the United States and east to Vienna, from where a young Freud came to study with him and later translated his work. In France, that fame was veritable celebrity: before the age of television medics, the 'Napoleon of the Neuroses' could be spotted in a crowd. His public lectures at the Salpêtrière – where his hysterics were diagnosed, in part through their susceptibility to hypnosis, and taken through the signs and manifestations of their condition of *grande hystérie* – were attended by *le tout Paris*. The spectacle of a scantily clothed, hypnotized hysteric moving a limb paralysed just moments before, or being prodded with a needle without responding to the sensation, or enacting a post-hypnotic suggestion, could easily vie with any drama at the theatre. It might even equal that other kind of reality spectacle, the courtroom.

Depicted and studied via the new quasi-scientific technology of the camera, Charcot and his team's hysterics (a significant proportion of whom were men, though being of that gender and working-class, they had less celebrity appeal) provided images to equal illustrations of music-hall stars and dancers, and women wielding revolvers or vitriol. Any of these might appear side by side in street hoardings advertising newspapers, magazines or spectacles. Charcot was a rigorous clinician who had cast light on a number of important neurological diseases: until late in his career, he was convinced that *la grande hystérie* was due to brain lesion and not to any psychological factors. The trauma his hysterics had often suffered, he long held, had had a neurophysiological impact on their brains – which pathologists also studied in the Salpêtrière laboratory. Whatever the scientific 'seriousness' attributed to the Salpêtrière team, Charcot and his investigations had a high popularity rating.

Already in 1883 *Le Figaro* had devoted much of the front page of one of its issues to a scathing article about 'the great doctor who is Napoleon's look-alike' under the less than respectful headline 'Cabotinage', or 'Hamming It Up'. The gist is that Charcot – on the point of being admitted to the elite Académie des Sciences – has perfectly understood his times, recognizing that this is the era of medicine – not of the red and black of soldiering and priesthood, or even of the law. No, this is the epoch of the medic, in other words that scientist who can 'act' on women. Charcot, the anonymous *Figaro* writer notes, has studied the great contemporary malady hysteria, and it took him only a very few years to attain popular fame.

Although back in 1878 the *Dictionnaire des contemporains*, the *Who's Who* of the time, didn't even mention his name, by dint of setting up his students in professorships around the country, by popularizing such concepts as 'cerebral localization' and by displaying nude women in the phases of the hysterical attack to such luminaries as the great actress Sarah Bernhardt – indeed, by surprising the men and frightening the women – he has monopolized hysteria and swayed public emotion.

The conservative *Figaro*'s criticism of Charcot is based on his atheistic ungodliness. In the process, however, the paper initiates readers into his medical theatre, describes the fetching half-clothed phases of hysterical hypnotism: from the insensate catalepsy with its rigid physiology-defying postures; the swooning lethargy, the obedient somnambulism, as well as the contortions of a major hysteric attack – *à la* Charcot – from the arc, to the *attitudes passionnelles*, to *clownisme* and the final orgiastic laughter. The writer evokes the hypnotic sound of Charcot's voice and likens it to Dante's Virgil leading us all into the Inferno.

Such articles helped to popularize and also trivialize what the medics were doing: in the process they made hysteria and hypnotic suggestion exciting, available to imitation, as well as frightening. They also offered categories of explanation and argument to the courts, where the debate about hysteria, consciousness, criminal responsibility and hypnotic suggestion took on a different kind of public prominence.

In 1884 Jules Liégeois, a professor of law from Nancy, argued in an influential and much contested speech to the Academy of Moral and Political Sciences that any person put into a somnambulistic state becomes in the hands of the experimenter a 'pure automaton both physically and psychologically'. It follows that crimes can be committed in a state of hypnotic suggestion.

Liégeois was a follower of Nancy's most famous doctor, Hippolyte Bernheim (1840–1919), chief of the Nancy faculty of medicine. Bernheim was a one-time student of Charcot's, but a generalist rather than a specialist in nervous diseases. He had been influenced by the saintly

Ambroise Liébault, a local philanthropist, who had been curing the poor with hypnotic treatments since the 1860s. In turn, Bernheim practised a therapeutic hypnotism which seemed to better a wide variety of ills and had nothing, as far as he was concerned, to do with hysteria. Most people, he declared, were hypnotizable. The Nancy school was thus at loggerheads with Charcot and his followers and their view that susceptibility to hypnosis was a sign of hysteria and that hypnotism had no uses outside of the diagnostic one. Charcot, like his most famous disciple Gilles de la Tourette, did not believe, for instance, that a person under hypnosis could undertake a crime he wouldn't undertake in a conscious state. The only 'crime' that a person might be led to commit in a condition of hypnotized lethargy – where complete unconsciousness coincided with muscular relaxation, and no memory followed – was the 'crime' of succumbing to rape: women's control here was, in any event, unreliable. Enter a whole new way of approaching woman's sexuality and assessing her virtue.

23. Hypnotic Murders 1: The Chambige Affair

The Chambige trial brought the debate about the powers of hypnotism to a wide public, amongst whom leading intellectuals and writers featured. The case raised troubling questions about the nature of female desire and maternal virtue; how the first could override the second. Because the murderer was a young man of refined talent and nervous sensibility, the whole affair also cast a disturbing spotlight on what seemed to be a new kind of individual – neurasthenic rebels against the bourgeois order for whom death and murder took on aesthetic rather than moral dimensions.

On 25 January 1888 in his family's stately villa in the town of Sidi Mabrouk, the twenty-two-year-old Henri Chambige, studying psychology in Paris and spending the summer with his mother in his native Algeria, was found wounded and in a state of disarray. He had shot himself through the mouth, and two bullets were lodged in his cheeks. In front of him on a bed lay a half-naked woman with a peaceful expression on her face. In fact she was dead, two neat bullets through her temple. When the doctor lifted her eyelids it was to encounter an expression of such ecstatic happiness that she looked magnetized.

The woman was Magdeleine Grille, a pretty, upright and Protestant thirty-year-old, devoted mother of two and wife of a prominent citizen of the region. Two explanations were given for the crime scene and the drama it conjured. The first came from Chambige, who wouldn't allow himself to be torn from Magdeleine's presence when officers attempted to do so. He was a literary young man who had written subtly on the Goncourts and Modernism, and whose poetic imagination was peopled by figures of romantic despair. According to Chambige, he and Magdeleine were passionately in love: she had proposed that she become his mistress and then, so as not to be dishonoured, since they couldn't live together, they would engage in a double suicide. Yes, he had killed her, though it was she who had held the gun to her temple for the first bullet at least. But he had failed in killing himself, and he begged those who had arrived on the scene to do it for him. He even attempted to grab the medical instruments being used to suture his face. A suicide note asking his mother to forgive him and to remember him to his best friend was found next to Magdeleine's neatly folded clothes.

Magdeleine Grille's family, known and respected in the Constantine area, did not accept Chambige's view of their near one's death. Her husband, a handsome, well established and much liked inspector of mines, claimed that his wife, a good and beautiful woman, beloved by everyone, had even sometimes complained of the boy's presence. In the trial, the family acted as civil plaintiffs and contended that a nervous and impressionable Magdeleine Grille had been hypnotized by Chambige, lured by his gaze to his house, perhaps drugged, and then raped. She had always talked of Chambige as a young madman. He had never spent any time completely alone with her before. He was imagining it all and had murdered the poor woman, after having hypnotized and raped her, since she was the only witness to his machinations and didn't return his love.

Ever since she had lost her little son, a nervous and mourning Magdeleine had been interested in hypnotism, her husband and mother attested. She had read tracts on suggestion. She borrowed one from Chambige, who lived only a ten-minute ride away. She had suffered a fainting spell while watching displays of hypnotism given by a troup of Arab travellers. She could go into a sleep state instantaneously, under the influence of unknown forces. She had told a friend that although she couldn't stand the radiance of Chambige's gaze, she was fascinated by it. So powerful was it, that only after he had gone back to Paris could she pull herself together.

The family's lawyer, Ludovic Trarieux, was intent on establishing Madame Grille's irreproachable honour. He himself was an eminent *député*, who later founded the League for the Rights of Man. He argued

that Madame Grille had resisted Chambige's advances on that fatal
afternoon, so he had hypnotized her in the way that the experiments
at the Salpêtrière exemplified. The crime scene showed no signs of any
struggle: every item of her clothing, even the buttons, were intact. So
she must have fallen into a cataleptic state under hypnotic influence,
after which Chambige had undressed her and twice had his way with
her. Her doctor testified that her expression was certainly not that of
a suicide and had more in common with a magnetized state. Her husband, who upheld her honour absolutely, testified that she could have
used her own money to go away with the younger man, if, as
Chambige claimed, that were really what she had wished. Their departure had been foiled because Chambige couldn't come up with funds,
yet she had two thousand francs in her desk. Nor had she packed anything. On the stand, Chambige refused to contest Monsieur Grille's
view of things. He embraced his guilt, wanting only the death he had
failed to inflict on himself.

The *Figaro*'s own Albert Bataille reported on the case as well as on the
trial, which began on 8 November 1888. Debate raged from Algeria to
Paris and beyond. Bataille's reports contained long extracts from
Chambige's jail diary, a remarkable document, at once prison writing
and romantic confessional, which formed part of the instruction. When
it was later published in book form it was prefaced by the famous novelist Paul Bourget (a writer the youthful Proust admired), who wrote a
novel inspired by the Chambige affair, *Le Disciple* (1889). On the stand,
Chambige, according to Bataille, was a captivating, indeed hypnotic,
defendant. His speech was superior even to his pen, while his telling of
his tragic tale, punctuated by weeping and trembling of hands, was
deeply moving and felt utterly sincere. The love story Chambige
evoked on the witness stand, between a nervous, hypersensitive student
and a tenderly kind older woman, his much mourned sister's closest
friend, had echoes of any number of fictions. When on his second
summer in Constantine he had whispered to Madame Grille that he
loved her, she had responded, 'Let us love each other like brother and
sister', but it was then that she kissed him for the first time.

Towards the end of the trial the eminent novelist Anatole France covered the case in *Le Temps*, while the influential Maurice Barrès evoked Chambige's 'sensibility' in the *Figaro*. Like so many artists fascinated since the Romantic movement by criminals, who seemed, like them, to be exceptional beings, France and Barrès were tantalized by the young Chambige. Here were criminality and talent in one – a perfect example of the decadence then coming into vogue, and often inmixed with a transgressive sexuality.

A melancholic, whose father had committed suicide out of an unshakeable sense of the horrors of the world, the young Chambige, according to France, had written a brilliant unfinished novel, 'The Infinite Dispersal of the Heart', which he had read out loud to his riveted student friends. '*C'était un malade et un orgueilleux,*' France cites the prosecution as saying, and draws the time's preferred image of the artist as sick, troubled and proud. Chambige's prison memoir, France writes, shows his progression from a sensitive, chaste, pious, scrupulous and anxious youth of sixteen to a young man whom confrontations with reality had filled with despair, turning him into a 'living tomb', trapped in eradicable mourning for his innocent childhood. Embracing the period's fashionable tropes, this young Chambige states with nihilistic aplomb, 'Even more than women, I loved lies.'

Chambige's early nihilism stemmed from a lost faith in both God and love after a tawdry sexual encounter. With Madame Grille, he was reborn into innocence. They had both recently suffered terrible losses: his beloved sister, and her close friend, had just died, while Magdeleine had also recently lost her son. Both had talked to their friends of suicide, and both were brought to life again through their growing intimacy. A chaste tenderness saw them through one summer and then much of the next. She listened maternally to his outpourings and eventually also confided in him. At the end of the first summer, she gave him a lock of her hair and her photograph. They vowed themselves to a pure love, not unlike that between Julien Sorel and Madame de Rênal in Stendhal's *The Red and the Black*. Like that love, theirs became fatal once it acquired an obsessive cast.

Unable to live without Magdeleine when he returned to Paris in the second year of their chaste relations, Chambige made it clear enough to his friends that he wanted to die. She was in turn obsessed by him and wrote him odd scraps of secret letters or passed him notes when they were together *en famille*, though her husband protested at all this, and local 'experts' denied it was her writing. When Chambige was called back to Algeria from Paris in December of 1887, they decided to run away together, or so he claimed. But he couldn't raise the necessary money, and seeing that he had a gun in his pocket when he came to say goodbye, she decided to accompany him on that final voyage. While they were locked for two hours in his bedroom in the family house, the coachman waited outside ... He heard no sounds, certainly no screams: there were only those final pistol shots

Anatole France is sceptical of the mind doctors and the idea of seduction by hypnotism. He doesn't deny that the experiments of Charcot, Liégeois and Bernheim show the power of a strong will over a feeble subject. But he doesn't believe that what takes place in clinics happens in the same way outside them.

There are no new 'expert' secrets in how to seduce women. It would be too strange if contemporary doctors alone had access to such secrets, and if lovers after centuries of wooing had never come across them. 'It's wiser to believe a little less in the academies and a little more in nature,' France advises. 'For me, the eternal and unique form of hypnosis is love.' And Madame Grille, like her admittedly neurotic lover, was drunk on literature and on the death in love of the poet Alfred de Vigny's 'Les Amants de Montmorency'. Passion trumped Madame Grille's affiliation to respectability. But Anatole France stops short at glorifying Chambige for his passionate crime – unlike some other young writers and friends. Chambige is a sad and guilty man, whatever his talent or the mitigating circumstances.

Gabriel Tarde (1843–1904), France's great jurist and criminologist, best known for the distinctions he drew between the crowd and a public, was asked to reflect on the case some years later in the journal of his profession, *Archives d'anthropologie criminelle*, edited by his friend Alexandre Lacassagne (1843–1924). Lacassagne was a talented forensic doctor and head of the Lyon school of criminology, which emphasized the environment's influence on crime and the criminal. For him, the criminal was less 'born' *à la* Cesare Lombroso than made, though the making had physiological repercussions. Tarde himself had even less time than Lacassagne for the biological positivism of the Italian. He was a social thinker, but also a psychologist in the classic literary way of the French, and would contend in his *Penal Philosophy* of 1890 that behaviour, including criminal behaviour, is in part caused by imitation. The poor, a few generations along, imitate the rich, whose vices have descended to them – 'one kills oneself or does not kill oneself, because of imitation'; and this is especially so in the great tumult of the cities, where that strange phenomenon of the mob – a single unit made up of heterogeneous elements – can rule. Literature, the press and conversation foster imitation and can make the far, near.

Tarde is clear that Chambige and Magdeleine Grille were caught up in an imitation of the great literary love stories. That Chambige is sincere in the story he tells of the failed double suicide is visible from the style of his written confession: he is a talented youth who suffers from a morbid ideal of extreme and unique sensation. Though he doesn't express this overtly, Tarde, writing in a professional journal, can allow himself to imply that Chambige experienced the boarding-school homosexuality of the nervously refined youth, which predisposed him to later mystical and ecstatic loves with women. (In one of his confessional remarks, Chambige had bemoaned the fact that he was constituted like a woman and could not stop weeping.) As for Madame Grille, Tarde notes that love itself is a form of hypnosis, and doctors aren't essential to describing its ways. And though he denies the mind doctors' views on hypnosis, he uses alternative psychiatric language to describe Madame Grille as a double personality: in this description, she suffers from a hysteria that allows a split between the virtuous mother and the *bacchante*, so that both coexist without one being aware of the other – in the way of the notorious Felida X

diagnosed with a '*doublement de la vie*', a doubling of life, and some of
Pierre Janet's famous alters. Whether it's psychiatrists or sociologists
who provide the analysis, women's passions are unnatural and sometimes fatal.

The jury were harder on Chambige than the literary men might
have liked. After a four-day trial they came back with a verdict of premeditated murder with mitigating circumstances. Chambige was
sentenced to seven years' forced labour in the notorious prison colony
of Cayenne, while the family received the compensation they had
asked for – a single franc together with the now confirmed assertion
that the lovely Madame Grille remained a woman of honour to the
end. But when Chambige's lawyer petitioned the President of the
Republic for mercy, the sentence was converted into a simple seven
years in prison in Algeria, despite protests from Madame Grille's husband. In fact Chambige was conditionally freed in 1892. In 1895 he
came to see Zola to take advice on how to restart his life: his new
name was Marcel Lami, under which he published several books, some
of which only appeared after his death in 1909.

Interestingly for a judge and criminologist, Tarde understands
Chambige's sentence as a response to a psychic need for punishment
on the part of the jury, the family and the public. In a fully rational
system, he argues, there would be no need to imprison Chambige at
all, since he would engage in no further 'suicide pacts': his punishment is not preventive but symbolic, as it is in other crimes of passion.
This suggests that when the jury acquits, that too may well act as a
symbolic assertion that justice needed to be done and has been carried
out by the avenging criminal.

24. Hypnotic Murders 2: L'Affaire Gouffé

The anxious debate about love, the power of hypnosis to instigate crime (or crowds), and the question of the suggestibility of the hysteric – a figure that could be extended, by slippage, to the female gender as a whole – continued in the French courts in the notorious but unlikely case of Gabrielle Bompard and Michel Eyraud, a twosome who in their aura resembled a *belle époque* Bonnie and Clyde.

Theirs was not exactly a crime of passion, though various passions, as well as sex, were involved. It triggered a major confrontation between opposing medics of the mind in both assizes and press of all brows. The medics warred so as to determine whether Bompard could have killed while under the hypnotic suggestion of her lover. Just as in the Myra Hindley and Ian Brady trial for the Moors murders, there was some difficulty in believing that a young woman from a bourgeois family, and not under the sway of a hypnotic male, could have performed the brutal murder, let alone engaged in a great escape that included cross-dressing. After the Eyraud–Bompard trial, all of France and beyond would know that the Paris school and the Nancy school of mind doctors had opposing views on the power of hypnotism and the criminal responsibility of hypnotized subjects.

It all began in high summer, during the heady days of the 1889 Exposition Universelle, celebrating the centenary of the Revolution. Hundreds of thousands poured into Paris to gaze at the newly completed Eiffel Tower and other wonders of technology. On the evening of 27 July, the womanizing widower and bailiff Toussaint-Augustin Gouffé, father of two grown daughters, was lured to a ground-floor flat at 3 Rue Ducoudray in the 8th arrondissement by the pertly attractive twenty-one-year-old Gabrielle Bompard, runaway daughter of a prosperous Lille metal merchant.

Once there, the forty-nine-year-old Gouffé lay back comfortably in a chaise longue in front of a heavy alcove-dividing curtain, while the enticing négligé-clad Bompard perched on his lap. As he fondled her, he allowed her to loop her red and white silk belt round his neck. Seconds later, the belt was latched into a complicated pulley system manipulated by Bompard's hidden forty-five-year-old lover, the conman Michel Eyraud, who promptly used it to hang Gouffé to death. Not finding the ample cash he had hoped for on Gouffé's person, Eyraud then rushed to the Rue Montmartre to the apartment of the man he had occasionally worked with, and searched for the anticipated monies there. To no avail.

Back at the site of the ambush, Gouffé's body was folded into a sack, made by Gabrielle. The hapless bailiff was placed in a capacious yellow-trimmed cabin trunk, which Eyraud had bought in preparation in London a few weeks before. This was transported to Lyon by train the next day, and from there some twelve miles by carriage to the remote and hilly outskirts of the town of Millery on the banks of the Rhône. Here the body lay in its sack: it had caught on some acacia bushes instead of tumbling into the river as Eyraud had intended. Its smell eventually alerted passers-by, who found it some three weeks later. A few days after that, snail hunters came upon the broken-up cabin trunk.

At a first autopsy the body was not thought to be Gouffé's but that of a much younger man. It took the investigative persistence of Marie-François Goron, the Paris Sûreté's talented chief, who put together evidence of the trunk's movements and the disappearance of Eyraud and Bompard, to ask for the body to be exhumed four months after it was first found. It also took the scrupulous forensic talents of Alexandre Lacassagne, who performed the examination, to deduce through the new science of anthropometric correlation, plus careful washing, that the short cadaver with the black hair was in fact the taller and auburn-haired Gouffé. The clinching proof came when Lacassagne identified that the cadaver had limped, something that Gouffé's daughters confirmed.

Meanwhile, Bompard and her lover had fled to England, then New York, north to Canada and finally across the country to Vancouver and San Francisco. Bompard often dressed very happily as a boy or pretended to be Eyraud's daughter or niece. The two had no money except for what accrued from the cons they executed along the way. In Vancouver, Gabrielle was paid court to by a rich adventurer, a Monsieur Garanger, whom Eyraud had extracted money from and wanted to persuade into a bigger con by having him invest in a non-existent cognac distillery. Garanger eventually wooed Gabrielle away, not realizing for some time who she really was. When he did, they returned to Paris and he persuaded her to go to the police to give herself up.

The French papers were so full of the crime, the identification of the body, the hunt for the alleged killers, that when Gouffé's body was exhibited in the Paris morgue, as bodies involved in crime customarily were, some twenty thousand people filed past to have a closer look. The international chase required cooperation between police jurisdictions and the dispatch of French officers to North America and ultimately to Cuba. The shady doings of a criminal underworld kept the public entertained for months. The seedy, corpulent Eyraud, evidently a talented and multilingual scammer and masquerader, as well as a fallen prodigal of the middle classes, was finally spotted and stopped in Havana on 20 May 1890, ten months after the crime was committed.

It may well be that Gabrielle gave herself up in December 1889 not only at the promptings of her new lover, but because she wanted to be fully present at her own sudden fame. Excited modern girl that she was, she thoroughly enjoyed her celebrity both from a distance through the press and, once arrested, through the lengthy pre-trial period. Her fame escalated to new heights when in answer to the charge of murder, her defence lawyer claimed she was innocent. The blame for the murder was all that notorious rogue Eyraud's. He had hypnotized Gabrielle and implanted a suggestion that she had then acted upon. Under the power of suggestion, she had enticed Gouffé to her apartment and stood by while her lover murdered him.

Gabrielle's pre-trial dossier is extensive: witnesses give contesting descriptions. Murder apart, she sounds not unlike a rather wildly rebellious contemporary teenager who, after a childhood partly spent 'in care', has fallen in with the wrong crowd. Her penchant for excitement has brought her to sorry ends.

Daughter of a prosperous widower who took up illicit relations with his housekeeper, Gabrielle was sent as a small child to live with her aunt in Belgium. Here she was schooled by nuns, and seemed to thrive. But her father decided to bring her home to live cheek by jowl with the housekeeper, whom Gabrielle hated. Her wayward behaviour, her flirtatiousness with customers in her father's shop, her constant reading of romances, saw her expelled once more – this time as a young teenager to the confines of a strict convent for wayward girls in Arras.

When the sisters tried to have her conform to their rules, they singularly failed. There are complaints of her lewd language and the way she stirred up her mates. She had to be carefully watched at all times. Only one nun noted that Gabrielle had a good heart, if a frivolous one. Sent home, Gabrielle behaved badly once more, openly rebelling against propriety and starting an affair with a local merchant. When this went wrong, she ran off in July 1888 to Paris, stopping at Arras to see a friend whom she convinced to come with her, though the girl stayed with her only a little while.

Finding work and being a young woman alone in Paris wasn't easy. Some reports say Gabrielle turned (or fell) quickly to prostitution, later abetted or pimped by Eyraud. Her father had sent a little money, but when she asked to come home, Gabrielle claims, he didn't reply: his version is that she only ever wanted money. Clearly, this was no Marie Bière. Witnesses talk of Gabrielle's 'dubious morality', her lying, cunning and coquettishness. One landlady says she was clever and read a great deal. Both descriptions are probably true.

According to her own testimony, Bompard met Eyraud when she answered an ad he had placed for a 'manager' in a paper: he had indeed placed the ad, so it could be true, though Eyraud, once the two had fallen out, claimed he had picked her up on the street. He was already married with two children. He had lost his wife's sizeable fortune in various badly run businesses and in general dissipation. He and Bompard, often passing as uncle and niece, moved in a shady milieu of gangsters, embezzlers and petty thieves. Their eventual victim, Gouffé, though richer, was part of the same circle. The motive for the murder was theft: Eyraud had heard that Gouffé would have a fair sum on him that day. In the event, he didn't: nor did Eyraud find the money in his late night search of Gouffé's home – though it was apparently there.

During the instruction period and in court, each half of the couple blamed the other for Gouffé's actual murder and for most of the premeditation. Bompard talked of Eyraud's brutality – he would tie her up and beat her. He talked of her cunning – she had left him because Garanger was richer – and her sexual hold over him. What lifted the case out of the lower depths of ordinary avaricious crime into a realm at least related to passion and the uncontrollable was the hypnotism defence. This brought a new twist to the insanity defence quite in keeping with psychiatric fashion. It also allowed each of the defendants to deny responsibility, since each – Gabrielle through her defence lawyer, and Eyraud acting in his own defence – claimed to have been hypnotized by the other.

Amongst the ninety or so witnesses, a former lover of Gabrielle's stated that he could put her easily into a somnambulistic state. More reliably perhaps, her childhood physician, one Dr Sacreste, who was also a friend of her father's, claimed that Gabrielle was an extraordinarily sensitive hypnotic subject: staring at her for a few seconds precipitated her into a state of catalepsy. Dr Sacreste's testimony provides fascinating evidence of how, even in provincial France, hypnotism had become something of a craze. He recounts how he once put the girl into trance at the end of dinner and carried out what he called 'society experiments'. He stuck a pin into Gabrielle's fist. He had her eat a raw potato, pretending it was a delicious fruit; and drink a glass of water, pretending it was champagne. Another time, he put her to sleep for a very painful operation, which she underwent, completely insensible to the pain.

Her father, who was interested in these experiments, asked him if he could have recourse to hypnotism to change her character, which seemed already to be veering towards the perverse. Could Gabrielle be inspired to behave more appropriately? Dr Sacreste tried, though the girl wasn't particularly willing: when she went into what he called a 'hysterical sleep', he advised her to stop making rude remarks to the youths in the street and to stop thinking of running away from home. He got no conclusive results. But one day after he had woken Gabrielle from her hypnotic state, she burst into tears and told him she had been hypnotized by a merchant from Lille who had made her his mistress! Perhaps for the youthful Gabrielle, brought up in an atmosphere where feminine virtue was aspired to but nowhere to be found in the family circle, sexual desire and sexual acts always had to be attributed to the other – the hypnotic male.

Dr Sacreste told the court that though he had largely lost touch with Gabrielle after she had moved to Paris, she had written to him on occasion as a friend to beg him to intervene with her father and have him send some money to her. The doctor was certain that her confidence in him was linked to his influence as a magnetizer. He was also convinced that Eyraud, who had known Gabrielle so well, could easily have had the power of hypnotic suggestion over her.

The president of the court intervened in Sacreste's testimony, to say that it had already been established that Eyraud had never put her under hypnosis. Her lawyer responded: That may be what she says, but how are we to know that what she says here isn't the result of a command, in other words a post-hypnotic suggestion? Suggestion, invisibly carried out, was a slippery matter for a courtroom, supposedly intent on establishing responsibility for crime. Expert opinion was necessary.

Gabrielle's susceptibility to hypnosis was utterly denied by the three expert psychiatric witnesses sent to examine her in prison on several occasions. Dr Gilbert Ballet and Dr Motet were led by the most important of France's medico-legists, Paul Brouardel (1837–1906), a good friend of Charcot's as well as Dean of the Paris medical faculty and professor of legal medicine.

Brouardel was willing to concede that Gabrielle – who had undergone a very visible nervous faint in court – might be 'a little hysteric'. But she was no full-blown *grande hystérique* and had experienced no diminishment of intellect. He considered her not only fully responsible, but also highly intelligent and fully aware of what she was doing. True, she was a woman who suffered from the effects of early perversion and debauchery. True, she had a libidinous imagination, always engaged with fictional fantasies. She also wrote with great facility, and had a startlingly good memory. Physiognomically, her development stopped at a boyish thirteen, though her periods had begun when she was eight. Brouardel found nothing peculiar in that.

With the consent of the accused, the doctors – promising not to make use of what they might thus learn or to attempt a confession along the way – had put Gabrielle into a state of hypnotic sleep. While she was under, they talked of her childhood. But, Brouardel claimed, at no time during her hypnotized sleep state was Gabrielle fully unconscious. This caused a commotion in the courtroom, since popular preconception elided the hypnotized state with unconsciousness. Brouardel's evidence for Gabrielle's at least partial consciousness under trance rested in physiology. Using the same physical test as Charcot used at the Salpêtrière, he concluded that there was no lack of sensation on Gabrielle's skin. In fact it remained highly sensitive: she was downright ticklish, unlike any fully hypnotized grand hysteric, who would suffer from anaesthesia. As regarded what was medically evidenced hypnosis, the Paris school set the bar high.

The dependence on a physical test to determine the patient's state – to diagnose that hysterical illness of which hypnotizability is one sign – points to the underlying difference between the Salpêtrière and Nancy schools: the first is ultimately neurophysiological in its explanations. Hysteria or insanity are mental states based on neurological disorder. The Nancy school is more psychological: for them, ideas can influence the patient's body, her physical state. Freud, though he studied with

Charcot and admired him, was to be more greatly influenced by Bernheim, the leader of the Nancy school, whose work he also translated and went to see in 1889. The experiments he witnessed in Nancy gave him 'the profoundest impression of the possibility that there could be powerful mental processes which nevertheless remained hidden from the consciousness of man'.

In court, when asked whether Gabrielle had told him that she sometimes simulated hypnotic sleep, Dr Brouardel smiled and answered: 'That's what all the women we put to sleep say. They seem to be both capable of being put to sleep and capable of pretending to be asleep.'

Brouardel's reply teases: he wants to suggest that all women are hysterics to a degree – though not necessarily *grandes hystériques* – and that all women lie, which would also seem to devalue the use of hypnosis as a diagnostic tool for hysteria. But Brouardel was a follower of Charcot's, and adamantly opposed the Nancy doctrine that everyone was hypnotizable. To a jury member's question about whether it was absolutely necessary to put a person to sleep in order to impose one's will on her, Brouardel responded in the affirmative. He did not hold with the Nancy school's notion that suggestion could secretly be practised on people who were fully conscious – that is, in a state of alertness. At the Salpêtrière, they had never seen a person who was awake and alert succumb to suggestion. It might be that a person in a somnambulistic state could be asked to perform a very simple act once she was awake – for example, kissing someone or pulling his ears, an act that was in no absolute contradiction with her temperament. But no more than that. Even patients under hypnosis sometimes refused the suggestion that they should undress. Their modesty, their inner morality, trumped the suggestion.

Dr Motet backed up Brouardel's comments: Gabrielle Bompard was not insane. She had a lively intelligence, neat and precise, and could perfectly well distinguish good from evil. Only her moral sense was perverted: it was her desires, not her intelligence, that had made her a prostitute. Dr Gilbert Ballet added that no morbidity, no hallucination or delirium, had been found in Gabrielle. She might suffer from a *petite hystérie*, which manifested itself in a nervous disposition, exacerbated by lasciviousness. But there had been no crime committed under the influence of suggestion.

The Paris doctors were emphatic in their testimony. They could also impress the jury and the public with the fact that they had had access to Gabrielle over five months. Charcot, interviewed before the trial by the popular paper *L'Intransigeant*, could of course say all the same things without ever once examining Gabrielle in the flesh. 'A priori I'm sceptical about her and for the moment, I think of her as a mischievous and cunning woman, who suffers from what the English were first to call moral madness.' The public, according to Charcot, had an altogether mistaken idea of hypnosis. There was no proof that crimes were, or could be, committed under hypnotic suggestion, whatever the Nancy school claimed. Under laboratory conditions it might be possible to give a hypnotized woman a paper-knife and order her to strike the man across the room – as Gilles de la Tourette had shown – but if she did, she wouldn't strike very hard.

Charcot emphasizes in his interview that there is an underlying 'honest instinct' in most people which can't be turned to crime while they're in a hypnotized state. Even amongst some of his most extraordinary somnambulistic patients at the Salpêtrière – who had a predisposition to be *la chose de quelqu'un* (someone's (controlled) thing), mere puppets who went off with charlatan hypnotists to be exhibited in fairgrounds because they needed to lean on someone – he had heard of none who had been turned to crime. If Eyraud really was a hypnotist and Bompard as susceptible as had been claimed, he would never have had any need to hit her. Violence, Charcot implies, sways far more adequately than hypnosis.

Finally, Charcot states that perhaps Bompard suffers from a *folie lucide*, a madness without delirium that entails excessive emotion and perhaps some delusion, though whether this is severe enough to undermine 'responsibility' he very much doubts. He's not saying she should have her neck severed, but she does merit punishment. As for what the interviewer calls her *monomanie de mensonge*, her mania for lying, Charcot reaches for the accepted common knowledge about ordinary 'little' hysterics: Gabrielle's lying can simply be attributed to her need to make herself interesting, to be talked about, to play a part.

If Charcot was to have his say out of court and before the trial, the French press thought it only fair that Hippolyte Bernheim, should also have his. Asked to give an expert opinion from Nancy for *L'Intransigeant* on 28 January 1890, Bernheim noted that he could have no firm view, since he hadn't interviewed Mlle Bompard personally. He could only give an impression, which he might have to modify when more material came to light. He compared Bompard to Madame Fenayrou, the accused in a recent murder case, who under her husband's influence had set a trap for her lover, after which her husband had brutally killed him. Like this woman, Bompard might have no underlying moral sense that could serve as a counterweight to any implanted suggestion.

Bompard's psychic state, like that of a sleepwalker, was one that would easily succumb to any external forces. She suffered from an *imbécilité instinctive* – an imbecility of the instincts to which, from an early age, she had abandoned herself. She had no sense of the monstrosity of her crime. She had spent a night with a murdered corpse. She was astonished that she was to be held in prison until her trial. She had no moral conscience. Her suggestibility was evident in the fact that she – a young, personable woman who could have succeeded in the demi-monde – gave herself up to the domination of a man who beat and exploited her. She followed his lead. Submissive to Eyraud's suggestions, she brought the bailiff to him, helped or collaborated in his murder, wasn't haunted by any regrets. She followed her lover across two continents, allowed him to throw her into other men's arms, and finally found herself in the arms of an intelligent man who captivated her in turn, and who, having learned of her crime, had her deliver herself to the Paris police. A woman who wasn't suggestible would never have accepted this last suggestion.

Bernheim elaborates the broad force of the suggestibility he understands as underlying Gabrielle's acts. It is a suggestibility that has no need of hypnotic sleep. 'In a state of perfect wakefulness, by simple affirmation, I obtain anaesthesia, contracture, and hallucinations from my patients,' Bernheim states; he adds that, like Gabrielle, 'suggestibles' lie all the time because they are the dupes of their own imagination. If he suggests a false memory to them – which he dubs a 'retroactive hallucination' – they develop that theme, which has been accepted by their imagination as their own. They really think it happened to them. It's quite possible that Gabrielle, prodded by the interrogation first one way, then another, and also instinctively animated by her desire to wipe out any criminal part she may have played, creates memories in her imagination that she accepts as realities. She can no longer untangle the lived truth from the falsified truth, as she sees it through the autosuggestion of her labile imagination.

All this bears an uncanny resemblance to those other 'imaginative' women letter and journal writers – Mrs Robinson, Christiana Edmunds – faced by the rigours of legal testimony. It also brings to mind the procedures of the infamous memory trials in the US in the 1990s, in which women claimed to have been abused as children by their fathers. In some of these cases, false memories, experienced as real by the subjects, seem to have been implanted via the therapeutic process – though in this slippery area of suggestion and sex in the family, definitive determinations of the 'truth' of memory and imagination are ever difficult to unravel.

Bernheim repeats the question put to him. 'You ask me if a hypnotized subject can be led to crime under hypnotic influence, without his own sense of responsibility coming into play?' But this question, he counters, 'can't really be put about Gabrielle Bompard . . . In her the absence or the perversion of any moral sense leaves the terrain open to receive criminal suggestion.' Bernheim draws a contrast between a person who has a developed moral sense and therefore cannot have it annihilated and be led by suggestion to commit a crime, and those other subjects who are gifted with a nervous impressionability which makes them susceptible. He makes an analogy with ordinary dream states. Some dreamers are not completely identified with the dream;

they know they're dreaming and playing a part, and their habitual consciousness subsists next to the dreamt one. But with other dreamers, they're incarnated heart and soul in their new role, and their former consciousness is annihilated. These latter would move into crime like 'impulsive epileptics'.

Bernheim was ill during the Eyraud–Bompard trial and couldn't attend to give his expert witness himself. Jules Liégeois, the member of the Nancy school mentioned earlier, though not a doctor, came in his place. He was not permitted access to Gabrielle, but he nonetheless took up his right to speak without interruption. He did so for four hours, describing the doctrine and history of the Nancy school at great length. According to Bataille, his address was so soporific that no enactment of hypnotism was needed to put Gabrielle, as well as much of the audience, to sleep. He was refused permission to hypnotize her in court, so that he could re-enact the murder scene with her.

Liégeois described experiments showing how he had completely annihilated his subjects' individual will and liberty and had them commit terrible if unreal crimes. For example, he had a nephew poison his uncle – though the substance used was sugar not arsenic. He showed photographs of women who – through suggestion – had made flaming red words or marks appear on their backs, like stigmata. As for rape under hypnosis, even the Paris school allowed that this took place. Liégeois argued that Bompard had been hypnotized into an *état second* of long duration – an altered, or second, state of consciousness of which she could have no recollection and during which she participated in the murder without the knowledge of her 'first', or ordinary, conscious self. Her lying was in fact an inability to remember events clearly. Throughout, she had acted unconsciously under Eyraud's command.

Brouardel's response to this was to mock and to state emphatically that what Liégeois called 'suggestibility' was simply doing something that you were inclined to do in any case under the influence of someone who had a certain sway over you. Lovers and adolescents were contantly acting under the influence of others. This did not mean their acts were involuntary or unwilled. They were not in a sleep state: Bompard was a willing accomplice, and though she might be something of a moral imbecile and depraved, she was not mentally disordered.

The president of the court was dismissive of Liégeois's expert opinion: 'The one outstanding fact that has been true for six thousand years is that the stronger will can possess the weaker: that is no peculiar part of the history of hypnotism; it belongs to the history of the world.' This was tantamount to saying that one didn't need newfangled 'medical' notions to confirm that women were vulnerable to predatory men. That fact, however, could not absolve them of all responsibility for crime.

Wild, amoral, Gabrielle was not to win over the compassion of judge and jury: she was simply not a woman in the virtuous image that the times wanted.

Then, too, Liégeois's assertion that any nervous woman could simply be hypnotized into succumbing to seduction and rape by the steady gaze of a man overreached and elicited a negative reaction from both judge and jury. Too much was at stake. Not only the freedom of the individual mind, but the stability of the bourgeois family and the virtue of wives and daughters. Hypnotism by gaze alone made women susceptible to any stranger on a train. The court negated such an inflated assumption.

Yet the dread of hypnotism's power continued: the huge success of George du Maurier's bestselling novel about the powers of the hypnotist Svengali to induce a sleepwalking and singing trance in his subject, Trilby, is only one example of the idea's spread. Society's underlying fears about women's vulnerability to predators and mental fragility, a worry too about their unconscious or unspoken sexual desire, together with a concern about an insufficiently educated and 'degenerate' underclass – all coalesced in the idea of hypnosis. And all this brought in train an anxiety about the stability of the bourgeois family, which was premised on women's virtue.

This fear of hypnosis and the power of the gaze is not so remote as it may seem: in the 1980 and 1990s — another moment of change and anxiety about women's place, when questions of fundamental weakness or strength went hand in hand with demands for equal rights — American campuses were subject to a wave of accusations of 'ocular harassment', in which women students and staff accused more 'powerful' male professors of attacking their integrity by staring at them.

After Liégeois's sorry performance, Gabrielle's lawyer put aside the hypnotism defence in his final appeal to the jury: instead he focused on Bompard's weakness and youthful moral irresponsibility. The president of the court declared that though it was his duty to call for the ultimate sentence, he would be happy if the jury did not take him up on it: his feelings as a compassionate man were not in synchrony with his stern duty as a judge. The jury took up his lead and brought in a 'guilty with extenuating circumstances' verdict for Gabrielle Bompard. She was sentenced to twenty years' penal servitude. Eyraud, whose lawyer had tried to prove that far from being Gabrielle's master, he had been her slave, completely in thrall to her seductive charms, was given the ultimate sentence. Though he appealed and gained a little time, he faced execution — apparently with great dignity — on 3 February 1891.

The Paris jury had refused to buy into a psychology which emphatically stated that all humans were suggestible to forces outside their control. But the fear persisted beyond the courtroom. It even reached Parliament, where one deputy demanded that Liégeois and the Nancy school be banned from teaching their doctrine, since it had a destabilizing effect on the nation. In November 1892, France outlawed theatrical performances of mesmerism and hypnotism, in a bid to keep the practice under medical control. The move was echoed throughout Europe.

Liégeois's performance in the courtroom showered mockery on the Nancy school. The papers had a field day over the learned professor, and for a while he disappeared from the public eye. But he returned. In 1892, he called for a public programme of 'moral vaccination' to protect every nervous woman in the country from the gaze of dangerous magnetizers who might proceed to rape them. The process of inoculation would mean that a nervous woman would first be hypnotized by a reliable practitioner, who would insert a suggestion that immunized her against any later hypnotic influence. His project, of course, was never taken up: underlying it, however, we see the social imperative of the French medico-legal profession: it was their duty on behalf of the state to be responsible for whole populations, not only disturbed individuals.

In 1903, when Gabrielle was released from prison on parole, Liégeois at last had his opportunity to hypnotize her. She apparently relived the scene in which the murder of Bailiff Gouffé was suggested to her by Eyraud. Dr Albert Moll, in his updated 1909 history, *Hypnotism*, considers this re-enactment doubtful, particularly with a woman as mischievous and untruthful as Gabrielle; but he states that the possibility of a crime carried out under hypnosis cannot be ruled out.

Less than three years after the Bompard trial, the moral panic around hypnotism in France occasioned a near-tragedy, this time enmeshing a patient and targeting one of the very medics who had investigated its use.

At about 6.45 on the evening of 6 December 1893, a young woman walked into the consulting room of Gilles de la Tourette, Charcot's colleague at the Salpêtrière, and asked if he was the author of works on hypnotism. When the doctor said yes, the woman told him she had been hypnotized by various practitioners, that she was now in a parlous state and needed a loan of fifty francs. He asked her to leave her name and address and he would see that she got the money. As he stepped towards the door, the woman pulled out a revolver and shot at him three times. He managed to get into the hall before he collapsed.

Apprehended, it turned out that the woman had been a patient both at Sainte-Anne and at the Salpêtrière, where she had suffered from, amongst other symptoms, delusions of persecution. When released she had decided to avenge herself on her persecutors, whom she imagined had practised hypnotism on her. She was once again confined, and Gilles de la Tourette, the bullet lodged in his neck removed, healed and returned to his psychiatric practice. Distancing himself in his writing from any belief in criminal suggestion had not saved him from the slippery side-effects of hypnotism. The press furore around the subject had not only stirred debate but heated unstable minds.

IV

Naturalizing the Impulsive Feminine

In the ultimate pre-First World War trial of passion, it was the press itself that took on the aura of a betraying, abusive and hypnotically suggestive power to become the object of a passionate crime. Restoring female honour here was not a question of avenging seduction and abandonment, or an unrecognized child. By the turn of the century, the passionate female criminal had a sense of 'reputation' as finely honed as any male engaging in a duel. For Madame Caillaux, wife of a cabinet minister, this entailed targeting the newspaper editor who, she felt, had slandered her and her husband. The democracy of free expression, and a press that had fewer worries about privacy than has ever since been the case in France, were suddenly under direct attack. It is as if one of the victims of British hacking in 2012 had stormed into Rebekah Brooks's or Rupert Murdoch's office, taken aim, murdered and been acquitted – on the grounds that this is how nervous women behave under pressure.

As the *belle époque* drew to its end, the alienists' understanding of women who committed passionate or impulsive crimes had infected what had been the norm. A 'real woman' had now become simply that nervy, emotional, suggestible, virtuous, domestic creature, hysterical by turn and weak of intellect, and ever subject to impulses beyond her control that made her either succumb to tears or explode in murderous rage. Examination by psychiatric experts was scarcely necessary to mitigate a crime that just couldn't be helped, especially if the woman was honourable and married to a leading politician.

But this somewhat nostalgic vision of the feminine, as it played itself out in violence and in courtroom drama, was far more public wish than private reality. With feminism on the rise and war on the horizon, gender anxiety was electric. Had French Republican masculinity grown even more effete and decadent since the Franco-Prussian War of 1870? Had France become feminized in comparison to its enemy other, the bullishly masculine Germany? For a moment, it even seemed as if, while fearing the denaturing of male and female, at the same time the country secretly wanted its women to be pistol-wielding viragos adamant about honour – their own and their husbands'.

During the week of the Henriette Caillaux trial, 20–28 July 1914, no paper headlined the massing of troops more prominently than the murder case. France's attention was on a courtroom where even the President of the Republic testified on behalf of the accused. Listening to the ricochet of Madame Caillaux's bullets, the country seemed to want to blot out that other shot aimed at Archduke Franz Ferdinand, which rang out from Sarajevo and around the world. On the day of Henriette's acquittal, Austria-Hungary declared war on Serbia. One kind of passionate madness would soon be displaced by a more tragic one.

25. Henriette Caillaux Meets the Press

On the afternoon of 16 March 1914, a wealthy, well dressed blonde nearing her fortieth birthday walked into Gastinne-Renette, the small-arms shop in central Paris, and bought a Browning automatic pistol. She tried it out in the shop's basement shooting range and managed to get three out of six bullets into the target figure. Then she went home to the Rue Alphonse-de-Neuville in the leafy 17th arrondissement, donned a formal tea gown, and wrote her husband a note: 'If this letter is put into your hands, it's because I will have done or at least attempted to do justice.' Her chauffeur then drove her to the Rue Drouot, site of the offices of *Le Figaro*, no scandal sheet but a centre-right newspaper of record. Here she asked to see the editor, Gaston Calmette, gave her card to a receptionist and waited patiently, her gun invisible behind her capacious furs and muff.

The day before, Gaston Calmette had daringly crossed a line, violating a privacy of a sexual nature at a time when sexual matters were confined to the brothel, the bedroom and the confessional – or to the steamier pages of fiction, where the transgressive could be made to suffer for their sins. The front page of his paper had carried a facsimile of an intimate letter from the Minister of Finance, Joseph Caillaux, written thirteen years earlier to his then married mistress, Berthe Gueydan, who had subsequently become his wife, before she in turn a few months later was displaced in his affections by Henriette Rainouard – the woman who in 1911 would become his second wife, Henriette Caillaux. The published letter, signed '*ton Jo*', the name it thereafter bore everywhere, was announced as the first of a promised series. This, Henriette Caillaux feared, would bear scandalous revelations of her own sexual nature.

The '*ton Jo*' letter contained cloying endearments, as well as the boastful revelation of a political ploy by the brilliant politician who would come to head the Radical Party. In 1914 when the *belle époque* had moved into a moment in which traditional Catholic family values had once more acquired power, Caillaux's adulterous and divorcing past acted to besmirch a politician many applauded as a man of superb skills.

In 1911, when Caillaux had briefly been Prime Minister, he had managed by diplomatic means to avert an armed encounter with Germany over the latter's sending of a gunship to Agadir in French Morocco. This feat of diplomacy lost him the premiership: he was soon pushed out for being too accommodating to the Germans. Although *Le Figaro* had, back in the mid-nineties, supported Captain Dreyfus when he was accused and then convicted of treason on fabricated evidence, and had indeed supported Caillaux, himself, over Agadir, as war approached, it took on an increasingly conservative cast. The paper now allied itself with the elite sectors of the nationalist right. Caillaux's radical stance on progressive taxation, the first of the kind we recognize as altogether ordinary today, together with his stand against increased government funds for the military, had brought him their enmity.

In December 1913, *Le Figaro*'s Gaston Calmette turned against the popular minister with a vengeance: each day brought new revelations and slanderous headlines, alleging collusion with the Germans, bribery, the theft of millions, sexual hi-jinks and illicit contributions to election campaigns. Caillaux, his cabinet colleagues and the President all feared that it would end, as Calmette threatened, with an exposé of intercepted cables and secret documents proving that France had engaged in spying on Germany.

Taxed by her husband's worries, confronted by what she experienced as the mockery of everyone in her circle as the libellous accusations of Calmette's paper soared, Madame Caillaux could face the loss of her reputation no more. The threat *Le Figaro* had made, that more sexual revelations were to come, bringing her own intimate and adulterous past into the public arena, was the step that toppled her hold on reason. So she waited in a trance-like calm for the newspaper's editor to return to his office. At six o'clock Calmette arrived, accompanied by the novelist Paul Bourget. When given Henriette's card, the ever gentlemanly Calmette remarked to Bourget that he really couldn't refuse to see a woman. Henriette was ushered in. No more than a few words were exchanged – 'You know why I have come?', to which he purportedly answered, 'Not at all, Madame' – before she pulled out her automatic and shot him six times.

Four bullets reached their destination. Moved from the offices on a stretcher, Calmette was heard by employees to be saying, 'I only did my duty.' At the clinic in Neuilly, he died later that night on the operating table. When Le Figaro's employees apprehended Madame Caillaux, she shrugged their hands off and exclaimed, 'Don't touch me! Je suis une dame. I am a lady.' Then, 'Since there is no more justice in France, only a revolver could stop this campaign.'

Henriette waited quietly for the police to arrive. But when they did, she insisted that her own chauffeur would ferry her to police headquarters. Here she was promptly charged with murder and taken to a cell in Saint-Lazare.

Henriette Caillaux, as her testimony explained to the magistrate and eventually in July to the court, had suffered an overwhelming sense of shame at Le Figaro's attacks. She was a bourgeoise, after all, and the mother of a nineteen-year-old girl, whose mental purity (and, of course, her virginity) also had to be protected from the slander that was drowning the family. Henriette couldn't bear going out in public any more and hearing the derision. She couldn't tolerate the shouts in the Assemblée's visitors' gallery of, 'Go back to Berlin!'. She felt intensely implicated in what was said about her husband. 'I was forced to steal away in shame. I didn't want to say anything; I was like a mad crazy person . . . I was overwhelmed by emotion.' She was also overwhelmed by the dredging-up of unseemly past affairs. 'They will finish by killing him,' she told a friend. Furthermore, Le Figaro's exposure and direct evocation of her husband's relations with Berthe Gueydan, the woman who had preceeded her as mistress, then as wife, may well have rekindled the turbulent jealousy that must have accompanied her early years as Joseph's mistress. Their affair had flaunted social codes and involved not a little brazening out: the nationalist right would use this earlier history to cast aspersions and moralize.

Back then, in 1907, when she and Joseph were first lovers, Henriette had been married for thirteen years to the writer Léo Claretie, nephew of the more famous Jules. Ironically, Léo wrote quite often for Le Figaro. The couple had two daughters, one of whom died around the time that Henriette and Léo divorced, in 1908. The guilt over the death must have been considerable. Nor would Berthe consent to divorcing Joseph in haste. Moreover, he put politics first, and so waited until after the election of 1910 to obtain his divorce. These must have been difficult years for Henriette, but once they married in 1911 she claimed true happiness had arrived, not to mention a joining of fortunes which made them one of the richest families in their circle.

Since it was clear, indeed confessed, that Henriette had killed Gaston Calmette, the court case in July seemed to hinge on only one question: was Henriette a 'real woman' – une vraie femme? A real woman, it seemed, was one who honoured her domesticity, was moved by emotion, and had fragile nerves and a weak mind that could be overwhelmed by a tide of feelings and spontaneous impulses. Or was Henriette a cold, calculating divorcée, an unsexed and manipulative virago, who, having already committed a crime against the family and thus the nation, had now planned her act meticulously and murdered a good man in cold blood?

These two popularly opposed stereotypes of the feminine still too often play into a court's determinations of fundamental – rather than evidential – female guilt and innocence.

There was an additional moral question concerning Henriette's character that hovered over the court proceedings: as a one-time adulteress, was she simply the wrong kind of woman, more demi-mondaine than the domestic angel her husband claimed? For all its romp and playfulness, the belle époque continued to pay heed to France's Catholic heritage and at least in public separated reproduction from pleasure: a virtuous baby-bearing sexuality and maternity were for wives; pleasure, for prostitutes or mistresses. All the period's contradictions, delusions and confusions about what women were and what they were meant to represent played themselves out in the spectacle of the trial and its coverage.

Henriette's deed done, Caillaux had offered his resignation to his Prime Minister, but it hadn't been accepted and the newspapers now lined up either for or against his wife and him. The left-leaning ones painted Henriette as the loyal, highly emotional wife, driven into a mad state by sleeplessness and slander. Her calm, her crossed hands and bowed head in the courtroom were a signal of her love of privacy and of her devotion to her husband, whose honour she wanted to salvage. Had he avenged himself in a duel with Calmette, the Republic could have lost one of its greatest men. So Henriette's deed, as she stated in court, was also an act of patriotic sacrifice.

The nationalist right, on the other hand, led by the oft-rabid columns of Le Figaro, saw in Henriette a cool, self-controlled and cheating harlot – a whorish Hedda Gabler with unerring aim – married to a dishonest, sinful politician who had precipitated two women into divorce. Even the newspaper illustrators and photographers whose images now adorned front pages to such effect, represented Henriette in her lushly feathered hats and studiedly sober elegance either as a German-loving Valkyrie or as a sweet and demure Parisienne de bonne famille, whose old-fashioned father, had he still been alive, would have disowned her at the exposure of her dishonour.

26. A Woman's Honour

The renowned advocate Fernand Labori represented Henriette at the trial, which ran from 20 to 28 July. The man who had so effectively battled for Dreyfus ran a straightforward argument: Henriette's fear of a greater scandal, in which Calmette would publish her private letters and expose her early intimacy with Joseph, had overwhelmed her reason. Already suicidal at the first invasion of her privacy, it was this fear that had driven her to shoot Calmette the night before the announced letters were scheduled to appear. In effect, she was acting in self-defence. She was protecting her husband, her family and her woman's honour. In this she was also defending France.

The matter of honour, as France moved inattentively towards war, played a substantial part in the trial's proceedings. There was female honour – which meant standing up for one's own unsullied reputation, that of one's family and one's husband. The *crime passionnel* was one extreme way of avenging it. There was male honour – which meant making a show of one's courageous masculinity and reputation by finding satisfaction in a duel. An illegal but socially sanctioned and oft-engaged-in process, duelling perpetuated an old aristocratic practice within a Republican France that many felt had lost its sense of hierarchy and value by embracing Godlessness and mere riches. This same democratic France, particularly in Paris, as Proust's opus so vividly reflects, adored its aristocrats. Born to solid rank and not just to the evanescent fluidity of capital, the crème de la crème, perception was, inhabited a world of honour and repute, of brave and dashing manliness and subtle gradations of female virtue. But honour and reputation were at the mercy of an unfettered press, which sullied what it touched, turned the private public, and just as in our own day, loved creating celebrities in order then to trash them, to the delight of its readers.

These readers were legion in a country of forty million where literacy was almost total. The four main papers alone printed some 4.5 million copies a day; each was probably read by at least two adults. Given the large number of other papers, both Parisian and regional, this meant every adult read at least one paper. This was mass circulation on an unprecedented scale, and the power of the press – which like *Le Matin*'s motto claimed 'to see, know and say everything' – was vast. Nor were there any libel laws in the Napoleonic Code to allow redress, or right of reply – and so men fought duels; and women like Henriette Caillaux could be driven to kill so as to preserve their reputation. Politicians often engaged in duels: Georges Clemenceau, twice Prime Minister and principal author of the Treaty of Versailles, fought twenty-two. As Gabriel Tarde, the jurist and sociologist, noted in his *Études Pénales et Sociales* (1892), the first part of which is entitled 'The Duel', the new culture of honour and duelling was the product of an unstable world of mobile capital, but in particular of the newly powerful press, 'a steam engine for the fabrication and the destruction of reputations on an immense scale'. Like wealth, honour could be destroyed overnight. Defamed and dishonoured, citizens looked for redress beyond the law.

During the trial, it became clear that Joseph Caillaux had talked of sending his seconds round to call on Calmette. He had decided against it, because to fight a duel would be to raise Calmette to his own level. He had no fears: he was a first-class shot, as the attendants at the firing range at Gastinne-Renette where he practised daily, confirmed. But Calmette was beneath him, a fraudster of sorts. The editor had acquired millions during his tenure at *Le Figaro* – sums, as Caillaux revealed, having managed to access his will, that it would take an ordinary bourgeois family 150 years to acquire. Caillaux himself, however, had no more money now than the millions he had inherited from his prosperous family.

The slur from the nationalist press that German-lover Caillaux had been emasculated, was less than a man, and so his wife had had to go out and retrieve his male honour for him, nonetheless made the rounds. This was just one more reason why Henriette had doubly to prove that she was a true, meek and mild, submissive woman, despite her outing with the Browning pistol. Honour took on even greater amplitude on the fifth and sixth days of the trial, when the president of the judges, Louis Albanel, suffered what he felt was an insult from a deputy judge. The latter instantly apologized, but exposed his disagreement with his superior, in full and in public, in the pages of *Le Figaro*. Albanel called for satisfaction in a duel; his deputy countered that his own seconds would be calling. The duel was delayed only by the arrival of war – that far larger playing field on which masculinity and honour could be tested.

Henriette stated that she had shot Calmette in order to restore honour to her husband and herself. During the instruction period, she had explained to the investigating magistrate that Calmette's frenzied and unabating attack on her husband had driven her mad. She felt that her body was inhabited by two opposing forces, the irrational one being the stronger of the two. 'It was like having two separate beings inside myself, like two separate wills. On the one hand I wanted to go to an afternoon tea a friend had invited me to, and I put on a town dress; if I had intended to go to the *Figaro* . . . I wouldn't have dressed up. On the other hand, I felt a greater force take hold of me and this was the one that drove me on.'

Madame Caillaux's language is one learned from the epoch's mind doctors and other much reported crimes of passion. There is a certain irony in her having killed a newspaper editor, since it is the sensational coverage given to such crimes that furnishes her with the responses and explanations of her behaviour she needs. Nonetheless, she inflects the popular scenario with elements of her own particular case. She kills, she says, as if in a dream, overwhelmed by emotions alien to her ordinary self. She is in a second state, a trance, like that of a hypnotic subject, but also like those of the doubled personalities that Pierre Janet had investigated and made graphically public. Her automatic weapon corresponds to her own unconscious mental state:

once given the space, it has a will of its own. It takes her over. She is, to use our own colloquialism, on automatic pilot. She talks of feeling hypnotized by a 'cinematographic film . . . that flashes before her eyes' in which she sees her husband kill Calmette, and she forces herself to position herself in her husband's place. She is in that sense both man and woman.

On the sixth day of the trial, Henriette gave visible evidence of her own excessive lability. The terrible moment had come when the let-ters – obtained from Caillaux's first wife – that she had so feared Calmette would publish in Le Figaro, were to be read out in open court. They would thus be available to every newspaper and every reader in France as well as abroad, where the trial was much reported. These letters detail the early days of Henriette's affair with Joseph, their very physical love: they show him asking her to wait for his divorce because of the impending election. As her own lawyer, read-ing out two of the letters, reached a point where Joseph landed 'a thousand million kisses all over your adored little body', Henriette fainted in her chair.

In his summing up, the Calmettes' family lawyer, Maître Chenu, tried to paint Henriette as an ogre of deliberate and calm calculation, propelled into her deed by a debauched husband whose ambition reached the skies and which she shared in an utterly unwomanly way. During his peroration, Henriette fainted once more.

Maître Labori countered by talking, amongst much else, of his admiration and friendship for the editor of the Figaro. Without wanting to blame him in any way, it was clear to Labori that where Caillaux was concerned Le Figaro had allowed its politics to outstrip the bounds of an otherwise estimable free press. Labori also instanced prior crimes of passion, in particular that of Jeanne Clovis-Hugues, the wife of a radical member of the Assemblée. Falsely accused of fornication by a private investigator, she had in 1884 shot him six times as he was leav-ing the Palace of Justice, despite the fact that the court had just convicted him of defamation. She was acquitted, and her husband was proud that she had redeemed her honour in this way.

In order to make sure that the jury was convinced Henriette fell within the same passionate rubric, Labori reminded the good men and true of her uncontrollable, irrational, sexually fearful and very feminine emotional volatility. She was a fragile woman who had been driven over the edge to breakdown by the public revelation of an intimate letter that scandalously compromised her virtue and her honour. Labori even introduced new evidence: he cited a psychiatrist he had consulted, a specialist from the faculty of medicine, who had provided him with an expert opinion. This stated that on the afternoon of 16 March 1914, Madame Caillaux had been guided by 'a subconscious impulse that resulted in a *dédoublement de personnalité* – a splitting into two, so that two beings and two wills inhabited her. Her own "automatism", her trance state, was an echo of her Browning automatic.' It was a statement which the *Figaro* would treat with mocking hilarity the next day, but which *Le Matin* quoted with perfect respect.

But then, *Le Figaro* could hardly allow itself to be generous to the Caillaux couple, whom it continued to libel in a manner far more emphatic than most editors would allow even today, and certainly never in Britain while a trial was still in progress. It didn't cite Maître Labori's final plea for a good ending to the trial: this would entail an acquittal for Madame Caillaux, who would inevitably evermore bear the scars of her act. But the good outcome would also entail a purified press. *Le Figaro* did, however, cite with just a smidgen of approval Labori's concluding words: a plea for concord between opposing factions in the greater conflict that was around the corner: 'Let us preserve our rage for our external enemies,' he urged, 'and proceed united . . . towards the dangers that now threaten.'

The issue of *Le Matin* on the day after the verdict, 29 July, carried a front page divided in half. On the left the headline read: 'Austro-Serb WAR declared: Europe-wide War may still be averted'; on the right, 'Madame Caillaux Acquitted'.

The jury had been out for just over an hour before it delivered its verdict to a rowdy and divided public. The vast numbers present spilled out into the streets, where a large crowd had long been gathered. According to *Le Figaro*, cries of 'Assassin!' greeted Caillaux, as he emerged from the court. For a while, they were to plague him wherever he went. In the rage that erupted against her husband, Henriette was all but forgotten, as if whatever the jury had declared, she was a mere female pawn in a male political game – and Caillaux himself the murderer, not only of Calmette but of all the patriotic values the *Figaro* editor had liked to associate himself with. When the socialist leader Jean Jaurès was assassinated on 31 July, political allies urged Caillaux to leave Paris. His initials were on the murderer's second gun.

Suspicion continued to hover over Henriette's acquittal – and not only that suspicion linked to her determining plea of *crime passionnel*. Rumours persisted that Caillaux had called in favours. The president of the court, Louis Albanel, was one of his friends, and it may not have been by chance that he was presiding. Just before the trial, the prosecutor was elevated to a higher rank in the Legion of Honour. There were rumours, too, that the jury was chosen with an eye to their Republican sympathies: the urn from which the names were drawn was broken.

Whatever the case – and with a viciously divided press, sifting fact from slander remained difficult – Caillaux was arrested in January 1918 for 'intelligence with the enemy'. Despite lack of evidence, he was convicted in 1920 and served a three-year sentence and a five-year proscription from politics. Amnestied in 1924, he returned to the Ministry of Finance. But it was clear that politics in an era that was not only postwar but post-Russian Revolution had moved to the left of him, while he had moved to the right. He outlived many of his cohort, and heading up the Senate's finance group in 1940, he even became a supporter of Maréchal Pétain.

As for Henriette, if love for her husband may not have endured his continuing extramarital frolics, she did retain her domestic role. She also began to use that volatile mind of hers. She completed a degree in art history, lectured and wrote a book. But her reputation as the woman who had killed the editor of *Le Figaro* continued to haunt her.

Restaurants and hotels on occasion refused to serve or admit her, and as late as 1934 when she was to give a lecture on Van Eyck, hecklers from the right-wing Action Française stopped her in her tracks, shouting, 'You belong in prison!' Perhaps a part of her agreed that she did.

27. Into the Sexual Century

Much had changed during the years that had elapsed between Christiana Edmunds's and Madame Caillaux's ordeal before the gathered force of judge, jury, press and mind doctors. The public visibility of the doctors, and the diffusion of their ways of thinking, had introduced new arguments about how the mind and the emotions worked, and cast them into the public arena. Along the way, the psychiatrists had medicalized sexuality. In doing so they had brought the discourse about sex and love into the open, even if their views and emphases, whether on 'perversion' or on the disturbances of love, differed markedly. By the first decade of the twentieth century Christiana would arguably have been allowed to speak her love in an English court, even if the verdict of the jury in the end went against her.

When, in 1902, lowly milliner's assistant Kitty Byron stabbed her violent, alcoholic, cohabiting stockbroker lover after he threatened to desert her, the press were kind to her; and though she was convicted of murder, the jury called for mercy. Mass petitioning resulted in the Home Secretary's clemency and what was a very brief seven-year sentence, with a final year off in a remedial centre. The press understood that the 'cad' could have driven the 'waiflike' Kitty mad; one of the petitions to the Home Secretary talked of how his repudiation of her had reduced her to shame and sorrow, 'followed by a terrible loss of mental control so as to make it well nigh impossible that she in any sense could realise the serious result of [her] offence'.

In a letter appended to the petition, a woman wrote that it was her 'firm belief that the poor creature was temporarily insane when she killed Baker'. Another, that she had been driven mad for a short time. There was also a general insistence on her feminine frailty and her 'hysteria'. Henry Maudsley, who alongside Dr J. J. Pitcairn had

examined her on arrest, considered her legally sane but in 'a transport of passion'. His younger colleague (who may also have doubled
as the detective fiction writer of the same name) was more interested in her sexual behaviour, noting her precocious activity 'for
libidinous purposes with youthful and older men' and her 'unnatural
practices with persons of her own sex'. These he considered to be
signs of her precarious mental disposition. He may have been right. In
the charity home where she spent the last year of her brief sentence,
Kitty Byron fell madly in love with a nurse of whom she grew obsessively jealous: she proceeded to attempt to poison her . . .

The influential Austrian forensic psychiatrist Krafft-Ebing begins his
monumental *Psychopathia Sexualis* (1886–1912) by forefronting the
importance of what Freud would call 'libido'. 'Sexual life no doubt is
the one mighty factor in the individual and social relations of man . . .
Sexual feeling is really the root of all ethics and no doubt of aestheti-
cism and religion.' But while stressing the importance of the sexual
instinct, Krafft-Ebing also wants to limit its expression in women: 'If a
woman's mind is normally developed and if she has been brought up
properly, then her sexuality is not very well developed. If this were
otherwise, the entire world would just be one vast brothel, and marriage and family life would be impossible.'

Women are part of society and, like men, including lawyers and
judges, they buy into a prevailing ethos. Arguably one part of Madame
Caillaux agreed with Krafft-Ebing. Exposure of her early sexual desires
on the front page of *Le Figaro* would be an exhibition of a shaming
abnormality, a perversity. Fear of the exposure of that secret past life
toppled her into what the medics chose to call an 'automatism', an
altered state in which she committed murder. According to the view
that predominated at her trial, her mind, already doubly frail by virtue
of its femininity and her earlier sexual excess, was temporarily overwhelmed.

The turn of the century had brought with it hypotheses about the
neurology of passion and its unbalancing sway. In a 1910 medico-legal

treatise, for example, Hélie Courtis linked passion to debilitating changes in circulation that produce physiological impulses, which in turn overwhelm moral and intellectual resistance and induce a temporary mental disorder in which consciousness is lost. And so passion had a physiological reason for leading to crime.

Perceptions about the frailties of the female mind and its predisposition to be overwhelmed by passion were, of course, fiercely disputed by a growing body of vocal feminists. They pointed to social factors and double standards in love and marriage as the source of women's ills: it was the resulting suffering that led to the need for revenge and justice. If love proved malignant for women, it was neither because they were fundamentally asexual or because their minds were frailer than men's. It was more often because they were trapped in the conflicts created by their time. The virtue demanded of them, their idealized position as bearers of family honour, paid no heed to their desires, which really did exist. Then, too, there was the ill-treatment of lovers and husbands, the failure of the marriages, and their inability to earn their own keep.

In effect, Madame Caillaux's crime was the last to bring together all the *belle époque*'s contradictory understandings of madness, feminine psychology and sexual relations. Meanwhile, the place of the medicolegist in the legal system had become solidly entrenched. In the country of reason, the rule of law and its emphasis on the rational man had given way in certain instances to the power of passion and of pistol-bearing, vitriol-throwing women with which the era chose to incarnate itself . . . just as Marianne with her streaming hair and bared bosom had come to stand for revolution.

When the mind doctors came to deal with male passions in the law courts, the clinical picture often looked substantively different. In the noisily antagonistic debating chamber that was the American courtroom, the varying views that the alienists took became headline news and served to educate the nation in the vagaries of the human mind.

THE PARANOIA OF
A MILLIONAIRE

'Murder as a cure for insanity is a new thing in this jurisdiction, until with Dementia Americana, it was introduced by my learned friend.'

DA William Travers Jerome

V

Brain Storm over Manhattan

28. A Voluptuary's Retreat

In the early 1900s New York's Madison Square Garden was located at Madison and 26th Street at the edge of the neighbourhood nicknamed the 'Tenderloin'. This was the raucous entertainment centre of America's Gilded Age. Known to Manhattan's anti-vice brigades as 'Satan's Circus' or 'Gomorrah', the area teemed with brothels and casinos, theatres and music halls, bars, hotels and clubs. Here poverty jostled against wealth, and crime was rife. So too was corruption. Protection rackets thrived and the police fattened themselves on bribes. Indeed the area had got its name from 'Clubber' Williams's comment on arriving at his new police precinct in 1876: he had thus far lived on chuck steak, he said, but now he'd be having a bit of tenderloin.

There wasn't much of that for the working class of the area, and as the century turned, organized strikes and protest grew – amongst newsboys, women in the garment industry and 'rapid transit' workers, to name just a few. Sometimes public protest spilled over into the Square after which the Garden was named. But with the years, that area grew increasingly affluent: Willa Cather in her *My Mortal Enemy* would evoke it as 'an open-air drawing room' – one where women's virtue was ever an issue.

Built in 1890 to replace a prior sporting and entertainment complex, the new and gracious 'Garden' was in the latest European Beaux Arts style. It was topped by an elegant cupola modelled on the minaret-like bell tower of the Cathedral of Seville. The style expressed the aspirations of the city's elite, those 'four hundred', as Mrs William Backhouse Astor's mythical number had it, who could receive an invitation to her Patriarch Balls on the strength of being the crème de la crème of society, not just money-grubbing, newly rich arrivistes. Luckily, 'new' was a fluid term.

At thirty-two storeys, the Garden was Manhattan's second-tallest building, and it came in at a cost of three million dollars to the financial group that backed it – one that included America's leading financiers: J. P. Morgan, Andrew Carnegie, W. W. Astor amongst them. The cost of such a building project today would probably be between $365 and $596 million. But this was America's Gilded Age: for the rich of that era before income tax, money accumulated unstoppably. The Garden's main auditorium seated eight thousand and had floor space for thousands more. It had a twelve-hundred-seat theatre, a larger concert hall, the city's biggest restaurant, and a roof garden-cabaret where champagne flowed and chorus girls sang.

The building's architect was the time's most eminent and the most beloved of its aristocracy of wealth. The name Stanford White (1853–1906) was a byword for taste and elegance. His firm McKim, Mead & White had designed Tiffany's, the New York Herald Building modelled on the Doge's Palace in Venice, the graceful Washington Square Memorial Arch and a host of plush restaurants, public buildings, churches and amenities, not to mention opulent mansions both on Fifth Avenue and in the country. Unlike other architects of his day, White also designed interiors and sumptuous parties, such as might transform a New York restaurant into Versailles's Grand Trianon and feature lavish spectacles of music and ballet. Of course, he attended these as well.

Many of White's gracious buildings have now vanished, but two country establishments have been restored and give a flavour of the

'American Renaissance' style in architecture which he helped to shape. Astor Courts, on John Jacob Astor IV's 2800-acre estate, Ferncliff, combined classical colonial with Beaux Arts to create a luxurious summer residence. It included the first indoor pool, as well as a bowling alley and shooting range. For the Vanderbilts, there was a columned limestone mansion on the banks of the Hudson River, now a historic building in which Stanford White's interiors remain largely intact.

Tall, rugged, mustachioed, his reddish hair brush-cut, his suits impeccable, White was a gentleman and an aesthete who knew Shakespeare by rote from his scholar father and was familiar with the museums of the world. He was charming and cultivated. He was also something of a voluptuary. A regular at the extravagant festivities the great hostesses of the day provided, White was a lover of the best cuisine and a collector of the most beautiful women. The cities of Europe were his regular haunts – shopping grounds for style as well as for objects to be shipped home to embellish the houses of rich clients and his own. He had a luxurious multi-gabled estate in Box Hill on Long Island, a three-hour journey away, a well connected wife, Betty Smith, and a much loved son. He also had a town house on East Twenty-first Street, a bachelor flat for private entertainment and an apartment for his own use at the very top of the Madison Square Garden.

A lift brought you up the eighty-foot tower, where White's rooms were built in horseshoe shape around the shaft. Blue and emerald-green Tiffany dragonfly sconces lit the space, their light reflected in a wall-sized gilt mirror. A moss-green tufted velvet sofa, an ebony grand piano on which a bronze Bacchante sculpture by a famous artist was poised, a rosewood table, exotic flowers, and bird-of-paradise plants brought from Florida . . . All this is what met the large, waif-like eyes of fetching sixteen-year-old Evelyn Nesbit when she first entered White's sumptuous apartment in the autumn of 1901. A lauded recent addition to the chorus of the hit show *Floradora*, Evelyn was already a much sought-after artist's and photographer's model. She had been dubbed 'the most beautiful specimen of the skylight world'.

The further climb up a narrow wrought-iron spiral staircase to reach the turreted top of the Garden's tower would have been easy for the nimble Evelyn. From here, you could have a close-up view of another nubile beauty – a shining, virginal Diana, who spun with the wind, her bow and arrow ever at the ready. She was the product of the time's most famous artist, Augustus Saint-Gaudens. The Puritan guardians of New York's virtue, led by the redoubtable and vociferous anti-vice campaigner Anthony Comstock, had protested against the statue's brazen glittering nudity. In provocative response, White and Saint-Gaudens had decked Diana in gauzy drapery. But her robes blew away within weeks, and Diana's champions proceeded to illuminate her so that she became brilliantly visible, even at night. Back when Diana had first arrived atop the tower, a *Mercury* reporter had written, 'The Square is now thronged with clubmen armed with field glasses ... No such figure has ever before been publicly exhibited in the United States.'

White, who was a connoisseur of the female form as well as of architectural structures, knew that this first Diana, who weighed in at 820kg of copper gilt and measured 5.5 metres in height, was too heavy to spin on the globe pedestal provided for her, and in 1893 she was replaced by a smaller, hollow version of herself – the one young Evelyn Nesbit gazed on during her visits to White. Whatever might be going on below her, Diana chastely turned with the wind here until 1925, when the building was pulled down. By that time, Stanford White was dead, murdered in the very Garden of which he was so proud by a millionaire who didn't approve of his penchant for youthful female beauty.

Evelyn Nesbit's biographer, Paula Uruburu, likens Evelyn's photogenic appeal to Marilyn Monroe's: Evelyn's, too, was a presence the camera loved and made iconic, though unlike Marilyn she was initially perhaps more fatal to the men around her than to herself. Born in 1884, she outlived Marilyn by some five years and would have liked Marilyn to play her in the 1955 film about her early life, *The Girl in the Red Velvet Swing*, rather than the chosen star, Joan Collins.

Slight, fragile, with supple childlike limbs, copious hair that in the light moved from chocolate to auburn, a full mouth, glowing dark-hazel eyes and an inherent love of dressing up, this 'American Eve' had, in the early 1900s, an allure that met the period's demands for naughty but nice: she was both enticingly seductive and charmingly innocent. Evelyn could be chaste shepherdess, classical nymph, ragged Gypsy or playful coquette. She could wear the clothes the newly bur-geoning fashion magazines demanded, yet needed none of the day's corsetry to advertise any of many products – soap, furs, chocolates, toothpaste.

She was the 'modern Helen', a dreamy, pouting pin-up girl for the new century. Dressed, half-dressed, veiled, behatted, chaste or seduc-tive, Evelyn graced everything from tobacco and playing cards to calendars for Prudential Life and Coca-Cola. Charles Dana Gibson, illustrator for the mass market, twisted her hair into a question mark and transformed her into 'Woman: the Eternal Question'. Her face came to embody the very mystery the eternal feminine posed. Eventually, even hard-bitten journalists would wax lyrical over her ingenuous charms. These were accompanied by a sharp, unschooled intelligence, which Stanford White, a Pygmalion to her Galatea, helped to educate, extending her native American to Shakespeare.

29. Murder in the Garden

The evening of Monday, 25 June 1906 was unseasonably hot. It drove the rich to their Long Island homes and the rest to Coney Island. The day before, a hippo in the Brooklyn Zoo had expired in the heat, but on the 25th a sea wind tempered the weather just a little. Stanford White, then fifty-two, had taken his nineteen-year-old son Laurence and a friend, both students at Harvard, to dinner at the stylish Café Martin, a Paris look-alike establishment which even boasted a space devoted to women without escorts. Dinner over, White had dropped the younger men at the theatre they had chosen over the opening of what was advertised as 'a sparkling musical comedy' in the rooftop space of Madison Square Garden.

The roof garden was a glamorous open-air cabaret-theatre. White's tower apartment and his luminous Diana overlooked it, and provided some of its visual drama. Lights of many colours twinkled and swayed amidst luxurious potted plants. Waiters carried drinks to the tables that took up the central space, and there were rows of seats at the sides. A special table was always reserved for White, the garden's creator. He was there for only part of that evening: he had seen bits of *Mamzelle Champagne* in rehearsal and it fizzed rather less than its title and advertising. But he was interested in one of the chorus girls, a seventeen-year-old new to the city, so he returned at eleven o'clock.

Soon after, a large muffled figure, with an unseasonable long black coat over his tux and a panama pulled down over his head, approached White's table from the lift towards which he and his party had seemed to be heading just moments before. A tenor was singing the ironically appropriate 'I Could Love a Million Girls':

'I've heard them say so often they could love their wives alone,
But I think that's just foolish; men must have hearts made of
   stone.
Now my heart is made of softer stuff; it melts at each warm
   glance.
A pretty girl can't look my way, without a new romance . . . '

A gunshot exploded in the night air, louder than both orchestra
and crooner. It was quickly followed by two more. A woman
screamed. Others joined in. White slid from the table, overturning it
as he fell. Glass splintered everywhere. A doctor raced through the
rising tumult to find him lying in a pool of blood, his face partly annihilated and blackened with powder burns. He was palpably dead and
his killer stood beside him, his pistol now turned upside down, his
arms held up over his head. He had been a mere two feet away from
his victim and had put a first bullet through his left eye, a second
through the mouth and a third through White's left shoulder. Some
reported a look of glee on his face.

The theatre manager had ordered the orchestra to resume their
playing and the chorus to be brought back on, but the performers
were already leaving, joining the frightened crowd in what would at
any moment turn into a stampede towards the exit. Others fainted on
the spot. The mother of *Mamzelle*'s lyricist, having watched the audience's hostile response to her son's opening night, feared he had been
the object of attack and screamed, 'They've shot my son!'

But it was unmistakeably Stanford White who was dead. Now, a
woman in a striking black hat piled high with a gauzy veil and wearing
an embroidered white satin gown that clung to her with 'sculptural
indiscretion' was heard, from the entrance to the roof theatre, to
scream, 'My God, Harry! What have you done?' The woman was
Evelyn Nesbit, now twenty-one years old and married for just over a
year to the Harry she was exclaiming at: Harry Kendall Thaw, the
thirty-four-year-old millionaire son of a Pittsburgh railroad and
mining dynasty, favourite of his strait-laced and Presbyterian widowed

mother, the redoubtable Mrs William Thaw, who would have far preferred her son never to have met the lovely Evelyn with her less than
respectable past.

There are varying accounts of how pasty-faced Harry, who had
drunk several bottles of champagne that evening and whose hands
and arms were twitching markedly, responded to Evelyn's exclamation. Over the coming months, up to the first trial and then through
the second, a rampant tabloid press as well as higher-brow one would
have a field day covering the lives, the hows and the whys of all the
principals, and often disagreeing not only in their points of view, but
also on chapter and verse.

Evelyn Nesbit's own remarkably well written first memoir of 1914,
The Story of My Life by Evelyn Thaw, is filled with literary and artistic allusions – to Flaubert, Shakespeare, the painter and diarist Marie
Bashkirtseff, for instance – and presents an endearing picture of an
astute young woman, sensitive to the life around her, to Harry's acts
and to what can be revealed and what can't.

Evelyn's *Untold Story* of 1934 (entitled *Prodigal Days* in the US) is more
sensational and direct, whether because of changes in the author herself, or in the times – or perhaps in her ghostwriter? – is not altogether
clear. Harry Thaw's revealingly peculiar self-published account, *The
Traitor* (1926), both simplifies events and complicates the picture
because of its palpable oddity: it reveals a man of determined views but
disordered intelligence, to whom money and mummy give inordi-
nate power. There is also the Edison Studios film, *The Unwritten Law*, of
1907, first of several movies. Then there are the various accounts over
the years of the landmark trial itself.

It seems that by the time Harry responded to Evelyn's cry he had
already been disarmed by the closest uniform to hand. Paul Brudi, a
New York City fireman, had the presence of mind to take Thaw's gun
and walk him towards the lift. Thaw may then have hugged and kissed
his wife and said, according to his memoir, 'It's all right, dearie. I have
probably saved your life.' When a local policeman, Officer Anthony L.
Debes, then arrived to arrest him, Thaw declared that White deserved

his death. 'He ruined my wife and then deserted her,' he said in complete calm, though the officer didn't know whether he'd heard 'wife' or 'life'. Both have a kind of accuracy.

Debes agreed to Thaw's request not to handcuff him. He was a millionaire, after all. They went down in the same lift as Evelyn and the two friends who had accompanied them to the roof garden. When they reached the ground floor, Thaw lit a cigarette and asked the officer to phone his friend George Lauder Carnegie — his brother-in-law and nephew of the great Andrew Carnegie — to tell him that he, Harry, was in trouble. Trouble was not a rare event for Harry. Earlier that week he had already had several altercations in Pittsburgh, including one with a bank employee who couldn't provide the cash he wanted within fifteen minutes, and another with a café attendant when the establishment didn't have any of his favourite cigars, so he had proceeded to ransack the place. He had also become so abusive with a tram driver that he had had to be forcibly ejected from the vehicle. His rages were common knowledge in his hometown, but also in New York and even London and Paris.

In New York, earlier in his career of havoc and mayhem, he had driven a car through a display window, attempted to ride a horse into an exclusive club that had failed to make him a member, and engaged in numerous fisticuffs. Some of these rows took place during gargantuan drinking sprees, which along with poker nights had comprised the larger part of his university education. His mother always came to Harry's rescue. Before his death when Harry was eighteen, his father had cut his monthly allowance down to $2500 – until he showed himself responsible enough to be entrusted with his share of an estate valued at $40 million. But after his father's death, Mrs Thaw restored her son's monthly $8000, only to withdraw it again when she didn't approve of his choice of women. All this was at a time when a good annual salary was about $500.

Down in the street, officer and prisoner managed to avoid the crush of people and carriages, as well as most of the reporters who had quickly gathered. They walked through the Tenderloin along Thirtieth towards Sixth Avenue to the police station. Here Thaw first identified himself as John Smith, an eighteen-year-old student from Philadelphia, something his calling cards instantly contradicted. (He later said that on the walk to the station, a reporter had told him not to give his real name.) When the press caught up with him, he declined to make a statement and simply sprawled back on a bench and smoked. His eyes were fixed in a stare, but he was otherwise calm. He treated the police politely, asked for water and a cigar, thanked the guard for both, then slept, his crushed hat pulled down over his baby face, until the coroner arrived.

The prosecution would later insist that Thaw was wholly in control: the fact that he refused to answer questions until he had seen his lawyers testified to that. Already rumours were circulating that he was a cocaine and morphine addict who had killed under the influence. He was 'kinda spooky', a policeman testified at the trial, with a far-away look in his 'bulging eyes'. But the coroner's first public statement put paid to gossip about drugs or insanity, at least for the time being. Mr Dooley arrived around one in the morning and at three was joined by witnesses, who identified Harry as the murderer. This permitted him to be officially charged. He was then walked across the so-called Bridge of Sighs, below which crowds would gather during the trial so as to look up and catch a glimpse of him, to a cell in the city prison, the Tombs.

The coroner told a questioning reporter that Thaw seemed 'perfectly rational'. 'His eyes were shifty and bleared, but he talked like a sane man, and I am convinced the killing was deliberately planned.' In his memoir, Thaw claimed that in the night, despite it being a men's prison, he had heard young women's voices uncannily like his wife's: one called out 'She's ennercent [innocent]!' His wife's chastity and innocence had in his dreaming mind long stood in for his own.

Meanwhile, Stanford White's son Lawrence was taken to the crime scene. He had never heard of Harry Thaw. He wished his father had gone to Philadelphia on planned business rather than staying in New York to see him. In a state of shock, he stood, for the length of the night, over his father's dead and disfigured body – which White's own brother-in-law, who had been in the audience that evening, had failed to recognize. As for Evelyn, reporters gathered en masse at the hotel where she and Harry had been staying – the Lorraine, a plush establishment on Fifth Avenue, where they had a suite together with rooms for maid and valet. They waited for her in vain. She had had the presence of mind – in *The Traitor* Harry says it was on his advice – to slip away and stay with one of the few remaining friends from her life in the theatre, May McKenzie.

Across the US, newspapers the next day, both broadsheet and tabloid, led on the lurid story. Reporters had been busy throughout the night gathering background material and responses to the event, interviewing possible witnesses, friends and, where they could, members of Harry's and Evelyn's families in Pittsburgh, Pennsylvania, and White's in Manhattan and Long Island. In status-conscious New York, White's obituaries noted, amongst much else in his luminous career, that the London *Spectator* had called his father 'the most accomplished and the best bred man that America has sent to England within the past generation', though the financial difficulties the elder White had encountered had meant that Stanford couldn't pursue his dream of being an artist. The *New York Times*, hinting at Stanford White's secret life, stated that he and his wife 'had not been living together recently' and that 'for a busy man, who worked hard and achieved notable things, he gave up a great deal of time to the pleasures of sociability and friendship'. Madison Square Garden where he kept a 'suite of apartments' was now described as his 'pleasure house'.

The full description of the kinds of pleasures Stanford White enjoyed there would not come out until the trial, but the press would soon hint and smear. If messages of condolence at first arrived at the famous architect's house in huge number and from around the world, the very fact of murder, combined with the insinuating press coverage and the Thaws' fortune and public relations machine, would soon taint White's reputation. Too mighty to provide comment, his influential friends and rich clients melted away. As if they, too, could only be maintained by a belief in their architect's virtue, many of his buildings were left to crumble and disappear.

Press descriptions of Harry Thaw had little but the size of his fortune to counterbalance the horror of his crime. But that and the family's reputation went some way towards shielding him from the worst. The report sent to the *New York Times* from his native Pittsburgh – where one of his brothers was seriously ill while the other, like his mother, was happily away – calls Harry the 'black sheep' of the family. One of his sisters had married a Carnegie, after all, the other the Earl of Yarmouth, avid for American millions, but nonetheless distantly in line to the throne. Harry had only a history of wildness and Evelyn Nesbit – the family, not altogether successfully, tried to massage away the less than impeccable reputation of each.

An unnamed member of the Thaw family, according to the *New York Times*, stated that there could have been nothing between Mrs Harry Thaw and Stanford White to provoke the shooting. The reverend who had married Evelyn and Harry, W. L. McEwan of the Third Presbyterian Church – the widowed Mrs Thaw's most enduring playing field – stated that when he had married the Thaws on 4 April 1905 their future had seemed rosy. The courtship, the reporter elaborated, had lasted three years, the couple having met when Evelyn performed in the musical *Floradora*. The two had been to Europe together, but Thaw's mother thoroughly disapproved of the relationship. On this occasion, she had cut her son's allowance herself: there would be no more coming to him from his father's forty-million-dollar estate unless he changed his ways.

What the paper didn't comment on is that, whatever her threats and Puritan rectitude, Mother Thaw continually bailed her eldest out – even after he had spent fifty thousand dollars on a dinner for the showgirls of Paris at which he was the only male and dessert came wrapped in diamonds. If, like the rest of the Pittsburgh moneyed classes, Mrs Thaw at first refused to accept Harry's 'chorus girl', she eventually consented to her poor besotted Harry's marriage. The newly-weds shared the Thaws' ample Pittsburgh mansion, where a campaign was promptly launched to make Evelyn conform to her mother-in-law's rigid ways.

But Evelyn had little patience for the stuffy Mrs Thaw, a woman who palpably loathed her and who was only interested in Church and status, the first being a version of the second: God was far easier to access than the snobbish New York elite who had never allowed her son entry. Effectively imprisoned by the older woman's ways while in Pittsburgh, Evelyn had been thrilled when Harry had decided on another trip to Europe. The week in New York was merely a stopover. It turned out to be a long one.

Harry Thaw had become increasingly obsessed with Stanford White. Thaw had White, as well as on occasion his wife, followed by agents. He referred to him as 'the Beast' or 'the Blackguard'. He insisted that Evelyn tell him when and if she saw him: when they were in restaurants with others and she spied the 'B', she was to pass him a note.

At dinner, before the murder, she had done just that.

In the days leading up to it, Evelyn had Harry's increasingly agitated state, and more, to concern her. He had developed an odd fascination with Truxtun Beale, one of the friends who had accompanied them to the Garden rooftop theatre. Beale was a native of San Francisco; he came from a diplomatic family, and had been named by President Harrison in 1891 Ambassador to Persia, then the following year to Greece, Romania and Serbia. He had also travelled to Siberia and written about his experiences, before returning home to practise law.

But Thaw was not interested in Beale's writing or his political past. What interested him was the scandal Beale had been involved in some years back. In September 1902, Truxtun Beale and the head of the California Jockey Club, Thomas H. Williams, had engaged in an act not unlike Madame Caillaux's. The *San Francisco News Letter*, a weekly, had printed a paragraph that Beale interpreted as casting aspersions on the honour of a Miss Marie Oge, the daughter of an eminent citizen who was a friend of his. Williams had rung Frederick Marriott, the newspaper editor, and he and Beale had been invited to visit his offices. When the editor opened the door, one of them punched him in the face. Marriott turned to run, but a gun was pulled out and he was shot four times in the back and thigh as he fled up the stairs. One of the bullets crippled him for life. Soon after the affair, Beale went to Washington and there married the very same Marie Oge.

What interested Harry Thaw and made Evelyn anxious was that Beale was so eminent that he had been acquitted under what Harry repeatedly referred to as the 'unwritten law': that higher code of honour, not unlike the one instituted by the Napoleonic Code, that permitted a husband or father to punish, even kill, the person who had dishonoured his fiancée, wife or sister. Thaw told Evelyn that public opinion had always been with Beale. There were people, everyone agreed, who deserved murder. In Thaw's view, Stanford White was one such: in his own eyes, ridding the world of White was a heroic act. Honour codes – the unwritten law – trumped the rule of law. It seemed that millionaires and outlaws have not a little in common, particularly if they can wave the moral flag for their team.

That famous head of the New York Society for the Suppression of Vice, Anthony Comstock (1844–1915), seemed – if not altogether to condone the murder – certainly to agree with Thaw about White. A US postal inspector and the time's leading campaigner against moral turpitude, Comstock even had a law named after him. It had been passed in 1873, the same year as his society had been created. This law forbade the posting of any materials that could be considered 'obscene, lewd or lascivious', or linked to birth control or venereal disease. In 1905, Comstock had campaigned against Bernard Shaw's play about prostitution, *Mrs Warren's Profession*, and had it suppressed. Shaw retaliated. pronouncing that 'Comstockery is the world's standing joke at the expense of the United States.' This hardly deterred Comstock from his determined attempt to wash America clean: his work led to some four thousand arrests as well as suicides, and the confiscation of approximately fifteen tons of books, plus pictures and press plates.

Alerted by Harry Thaw to his plight on the morning of White's inquest, Comstock sent one of his agents to the Tombs, but the man failed to gain access to Harry. Nonetheless, Comstock told the press that he was ready to provide the Grand Jury with evidence about Stanford White's nefarious activities. Thaw had alerted him to the architect's vices some eighteen months earlier, before his marriage to Evelyn Nesbit. He had done so, Comstock contended, on the 'purest' of motives. 'He seemed to think that White was a monster who ought to be put out of the community.'

Comstock had sent agents to stalk the apartment in Madison Square Garden as well as White's other haunts. Thaw knew of 'revolting orgies' and 'atrocities perpetrated on girls' whom White had invited home. Thaw had provided him with names, and Comstock had taken evidence from underage girls, of seduction or worse by White. But either because they were dissuaded by their families or had been bought off and made mysteriously to disappear, Comstock hadn't been able to mount a solid legal case against White. He was 'morally convinced' of the man's guilt, but he had had to drop the idea of having him 'indicted on the evidence I had obtained'. His lack of success seemed 'to depress Thaw. As to whether I believe this depression could cause Thaw to commit murder I do not care to say.'

Comstock stated that he was willing to appear before a grand jury to testify to White's 'atrocities'. In the affidavit he made to the trial in Thaw's defence, he also stated: 'The last time I saw Harry Thaw was only two or three weeks before he shot White. He appeared to be in a desperate state – like a man who is well nigh frantic. He said to me wildly, "You must keep on, you must stop this man, he must be stopped now – at once."'

Like Harry Thaw, the Reverend Anthony Comstock seemed to think that in the pursuit of a purer America, in the war on vice, murder was simply another weapon and need incur no punishment. He may not have considered Harry Thaw quite the valiant hero that half the press and Thaw himself seemed to want to make of him. But nor did Comstock pause to consider that his statement, which gave support to the murder being long premeditated, might send Harry to the electric chair – developed in the ever inventive Thomas Edison's workshop and in use since 1889. In the eyes of the law, only a plea of insanity might save him, and insanity meant that he could have no responsible understanding of his crime.

The wild and frantic Thaw that Comstock describes is consumed by passion. It is a passion that has lasted for years and overrides any common understanding of reason. But if the murder in the Garden was a crime of passion – an 'irresistible impulse' – it became increasingly clear that Thaw's passion was all about Stanford White. That passion certainly pre-dated any the renegade millionaire had for Evelyn Nesbit, the child-woman with the Renaissance angel's face, the woman he called 'Boofuls'.

The habit of being consumed by the vice of others while keeping one's own hidden, sometimes even from one's own eyes, was hardly new to Puritan America.

30. The Girl in the Red Velvet Swing

Fifteen-year-old Florence Evelyn Nesbit arrived in Gotham with the new century. She was the daughter of Florence MacKenzie and Winfield Scott Nesbit, a handsome, gentle and oddly unambitious lawyer who foresaw a Vassar education for his lovely, clever daughter. She was a girl who could dance and sing, play the piano and recite, and who, encouraged by him, loved reading almost as much as she loved her father's praise. Evelyn's two-years-younger brother, Howard – like his sister, delicate-limbed and with wide liquid eyes – was his mother's favourite.

The family first lived in Tarentum, a place and a part of her life that Evelyn remembers in her memoir as rustic and idyllic, though the town was only marginally less industrialized than Pittsburgh, some twenty-five miles away, and known as the nation's dirtiest city. The family moved to Pittsburgh (then spelled without its *h*) when Evelyn was around ten. A year later, her father suddenly died, at the early age of forty. Utterly unexpected, the death left the family grieving and destitute: it also robbed Evelyn of all sense of security, both psychological and material.

House and furniture had to be auctioned or sold, as did the books her father had given her. The next months and years were spent surviving on family handouts and loans, constant moves, a failed boarding-house enterprise, plus whatever scraps Evelyn's largely incompetent and lamenting mother could amass. The family often went hungry: one bare meal a day was all that there was to be had. When the boarding house was lost, the children were sent to live with distant relatives in the country. Evelyn's mother, once she had managed to closet away her tears, cut off all her old friends and dreamt only of being a fashion seamstress. She never succeeded: she had, after all, never been to Paris or trained to do anything, but she did go to Philadelphia to try her hand. Here she at last found a job at Wanamaker's department store and sent for her children. Both of them were now taken out of school and went to work in the store. Howard, ever frail, fell ill: labour and the continuing scarcity of food affected both children's health, but Howard seemed to suffer or was permitted to suffer more. He was sent to distant relatives again, this time in Tarentum.

A week before her fourteenth birthday everything began slowly to change for Evelyn. She was spotted in the street gazing into a shop window by a woman who asked her if she would like to pose for a portrait. Disbelieving, Evelyn in her tattered, mismatched clothes said she would ask her mother. When the latter learned that five hours of her daughter's stillness would earn the colossal sum of a dollar, she immediately sanctioned the work.

Now, every Sunday, Evelyn posed for Mrs Darach, a well respected local artist and miniaturist. One of her friends, the sister of the artist John Storm, then told her brother about Evelyn, who in turn introduced her to a local colony comprising talented women illustrators and stained-glass artists.

Evelyn's career was on its way: she had a respect for art; she was versatile; she loved dressing up and the attendant play of fantasy. If she sometimes got bored with the need for stillness, she was nonetheless good at reverie. With her porcelain skin, sultry gaze and pubescent charm she was striking to look at and loved being looked at − let alone being told she was beautiful. Evelyn could appear ethereal, or childlike and androgynous, or as an underage vamp. Violet Oakley used her as a model for her stained-glass windows in churches in Philadelphia and New York. The 'angel child' − a name Thaw also called her − was soon much in demand. She worked hard, posing five hours at a stretch, sometimes with no break, her neck aching and her stomach rumbling.

Evelyn's mother quit her day job to become her daughter's manager, despite her occasional disapproval of the work Evelyn did.

Willing to sell her daughter's charms, Mrs Nesbit yet had a need to appear respectable, most of all perhaps to herself. By the age of fifteen, Evelyn was supporting the family through her labours. She had no friends of her own age, and her greatest solace was reading: one book, Zola's *Nana*, his novel about an actress-prostitute who rises from rags to riches, had been left at the boarding house by a guest and Evelyn had retrieved it. She had dreams of fulfilling the paternal promise that she would someday go to Vassar. Meanwhile, there was not even the hope of high school.

As Evelyn's brilliance at posing in the 'skylight world' of the studios became known, it was suggested that photographers, too, might be interested in her. Philadelphia's Ryland Phillips had her in to pose: he made her up for the first time and dressed her in floor-length white satin, draping it so that his model resembled 'a young Aphrodite'. The photos were reproduced for years, and the local papers talked of this 'strange and fascinating creature' with 'a remarkable maturity of repose' for one of her youth. The rare young Pittsburgh beauty with her 'enchanting combination of youthful innocence and colossal self possession' found herself much in demand, and gained an introduction to a leading New York artist.

Mrs Nesbit took herself off to Manhattan, purportedly to find work for Evelyn. Then, unaccountably, she did nothing for months, the excuse being that she was once more trying to set up as a fashion seamstress herself. The mother's ambivalence towards her daughter and her work was marked. Finally, when work didn't materialize and all Evelyn's earnings had been spent, Mrs Nesbit sent for her children.

Evelyn arrived in Manhattan in December 1900. Within weeks, she was posing for the respected and well connected James Carroll Beckwith. When her photographs appeared in a two-page spread in the *Sunday American*, and again in *Broadway Magazine*, she had started on her road to celebrity. Despite her self-deluding mother's ineptitude as an agent, her talent as a model shone. Evelyn would appear as Undine with water-lilies in her hair, in orientalist mode in a half-open kimono, or as an innocent all-American girl in a high-necked blouse.

She could appear in anything at all, and halt the gaze. She would soon become an icon of the new century, her nubile image distributed in any number of forms and settings.

But Evelyn grew bored with solitary modelling for ageing artists. It was a lonely life for a girl who had just turned sixteen. Her aspirations swung to the more exciting world of the theatre, and in May 1901, when the agent who had been wooing her said he had an offer from the producer of the Broadway musical hit *Floradora*, Evelyn made an initial foray onto the stage. At first, she was almost sent home. John C. Fisher, *Floradora*'s manager, thought this Evelyn, who looked barely pubescent, would bring Comstock's anti-vice squad down on the theatre. But by the end of an audition that included unschooled dancing and singing, he told her mother that if Evelyn would lie about her age, he would take her on.

The theatre marked Evelyn's first real encounter with a social group whose experience in any way reflected her own. In the chorus line there were other young women from the provinces whose family lives had been straitened by death and poverty. At first the older members of the troupe sheltered the tiny Evelyn, who was still little more than a child who loved mechanical toys more than much else. But she was also a thorough professional. She watched and listened and practised, growing into the exhilaration of music and her new craft. For the first time in her life, she started to go out with other young people. She revelled in the parties, the vibrant Manhattan scene. She loved the experiment that was this new independent life, even if her cautious and envious mother disapproved. Between the arduous routine of modelling all day and performing in the evening seven days a week, plus a matinée, it took a little while for the girl who was nicknamed 'the Kid' and who could nurse a single glass of wine until the early hours of the morning, gradually to lose her innocence.

Stanford White was a regular at *Floradora*, with its ever shifting chorus line. The little Spanish Gypsy that Evelyn performed caught his eye. Towards the end of September 1901 – that momentous month in which President McKinley was assassinated by an anarchist and that energetic Cuban War hero, member of New York's elite, Theodore Roosevelt, at forty-two the youngest president ever, was sworn in to breathe change into the new century – White asked a *Floradora* cast member, Nell King (secretly mother to Edna Goodrich, one of Evelyn's chorus-line friends), to invite her to a society lunch.

Evelyn's mother, perhaps fearful of the daily headlines pinpointing Comstock's vice-suppression squad, not to mention her daughter's reputation, withheld permission. She was interested in another suitor of Evelyn's, a rich banker by the name of James Garland, married and almost four times Evelyn's age, who had come to ask Mrs Nesbit's permission before approaching her daughter. His yacht was at their disposal for Sunday jaunts. Nell King, however, didn't like to displease the mighty Stanford White, and came personally in White's electric car to solicit Mrs Nesbit's approval for the lunch invitation. Mrs Nesbit gave in. Whether to emphasize her own fading youth or her daughter's innocence, she dressed Evelyn in a schoolgirl's sailor frock which fell just above the knee. She didn't know that White's tastes lay particularly in virginal waifs.

On the Sunday Edna brought Evelyn to an unprepossessing door on West 24th Street off Broadway. A toyshop window stood next to it and Evelyn was enchanted by the automata, the painted toys that moved and clattered. At the top of the stairs a second door opened magically and they were plunged into what Evelyn later described as a breath-taking space in a wonderful red, protected from the outside world by heavy red curtains and furnished with carved Italian antique furniture. Fine paintings hung on the walls. Illumination came from mysterious sources. Velvet divans, silk cushions ... The young girl thought she had entered a scene from *The Arabian Nights*, and waited for the carpets to fly. Stanford White, by contrast, seemed at forty-six 'terribly old', a potentate but no prince. Evelyn notes that she was equally disappointed when a second man came in, even older than the first, and no Don Juan either.

The food, however, shipped in from Delmonico's, was a revelation to the ever hungry young woman, who gorged herself on oysters and

Lobster Newberg, devilled eggs, sweetbreads, preserves and cherry pie
à la mode, washing it all down with the single glass of champagne that
White permitted her. The voluptuous corseted Edna, unlike Evelyn,
could only dip into cucumber salad. White was intrigued by this lithe
Twiggy of an adolescent. As Evelyn later reflected, comparing herself
to Edna and the popular type of the Gay Nineties: 'I was smaller, slen-
derer; a type artists and, as I learned later, older more experienced
men admired. I had discovered in the studios that artists cared little
for the big-breasted, heavy-hipped, corseted figure, preferring to paint
the freer, more sinuous, uncorseted one with natural, unspoiled lines.'

Welcome in the photographic twentieth century: thin women reproduce better, on film at least. White would soon recommend thinness
to Evelyn.

When the fourth member of their party left them for business on
Wall Street, White ushered the young women towards more splen-
dour, two floors up, at the top of the building. Here everything was a
deep forest-green, and at one corner of the studio space there was a
'gorgeous swing with red velvet ropes around which trailed green
smilax [a glossy vine], set high in the ceiling'.

'Let's give this kiddie a ride,' White said, and Evelyn jumped on. He
sent her soaring up towards a large many-coloured Japanese parasol,
which Edna controlled with an undetectable string. Evelyn was
encouraged to kick at it as it twirled before her eyes. She tattered several parasols and laughed uproariously at the game, as did White, who
also shuddered and clapped each time her foot tore through the
paper. At around four the game drew to an end. White had to go. But
before doing so he took Edna aside and told her he wanted her to
take Evelyn to the dentist to have a slightly discoloured front tooth
fixed, something the older woman only revealed to her once they
were on their way. This was a Pygmalion who loved perfection.

When Stanford White asked Mrs Nesbit to come and see him a few
days later, it seems neither she nor Evelyn suspected his motives. She
was altogether taken with White's courtesy and concern: he had once
more recommended his dentist, assuring Mrs Nesbit that he had

tended to the teeth of all the girls in *Floradora*. Only later did Evelyn take up the offer. But when White's next invitation to her came, her mother was happy to let her go and visit the man the newspapers described as intense and masterful. Evelyn liked him too. 'He was a compendium of information on all subjects, likely and unlikely. He was an authority and teacher . . . gifted by Nature beyond the average.' He was also very kind, as her mother had pointed out, and felt very safe. White was a 'charming, cultured gentleman whose magnetism undid all my first impressions of him. He emerged as a splendid man, thoughtful, sweet and kind; a brilliant conversationalist and an altogether interesting companion.'

White might have been all these things, and indeed was a more than suitable replacement father for an Evelyn who had lost her own and was eager for intellectual stimulus. However, if White was 'clever', and a useful patron and benefactor for a rising teenage star over whom he exercised a 'fatherly supervision', he was also a 'voluptuary' – something her other admirer, James Garland, informed her of in no uncertain terms, indicating that he couldn't carry on seeing her if she was frequenting Stanford White.

Evelyn wasn't sure what 'voluptuary' meant and far preferred the impressive White, who bought her intriguing automata every time they met and sent flowers daily. Nor was she interested in marriage to a man like Garland. Two weeks later, after another reminder from White, and with her mother now on side, Evelyn finally had her teeth fixed.

As if this was a sign that she would play Galatea to his lubricious whims, White then moved the Nesbit family, mother, daughter and son Howard whom he also befriended, into an apartment at the Wellington Hotel, which he had designed. Evelyn had never lived in rooms so opulent and enchanting. It was like inhabiting a fairy tale: her bedroom was draped in white (!) satin. There was a matching lace-topped bed, and a canopy crowned in white ostrich feathers. The forest-green living room had a piano, and White provided a teacher. Evelyn played Beethoven to please her patron. Soon after the move, he sent her a red cloak to wear to a party that Friday night. The big bad wolf came to pick up his Little Red Riding-Hood himself this time, instead of sending one of his emissaries – often enough mistresses on their way out. He took her to his Garden apartment. It was there that events would soon unfurl that would rivet millions when recounted in detail at Harry Thaw's trial in 1907 by an Evelyn who still looked like a schoolgirl.

Excited by the wonders of the Garden's treasure-filled tower, if bemused by the lack of party guests, Evelyn was comforted by White's promise that he would have her photographed – in her Red Riding-Hood cloak – by the time's best photographers, Gertrude Käsebier and Rudolf Eickemeyer Jr amongst them. He would keep his promise.

After one glass of champagne, the man who was now 'Stanny' took Evelyn home. She had to behave like a good girl, he told her. The next morning, he was there with books for her to read – an education that took in Shakespeare and Milton, Keats and Shelley, as well as Dickens. White thought schooling important and now began to finance Howard's, sending him to the Chester Academy in Pennsylvania. Soon after, he took Evelyn to Gertrude Käsebier's studio, where she was photographed in an Empire dress, demurely innocent, her hair coiled girlishly yet suggestively on her bare shoulders, and staring enigmatically direct at the spectator. White's seduction was the slow wooing of a man who understood his own pleasures.

Now, as the date marking the end of Evelyn's first year in Manhattan approached, White gradually convinced Mrs Nesbit to take some days to reacquaint herself with Pittsburgh and leave Evelyn in his care. Reluctant at first, the woman soon succumbed, invoking Evelyn to see no one but Mr White during her absence and to obey him. Indeed, as Evelyn writes in her memoir, 'He dominated me by his kindness and by his authority.' He dominated her mother too, who might have known better.

A few days after Mrs Nesbit's departure, White took Evelyn to Rudolf Eickemeyer's studio. Choosing her costumes himself, White had her photographed as a Turkish maiden, a demure Quaker girl, as

Little Red Riding-Hood and Little Bo-Peep, and finally in a lavish Japanese kimono on a bear rug where, exhausted after hours of posing, Evelyn fell asleep and gave Eickemeyer one of his most famous photographs of her as Little Miss Butterfly. A day or two later, Stanny's hold over Evelyn took on a new configuration.

Invited to a party in his 24th Street rooms, not for the first time Evelyn found herself alone. Stanny entertained her with tales, and this time she was allowed a second glass of champagne. When she wanted to go home, he suggested she stay, and took her up to a mirrored room she had never visited before. Tapestry hangings gave way to a four-poster bed, it too surrounded by mirrors on three sides, and on the ceiling rows of tiny differently coloured bulbs producing lighting in rose and blue – like a nymph's palace under the sea, Evelyn later wrote. Then came more drink, tasting bitter this time, but Stanny told her to drink up. After a few moments a 'curious sensation' overcame her. She felt 'dizzy and sick' and the room and its objects grew 'blurred and indistinct'. In her 1934 memoir she adds that Harry Thaw later maintained that the wine had been drugged, but she never altogether believed it.

Whatever the case, when she next woke, Stanny lay beside her exposing 'the naked body of his naked sins' still more or less in 'the full flush of his extraordinary physical powers'. She screamed in terror, started to cry in her confusion. A tender Stanny comforted her: 'Don't cry Kittens . . . Please don't. It's all over. Now, you belong to me.' He had good reason to try to comfort her. Under the law, since Evelyn was under eighteen, he had committed statutory rape.

Distressed as she might have been at the time, Evelyn never damned White for his 'deflowering' of her. Since she had fallen asleep, induced into unconsciousness either by far more champagne than she had ever drunk or by a drug slipped into it, she had never given her consent. But Evelyn was not one to press rape charges. In her 1914 memoir she wrote what she had earlier stated at the trial, 'Not even for the purpose of pleasing those who demand, according to the rules of melodrama, a more bitter and more prejudiced view, can I represent him other than he was. His failing we know – it was his one failing.'

That night, Stanny's making much of her didn't assuage Evelyn. She was in something like shock. Sex just wasn't talked about, so it was difficult to make sense of. She went home distressed, feeling 'nothing, neither repulsion nor hate'. An aspect of life had been revealed to her in a flash and changed her perspective on everything. Eventually, as she pondered Stanny's ways, this 'generously big man', who was kind and tender, yet 'preyed on the defenceless', she decided, 'He was a prodigious vampire.'

When he came to plead with her the next day, Evelyn sat very still. He explained to her that all people behaved like this: she translated him to mean that everybody was bad, but she must go on as if nothing had happened, since the worst sin of all was to be found out. Appearances were all. It was a difficult lesson for a slip of a girl. She continued to sit in stony silence, a numb, hollowed presence. But she listened to Stanny's voice of seductive authority and blocked out what was also a betrayal. Her childhood had taught her to swallow hard, say nothing, and move on. She might have lost that great female prize of virginity, but something in her prevented morbid introspection and utter defeat. White was like an 'earthquake', she wrote, a natural force. There was no resisting. You could only pick up the pieces and carry on.

Evelyn carried on, and she fell in love all over again with the charming, inventive Stanny who, for a little while, was utterly taken with his heart-rending child-woman whose praises the papers crooned – that 'fluttering fair flower of American girlhood' who had 'blossomed in a mud puddle'. He would tremble when he touched her, she wrote, he wanted her so naked, he took the pins out of her hair, all the while cultivating his Galatea, sometimes arranging her in poses that mimicked the world's great paintings or sculptures, or setting her gently, naked, on his red velvet swing. They laughed, talked and loved.

White's undoubted assets as a patron combined with Evelyn's own talents saw her into her next role, in a production called *The Wild Rose*.

Here, she played a winsome Gypsy girl. Promoted as 'a fresh and fascinating theatrical find', Evelyn made more headlines. They feted her birthday together in the Garden apartment, just before Christmas 1902: presented in a huge red velvet stocking were white fox furs, diamond rings and pearls. Evelyn dubbed White 'Stanny Claus', which he certainly was to her whole family . . . and the gifts and treats continued all year long.

But she grew restless with White's secretiveness, his constantly roving eye for new and fresh talent, even if she never complained of his marriage. Yet none of the 'millionaires' who wooed her had White's artistic ways and intelligence. It took the attentions of the handsome twenty-one-year-old actor John Barrymore to make her suddenly feel the attractions of a youthful and open romance – so open indeed that the papers happily charted the progress of their relations. For a brief while they 'did Broadway' together, but young Jack didn't have a penny to his name. When Mrs Nesbit found out about the romance, she upbraided her daughter, even going to White to ask for help in chastizing her! White did nothing, perhaps because he had been growing worried about the frenetic activity of the anti-vice brigades and his ongoing relations with an underage girl whom the newspapers adored. Then, too, he had severe financial worries and was overcommitted. Evelyn was distressed at his lack of any manifest jealousy, and like the teenager she was, pushed him and herself further.

It was only after Jack and Evelyn spent an entire drunken (but apparently chaste) night together, something that she had somehow never done with White, that on Mrs Nesbit's inducement White reacted. First he sent Evelyn straight to the doctor's, where she spent a day refusing to be examined. It's unclear whether White wanted to blame her missing hymen on Jack, or was worried that she might be pregnant, since she had been complaining of stomach cramps. In any event, White called the pair to the tower and reprimanded Barrymore for smearing Evelyn's reputation. The youth surprised everyone by asking Evelyn to marry him. She stammered out an inconclusive answer, and White asked what two kids like them would live on.

Barrymore promptly said, 'Love.' White 'got very mad and purple', took her aside to remind her that she wanted to be an actress – and to warn that there was insanity in Barrymore's family. Standing up to him, Evelyn told him she would do what she pleased.

Almost immediately after this scene, with the complicity of Mrs Nesbit who feared the youngsters might elope, Evelyn was told by White that, come October, her education needed to be seen to. She was being banished from New York to an all-girls' boarding school in New Jersey, run by a Mrs DeMille (mother of the future director). The papers talked of an interruption in her career while she followed her mother's strict orders.

It was during this difficult period of her life, while Evelyn was rebelling against White, all the while wanting his attentions, that she met Harry Thaw. He appeared first under the pseudonym of Mr Munroe, one amongst the innumerable array of stage-door suitors who sought the fetching young woman's notice. Thaw had first seen Evelyn in *Floradora*, probably alerted to her precisely because she had been selected out by Stanford White. Having watched her in some forty performances of the *The Wild Rose*, he began his suit by writing her anonymous letters. Thaw had learned of Evelyn's tastes by sending his Pinkerton detectives to spy on her: he proclaimed a love of animals and books. But Evelyn refused to meet him: she really had no interest in these fans. Thaw congratulated her on her refusal to meet strangers. It was now that he identified himself as Mr Munroe and put twenty-dollar bills in the letters he sent her. Evelyn returned them, as well as on one occasion flowers wrapped in a $50 bill – though her mother, ever hungry for cash, kept that bill without her knowing.

Imitating a Stanford White tactic, Thaw, still as Mr Munroe, through another chorine invited Evelyn to an 'early dinner' at Rector's Restaurant. Ever happy to eat, Evelyn accepted the distraction: she was depressed over her imminent removal to the New Jersey boarding school.

31. *The Pittsburgh Millionaire*

In his decidedly odd and peripatetic self-published memoir *The Traitor*, dedicated to his mother 'who stood by me to the last', Harry K. Thaw arrives at his first meeting with Evelyn about a third of the way through the book – after *Boy's Own* drinking bouts in Harvard, playboy treks across the name-dropping heights and depths of France, Switzerland, Austria and Hungary, and (largely failed) adventures in scaling the social heights of New York and Newport. Of his first encounter with the woman who so dramatically altered his life, Harry writes, in his idiosyncratic manner:

> It was good to see her. But I had heard of Stanford White, and I told her she should keep away from him, that he was very ugly, and not only that, he was married . . . She liked my wrists and hands. I was wrong, for I said my wrists should be thicker, and she said she was sorry as she liked mine, but she agreed with me.

Evelyn's recollection of this meeting is rather different. She is all ready to leave because 'Mr Munroe' is late, and she only stays because of the intermediary's insistence.

When Munroe does appear, he falls dramatically to his knees before her and kisses the hem of her skirts. Astonished and slightly repelled, Evelyn darts back and the man leaps to his full six foot two. At first, seeing him in his impeccable suit, she thinks he looks 'sweet', but at second glance there is something unsettling about the combination of manly height and child's podgy, unshaped face: she focuses on his smooth hands, which evidently 'had never labored at all in his thirty-two years'. Thaw's 'goo-goo eyes', silly grin and snub nose give the impression of a face that is both odd and has 'a sinister brutality about the mouth'. He gestures extravagantly and talks non-stop, his subjects piling one on top of the other, while he blinks frenetically. Evelyn reflects that this was a man who 'took his position in life very seriously and his world value too seriously'. When she contradicts his insulting view about a friend of hers who, he says, is 'fat', then his insistence that women shouldn't allow themselves to put on 'flesh', he seems utterly taken aback. Evelyn is by turn irritated and amused. In a comment as astute as that pronounced by any of Thaw's later psychiatrists, Evelyn writes in her first memoir: 'Men who acclaim their own importance persistently and with no sign of hesitation as to their own conviction on the subject cease to be nobodies and become somebodies. And the egotism which prompted Harry's sentences and which appeared in all his dealings with the remainder of humanity at once fascinated and annoyed.'

Harry Thaw, the delinquent millionaire, was rarely challenged by young women. If Evelyn was relieved to see the back of him and, as she told her intermediary, had no interest in seeing Munroe again, Harry was hardly a man who could be described as susceptible to cues. The next day, he was pressing his attentions on Mrs Nesbit, who had no trouble in recognizing a face she had often enough seen in the Pittsburgh papers. Indeed, at the lowest moment of her life she had been to the Thaw mansion to plead for rescue funds for her family, but had been turned away unceremoniously by Mrs Thaw, who on the whole didn't dispense charity that didn't earn her recognition.

Harry K. Thaw (1871–1947) was the eldest son of the Pittsburgh railway baron William Thaw (1818–89) and his second wife Mary Sibbet Copley. Perhaps because there had been a male child before Harry who had died in early infancy (purportedly smothered by the ample Mary's breast), Mary Thaw spoiled her surviving eldest and was ever ready to pull him out of disreputable scraps. His father was distant, stern and disciplinarian in the way of Victorian fathers. If trial evidence is to be believed, Harry was definitely an odd child, ever prone to twitching and temper tantrums – during which, following the maternal cue, he would hurl heavy objects at the servants. He suffered from sleeplessness and a kind of unstoppable erratic speech, punctuated by the baby talk he used throughout his life. There may have been some innate brain condition or an ingrained pattern of behaviour from earliest childhood, but whatever the reason, Harry Thaw was never less than peculiar. Teachers found him unteachable and he was moved from school to school: one later testified to his 'zigzag' walk, perhaps reflecting his erratic brain patterns.

Sent to Harvard, Thaw boasts in his autobiography that he spent his time boozing, womanizing, watching cockfights and playing poker, while lighting his cigars with hundred-dollar bills, and once even chasing a man who had cheated him out of 10 cents down the street with a shotgun (unloaded). He was expelled for 'immoral practices', despite his father's millions. He studied law, which he didn't take to, at Pittsburgh, and was only saved from bringing further ignominy on his family by being sent abroad. Though news of his antics in Europe, and his gargantuan expenditure, reached home soon enough.

Thaw's 'immoral practices' were exposed to Evelyn and the world only piecemeal. They had hitherto been successfully veiled by his millions and by the family's efficiency in finding lawyers to buy out the victims of Harry's excesses. But his sadistic orgies, which employed whips and handcuffs, were known to any number of 'thin' young women he had brutalized and paid for, as well as to the madames who supplied them.

In Paris, he was recognized as the most 'perversely profligate' member of the American colony. In the Tenderloin he would pose as a professor and have underage would-be actresses sent to him for 'tutoring': this included being tied to chairs, handcuffed, whipped and simultaneously harangued. Sometimes leg-irons were involved, or bathtub scaldings, a procedure that earned him the name 'Bathtub Harry' and might just have related back to those fraternity practices at Harvard, not unrelated to the form of torture that goes by the name 'waterboarding'. Around the time of Thaw's second trial, a woman called Susie Merrill who ran a house of ill-repute provided an affidavit relating to Harry's perverse practices over a period of two years and with more than two hundred girls. Merrill disappeared mysteriously before she could have her day in court, though she reappeared later.

Harry also had a penchant for boys. In London, after one bellhop lodged a complaint that he had been lured into Thaw's room, bound, placed in a bathtub, had boiling water poured over him and been whiplashed into near-unconsciousness, some five thousand dollars had to be paid out. On his trips to Europe, Harry ran through valets, too, with great speed: during his trial, the one who had served him longest at home suffered a sudden and mysterious death, perhaps because there was too much that he could reveal, most of it outrageously sadistic.

Whether he performed his brutal acts in a manic fugue or in a drugged state, whether he successfully split them off from the life his mother (and he) approved, readily disavowing them while he led his ordinary existence under cover of an idealized self image and unreconcilable notions of good and bad – or whether he lied and deluded himself in some simpler way – is inevitably difficult to penetrate at this distance. What is certainly clear is that for Harry Thaw Stanford White stood for all the bad he couldn't acknowledge in his own life.

Thaw's obsession with White had come into being at the cusp of the century. It may have coincided with or been exaggerated by his use of cocaine, a substance it is almost certain he injected, given his behavioural patterns and the fact that Evelyn had found a syringe amidst his things. But there are other elements in play in Thaw's obsession. As the constant name-dropping in his memoir underscores, he had taken on his mother's aspiration to be accepted by the crème – the Fishes, the Vanderbilts, the Astors. Neither he nor his mother were of that class, and the fact rankled – dangerously, in Harry's case. Nor was Harry, expelled from Harvard and known for his bullying antics, allowed into New York's elite men-only clubs. The one club that had him as a member, the Union League Club of New York, revoked his membership when he rode a horse up its front steps and through the front doors.

Thaw became convinced that his rejection by the New York elite was all due to Stanford White, the cultivated *bon viveur* who was welcomed by the mighty and went unpunished for vices that the young scion of strict Pittsburgh Presbyterians shared, but couldn't allow himself to admit. In a paranoid twist, White became Thaw's double: he had what Thaw secretly wished for and wasn't permitted. So he imagined White was persecuting him for those same unconscious wishes: White's agents followed him, he said, and the architect had turned Manhattan against him.

An instance that could only have exacerbated the situation occurred when Thaw invited a showgirl with her fellow lovelies to a gala party he was throwing for his circle. Just before, lunching with a respectable friend from his social, not his sexual, world, he had refused to recognize the woman when he saw her at a restaurant. Angered by the slight, she took her party girls to a gathering at White's tower instead, while Thaw waited in vain for the 'girls' he had promised his friends.

Now, a humiliated Harry knew for certain that the world had to be rid of White. It was White, he was convinced, who had set out to shame him. Who had turned both the woman and all of New York society against him. If Harry could rid the world of White, that despoiler of virgins, he, Harry, would become the city's saviour. He sent both money and information to Anthony Comstock so that the vice-hunter's agents would follow White and out him. He was convinced that White was having him followed in turn, and setting his own agents against him.

Historical moments and their social mores undoubtedly affect both the expression of psychological disorder and the terms in which it is understood. Harry Thaw is a figure contemporaneous with Krafft-Ebing's expositions of criminal perversion and paranoia, as well as Freud's first reflections on the subject. On 24 January 1895, Freud had written to Wilhelm Fliess suggesting that 'people become paranoid over things they cannot put up with'. Paranoia in this light begins as a defence against painful experiences, particularly of embarrassment or humiliation, which could destroy the ego. When there is an internal change, the subject has to make a choice as to whether the cause is internal or external: the paranoid person, in order to preserve his narcissism whole, or prevent any experience of deficiency within the self, attributes it to the external, 'what people know about us and . . . have done to us'. Grandiosity is part of the clinical picture, as is a distinct emphasis on projection onto the other of the defects one cannot afford or bear to see in oneself. Harry projects his own envious hatred onto White, imagines himself both hated and in danger, and so needs to strike out at the vile predator first.

32. Pursuing Evelyn

How did the young, but relatively sensible, Evelyn allow herself to become prey to Harry Thaw's designs?

With the punishment of removal to Mrs DeMille's school awaiting her, the romance with Barrymore over and the sense that White was tiring of her, Evelyn was more susceptible than she might otherwise have been to Thaw's pursuit of her. About a week after their first meeting, they met again at a pre-theatre supper party when Mr Munroe sat next to her. On the way to the theatre, he unveiled himself as Harry Kendall Thaw of Pittsburgh. According to Evelyn, the revelation was full of theatrical panache and pride. He clearly assumed, as if he were like some Superman emerging from his disguise as Clark Kent, not only that Evelyn would now instantly recognize him, but that she would also instantly acquiesce to his suit.

Evelyn was only very hazily aware of Harry's dark side. Her own mother's adamant objection to his attentions, perhaps in part fuelled by Stanford White's disapproval and a greater knowledge of the millionaire's background, only elicited rebellion in the young woman. It allowed her to see the more gentlemanly aspects of Thaw, what she eventually called his 'kind, sweet, generous, and gentle side'. She often thought of him as something of a large child; his propensity towards idées fixes and explosions had not yet become visible, though, of course, he had told her to beware of Stanford White. In this, Thaw, as she put it, 'played at the reformer with all the enthusiasm of a Savonarola'. Harry also encouraged her return to school and seemed to be genuinely interested in her well-being.

Just before she left for New Jersey, in October 1903, Harry proposed marriage. Evelyn refused. Her life was already too complicated.

She got on well at school, where the other girls loved the fact that she was an actress. Thaw wrote moralizing letters and Stanny, when she didn't see him in New York, came to visit – though after one racy excursion with classmates in a fast car with Stanny at the wheel, parents complained vehemently and demanded that Evelyn be sent home. While Mrs DeMille was trying to decide how to handle the situation, Evelyn fell seriously ill with stomach pains and vomiting. The school nurse rang her mother and told her it might well be appendicitis. When Mrs Nesbit, who always contacted White when any problem arose, tried to reach him, he was out of town. No one knows if she hesitated before ringing Harry Thaw, recently back in New York after some months on the French Riviera.

Thaw was at his best in an emergency that demanded money be thrown at it. A leading doctor and two nurses were instantly found, a makeshift operating theatre was set up in a classroom; then chloroform was administered and Evelyn was operated on, apparently for a burst appendix. There were rumours that the operation was in fact an abortion, but Evelyn denied this under oath at the trial, as did Barrymore. Whatever the exact nature of the ordeal, it soon robbed Evelyn of her wondrous hair, which fell out in clumps and had to be shaved off. Thaw promised expensive wigs. We might wonder whether Harry perhaps preferred her as a brush-haired boy, something she herself intuited: seeing herself in her short hair, Evelyn thought she looked exactly like her little brother. Incongruously, Harry then chose a blond wig for Evelyn, perhaps in an attempt to baffle White and an ever inquisitive press, who loved nothing more than stories of their favourite pin-up.

Evelyn's operation, and the morphine and laudanum given to her afterwards, left her gravely weakened and as a consequence indebted to an attentive Thaw. He now made a concerted play for her, offering her and her mother a recuperative cruise on an ocean liner, topped by a trip to the European capitals Evelyn had long wanted to visit. White had sung their cultivating charms and Evelyn was keen at the prospect. Her mother, reluctant at first, accepted, not realizing that Thaw planned to accompany them, if initially on a different liner.

Despite Thaw's millions, Mrs Nesbit remained loyal to the charming Stanford White, who never proposed to her daughter, but supported her son. She would fall out with Thaw even more severely during their stay in Europe, accusing him of exhausting her daughter with his manic form of travel.

She returned home without Evelyn, despite voicing her worries about her daughter's reputation, to complain bitterly to White, who had given her and Evelyn a letter of credit in case they needed it during their travels. Mrs Nesbit's dislike of Thaw was returned by him; when he heard from an embarrassed Evelyn about White's long arm, he promptly tore up the letter of credit.

In his memoir, Thaw underscores how Mrs Nesbit continually let her daughter down, first of all in closing her eyes to her relations with Stanford White, then in abandoning her without a chaperone in Europe. Whatever his proclivities and state of mind, Thaw was ever alert to reputation, and would have been happy to blame the hapless Mrs Nesbit for a good portion of Evelyn's downfall. But since Evelyn defended her 'naive' mother, and remained loyal at least until the trial, he couldn't condemn Mrs Nesbit outright.

Thaw had proposed to Evelyn before the voyage. Evelyn had refused, as she was to refuse again in London and again in Paris, whatever pressure a peristent Harry applied. She couldn't marry a man unless he knew everything there was to know about her, she wrote. 'This was a matter of common honesty, and I take no credit for desiring to be frank and above board with my future husband.' Perhaps, too, she was instinctively fearful of Thaw's obsession with virginity, which manifested itself early in their relations – though she didn't then realize that he already surmised the nature of her relations with White in his 'lust nest', having had the architect watched even before he had formally met Evelyn. On top of that, something in Harry's manner when the bellboy incident came to light, whatever gloss he put on it, may have frightened Evelyn. Tempting as it might be to succumb to a millionaire who would provide that ever-elusive sense of security she so needed, particularly now that Stanny was less attentive, Evelyn resisted.

Whether her resistance had anything to do with spurring on the bellhop incident is unclear. The perverse Thaw had set a brutal trap for the boy. He called him to his hotel room, left money lying in a tempting heap on a table, and hid. Thinking himself alone, the duped boy dipped into the cash. Harry leapt out, heaved him into the bathtub, stripped and flogged him, perhaps more. The legal claim afterwards had Thaw settling for damages. Plaintively, he told Evelyn this was ever the fate of the millionaire: people exaggerated stories and made claims for injury.

Harry continued to hound his 'Angel-Child', demanding to know why she wouldn't have him. Torn apart by the battling between Harry and her mother, further debilitated by Harry's frenetic partying pace and constant changing of hotels even in the same city, as well as frightened of the explosive violence he could exude in his bullying and his agitated pacing up and down, ever accompanied by wayward babble – Evelyn, primed by drink, finally gave in one night to his direct question: 'Is it because of Stanford White?'

She then told him the story of the girl on the red velvet swing, the drink, the possible drugging, the deflowering. This was the very narrative that was later allowed into court because, despite its licentious content, it laid the ground for what purportedly had provoked Thaw to murder the older man and to avenge his by then wife's honour. For Thaw, Evelyn's story provided confirmation of everything he had imagined about White and the vicious prodigality of the 'Beast' he both loathed and desired to be, the 'ravisher' who 'boasted of having taken advantage of three hundred and seventy-eight girls'.

In the course of the long, stammering, tearful narrative of her 'filthy ruin', Evelyn revealed how she had been innocently seduced; how, when her mother had left her in White's care, he had fed her champagne; how he had 'had his way with her' while she was unconscious; how she had then stayed with Stanhope White despite all of that. As she described it in her first memoir, Harry's response was to gape open-mouthed, to shudder, to go limp – and when she had reached the climax of her story, to rise, then plunge into a chair and sob loudly, muttering 'Poor child!' repeatedly. Then he began to shake uncontrollably, his face 'ghastly' as he walked up and down the room, gesticulating and muttering. He made wounded-animal noises while she wept. He wrung his hands and gnashed his teeth. He questioned her about her mother, accusing Mrs Nesbit of terrible negligence, assuring Evelyn that no decent person hearing her story would say it was her own doing. She was not at fault. His respect for her had not lessened, he would always be her friend.

As the dark night dragged on and then turned into morning, an exhausted Evelyn clutched at her scars while Thaw cursed Stanford White, whom he had of course suspected all along of foul deeds. The more he pressed Evelyn to confess, the more he rambled on incoherently. When she had finished, he knelt at her side and took her hand. Evelyn states that she was utterly swayed by him then, 'all that was best in Harry Thaw . . . all the womanliness in him, all the Quixote that was in his composition' was then evident. In *The Traitor*, Thaw wrote that his Angel-Child's 'hideously awful tale' was one in which she had never acted of 'her own volition unless she had refused point blank her mother's order to obey a beast'.

But Thaw's gentleness, once he had Evelyn to himself and totally in his sway, metamorphosed in grotesque ways. His references to virginity escalated. At Joan of Arc's birthplace he wrote in the guestbook, 'she would not have been a virgin if Stanford White had been around'. He showed Evelyn all the statues of saints and martyrs who had chosen to die rather than give in to sin. His idée fixe and his wild murmuring made her increasingly nervous. They didn't share rooms, either in Holland or on their restless travels along the Rhine to Munich and Innsbruck, a journey that did Evelyn's health no good.

Then Harry rented a lonely castle in the Tyrol, Schloss Katzenstein, for three weeks. At first Evelyn, her youthful imagination steeped in romance and musical comedy, had fantasized a romantic retreat in which her exhaustion would dissipate and she would finally be able to convalesce. Instead, the castle was up a steep mountain and remote from everywhere, made of cold stone, dimly lit, and with long drafty

corridors. It came with a staff of two who lived at one end, while
Harry and Evelyn had separate rooms at the other. Evelyn had entered
a Gothic horror in which the all but orphaned damsel was at the
mercy of a monstrous Bluebeard.

On the second night of their stay, after a long day of sightseeing in
the forest nearby, Harry dismissed the servants with 'high-handed
Teutonic severity'. Tired, Evelyn ate quickly, and having accepted the
usual chaste goodnight kiss on the forehead, she went to bed. Wig
off, nightie on, she fell asleep instantly, only to be abruptly woken a
very short time after by an apparition. A stark-naked Harry was loom-
ing above her, a leather riding crop in his hand. Its slash across her legs
was what had woken her, and now she leapt up with a scream as a
raging, 'bug-eyed' Harry tore off her clothes, all the while landing
violent blows on her body with his crop.

Later, Evelyn thought that the sight of her thin naked body, so like
a boy's with its shorn hair, excited him all the more. In any event, no
protest or pleading could persuade him to lessen the blows. Quite the
reverse. Her pleas spurred him on. His pupils were vast and he was
sweating profusely. All the while, a diatribe against sin and indecency
poured from his lips. Evelyn had the impression he couldn't hear her,
nor always recognize her. She stood in for all nether and immoral
beings, perhaps for himself too. At the end, he threw her, bleeding,
back onto the bed and, pinning her down with his riding crop, raped
her. His railing never stopped. Punishment, penance, retribution,
Stanford White, virginity – Thaw's preoccupations were ever on his
lips.

Evelyn wrote that as she faded in and out of consciousness, and
wondered whether her life was about to end in Schloss Katzenstein,
she also thought that this must be her punishment for what she had
revealed about White and herself; and for allowing herself to accept
Thaw's generosity.

Inquisition followed rape, as if she weren't sufficiently battered.
'Did you really believe White when he told you everybody did the
things you had done? Did you? Is it possible?' Evelyn, barely sixteen

when she first met White, stammered a 'Yes'. Thaw rose to his full height and, towering above her, looked as if he were about to land more blows. Instead he raged: That was a lie, a dirty lie. There were many pure and decent women in the world – 'his mother and his two lovely, decent sisters' prime amongst them.

The splitting of women into two – the chaste and the sullied – so pervasive at the time, is hardly altogether gone today. There are those pure women who are untouchable and to be respected and who are beyond desire; and those who are desired, desiring and thus dirty, but who alone can provide sexual satisfaction for the male. Evelyn suffered from this split at the hands of Harry Thaw. Nor would his obsession with the purity he himself so lacked cease with his punishment of her.

After Evelyn's trial by flogging and brutal rape, Harry Thaw locked her into her castle room and left her, bruised, bloodied and helpless. Without her mother, without friends or funds, she was effectively a hostage. Like so many abused women, she both felt that the punishment was somehow deserved and was terrified that the avenging Thaw would return to her room. For some three weeks, she didn't leave it. The only medication for her welts, cuts and scabs was a stinging ointment that an utterly unrepentant Harry applied. He acted as if nothing was amiss. But he did not attack her again.

At the end of that time, he took her to Zürich. There, one day, he 'exploded' into blind rage once more. He had been accused of having pushed a carriage off the road with his rented car. As ever, he was in denial. He exonerated himself, blanked and twisted matters, so that the event became one that he had seen only from a distance. The world had it in for millionaires, forcing them to pay for everything. In fact Thaw's lawyers paid out hush money. Evelyn was reminded of the episode with the bellboy in the London hotel and of her own brutal rape. This was never mentioned by a daytime Harry, adept at splitting and defending himself against his own worst excesses.

When, worried about her lacerated body and her operation scars, Evelyn asked to see a doctor, she soon realized that the physician knew Thaw from previous trips and was in his pay: he never commented on her scars and bruises. Trapped, apprehensive, in a state akin to shock, Evelyn was now forced to accompany Thaw on moralizing trips up the 'virginal' Jungfrau.

In his memoir, Harry comments on her unhappiness but never attributes it to his own actions, all the while sermonizing about Stanford White: 'I remember poor Evelyn crying because we could not settle down to live like other people. I did too; but you know when a girl dies one is saddened to think how pretty and happy she might have been ... and yet it is a hundred times worse when it is not death but the hellish selfishness of Stanford White that ruins girls' lives.' In the murky reaches of Thaw's mind the battle of good and evil, projected outwards, puts all the evil on White's side. Death, for ravished girls at least, is better than immorality.

In Paris, Evelyn met some acquaintances. She broke down and recounted her story. They determined that she should return with them to New York. Probably realizing that if his relations with an underage girl were made public, he could be prosecuted, Harry allowed her to go, paying her fare, as well as for a chaperone.

Home in New York, life proved difficult for a strained and still suffering Evelyn. She was estranged from her mother, who was now only interested in pursuing her affair with an old admirer whom she would soon marry. Mrs Nesbit had claimed that Evelyn had been kidnapped into going to Europe with Thaw. White knew better, but pretended not to. After a chance encounter with Evelyn on the street, he insisted on seeing her and revealed what he should emphatically have told her about Thaw beforehand – that the 'Pennsylvania pug' was dangerous, that he took morphine and other substances, that his habits were less than salubrious.

After hearing more of the same from others, Evelyn stayed away from Thaw, but it was not clear that she could rely on White either. Despite his help in finding work for her, Evelyn recognized that her charm and hold over him had waned. She was almost eighteen now, bruised, battered, no longer quite the little girl White had fallen for.

The fact that she was still legally underage, however, made her potentially dangerous to both men. White, without explaining to her what he was doing, had her see the notorious lawyer, the 'slimy shyster' Abe Hummel, a frightening dwarf-like man, who would eventually be disbarred. Having elicited the story of her terrible adventure with Thaw, Hummel embroidered it with even greater dramatic violence and represented it to her as an affidavit to be signed. He recommended that she use it against Thaw in a breach-of-promise suit. A frightened but honest Evelyn refused, claiming she was the one who had not agreed to marry Thaw, not the other way round. Then White, who sensed that the ever truthful Evelyn could well have exposed him to a suit for immorality through her relations with Thaw, asked her if she had any letters from Harry. These, like her affidavit, would give him bargaining power, if the matter were ever revealed.

Evelyn continued to be pulled apart by the two men, each fearing that the other might trump him in her favours and in revelations about illicit acts.

After she had refused to see him for some time, Harry came to her in his kind and gentle guise. He offered her a weekly allowance if she gave up the play she was in. In response to his pleading, she eventually handed him some of Stanford White's letters to her. Thaw was on his best behaviour. At home in Pittsburgh without Evelyn during the time that she wouldn't see him, he had fallen into so marked a depression that his mother feared suicide. She hardly wanted a rank chorus girl, or, in her words, 'a social-climbing soubrette', in the family and had thus far refused to give her son permission to marry the woman she saw as a fortune-hunting strumpet. Now recognizing the scale of her son's obsession, the ever snobbish Mrs Thaw melted a little. As for Harry, once Evelyn allowed him access, he sought to prove that he was no longer the man who had whipped her and locked her inside a cold castle room. All that was only because Stanford White had driven him to madness. He even paid for Evelyn to take a European study trip without him, accompanied by a chaperone: to gain the tight-laced

Mrs Thaw's favour, not to mention her purity-loving son's, Evelyn had
to give up the stage.

Finally, like some of the other attractive chorus girls of the time,
Evelyn made her decision to become a 'mistress of millions' and move
into the financial security that she had lost with her father's death
when she was ten. Sanctioned by his mother, Harry K. Thaw was prepared to have her, despite the stain 'the Beast' had cast over 'Boofuls's'
past. On 4 April 1905, they were married. Harry had decreed his bride
wear black – an 'opera coat trimmed in rare lace with Persian floral
designs and a velvet hat with a silk entwined brim and a gorgeous
feather of three shades of brown'. Evelyn might well explain to
reporters that the absence of white was due to the couple's haste to
depart on their honeymoon, but Harry's taste had a distinct shade of
punishment about it, certainly of mourning for some lost hymen.

They took up residence in a wing of what was according to Evelyn
the charmless, damp, gloomy, ivy-clad Thaw mansion in Pittsburgh.
This was the very same 'Lyndhurst' that Mrs Nesbit had come to some
ten years back to beg for charity. That fact brought Evelyn no sense of
triumph.

For the first months of their marriage, played out under the con-
straining maternal wing, Harry was a pious, virtuous son – and a
largely patient, tactful husband, expending his energies on charity
work for the Presbyterian church that figured so large in his mother's
eyes. Evelyn found the life there one of mindless tedium, and rank
with hypocrisies. There was a regular procession of ministers whose
wives 'said things with a monotony and a sameness which leads me to
suppose that there existed somewhere in America a school for ministers' wives where they were taught to say the same things in identical
terms'. The Thaws themselves were utter materialists, hardly 'intel-
lectually and socially among the gods'. It's clear that Evelyn missed
Stanford White's cultivated intelligence and taste, let alone the excitements of New York life. As any young woman might, she had hoped in
marrying Thaw that there would be not only stability, but also the
chance of trips to Europe, balls and shopping sprees. Now there was

only boredom, and towards the end of 1905 the reawakening of Harry's crusade to do away with his very own fiery dragon, Stanford White.

Thaw now started a correspondence with the vice-hunting Anthony Comstock and paid for a campaign to expose White. The very process of surveillance increased his own anxieties: he grew convinced that the older man was out to kill him and had hired members of the infamous Monk Eastman gang to carry out the murder. A paranoid Harry began to tote a gun. He did target practice at the back of the house.

In conjunction with the gun toting came renewed and assiduous questioning of Evelyn whenever they were alone. Harry would wake her in the middle of the night and demand the narrative of her life with Stanny. He wanted details of every aspect of her modelling and her meetings with White, and in particular of the fatal night, repeated over and over again. The repetition aroused him and terrified Evelyn, not on behalf of the man she was now only allowed to call 'the Beast', but on her own behalf. Harry was patently jealous and obsessed with White: Evelyn's ravishment was 'never absent from his mind'. Imitating the more powerful man, he had Evelyn photographed by various professionals. Usually, he wanted his Angel Child dressed as an innocent girl in frilly white. But in the set of photographs that most excited him, Evelyn appears bodiless, only her 'decapitated' head visible through the hole in a sheet, her hair pinned up above. 'I am Bluebeard,' an excited Harry had declared as he rushed her into this particular photo session. On another day, he forced her to the dentist's: he had directed the man to undo all the work Stanford White had first had carried out on her. It took over a month.

No surprise that Evelyn had begun 'to fear for his reason', and increasingly for herself. But on 25 June 1906, when Harry K. Thaw used his gun for more than target practice, it was 'the Beast' he aimed at and not his 'Boofuls'.

33. The Trial of the Century

Six months passed before Harry K. Thaw came to court, on 23 January 1907. What unfolded over the following months came to be dubbed in the far-flung newspaper coverage, 'the Trial of the Century': America's entire value system was in the dock. Beliefs, morals, hypocrisies were openly and widely debated. What constituted masculine and feminine virtue? What did wealth permit? What was bad and what mad? What depraved and what deranged?

The Europeans, too, were interested. The criminologist Cesare Lombroso weighed in with a long-distance diagnosis of Harry Thaw. In an article in the *New York World* that month he analysed photographs of Thaw and, true to his own preferred diagnoses, named him 'a true epileptic moral maniac' whose 'revenge and hatred are excited by the smallest causes or even without any apparent cause'. Lombroso had deduced all this from the sparseness of his beard, the lobeless ear close to the head, 'the species of forehead that bulges on the right temple . . . the great projection of the jaw . . . The nose . . . is somewhat displaced to one side.'

At the pre-trial hearing before the Grand Jury, just after the coroner's inquest, Evelyn had adamantly protested that they could send her to jail but she would not testify against her husband. 'I will never do anything to harm Harry,' the loyal wife measuring five foot nothing stated. She was as good as her word, but in telling the truth of her story so cogently she rocked the strongholds of the rich and their armour of moral rectitude, as well as introducing America to a new kind of woman. Little wonder that in giving Evelyn fictional life, the novelist E. L. Doctorow counterpoints her with the free-thinking anarchist Emma Goldman. If Evelyn was a bad girl, then 'bad' had to take on new meanings. Meanwhile, Harry

Thaw's murderous rectitude brought into the public sphere a psycho-sexual dynamic that only the mind doctors would want to label 'mad' – rather than, as many papers initially thought, heroically virtuous.

Some thousand people thronged outside the Criminal Branch of the Supreme Court of New York, hoping to catch a glimpse of the star players as they drove up and made their way into the courtroom; or indeed, as a clean-shirted Harry, whose waiting time in prison had been eased by meals sent in from Delmonico's, by whiskey and by workouts with barbells, made his way across the Bridge of Sighs. The court was packed with extra chairs for the huge numbers of witnesses, family members, possible jurors and reporters. The media frenzy hadn't let up and it continued during the many months and more of this 'Trial of the Century'. As had happened with the earlier trial of Dreyfus in France, a special telegraph room was set up in the main hall of the court: proceedings were 'being reported to the ends of the civilized globe', the *New York Times* commented.

So heated and sensationalist was the media build-up, so intent was America on thinking about itself afresh and debating its vices and virtues through the trial's key players, that for the first time in history an American judge, Justice James Fitzgerald, sequestered the jury, once it was finally selected after two weeks of careful consideration. If free to leave the court precincts, the jury's views would inevitably be influenced by what they might read. So instead, they were housed under guard at the Broadway Central Hotel, and could not see their families except under supervision.

Once Evelyn's clear and moving account of her relations with Stanford White and the fatal night of her undoing was allowed in as evidence for the defence, as well as eventually her ordeal with Harry Thaw at the Schloss Katzenstein, it seemed there was little other news left in America for the papers and magazines to headline. This was explosively sexual material of a kind never before made quite so public in newspapers available to women, and in certain instances through articles that had been written by women. The religious lobby from as far away as Tennessee grew heated. President Theodore Roosevelt was asked to censor the coverage. Roosevelt was indeed worried about the printing of the 'full disgusting particulars' of Evelyn's testimony, and could have controlled the mailing of obscene material under Comstock's law, but the threatened censorship never materialized.

The press – which carried not only reports, but also in some cases, like the French did for major trials, full verbatim accounts of proceedings – noted certain oddities at the very start of the trial. Evelyn's mother, now Mrs Holman, was absent. She remained loyal to White, and refused to give evidence that might prejudice either side, or so she said. The press were hard on her, branding her 'an inhuman monster and a wretch' who had bartered her child to satisfy her greed.

Nor was Mrs Stanford White in the courtroom: she had moved to Cambridge, Massachusetts, closer to her son and to escape any more anguish. Evelyn's nineteen-year-old brother was, however, present. He told the press he had come from Pittsburgh to 'do what I can to vindicate the memory of Mr White', who had done so much for him and his family. 'Why is it that people always put the worst construction on a man's motives in a case like this? Aren't there any honest, decent men?' Howard Nesbit, who was the spitting image of his sister, sat next to Charles Harnett, the man who had been White's secretary and was now Howard's intimate friend.

Evelyn herself on the trial's opening day was waifishly pale and without make-up. Beneath her dark coat she was wearing a navy-blue schoolgirl shirtwaist topped with a starched white Buster Brown collar. Wedged in between Mrs William Thaw and her more flamboyantly attired theatrical friend, May McKenzie, in lavender suit and lavish ostrich-feathered hat, she looked like a demure innocent, 'a fragile white-faced child', but she paid attention to the proceedings with her usual intelligence. She was also constantly alert to Harry, prompting him in the selection of jury members and soothing his nervousness with glances.

The Thaw legal team was substantial: Harry had already fired his first lawyer, Lewis Delafield – the man he later designated 'the Traitor', the very name he gave his memoir. Delafield's 'betrayal' had to do with the fact that he had agreed with the prosecution's initial stance: to forgo a trial by declaring Thaw legally insane, thereby preventing a death sentence in one of America's major families. As for District Attorney Jerome, despite his reforming hopes, the prosecutor was worried the evidence that would come out at the trial would not only provide acres of smut for the press, but would also blacken the reputation of some of New York's elite. White had hardly been alone in his extracurricular activities, and his parties were attended by any number of Manhattan's crème.

Thaw adamantly refused the insanity plea, though his family might at first have preferred a swift ruling without a public trial and the mass exposure that would so damage their reputation. Harry was convinced that the 'Traitor' was briefing the press against him, calling him 'a lunatic murderer' and Evelyn 'an abandoned woman who led to my downfall'. On top of that, Delafield was costing him the princely fee of $10,000 dollars and a promise of $15,000 – though it's not clear that any of it was actually paid. Delafield wanted, Thaw claimed, nothing more than 'to railroad me to Matteawan [State Hospital for the criminally insane] as the half crazy tool of a dissolute woman'. With Stanford White dead and no longer dangerous, Thaw could focus on White's good points, the ones that had initially singled the man out to him. He was now transferring his persecutory delusions to the attorney he had himself chosen. In his memoir he writes that Delafield 'was a creature far meaner and uglier than Stanford White'; for, 'aside from White's one vice . . . his slaughter of virgins . . . White was a man of many attractions . . . You could not say of White that he was utterly rotten in character, because he had his good points. The Traitor had no excuse whatever.'

Even without Delafield, Thaw's defence team when the trial opened was six-strong, though almost none had any real experience of the appropriate kind. The exception was 'the Napoleon of the Western Bar', Delphin Michael Delmas, a small man with a big voice and a fine rhetorical style who had a record of nineteen acquittals in nineteen murder cases. Delmas's fee was purportedly a hundred thousand dollars, but then Mrs Thaw had already financed a play at the Amphion in Brooklyn, and much else, to promote her son. The play ended with the line, spoken by its hero, one Harold Daw: 'No jury on earth will send me to the chair, no matter what I have done or what I have been, for killing the man who defamed my wife. That is the unwritten law made by men themselves, and upon its virtue, I will stake my life.'

Mother Thaw had also spent money buying from their recipients any incriminating letters, buying out harmful witnesses, and generally buying her son off an indictment, while having White slandered. Only Evelyn was kept on a tight financial leash. Yet Matron Thaw was forced to be at least polite to her daughter-in-law, or her testimony might go amiss. Evelyn, rumours had it, was promised some twenty thousand dollars if she behaved well in court, and the figure would sky-rocket if she promised eventually to divorce Thaw. For the time being, it seemed Evelyn was genuinely determined to abet her husband's case, even while she loathed being under Mrs Thaw's thumb. Sitting at a table in gestural proximity to Harry in the dock, she calmed her ever fidgety husband with her glances. To be fair to Harry, he recognized how badly his mother treated Evelyn, and tried to allay the worst.

The chief prosecutor, District Attorney William Travers Jerome, was a man who bore a passing resemblance to Theodore Roosevelt. He came from the same social class and had a similar zeal for political reform. He worked to free Manhattan of police and political corruption and had no time for those who wanted to buy justice. He was also a man of great verbal skill and wit, a determined cross-examiner, and didn't suffer fools gladly. But fighting the Thaw millions and the press love affair with the trial's principals would not prove easy.

It was Jerome's assistant DA Garvey who, the jury having at last been selected, on 4 February opened the proceedings for the prosecution. The shooting of White by Harry Thaw 'was a cool, deliberate, malicious, premeditated murder, and we shall ask for a verdict of murder in the first degree,' he stated.

Witnesses to the murder in the Garden followed. After lunch, it was the defence's turn. Everyone had been waiting to hear Delmas, but instead John B. Gleason led the proceedings. A practised lawyer in civil fields, this was his first criminal case, and he rambled on mercilessly, stating that the defence would prove that Harry was insane when he killed White, and 'not accountable for his actions': his client was acting 'under the delusion that it was an act of Providence; that he was the agent of Providence to kill Stanford White'. At the time he didn't consider the murder wrong: he acted 'without malice and without premeditation and in the belief of self-defence, induced by the threats of Mr White to kill the defendant'.

Whether Gleason thought there was actual 'provocation', or merely Harry's delusion of provocation, isn't altogether clear. But the main thrust of his opening argument was that Thaw had a 'psychopathic temperament . . . a temperament liable to a mind diseased', the result of 'his insane heredity'. 'It was an act justfiable in itself, yet nevertheless performed by a man who had no control over himself or his acts at the time.' Robert Louis Stevenson, Shakespeare and Goethe came to Gleason's aid in his attempt to convince the jury that 'upon the evidence it will be impossible for you . . . to say that this man at the time he shot Stanford White was sane beyond a reasonable doubt'. 'It is a maxim of Roman law that a madman's punishment is his own misery. It is a rule of the common law that the intent of the party is a part of the alleged crime,' Gleason added, reminding the jury that madness was a mitigation.

Harry sat rigid and stony-faced, staring at the floor, while Gleason spoke. The press would report that his case had had 'an inauspicious beginning'. The team's choice of witnesses, Gleason's questioning, all were somewhat shambolic. But despite Gleason's unhappy style, 'temporary insanity' was indeed the defence's plea, and they would go on to show that what had derailed Harry, who had a marked tendency to be derailed, was an honourable intention – one with which the jury could sympathize. The 'unwritten law' had no statutory force in the US (except briefly in Texas during the 1920s, when murder was reduced to manslaughter if a husband shot his wife's lover in flagrante delicto, a very French dispensation for a state that might not now like to admit the link). The term 'crime of passion' was never used. Nonetheless, the defence strategy was to prove that Thaw had been driven temporarily mad by the behaviour of a vicious Stanford White. He had been justified in taking action against this evil rapist who had humiliated and disgraced his beloved wife, thereby ridding the world of a foul Lothario. The act done, Thaw was no longer insane and needn't be institutionalized.

This defence, which combined an appeal to the 'unwritten law' – the duty of a man to keep his family sacred, defend his wife's chastity and through that his own honour – while pleading temporary insanity, was not new. In a famous 1859 case known to Thaw, who cited it at a later trial, Lincoln's future secretary of war Edwin M. Stanton won a not-guilty verdict for one Daniel Sickles, who had killed his wife's lover in full view of the White House, the day after she had confessed to adultery. Sickles was a Congressman, his victim, Philip Barton Key, an attorney for the District of Columbia. Sickles had huge public support for his act, and the plea of temporary insanity in a man driven into 'uncontrollable frenzy' by his wife's infidelity got him an acquittal from his jury in just a few minutes. In the aftermath of the trial, the more responsible papers worried over the impact of a ruling that sanctioned murder, an act often committed in a state of uncontrollable frenzy.

In another case, in 1875, a San Francisco jury had effectively arrived at a verdict of 'justifiable homicide', and acquitted the pioneering photographer Eadweard Muybridge after he had killed his wife's lover on discovering that their baby had in fact been fathered by the man. Muybridge's attorney had run an insanity defence, bringing witnesses to testify that ever since a stagecoach accident in 1860 Muybridge's personality had changed. Having been a genial, pleasant businessman, the accident had turned him into a risk-taker with an explosive and unpredictable personality. It may well be that Muybridge had sustained damage to the orbitofrontal cortex, the anterior part of the frontal lobe. Whatever the actual ailment, however, the jury wanted to find him neither guilty nor insane. Though it was never called such, his 'crime of passion' was considered justified. Muybridge's wife died a few months after the trial; he went on to become a world famous photographer.

There were major differences in the Thaw case, however. Not only had the turn of the century and the passing years of the new one brought a slightly more liberal moral regime into being, particularly in that twentieth-century enclave Manhattan. But, more importantly, five years had elapsed between Evelyn's sexual coercion by White and Thaw's murder of him. Nor was Evelyn at the time of her affair with White either married to Thaw or even aware of his existence, except perhaps via gossip. To win the sympathy of jury and public concerning a murder propelled by vengeance for an act long past and committed on a chorus girl then not even met, while pleading temporary insanity, would be an uphill struggle – particularly under New York jurisdiction, which followed the old British M'Naghten test of insanity measured as an ability to understand right and wrong. Nor did New York law equate 'irresistible impulse' with insanity.

Yet the press, and particularly the women reporters, were sympathetic to Thaw. He, in turn, loved the attention and put out many a press release. He was in his 'heroic mood', Evelyn noted. William Alanson White, a future president of the American Psychiatric Association (APA) and one of the ten expert psychiatric witnesses hired by the defence, summed up the role of the press and the public response to the defendants. When negative feelings towards the accused are stirred, he commented, the verdict is usually that he's responsible for the crime. 'If sympathetic emotions are more stirred, then the verdict is that he is irresponsible, that is, insane.'

34. Mad Harry: American Psychiatry Meets the Law

Harry K. Thaw's trial provided something of a congress of psychiatry for the 1900s. It might not retrospectively have had quite the historical cachet of the occasion on which Sigmund Freud delivered his September 1909 lectures at Clark University, but the Thaw trial gathered together many of the best-known alienists – or 'bug-doctors', as Harry would have it – of the period. Some of them were traditional, some more experimental. Their diverging diagnoses and analyses of Harry could be seen to reflect a 'disorder' in the field; or they could equally be seen as indicating a buoyant phase of debate and experimentation, alongside a wish that the legal system were less rigid in its understanding of the human.

It was an exciting moment for the field of psychiatry. New ideas were rapidly being generated. Many alienists and neurologists had grown demoralized by the therapeutic possibilities of the vast asylums. Once considered sanctuaries both for the indigent poor and for those who could pay, many were no longer fit for purpose. By the turn of the century medical (as opposed to mind) doctors had risen to a high social and scientific status: with the germ theory of disease to hand, medics had developed a surer grasp of the origins and aetiology of disease, and were no longer relegated to the mere assuaging or description of symptoms.

The mind doctors, by contrast, were well aware that they were too often mere hospital superintendents overseeing storage bins for idiosyncratic (and unwanted) human life. Scientific knowledge was needed. So were new therapies. The period's most enterprising psychiatrists were alive to the possibilities of both. They wanted new ideas and techniques that would permit them, like their medical kin, to investigate the anatomy and physiology of the nervous system, all the while treating their patients. A first centre for psychiatric research had been set up in 1895 in New York, the Pathological Institute, attached to the New York Hospital. One of Harry Thaw's future medics, Adolf Meyer, took over its headship in 1901.

Meyer, like many of the younger members of the profession, was not interested in administering the large populations of the asylums. He was interested in the individual and the new psychodynamic and psychoanalytic ideas coming from Freud's Vienna, from Paris, and from that leading institution for research and treatment, Zürich's Burghölzli, where Eugen Bleuler and C. G. Jung were at work. Jung would come to the US with Freud in 1909 and return once more in 1912 on the invitation of Smith Ely Jelliffe, another of Thaw's psychiatrists.

The possibilities of individual practice and new-style private clinics also beckoned to the psychiatrists. Meanwhile, the challenges of working within a forensic environment were being tested out. The relationship with the law was hardly an easy one, as the Thaw case would prove. But the very exposure in the public domain that the case provided inevitably served as something of a stimulus to the rapidly changing field.

Harry K. Thaw was examined by no less than thirteen experts – medics with a knowledge of psychiatry and neurology or experience with work in asylums. Ten of these were hired by the defence at an expense of, purportedly, ten thousand dollars a day (or approximately two hundred thousand dollars in today's terms), the others by the prosecution. Each side thus had their own experts whose 'opinions' were tested in cross-examination by the other side, though not all the medics were called to testify.

Allan McLane Hamilton MD (1837–1919) was the first of the doctors to examine Thaw in the Tombs. Hamilton saw him on 27 June, two days after the murder, and then on three other occasions. He also consulted with the Thaws' family doctor to get a fuller picture of Harry's mental history. Remembered by his colleagues as a tall, distinguished and imposing man, Hamilton was professor of mental diseases at Cornell University, and as the grandson of Alexander

Hamilton, one of America's founding fathers, well respected. A seasoned expert witness, he had appeared in two of the three American presidential assassination cases and had looked into the sanity of Mary Baker Eddy, the founder of Christian Science, whose son wanted to prove her mentally incompetent.

Hamilton, it was said, could withstand days of cross-examination by 'pompous and conceited' lawyers. He was highly critical of a system in which expertise could be 'bought' by attorneys, and wished for an arrangement like the French, which made the experts 'objective' servants of the court. He also considered the English 'guilty but insane' ruling far superior to the American 'not guilty, because insane'. He thought DA Jerome an honest man, but one who was misguided in his scoffing at Thaw's 'mental degeneration' by naming it a 'Pittsburgh Insanity'. He judged the Thaw family far more severely. Their 'lavish use of money' enabled the hiring of a 'perfect cloud of so-called experts, the testimony of some at different times being contradictory and worthless'. Hamilton took himself off to North Africa so he wouldn't have to testify – and only did so later 'under compulsion', when he had to join the commission of expert witnesses. The case, from his point of view, was 'a gross illustration of the evils of expert testimony'.

Hamilton, who held eugenic and hereditary ideas not unlike Maudsley's in England, was convinced that Thaw's insanity was not of the temporary kind. He understood him to be 'hopelessly crazy', 'a paranoiac in an advanced stage', and he wouldn't allow his opinion to be bought for lucre. Nor did he have any time for the so-called unwritten law, which countered the rule of law. Harry Thaw's opinion of him was inevitably not very high: he thought this 'bug doctor' was a queer person, and in collusion with the 'Traitor', his first lawyer.

William Alanson White (1870–1937), Charles G. Wagner and Charles W. Pilgrim – all three future presidents of what was the American Psychopathological Association and became the American Psychiatric Association – as well as a past and future president of the American Neurological Association, Graeme M. Hammond (1858–1944), chair of neurology at the NYU School of Medicine, and Smith Ely Jelliffe (1866–1945), all provided expert assessments on behalf of the defence. There was also Britton D. Evans, for the last fifteen years superintendent of the 1850-patient New Jersey State Asylum at Morris Plains, and an experienced forensic witness.

White and Jelliffe were interested in psychoanalysis and in psychodynamic ideas that situated disorder in the individual's lived history of family life. In 1913 – after Freud's 1909 Clark Lectures (later published as his *Introduction to Psychoanalysis*) and Jung's lectures of 1912 at Fordham University in New York, which were initiated by Jelliffe – they founded the first *American Psychoanalytic Review*, an eclectic publication that was never less than heterodox. Both men also took an active interest in forensic psychiatry as well as in 'mental hygiene'.

In 1910, having recognized that there were no black psychiatrists in the US although there was a need for them, White opened his lectures and teaching clinics to black students. The racist backlash from some students and staff was noisy, so seeing no other solution White offered to teach the black students at Howard University separately. He also spoke out against the gathering pace of the eugenicists who would sterilize the 'defective' population, and claimed that there wasn't 'the slightest particle of justification for the mutilating operations that are being advocated and broadcast over the country at this time'. All real evidence of what could be inherited had been brushed aside 'for the purpose of satisfying a sadistic orgy of cutting out testicles and ovaries'.

At the time that he attended the Thaw trial, White was professor of nervous and mental diseases at Georgetown University and also held a chair at George Washington University, all the while acting as superintendent of the Government Hospital for the Insane in Washington. His much reprinted *Outlines of Psychiatry*, published in the year of the trial, became a classic of the field, influencing a generation of practitioners. So, too, did the text he co-authored with his colleague Ely Jelliffe, *Diseases of the Nervous System* (1915). Ely Jelliffe was an energetic impresario and publisher, who for forty years edited the influential *Journal of Mental and Nervous Diseases*.

At the time of the trial Graeme M. Hammond was the best-known of these many neurologists and alienists, though perhaps as much for his sporting as for his medical feats. His father, William, had been the US army's Surgeon General during the Civil War and as a boy, Hammond had accompanied Lincoln on visits to the Front. Later, during the Great War, Graeme Hammond worked with soldiers suffering from shell shock.

The prosecution's experts were scarcely less illustrious. Carlos F. MacDonald, who had seen Thaw just after his arrest, was Bellevue Hospital's emeritus professor of mental diseases and medical jurisprudence. Just six years before, in 1901, he had served the defence team working for Leon Czolgosz, the anarchist assassin of President William McKinley – 'the president of money kings and trust magnates', as Emma Goldman called him. Czolgosz had refused to speak either to MacDonald or indeed to his defence lawyers, and the attempt to plead insanity in his case failed utterly. MacDonald determined him sane – appropriately, since it's said Czolgosz's last words, before he was electrocuted, reiterated his political beliefs: 'I killed the President because he was the enemy of the good people – the good working people.' Dr MacDonald had also served as consultant to several hospitals and had headed the New York State Commission in Lunacy, set up in 1899 to improve the treatment of the mad in the state of New York. He was to become president of the APA in 1913.

On the witness stand at Thaw's trial, it was two other physicians who would dominate expert witness for the prosecution. Austin Flint (1836–1915), an expert in physiology, was an eminent and much published medic who had worked on the liver and the nervous system, though not all that much in the field of insanity. The younger man, William Hirsch, was a consultant at the Manhattan State Hospital and had links with Cornell University Medical School, where both men had been professors. Hirsch is also listed in the 1906 records of the American Medico-Legal Association, to which he belonged, as 'Neurologist to the German Poliklinik', a pioneering outpatients' facility.

In an 1896 issue of *Popular Science Monthly*, Hirsch argues against the scaremongers who see in the rise of statistics on mental degeneration proof of 'Epidemics of Hysteria' and neurasthenia. We just count better than we used to, he argues; plus more people, and in particular women, come more often to doctors. On the way Hirsch shows himself to be well acquainted with continental literature on the subject. In 1912, he published a book called *Religion and Civilization*. This sets out to argue that from the vantage point of science, delusion is at the heart of monotheism, while paranoia with its persecutory cast and its delusions of grandeur could explain many of the characters in the Old and New Testaments. Apart from their delusions, Hirsch points out, paranoiacs 'may appear perfectly normal', and only some suffer from hallucinations – that is, perceive the products of their morbid imaginations with their senses.

Whatever their vaunted credentials, the prosecution's position made its doctors' task of expertise difficult. For a murder verdict, Jerome needed the accused sane. Prodded into changing his position midstream, he wanted to prove that Thaw, if not fully responsible for his actions, was not only temporarily or partially insane – but wholly so. This position was akin to the one that the first examining psychiatrist, Hamilton, had taken. The difficulty for the medics on Thaw's defence team was that New York law – unlike the law in fourteen other states – did not recognize the 'irresistible impulse' test of insanity or the 'temporary' lack of mental responsibility, common enough in France.

35. *Experts on the Stand*

First on the stand for the defence was a Dr Charles J. Wiley of Pittsburgh, introduced as a specialist in insanity and nervous diseases. He had presumably been chosen to testify first because, unlike the other experts, he had experience of Harry outside the Tombs. He had seen him in a streetcar on the Fifth Avenue line in Pittsburgh during the summer of 1905. Harry had come aboard and peremptorily pulled up a blind, which had affected the 'motorman's' vision; when the conductor had stepped forward to pull it down again, Harry had exploded 'into a furor', giving Wiley the impression that he was both 'vague and irrational'.

Gleason then, in one of those excessively long questions that summed up the events of the crime from entry to roof garden to murder in one long breath, asked Wiley if he could give an opinion on the sanity of this man who, immediately after killing Stanford White, muttered as explanation that 'he ruined my wife'. Amidst a storm of interventions from Jerome, interrupted by several legal arguments, Wiley let it be known that he believed Harry Thaw was suffering from a delusion.

In his cross-examination, Jerome proceeded to tear Wiley apart. He pointed out that Wiley's 'belief' was immaterial: it was his 'opinion as an expert', as 'a scientific man', that counted. When Wiley restated his opinion that Thaw was insane on the night when he killed White, Jerome insisted that the State of New York penal code be read out to him.

Gleason did so:

Section 20: 'An act which is done by a prisoner who is an idiot, imbecile or insane, is not a crime. A prisoner cannot be tried, sentenced to any punishment, or punished for a crime, while he is in a state of idiocy, imbecility, lunacy or insanity, so as to be incapable of understanding the proceedings or making his defence.'

Section 21: 'A prisoner is not excused from criminal liability as an idiot, imbecile, lunatic or insane person or of unsound mind, except upon proof that, at the time of committing the alleged criminal act, he was laboring under such a defect of reason as either:

(1) not to know the nature and quality of the act he was doing; or

(2) not to know that the act was wrong.'

Section 23: 'A morbid propensity to commit prohibited acts, existing in the mind of a person who is not shown to have been incapable of knowing the wrongfulness of such acts, forms no defence to a prosecution therefor.'

Dr Wiley persisted in his opinion, despite Jerome's emphasis on Section 23. Grilling him on what exactly in this tricky domain of love and jealousy constituted the difference between madness and sanity, Jerome then asked: 'Do you consider that everybody who is actuated by jealousy is of unsound mind?'

When Wiley answered, 'No', Jerome continued: 'Would the mere killing by a man who believed his wife had been wronged in itself be evidence of insanity?'

Again Wiley replied in the negative. Pressing him further, Jerome asked what element on the night of the murder demonstrated that the defendant was insane.

'The declaration [to his wife] that "I have probably saved your life",' Wiley stated, showed that Thaw was 'laboring under a delusion'.

Jerome's tactics then shifted. To the amusement of the jury, he demonstrated that this trumpeted expert was no expert at all since he didn't even know what Jerome himself knew and asserted were fundamental texts, tests and authorities in the field. He questioned Wiley on Romberg symptoms. Wiley couldn't answer, though he claimed to be familiar with a book in which they figured. Jerome pushed him on

Dr Hammond's *Diseases of the Nervous System*, which Wiley couldn't recall, and went on to shame him thoroughly in a basic medical exam on nerves, spleen and kidneys. After nigh on four hours of such tactics, anything Wiley might have had to say on Harry Thaw's sanity was undermined, and the witness himself utterly humiliated. Jerome's tactics were not unusual when it came to cross-examining a purported expert.

The chief prosecutor was more lenient on the elderly family physician, Dr Charles F. Bingamon, who claimed that Thaw had as a child suffered from a 'neurotic temperament' and had bouts of St Vitus' Dance, one lasting four weeks; but he put a quick end to the testimony of a relative of Harry's who told the court that his father, a first cousin of Thaw's father, had been committed to an asylum. Jerome pointed out that this collateral branch of the family had no bearing on Harry's mental condition. Subsequent testimony about the mental state of an uncle was similarly objected to and the objection sustained by the judge.

At the end of the first day, the defence determined that the out-flanked Gleason would henceforth step down as their team leader and the acclaimed Delmas take over. Possessing the gestures and authority that had earned him his Napoleon sobriquet, he was indeed a more effective lawyer. Justice in adversarial systems has ever been affected by the brilliance of combative attorneys and their mustering of facts and emotions for jury and public. Delmas treated juries in the same way as he treated women, one reporter wrote – with the 'flattering unction that causes a washerwoman to forget that she is not a queen'.

36. *Star Witness for the Defence*

On his second day, Delmas called Evelyn to the witness stand. Outside, some ten thousand thronged to catch a glimpse of the famous model and star witness. Inside, her clear-headed, soft spoken testimony as well as her physical charm riveted courtroom, press and jury alike.

Delmas took her through the day of the murder, her background, her coming to New York, her meeting with Thaw. In a hushed courtroom, he guided her through the long night in which she had confessed to Thaw the full extent of her relations with Stanford White – the seduction, then sexual coercion, by the architect. Delmas's ploy was to demonstrate that Evelyn was recounting the entire story as she had told it to Thaw, since it was this narrative that had catapulted him on his journey towards murder. The truth content of the account, which the prosecution kept wanting to test, was irrelevant. This was a story told by a child-woman to the man who was to be her husband. Its salacious details were allowed only so that judge and jury could gauge the impact its telling had had on Harry Thaw.

Visibly, it continued to have an impact. Harry sat hunched and perspiring. He squirmed, fidgeted, and occasionally sobbed out loud. Evelyn's palpable nervousness as she spoke in public about matters that were rarely breathed, certainly not by a young woman, electrified the court. Here's how she narrated her numbed state in the hours and days after she had woken in bed next to a 'completely undressed' Stanford White.

Mr White came into the room and tried to quiet me. He got down on his knees beside me and picked up the ends of my dress and kissed it. I do not know how I got home. Next day he came to my home. I was quiet now and sat staring out the window. After a while he said, 'Why don't you look at me, child?' I said, 'Because I can't.' Then he began to talk to me. He told me that I must not be worried about what had occurred. He said that everything was all right. He said he thought I had the most beautiful hair he had ever seen. He said he would do a great many things for me. He said everybody did those things; that all people were doing these things, that that is all people were for, all they lived for. He said that I was so nice and young and slim, that he couldn't help it and so he did it.

Here, apparently, Evelyn gave way to the tears she had been trying not to shed and twisted her hands, only to resume her testimony. Its content cued the shift in taste that would mark women for the rest of the new century:

Then he told me that only very young girls were nice, and the thinner they were, the prettier they were, that nothing was so loathsome as fat, and that I must never get fat. He said the great thing in this world was not to be found out . . . He made me swear that I would not tell my mother, not to say one word to Mother about it, that I must not tell anyone about it, that people did not talk about these things, and did not tell about them.

Delmas didn't want to hand Evelyn over for cross-examination until the impact of her confession – on Thaw, let alone on the public – had been sifted by the psychiatric experts. Nor did he want any dissipation of the effect on the court of reading Thaw's syntactically bizarre letters to Evelyn – where he sometimes refers to himself as 'he' – and his equally deranged will, made on the day of his marriage. Here he orders, in good paranoid fashion, that if his death is suspicious, fifty thousand dollars or more should be used in discovering and bringing to justice the guilty party (White); and he leaves funds under Comstock's trusteeship to various young women to prosecute Stanford White.

So on Monday 11 February, Delmas called Dr Charles G. Wagner to the stand.

Dr Wagner, an experienced courtroom witness, was the super-intendent of the State Hospital for the Insane in Binghampton, New York, which housed some 1570 people. He stated that he had visited Thaw six times in the Tombs. He was about to narrate his conversations with the defendant during these visits when Jerome objected to such material being presented as evidence.

Wagner was nonplussed, and Delmas only retrieved his testimony by asking him a question that took sixteen minutes to put.

His question narrated the entire history of the case from the defence point of view – including Thaw's chequered heredity; illnesses during childhood; a meeting with Evelyn, always named as 'the child', and dating from when she was sixteen; his proposal in 1903, after 'the child's' operation; her declining of his suit, and then the reason for it, which propelled his plunge into 'profound grief'. Then came Thaw's learning on his return from Europe that there was a scheme afoot, 'that the same man who had previously assaulted her ... had laid a plan ... defaming the name and character of the young man' – viz. himself; he had then married her and subsequently learned on a visit to New York that White, or 'B', had been in touch; that the 'Blackguard' had renewed his suit. Then, on the night of 25 June 1906, after 'the child' had given him a note while they were in a restaurant, saying that 'the B has been here but has gone away', he had seen B in the Madison Square roof garden when his party was leaving, and had unloaded three shots from the pistol he only carried in New York where the B lived and where threats had been made against his life. Finally came the question, 'What, in your opinion, was the condition of the defendant ... at the time the fatal shot was fired?'

After Jerome had raised objections as to the factual nature of a great many of the points in Delmas's long question, the judge told Dr Wagner to answer the question, bearing in mind the objections: Did the defendant, at the time he fired the fatal shot, know the act was wrong?

Wagner replied that in his opinion he did not.

Was Thaw's failure or incapacity to know that the act was wrong due to a defect of reason under which he was labouring at the time?

Wagner answered in the affirmative twice, the question having been posed again slightly differently.

A flustered Dr Wagner had been a less than satisfactory witness. But Dr Britton D. Evans, of the State Hospital for the Insane in Morris Plains, was unflappable. Perhaps his star performance was due to the fact that he and Jerome had belligerent history in a prior case: indeed, the district attorney had refused to shake his hand the day before, and the doctor had noted the insult out loud, declaring in full view of reporters, 'You are no gentleman.' Evans would not allow Jerome to humiliate him.

Dr Evans had visited Thaw eight times in the Tombs, on six of those occasions with Dr Wagner. His testimony was cogent and energetic, beginning as mental-state reports do even today with a description of physical state, then behaviour, and finally moving inward to delusions and possible biological problems.

> I observed that Harry K. Thaw exhibited a peculiar facial expression, a glaring of the eyes, a restlessness of the eyes, a suspicious viewing of the surroundings and me, watching every movement. I observed a nervous agitation and restlessness, such as comes from a severe brain storm, and is common in persons who have recently gone through an explosive or fulminating condition of mental unsoundness. He exhibited delusions of a personal character and exaggerated ego, and along with them, delusions of a persecutory character, in that he exhibited the fact that he felt himself of exaggerated importance, and that he was subjected to persecutions and conspiracies on the part of numerous people. These were my observations on August 4.

Asked what he meant by some of his recondite terms, for example an 'exaggerated ego', Dr Evans replied:

> It is an exhibition of an exaggerated value put upon the ability, capacity and influence of one's own self out of proportion to that which can be given to that particular person under all the conditions and

propositions presented to the observer or examiner. An analysis of the person puts him upon an ordinary even plane. He himself believes that he is clothed with power, capacities and abilities far above him and out of proportion of a normal human being under the advantages of that particular person.

On top of this narcissistic disorder, Harry suffered from 'logorrhea', an abnormally rapid flow of words which Evans 'noticed were not characteristic of the healthy mind'. This went along with an 'abnormal excitement of the cerebral function, an abnormal or diseased condition of the brain, which is the organ of the mind'.

Asked to say more about what was abnormal about Thaw's ready flow of language, Dr Evans pointed to its comparative incoherence and lack of logic.

A man speaking with a diseased brain talks with words and ideas lumped one over the other in rapid succession, a flight of ideas, so that it ... tends to confuse the hearer and make him unable to grasp what the situation is, except that these rapid and successive states ... are the logical outcome of a morbid condition of the mind ... it is either a symptom or indication that the brain has undergone a recent terrible storm of an abnormal character, or is in its initial stage of disorder ... It is the twilight or the dawn of a state of mental unsoundness and mental explosion.

Evans also elaborated on what he meant by 'delusions';

I mean by a delusion a false belief, out of which you cannot reason a person by the usual arguments – by the usual counter arguments, by the usual methods that are used to dissuade a man from an illogical position or an error of judgment. The man who has any judgment, when you place before him a logical argument and show him he is wrong, if he is a normal man, he will see his error, whether he admits it directly at once or not ... [When you] dissuade an insane

man from his delusions or false beliefs, he still holds to it because it
is a matter of disease engrafted upon his mind, or his brain which is
an organ of the mind, and your arguments are of no avail.

On Evans's second visit with Dr Wagner, on 21 August, he
observed that Thaw was 'nervous and agitated and that he had that
peculiar glaring eye which is so well recognized by persons who
are familiar with conditions of that sort; that look of suspicion;
watching me, watching those about him; and still the exaggerated
ego.'

Perhaps not altogether unrelated to his status as millionaire son of
a doting mother, Thaw was far more disposed to telling Evans what to
do than to 'submit to me as an examiner'. He continued to exhibit
'delusions of an exaggerated ego' and 'delusions of persecution'. These
persecutions were 'unjust and unfair and attack the most vital interests of his being, and life, and his social welfare'. Thaw had no
hallucinations, which Evans glossed as 'false sense impressions'.

On his further visits to the Tombs, there was still much nervous agitation in Harry, but it had lessened, and after that, Evans found great
improvement: still less nervousness and none of the peculiar darting
looks into corners of the room. Harry Thaw's 'brain storm' had passed.
The term Evans had hit upon to describe Harry's state on the night of
the murder caught the journalists' and the public's attention. It stuck.
The 'brain storm of a millionaire' was to serve many a headline and
echo through the culture.

Pressed further by Delmas and keeping so tightly to the rules of evidence that there was no room for Jerome to object, Evans then
described the conspiracy that Harry Thaw believed to have been
mounted against him by Stanford White and which he thought
endangered his life, since White, he claimed, had hired the Monk
Eastman gang, notorious Tenderloin criminals, to do him in. The conspiracy extended to the district attorney's office, which initially hadn't
followed up his complaints about White's activities and had counselled him to let the matter drop. It now included all the lawyers on

his first defence team who had colluded with Jerome, he said, to have him declared insane.

Evans also testified that Harry had told him:

> I never wanted to shoot that man; I never wanted to kill him . . . but I did want through legal means to bring him to trial. I wanted to bring him before a court, that he might be brought to justice and suffer for that which he had done . . . Providence took charge of the situation; this was an act of Providence. Had it been my judgment, I would have preferred for him to suffer the humiliation and all that comes from laying bare this matter of his doings before a court and before the public.

All this, Evans concluded, he as a doctor considered to be 'a delusion . . . an insane delusion'.

When Delmas called Dr Wagner back into the courtroom, Wagner proceeded to iterate Thaw's delusions of persecution. The case for his temporary insanity was now strong.

In contemporary terms, Harry Thaw might well be classified as having what the World Health Organization's International Classification of Diseases (ICD) 10 calls a 'paranoid personality disorder', which may include brief psychotic episodes. It calls for at least three of the following characteristics:

1. excessive sensitivity to setbacks and rebuffs;
2. tendency to bear grudges persistently, i.e. refusal to forgive insults and injuries or slights;
3. suspiciousness and a pervasive tendency to distort experience by misconstruing the neutral or friendly actions of others as hostile or contemptuous;
4. a combative and tenacious sense of personal rights out of keeping with the actual situation;
5. recurrent suspicions, without justification, regarding sexual fidelity of spouse or sexual partner;

6. tendency to experience excessive self-importance, manifest in a persistent self-referential attitude;
7. preoccupation with unsubstantiated 'conspiratorial' explanations of events both immediate to the patient and in the world at large.

American alienists of the time, like Evans and Wagner, would most likely have read Valentin Magnan's classic descriptions of paranoia, and certainly Krafft-Ebing's. Such descriptions, even to the present day, link paranoia to excessive narcissism – that self-aggrandizement and exaggerated sensitivity to slight that often involves the person in splitting off the unwanted, as a defence mechanism. Magnan, in his *Délire Chronique* (1890), had broken down 'systematized delusion' into 'persecutory paranoia', 'ambitious paranoia', 'amatory paranoia' and 'litigious paranoia'. The amatory paranoiac is often chivalrous and idealistic, but feels persecuted by those who prevent the success of his desires, and may lose his self-control and resort to violence against his persecutors.

The death of a juror's wife resulted in a court recess over a long weekend. It was apparently an eventful one. At the Tombs, Thaw was frantic, fearing a mistrial. He shouted for Evelyn. Meanwhile the papers, which could not get enough of the case, talked up the possibility of a lunacy commission being called for: it looked to them as if the defence's 'temporary insanity' might really be a far more permanent form of madness. In addition, there were reports that Evelyn was being cited in the divorce case of the producer of *The Wild Rose*: the play had been named after her, it was claimed. Delmas squashed the rumours. Evelyn as a victim who needed rescue was crucial to the Thaw case.

When court reconvened on Monday, 18 February. Dr Evans was called back and now questioned about Thaw's will: this allowed Delmas to have this strange document read into the court records. Evans's view, in response to Delmas's question, was that this was indeed not the will of a sane man.

37. The Prosecution Counter-attacks

Both Evelyn and Evans had been so strong in the witness stand that the district attorney was left with his case floundering. If the jury bought the defence's 'temporary insanity' line, they might well release Harry altogether.

Jerome flailed. He called Evelyn back to the stand and tried to discredit her. His questioning was brutal. He was attempting to prove to the jury that she had been lying all along. Her 'confession' to Thaw had either never taken place, or it was not true to the facts. Delmas rightly objected, pointing out that Eveyln had been recounting what she remembered telling Thaw. Jerome paid no heed and sneeringly tried to blacken her character and destroy the illusion of innocence her childlike looks reinforced. He questioned her about the extent of her nudity when she had modelled, the risqué cafés she had frequented in Paris, her unchaperoned status, her late nights, her continued relations with Stanford White, a man she had described as 'kind and fatherly' despite the fact that he had 'wronged' her. He asked whether her operation had been an abortion. By the end, Evelyn was in tears.

But Jerome's bullying had gone too far, and it turned the court against him. One of the four or so women reporters allowed to stay in the courtroom during the confession of activities so inappropriate for chaste feminine ears, Nixola Greeley-Smith, wondered how Evelyn had been able to survive what was palpably 'torture' inflicted in the name of the law. She recounted how all the women in the room had writhed under the sting of Jerome's questions. His 'vivisection of a woman's soul' made it a duty to give this 'trembling, weeping woman any support that the presence of members of her own sex might afford'. Even the Reverend Madison C. Peters concluded that it was time to halt this 'disgusting barbarity' being inflicted on 'a helpless child', who was more sinned against than sinning.

Jerome, however, persisted. Through Evelyn's mother – whom the press now uniformly deplored as 'unnatural' – he had gained access to her teenage diary from her days at the DeMille school. This came complete with a mocking sketch of a nun. Jerome wanted to show that Evelyn was scandalously immoral, that she scoffed at her innocent schoolfriends whose ambition was to be mothers, while she herself was intent on performing on the stage.

He then asked Evelyn questions about Thaw's irrational acts. She said that he had carried a revolver ever since Christmas 1903, because he believed people were following him in order to do him harm. No, the pistol didn't frighten her, since she knew it was intended only for Stanford White. At this Jerome abruptly released her from the stand. He was getting nowhere.

The next day brought him nothing more promising. Delmas had called Evelyn back to the stand to show she wasn't implicated in any of her mother's arrangements with White concerning money for her or her brother. Jerome tried once more to impugn her honesty. Hadn't Evelyn told her brother, when she returned from Europe with Thaw, that he had treated her cruelly in order to make her confess that White had drugged her? But Evelyn stood up to him. As she said in her first memoir, she had learned how to be a confident witness by concentrating on the truth. The handwritten frontispiece of the book reads: 'Be truthful. Even a well made lie is easily broken down under proper and persistent cross examination. A witness who deliberately and knowingly commits perjury is not only doing a wrong but is a fool.'

Frustrated by the charming and clever Evelyn, Jerome then turned his ire on Dr Evans. Once more, he tried to discredit the expert. He wanted to make Evans admit that the conditions he had attributed to Thaw – melancholia and paranoia – were permanent, not temporary; and that 'brain storm' was a spurious invention of his own. But Evans held his ground, and the only effect repeating the term 'brain storm' had was to embed it in the language:

My observation of him and the facts I have heard, make me positive that in his abnormal, excited condition of mind he would not be accountable for his actions when he heard the mention of Stanford White's name . . . Constant brooding over the terrible story he had heard so sunk his soul to its lowest depths that he might be liable at any time to be plunged into a brain storm, and under its influences use upon his enemy a revolver which he had been carrying for self-protection.

Jerome got no further with Dr Wagner when he called him back to the stand. And now the judge was astonished to hear the prosecutor stating: 'If Thaw was insane on the date of the shooting and on the first three medical visits he sustained in the Tombs, he is now insane.' Presumably, an exasperated Jerome had now been squeezed into the position that it was better to have Harry K. Thaw in a psychiatric facility than out and about roaming the streets. It wasn't the electric chair, but it was certainly an alternative form of containment.

Meanwhile Thaw himself, who wanted not only to be exonerated but hailed as a heroic saviour of innocent damsels, was briefing the press: 'I am not crazy. I was not crazy when I shot Stanford White. I'm glad I did it. I was justified when I shot him. I was never insane and never said I was.'

Harry Thaw adored the limelight, and litigation continued to be his route into it.

To counter the son's ill-effects on his own case, Delmas called the mother. On the stand, the redoubtable Mrs William Thaw proved a formidable witness, one who spoke with utter rectitude and honesty. As Evelyn, who rarely had sympathy to spare for the woman, wrote in her 1914 memoir: 'Mrs Thaw made a good witness. She put up a fine fight for her son's life. Every motherly instinct was aroused. She is a kindly matron, with brown eyes and a pleasant expression. She was dressed in widow's garb with her black veil thrown back, disclosing a mass of silver-white hair. At all times she was perfectly self-possessed.'

Mrs Thaw told the court how, on his return to Pittsburgh in the autumn of 1903, she had picked up Harry's terrible state from the violent manner in which he played the piano, and then from his groans and sobs. He told her he couldn't sleep. Finally, on being pressed, he confessed that he had been thinking about 'a wicked thing the wickedest man in New York had done' and that this man had ruined his life by ruining the girl Harry loved. She was a girl with the 'most beautiful mind' of all the young girls he had ever known, and he would 'make it his business to see that this girl was not dragged down'. As Harry grew more and more depressed, overwrought and obsessed with the young woman, whose name and profession Mrs Thaw eventually learned, the family doctor too grew worried about him.

Jerome now leapt up. His intervention stunned the court. 'If it is presumed that this defendant was insane at the time of these conversations and continued insane right down the line until June 25, 1906, then it must be presumed that he is still insane, that he is insane today. In that case, it is time to stop this trial.'

Only the judge's irritation and refusal to appoint a lunacy commission ensured that the trial continued. Mrs Thaw was taken through her ultimate agreement to her son's marriage to Evelyn – on the condition that her past was never referred to and that her mother never came to visit.

After a long weekend recess, the court reconvened on the Monday. Jerome's tactic now seemed to be to tell the world the worst about Evelyn and about Harry K. Thaw's sadistic tendencies. Thaw's former long-term lawyer, whose firm had been fired before the trial commenced, was called and asked about the various claims he had settled for Thaw, including one brought by a girl alleging that she had been tied to a bedpost and whipped. Delmas's objections that such testimony couldn't be brought in rebuttal prompted only Jerome's plaint that he was trying to show that Evelyn's narrative about White couldn't have dislodged Harry's reason, since he was already familiar with such propensities in his own person.

One of Evelyn's photographers and Stanford White's brother-in-law were up next. The latter, just back from Europe, had been at the roof garden on the night of the murder. He had talked with Thaw just before, and claimed that he was neither drunk nor mad, though Harry had offered to introduce him to young women . . .

Jerome then called Abraham Hummel, the lawyer that Stanford White had sent Evelyn to for an affidavit as to what had happened to her in Schloss Katzenstein. Despite a slew of objections from Delmas, the court heard of the sexual violence Evelyn had been subjected to within the castle walls. Once out in the public sphere, the material was so scandalous that there was no point in trying to undermine the authenticity of the affidavit or the statement of a decidedly weaselly Hummel.

After that, Jerome called what Delmas named his 'squadron [or army] of experts', and the battle over Harry Thaw's sanity began in earnest.

Never had so many notable alienists been summoned to court at the same time, or appeared nationwide on the front pages. Never had the new psychiatry been so tested and at such length, its disparate views, diagnoses and terms trumpeted and pulled apart before so vast a newspaper-reading public. If the vagaries of the human mind had had an initial airing with Dr Evans's definitions of 'brain storm', melancholia and paranoia, they were now to be stretched even further, this time on the side of a rational ability to distinguish between right and wrong that coexisted with 'insanity'. Jerome forced the court to ask whether, given the logic of the proceedings, Harry K. Thaw was even 'competent' to brief his lawyers and stand trial.

Up for the prosecution were Dr Austin Flint, Dr Carlos F. MacDonald and Dr William Mabon, who had all been on hand since Harry's initial arrest. They were now joined by Dr William Hirsch of the Cornell University Medical School, Dr William Pritchard of the Polyclinic Hospital, Dr Allen Ross Diffendorf, superintendent of the Connecticut State Hospital, Dr Albert Warren Ferrie of the College of Physicians and Surgeons, and – Jerome's trump card – Dr Allan McLane Hamilton, who had been the first doctor on the defence team when it was still led by Thaw's 'Traitor', Delafield.

Jerome had prepared what the *New York Times* called a '12,000 word question' for the alienists, once they were sworn in en masse after the lunchtime recess. (Only Hamilton and MacDonald, who had helped Jerome prepare his case and therefore thought it unethical to testify now, were kept back.) The people's 'hypothetical' question incorporated all the events leading to the murder from the prosecution's point of view.

It took Jerome's second an hour and a half to read out what was in effect a pamphlet of thirty-nine pages; halfway through it, a brief recess was called. The question covered the whole story to date, including Thaw's sadistic acts and his demeanour in the Tombs when he refused examination. Asked at the end of the reading whether Thaw 'knew that his acts were wrong and knew the nature and quality of those acts', Dr Flint responded that he did. When the witness was handed over to Delmas, the defence attorney asked that the court be adjourned so that he could read the lengthy hypothetical question at least once before cross-examining the witness.

The next day all the other prosecution experts agreed with Dr Flint: Harry K. Thaw could tell right from wrong and knew what he was doing when he killed Stanford White. When Dr Hirsch came to the witness box on 15 March, he told the court that he had been a colleague of the famous Austrian neurologist Krafft-Ebing, who had been used by the defence to bolster the idea of a temporary insanity – their 'brain storm' theory. There was, he said, no such thing as a brain storm in any of the scientific literature. Nor did Thaw's case match the mild versions of temporary insanity that Krafft-Ebing mentioned in his *Textbook of Insanity*, which had been translated into English in 1904.

Dr Hirsch, who knew his continentals, did not know his Americans or English quite as well. The *Oxford English Dictionary* attributes the term 'brain storm' to a medical dictionary of 1894, while William James, who knew how to twist and shape the language as well as his more literary brother, had used it in his 1879 essay exploring the limits of consciousness, 'Are We Automata?'. Indeed, Evans in his evidence had used a metaphor similar to James's. In referring to Thaw's loss of willpower he had said: 'the person becomes a victim of his diseased condition, operating as a ship does without a rudder in the wind'. The inimitable James, so important to the establishment of psychology in the English-speaking world, ruminated on

> the notorious fact that the strongest tendencies to automatic activity in the nerves often run most counter to the selective pressure of consciousness. Every day of our lives we struggle to escape some tedious tune or odious thought which the momentary disposition of the brain keeps forcing upon us. And, to take more extreme cases, there are murderous tendencies to nervous discharge which, so far from involving by their intensity the assent of the will, cause their subjects voluntarily to repair to asylums to escape their dreaded tyranny. In all these cases of *voluntas paradoxa* or *invita*, [contradictory wills or invited ones] the individual selects out of the two possible selves yielded by his cerebral powers one as the true Ego; the other he regards as an enemy until at last the brain-storm becomes too strong for the helmsman's power. But even in the depths of mania or of drunkenness the conscious man can steady himself and be rational for an instant if a sufficient motive be brought to bear.

In this version, the brain storm overwhelms Harry and he becomes murderous, unable to escape the tyranny of a 'nervous discharge'.

The defence wouldn't be outdone by Flint, Hirsch or Jerome. They called Charles Pilgrim, president of the State Commission in Lunacy, and Graeme Hammond, as well as Ely Jelliffe and William A. White. While they all agreed, after a reading of both the defence and the prosecution's hypothetical questions, that Thaw was mad and not responsible when he shot Stanford White, they had a little more trouble agreeing in what that madness consisted or how to describe it.

The difficulties of expert-witnessing, particularly in this field of the mind, have not changed all that much – despite more widely agreed classificatory systems, with numbers attached. By 1907, the great psychiatric classifier Emil Kraepelin's terminology would have been circulating in English for at least five years, but new terms were constantly being tried out and debated.

Hammond, on the stand, admitted that classification systems in the field were not cast in stone: he wasn't familiar with the term 'brain storm', which the press and public had taken to with such rapidity that Evans became colloquially known as the 'brain-storm doctor'. Hammond thought it was probably akin to transitory mania, or psychokinesia, a term the researchers into automatic action and the paranormal also used at the time. He spoke of Thaw's 'maniacal furor' on the night in question and had no doubt the madness he suffered from was transient. William White concurred. Thaw's 'defect of reason', as far as he was concerned, meant he didn't have complete knowledge of right and wrong; nor did the fact that he could remember his actions discount a diagnosis of insanity. Ely Jelliffe pronounced that all of Thaw's intellectual functions were affected by his defective judgement.

The defence had now lined up one by one – all but the hugely respected Dr Allan McLane Hamilton, who was now subpoenaed into court. He had found Thaw to be suffering from dementia praecox – one of Kraepelin's two great disease categories, the other being manic depressive psychosis. In Kraepelin's view, dementia praecox – eventually reconfigured as schizophrenia – was a disorder of thinking, or cognition. Understood as a psychosis that had a paranoid subtype that Hamilton ascribed to Thaw, this was the late-nineteenth-century asylum diagnosis par excellence, and it was understood to lead to inevitable disintegration. Thaw's was no temporary condition.

Jerome insisted that Hamilton recount all his findings, not just what the defence wanted to hear and had hired him for. This needed to include the inherited component of Thaw's condition. 'If the real facts were known,' (about the madness in Thaw's family and Harry, himself) Jerome insisted, 'I would have no right to be here trying this man. He is incapable of advising counsel.' This last was, of course, the first measure of legal sanity – competence to plead. If Hamilton's diagnosis was to be taken on board, Thaw was incapable of standing trial.

Jerome, having undermined his own case, then waxed even more radical, questioning the ability of the M'Naghten rules to deal with contemporary psychiatric knowledge:

Dr Hamilton, having examined this defendant, was of the opinion that he was of unsound mind during, or rather, prior to the time that he committed the crime, that he was of unsound mind as he committed it, and that he is still today of unsound mind, within the meaning of the statute, and incapable of properly advising his counsel on the defence; he is of opinion in a general way that this defendant is suffering in general from a type or form of insanity known as paranoia, or a paranoiac condition; that in paranoia very often — until it has passed into the extreme stage or terminal stage — the person who has it knows the nature and quality of his acts, and knows that they are wrong, and does them under an insane delusion; that the matter is, for lack of a better term, called medical insanity ... Today we are trying a man who, under the law of this State, is absolutely sane and is not a paranoiac, and every competent medical man honestly giving his opinion in this case, with a full knowledge of the facts, would say that he knew the nature and quality of the act that he committed; and knew that it was wrong — and still he was insane!

Since the McNaughton [M'Naghten] case was decided in 1842 by the House of Lords, which is the basis of all our insanity legislation, the knowledge of scientific men has passed far beyond; they know today that many a man who is insane knows what he is doing and what is wrong.

On the stand, Hamilton confirmed what Jerome had said. Thaw was incapable of cooperating with his lawyers and was suffering from a form of insanity which allowed him to recognize right from wrong, but from which only 'two per cent might recover'.

The Sanity Commission

Trapped by these conflicting expert opinions and by the about turn of the district attorney, the judge had recourse to a 'sanity commission', which would evaluate the expert witness from both sides in the form of affidavits, and determine whether Thaw was fit to 'understand his own condition, the nature of the charges against him, and of conducting his defence in a rational manner'.

Harry Thaw had been removed from the court during these arguments. According to the *New York Times*, he was 'absolutely confident that he can advise with counsel, and believes that when that has once been proved it will be far easier for his advocates to convince the jury of the brain-storm theory'. His courage was kept up by visits from Evelyn, his mother and his sister and, the *Times* noted, by reading 'St George and the Dragon' from Percy's *Reliques of Ancient English Poetry*. Thaw deems himself the 'knight of courage stout' who went to the aid of the damsel enthralled by the 'fiery dragon'. Stanford White was now a dead fiery dragon, and Harry's view of himself as the grand and principled saviour never faltered.

Two eminent attorneys and the well known medic, Dr Leopold Putzel, conducted the sanity evaluation. Witnesses from the Tombs, including two chaplains and a doctor, claimed that Thaw was rational, even though they had seen whole chapters of the Bible pasted onto his cell walls, containing notes for his lawyers. There were also scores of newspaper clippings and literary references: the heroic rescuer's arsenal was all around him.

The experts, once more divided, mostly kept to their initial positions. The prosecution alienists as well as Hamilton contended that Thaw was suffering from an incurable form of paranoia. They added that 'he had a homicidal tendency, which if he were released, would be a menace to the community'. Britton Evans, Hammond and Jelliffe, meanwhile, stated that whereas Thaw was irresponsible during the killing, he was now able to understand the nature of the charges against him and to conduct his own defence in a rational manner. After the physical examination on 3 April, when Dr Putzel and the two commission attorneys found no abnormal symptoms and shook Thaw's hand, he issued a statement to the press claiming that he had 'firmly convinced all three of the Commissioners I am sane in every sense of the word. I believe that when the court convenes for my trial tomorrow morning, the Commissioners will make a unanimous report to the Justice that in their opinion I am mentally competent in every way.'

The commission did indeed find Thaw sane and capable of conducting his defence. Jerome was in a double bind: how to demand a death sentence for a man he now thought insane?

38. Climax: 'Murder as a Cure for Insanity'

Delmas's closing defence speech, which he made on 8 April 1907, drew a portrait of Harry K. Thaw as the best kind of American, a protector of 'the purity of the home and the purity of American women'. If this was madness, then it deserved a patriotic diagnosis of 'dementia Americana', he stated, launching a whole new form of lunacy for the newspapers to pounce on.

> It is that species of insanity which makes every home sacred. It is that species of insanity which makes a man believe that the honour of his wife is sacred; it is that species of insanity which makes him believe that whoever invades the sanctity of that home, whoever brings pollution upon the daughter, whoever stains the virtue of that wife, has forfeited the protection of human laws.

Some of the papers felt that Delmas, despite his rhetorical flair, was exaggerating just a little. He 'was straining the limits both of forensic and poetic licence when, in the morning hours, he had pictured as a veritable Sir Galahad, pledged to the knightly service of distressed maidens, this profligate, who for years had fluttered through the tawdry tinsel life of the Tenderloin, idly squandering such portion of a paternal fortune as a too indulgent mother had allowed him'.

District Attorney Jerome, nonetheless, had a difficult act to follow. He pleaded with the jury to remember that they were there to determine 'whether what the defendant did was, in law, justifiable or excusable'.

Five possible verdicts were open to them – murder in the first or second degree, manslaughter in the first degree, justifiable homicide or not guilty on the grounds of insanity. He pointed out that 'dementia Americana' did not equal justifiable homicide, which could only be carried out in self-defence: Harry's brutal murder of the great Stanford White certainly wasn't that. Nor was it excusable – that is, an accident. Jerome redescribed the murder. He tried to salvage White from the brutal image that Evelyn had painted of him: unchaste, yes, but violent no – after all, if he was such a heinous man why had the child she then was continued to see him? He then argued that the Thaw who had pursued young Evelyn and flaunted her through every European capital was no Sir Galahad either. If Thaw had been one of the more typical inhabitants of the Tenderloin, a son of a *padrone*, a godfather, and not of a Pittsburgh millionaire, if Mr White had been a modeller of plaster images and not a leading architect, there would be no talk of paranoia or brain storms, only of 'a vulgar, ordinary, low, sordid, murder'.

Jerome then poked fun at the experts who contended that a man could be insane when in love, insane when he was married and when he made his will, insane 'when he brutally and cowardly shot down his enemy whom he hated' – and then, suddenly, his insanity vanished. 'Murder as a cure for insanity is a new thing in this jurisdiction, until with Dementia Americana, it was introduced by my learned friend, Mr Delmas.'

When the time to instruct the jury finally came, Justice Fitzgerald reminded them that the law was there to protect everyone, no matter the character of the victim. He underlined that there was no excuse in law for 'an irresistible impulse to commit a crime, where the offender has the ability to discover his legal and moral duty in respect to it. Nor is it every weak and disordered mind that is excused from the consequences of crime.' Partial insanity – for example, if the defendant had an insane delusion as to the character of his victim – was no excuse for homicide. Explaining the brunt of the M'Naghten rules, the judge further reminded the jury that experts testify only to their own opinions. The jury was not bound, or indeed permitted, 'to accept testimony of opinions as you would accept testimony of facts'. Such opinions were merely an aid to their deliberations. If Thaw knew the nature and quality of the act he was doing and knew it was wrong, he had committed a crime.

The jury went out at five, couldn't reach a verdict by eleven, and were locked up for the night. They were sifting evidence that had accumulated over eleven weeks and four days, at a cost of a hundred thousand dollars to the state (two million at today's rates) and four times that amount to the Thaw family. Next day, looking haggard, the jury returned to the court and asked for further information. They didn't finally come back with their verdict until the day after, 12 April. Having deliberated for forty-seven hours, they now declared they had failed to agree. Seven had voted for murder in the first degree and five for acquittal on the ground of insanity.

A new trial was called.

39. Sexual Politics

The Thaw trial was kept in the public mind for months by a horde of reporters who not only commented on the look and statements of witnesses, lawyers and the accused, but speculated on or insinuated motives and meanings. The nature of madness and 'honour' killings, the fine points of expert analysis, what constituted female virtue and woman's place in the world, the definitions of perversity and perversion – all were debated in that democratic forum that is the press.

Criticized or admired, Evelyn Nesbit was at the centre of the media storm. Through her, America came face to face with its contradictory morality. The country was prepared to visit at the shrine of her nubile photographic image, but the very fact that Stanford White had been equally attracted and had stepped over the line from wish to consummation had not only destroyed his reputation as an architect, but in some quarters had turned his murderer into a hero. Meanwhile, Evelyn's calm refusal to condemn White outright as a horrendous beast tarnished her image. Female desire and desirability combined with female intelligence were simply too dangerous in one tiny child-woman. No one, however, seemed to be particularly aghast at the sadistic brutality of Harry K. Thaw: the existence of millions seemed to excuse a million ills. Perhaps the savage Thaw rather than the civilized White incarnated a preferred image of masculinity.

Yet even though the trial reporters, standing in for Everyman and woman, might turn against Evelyn, their depiction of her extraordinary calm and honesty on the witness stand came to embody a new twentieth-century manifestation of emancipated femininity.

Women reporters – like Evelyn herself, relatively new figures on the American public scene – were present in substantial numbers at the Thaw trial. Nicknamed the 'pity platoon', 'sympathy squad' or 'lady muckrakers', they were mostly excluded from the courtroom when proceedings grew too sexually explicit: the judge, unwittingly echoing Thaw's own feelings about women and virtue, ordered all but four of the most serious 'sob sisters' to leave. They sat at their own special table. It may have been the famous wit Irvin S. Cobb, then a rising journalist, who named the 'four fine looking girls who spread their sympathy like jam' 'sob sisters', thereby giving birth to a term that would long outlive its origin. Women's coverage was intended, like popular fiction, to elicit tears, a 'great depth of womanly feeling' – to show the human face of a story.

The Pittsburgh millionaire was uncomfortably popular with the romanticizing type of woman, unlike the marauding Stanford White – in the period leading up to the trial, many chorus girls had spoken out against him. Whether this was due to the Thaw family's financially seductive efforts or to White's actual seductions will never be known. Thaw's 'is a lovable face', wrote Beatrice Fairfax of the *New York Evening Journal*. 'Wilful, and perhaps weak, it is yet lovable. One can imagine that he was an easy boy to spoil ... The chances are that, even without his fortune, Harry Thaw would have been popular among women.' It may as easily be the case that the allure of millions in the Gilded Age happily stood in for any other lacks.

Of Evelyn, that slip of a girl who had run the whole gamut of emotions and 'crowded more into her few short years than other women go through in a lifetime', the same reporter emphasized her 'sad little face now, with all the joy and youth faded out of it'. She judged both Thaw and Evelyn to be two 'unruly natures' who, given their 'lack of self control', inevitably ushered in an unhappy end.

> The story of Evelyn Thaw's life is a lesson to every foolish little girl in the land who imagines that the greatest of joys lies in posing before the world as a famous beauty and receiving the homage and gifts of men whose attentions, did the girl but know, are an insult instead of an honor.

America and its women couldn't work out whether Evelyn was a vixen or a victim, an active beneficiary of her own rape, or its sullied loser. Whereas Stanford White was condemned as an ageing seducer and rapist, Harry Thaw's whipping and humiliation of Evelyn brought almost no comment: prevailing wisdom seemed to think it altogether unremarkable that a man might beat the woman who was, or would soon be, his wife. Domestic violence, after all, was not unusual.

Then, too, Harry blubbed and sobbed in court, while Evelyn largely maintained a reasonable composure, only once letting tears overcome her. Thaw's emotion garnered sympathy from the women reporters, while Evelyn's clarity, her intelligence, her stoical self-control through difficult cross-examination, her ability to speak calmly about sexual events, all rendered her more suspect: if not an outright liar, then a denatured woman. The QC Helena Kennedy, writing about women in the courts today, shows that things have not altogether changed: a cool distance, let alone overt sexuality and lack of fluffy emotion in a woman, can brand her as guilty and immoral just as easily now as it did then. While Evelyn spoke, the papers reported, the women in court bowed their heads, evidently in shared shame.

The headline to a report on the Thaw case by Dorothy Dix stated that an all-woman jury – there wasn't a single woman on the jury of the Thaw trial, of course – would certainly acquit Harry for killing Stanford White, since 'Killing through Jealousy Appeals to Female Heart' and 'Emotions Would Almost Entirely Govern a Decision by Fair Sex'.

In her analysis of the press at the trial, *Front-Page Girls*, Jean Marie Lutes quotes one of the most coolly analytical of the 'sob-sisters" assessments of Evelyn. Nixola Greeley-Smith of the *New York Evening World* wrote: 'I have no illusions about Evelyn Thaw . . . I think merely that she was sold to one man and later sold herself to another.'

The same Greeley-Smith (who met her soon-to-be husband, a fellow journalist, at the trial), during Evelyn's narrative of the horrors of her sexual victimization, writes of the duty of giving to the trembling, weeping woman on the witness stand any support that the presence of members of her own sex might afford. I think all the women present felt it, and only a sense of utter mental and physical nausea made any of them forget it and fly from the flaunted shames, the dark horrors of that court-room.

Moreover, they fled from it in vain. For these horrors followed them into the sunlit street, into their offices, back to their homes, and kept relentless vigil at their pillows, making them wonder if the iniquity through which Evelyn Thaw had passed was to leave a permanent polluting stamp on all who heard it.

At the heart of the trial was Evelyn's despoliation, to which White's murder came a poor second. When she recounted the sordid facts of her deflowering and broke into tears, the courtroom and the 'sob sisters' sobbed with her. Her 'wrenching tale of betrayal and debauched innocence' had an even more devastating effect on Harry, the papers reported: he broke down in tears, and uttered the sounds of a wounded animal. It was these sounds that garnered sympathy for Harry.

One other aspect of Evelyn's testimony had the women reporters split in their estimation of her. On the sixth day of her brave open testimony concerning her sexual life, DA Jerome once more set out to cast her as more sinning than sinned against. This time he used her schooldays diary to illustrate that she was not quite the home-loving would-be wife that her testimony might have been intended to evoke. At sixteen, commenting on her mates, she had written:

A girl who has always been good and never had a word of scandal breathed about her is fortunate in more ways than one. These girls are all just that kind. They have been kept from the world all their lives and know very little of the mean side of it. And then, on the other hand, there is not one of them who will ever be 'anything'. And by 'anything' I mean just that. They will perhaps be good wives and mothers and die good wives and mothers. Most people would say, What could be better? But whether it is ambition or foolishness, I want to be a good actress first.

All the papers reported, or printed verbatim, this moment in Evelyn's testimony. She had been unflinching in her response to questions about waking in Stanford White's tower after the rape, to insinuations that her 'appendicitis' might well have been an abortion or to inquisitorial probing about Thaw's whipping attack and rape – but this extract from her diary, it was said, was the one moment that brought a blush to her pale cheeks. Evelyn had been outed as a woman who harboured desires, evidently perverse for the time, to be more than a domestic appendage, a good little wife. Perhaps she was also flushed through worry that the court, in the light of her wishing to be an actress, might take her entire testimony as a performance.

But the women journalists didn't uniformly attack her teenage revelations. Hard-headed Greeley-Smith defended this schoolgirl's diary: 'Though Mr Jerome read the slangy passages of this interesting human document with as insinuating an emphasis as his varied voice could summon, the worst interpretation that Mrs Thaw's worst enemy could place upon it is that at sixteen her view of life was, as the New York vernacular phrases it, "hip".' To wish to have a working life carried no shame, this commentator thought: indeed, she herself would be wooed back into journalism after her marriage.

40. Expert Fall-out

Harry Kendall Thaw languished in jail for nine long months before his second trial began. During that time his affection for his wife, the newspapers reported, dimmed, and he took up the study of Christian Science. Meanwhile his lauded sister, the Countess of Yarmouth – whom Harry had held up to Evelyn as a counter-example to Stanford White's claim that all people really behaved badly in secret – was divorcing her husband on grounds of non-consummation of their marriage. Evelyn's relations with her in-laws grew no better, but as the second trial approached, they knew they had to rely on her once more for her testimony.

Principal players apart, it was the expert witnesses who seemed most appalled by the progress of the first trial. They were calling for reform. Writing in *The American Lawyer*, which devoted its July 1907 issue to articles on the 'fiasco of the recent Thaw trial', Hamilton reiterated his belief that Thaw was permanently insane. He attacked his fellow alienists for supporting the defence of temporary insanity. They had sold out to the highest bidder in what he described as 'the present prostitution of scientific testimony'. He and several other experts now voiced their opinion that impartial experts should be appointed by the court to examine defendants in a hospital setting.

Others objected to the form of the all-inclusive, multifaceted hypothetical questions that lawyers put to experts, demanding at their long-delayed end a yes or no response about the defendant's sanity. A human life could hang on this single response, which might include one or two hypotheses with which the expert simply could not agree. Looking back at the trial, though not naming it, at the sixty-fifth annual meeting of the American Medico-Psychological Association in June 1909, the defence's star expert witness, Britton D. Evans, objected to the hypotheticals, which grouped too many unknowns together and forced the witness to accept them all as facts:

> In a somewhat celebrated murder trial in which I appeared as one of the expert witnesses, a hypothetical question was so framed as to lead a casual observer to believe that it embodied all the essential facts which had been presented upon the witness stand, but in one part of it it had this phrase: 'and assume that this time he was suffering from a disorder of the mind'. Now whatever might have constituted the other parts of this lengthy question, since a 'disorder of the mind' is used to indicate mental unsoundness, mental derangement and insanity, it is clear that the witness, by the insertion of this one assumption, was left no choice as to a conclusion and was denied the right of discrimination and the opportunity of weighing the other parts of the question.

Evans was also aiming at the critics who wanted all experts to agree. New forms of selecting expert witnesses, perhaps by official boards, were being mooted; but these, Evans argued, would be selected by people who themselves might disagree with each other. If selected for life and thus responsible to no one, the experts could still find reasons to differ. In addition, there were other real difficulties in making the principles of medicine meet the requirements of the law.

The law too often ended up disarranging and misusing 'legitimate and reliable scientific findings in order that they may be made to meet the demands of established legal precedents or harmonize with court rulings, many of which are relics of antiquity'. The relationship of medicine to law may have begun in England at the Suffolk witch trials of 1665, when the natural philosopher and doctor, Sir Thomas Browne, had examined the accused. But medical science had grown in expertise since then. It was progressive. Evans went on:

> It does not depend on the dogma and theories of the middle ages; it does not even hang on the theories of the last decade, but accepts

that which is proven to be the soundest and best after it has been subjected to scientific scrutiny and careful analysis. In medicine no great authority of the past is allowed to retard the investigations and progress of today or to interfere with the steady strides which were made through scientific medical research in the interests of humanity.

For all the criticism, Evans underlined, the court needed its experts: and it couldn't expect them ever and always to agree. After all, judges at the Supreme Court didn't always agree either.

William A. White had already suggested in his article 'Expert Testimony and the Alienist' in the *New York Medical Journal* of 25 July 1908 that professional jealousy was hardly unknown, even amongst doctors. The specialist who hadn't been called to give his expertise to a court and consequently had not received 'large fees . . . can well afford to decry the lack of morals in his more fortunate brother'. Using his own psycho-analytic expertise, White had termed this a 'defence reaction' which allowed the unsummoned professional to 'spare himself the discomfort that comes from emotions that find no means of outlet'. A less techni-cal way of putting it was to say they were venting their spleen. Too often they had no understanding of the way the criminal law worked, and that what they proposed would mean its radical overhaul.

Evans, in his lecture, went on to re-emphasize that in all expert fields there are differences of opinion. In court, however, witnesses were badgered 'by pugnacious and aggressive lawyers' and sometimes had to react either combatively or submissively. If the latter, jury and public thought them ill-equipped and incompetent, not qualified to testify in the capacity of expert. Humiliation followed. If, on the other hand, the witness stood firm in his convictions and refused to be forced into a false position, he would then be criticized for arrogant lecturing, for behaving like an advocate or showing bias. Evans's recom-mendation was that experts needed to put their opinions in plain English, back them up, and be fearless of criticism or of the aggressive attacks of examining counsel.

In the discussion that followed the lecture, a Dr Stedman recommended that a court-appointed expert would be the surest means to 'secure unbiased expert opinion'. The employment of such an officer of the court would not preclude the hiring of further expertise by defence or prosecution, but for the jury the opinion of the court expert, since it was disinterested, would necessarily carry greater weight. A law in favour of the appointment of such experts had thus far failed to be passed, even though it would uphold the dignity of the medical profession. Germany had such appointees, and as a result their doctors were not held up to ridicule and cases were quickly settled. There, in difficult cases the accused would be sent to a hospital for some months for pre-trial observation.

Most telling of all the comments at this annual meeting was the criticism Britton Evans himself received. The specialists did not approve of his having coined a 'classification' on the witness stand, particularly one that had caught the attention of the media. Classifications had to be agreed upon by the learned society as a whole. As if they had arrived some hundred years early for a meeting of a *Diagnostic and Statistical Manual of Mental Disorders* task force, the good doctors scorned Evans's colourful notion of a 'brain storm' as a diagnostic category.

Although indignant about the publicly reported and undignified 'battle of the experts', the professionals were not averse to doing battle with each other. Nor, in time-honoured fashion, did they mind taking the more prominent physicians down a peg or two. Evans's reputation suffered, while White and Hamilton were bitter until the end about the humiliation the trial had brought. And on top of this professional malaise, all the experts claimed that the Thaw family had failed to pay them the agreed fees. Evelyn was to fare no better at the hands of the millionaires, insane or not.

41. The Second Trial of Harry K. Thaw

Thaw's second trial began on 6 January 1908. Though still much reported, it didn't consistently make the front pages – except when it was Evelyn's turn to come to the witness stand. It may have been the same navy-blue schoolgirl outfit she was wearing, but Evelyn, according to one reporter, appeared at the opening day of the trial like 'a new radiant self instead of the wan, pinched girl of the first trial'. Perhaps it was the lavish hat that made the difference: a vast black velvet topped with a lavender rose amidst a cluster of violets and draped with a newly fashionable motoring veil. Though the radiance may equally have been the effect of life at the Waldorf, her current address, and six months without Harry. As for Harry, in his place in the dock, he was both quieter and grimmer.

As before, some six hundred prospective jurors were summoned in order to find twelve good men and true. But this time, instead of Napoleonic Delmas at the helm of the defence team, the lead was Martin W. Littleton, a witty and agile attorney who, with the Thaw family's backing, would argue for a simple insanity verdict. There would be no attempt to argue temporary insanity or appeal to the unwritten law.

In his opening speech, Littleton stated that the defendant 'would make the simple claim that at the time he killed Stanford White he was insane'. This was effectively what Thaw's first and fired advocates had urged. Littleton had had prior discussions with District Attorney Jerome, and though the prosecution argued that Thaw's murder of White had been a premeditated act, the trial moved on far more quickly than its predecessor. Expert witnesses were limited by the judge, Justice Victor J. Dowling, to three on each side.

Littleton called his first expert witness on the second day. He was going down the well beaten path of inherited insanity. Dr Robert H. Chase of the Friends' Asylum in Frankford, Pennsylvania, testified to the mental incompetence of a cousin of Harry's father. She had been an inmate at the institution. Next came a nurse, Amy Gosette, who had attended Harry for three weeks under the auspices of one Dr Price Mitchell in 1897 in Monte Carlo, while she was working there. Jerome, being his usual argumentative self, objected to the violation of personal medical material without prior permission. A seemingly confused Harry was asked to waive confidentiality privileges. He eventually murmured the only words that would leave his lips during the trial, 'I do.' Nurse Gosette proceeded to describe how Harry, who was running a high temperature while under her care, had behaved in an entirely irrational manner, 'was very unsettled in his actions and direction of thought'. Against the doctor's orders not to leave his room, a wild-eyed, twitching Thaw had gone out, only to return to finish a quantity of letters that he then destroyed.

Witnesses, including a schoolteacher who remembered him for his 'backwardness', then all attested to Harry's incoherence of speech, his running-together of words, going off on wild tangents, failing to do the simplest things, and his crazy eyes. There were testimonies about relatives who had spent their lives in asylums, and the statement of the steward from Manhattan's Whist Club where Thaw came periodically, sometimes staying in the club rooms. He had been there on the day before the murder and on the actual day, and talked of Thaw's irrational speech and actions, his twitching and nervousness. A hotel switchboard operator stated that Thaw had made an outlandish seventy-five telephone calls in three or four hours. A second schoolteacher talked of his impulsive behaviour, his 'animal-like howls and his tearless crying. His eyes were wide and rolling.'

Harry's mind was patently unsettled, a view with which his mother in a letter to Harry's former teacher Abram Beck concurred. 'His mind is more or less unbalanced,' she wrote, adding that he 'ought to have been more closely reared and trained'.

Mrs William Thaw now rose from her sickbed and travelled from

Pittsburgh to take the stand. She was feverish and feeble, and her testimony was rather different from that given at the first trial. She spoke of how her 'nervous system' had suffered after the death of her first child and how she had been an invalid until six months before Harry was born. Though he seemed normally healthy at first, a congestion of the lungs at three months induced nervous problems and sleeplessness. He also screamed, was frail, had fits and what was diagnosed as St Vitus' Dance. Other members of the family were 'weak-minded', nervous or epileptic and had spent time in asylums.

Mrs Thaw stood down without cross-examination because Jerome had permission from Littleton to read before the court her affidavit for the *first* trial. This stated that there 'were no family secrets to be hidden' and that there had been no sign of insanity or epilepsy for four generations in Harry K. Thaw's direct line of descent. Evidently, definitions as well as declarations of madness were a moveable feast.

It is tempting to speculate, however, on the key to Harry's character that Mrs Thaw's new trial narrative provides. Her stress here on her suffering nervous system, on Harry as a swift replacement child after the death of her firstborn, on his succession of early illnesses, finds parallels in the troubled infancy of other 'deviant' subjects. The presence of a dead and much mourned baby between mother and Harry may well have contributed to his ever shaky sense of himself. Beneath the image of scion of the millionaire family, there often seems to be little more than a small boy thrashing about in a world he can't quite make sense of. His compulsive and perverse beating of young boys, the forbidden pleasure he takes in it, may well signal a wish to eradicate the ghost infant who had preceded him in his nervous mother's affections.

More witnesses followed, to testify to Harry's insanity. At Claridges in 1899, he had been in so excited a state that a Dr Wells diagnosed subacute mania and had him transferred to a nursing home, where for six days he made preposterous demands. A physician from Paris's Hôtel d'Orsay stated that he had attempted suicide by swallowing poison when there with Evelyn Nesbit. A British doctor, in Rome, had diagnosed a case of mild mania.

The vice crusader Anthony Comstock had not been well enough to testify at Thaw's first trial, but this time he appeared. He recounted Harry's coming to his office and detailing the vicious sex life of Stanford White. He had also told Comstock he was being shadowed. Perhaps only this last accounted for the personal blow for Harry from the Comstock he admired: 'I thought his mind was unbalanced.'

It was Evelyn's testimony that once more drew vast crowds to the courthouse, as well as legions of journalists. It also drew Prosecutor Jerome's most heated cross-examination. The papers, this time, were less sympathetic to Eveyln. She appeared too composed, too strong, no longer the little girl but the contained, confident woman. The press on the whole didn't approve. The *New York Times* stated that 'she was flushed of face, but the flush was the mantling of the cheeks of a woman angry at heart and not the flush that comes with a sense of shame'. The first time, the paper reported, she 'lisped in constant suggestion of childish innocence'. The details were given 'with a calmness and poise that made them all the more thrilling and horrible'. This time round there was no lisp, the cynical *Times* underscored: 'she was no longer in the role of a child', even if her attire showed that 'her feminine heart was still attached to the juvenile in the matter of make-up'.

Perhaps Evelyn really had grown up; perhaps too, she had had her fill of the Thaw family and its mean millionaire ways.

Littleton, intent on proving Harry insane, not a jealous man who had rescued his wife from dishonour, quickly took Evelyn through her testimony. The effect, according to the *Times*, which nonetheless carried the trial on its front page for the first time since its second round had started, was that 'where women in the courtroom – newspaper women accustomed to the sensational – had bowed their heads and gasped a year ago, they maintained a stolid indifference this time'. Evelyn shed no tears and didn't collapse, and her sexual congress with Stanford White in this current rendition seemed less important than the details of the furnishings in his apartments.

Evelyn stood her ground remarkably well against Jerome's

haranguing objections – so marked that in his summing-up Littleton complained of his attitude of 'unofficial antipathy' towards her, as if his entire case rested on Evelyn's morality, not on Thaw's sanity. Evelyn herself, in this trial, emphasized the signs of Thaw's madness and the fact that everyone had told her 'Harry was crazy'. Harry's attempted suicide by overdosing on laudanum in the Hôtel d'Orsay was now narrated in detail; as well as a plan that they commit joint suicide at the Waldorf – on the very day when he had made those seventy-five telephone calls.

Jerome's cross-examination began promptly at three, and was intended totally to subvert any possibility of the jury trusting in Evelyn's honesty, or indeed innocence. She was, he set out to prove, a hardened money-grabbing schemer already immersed in vice, whose account of why she had initially refused to marry Harry and what she had told him so as to tip him over the edge was a pack of lies. According to the New York Times, he 'hammered mercilessly on the question of the witness's conception of what was moral in the matter of the relation of the sexes, and quoted from her former testimony that illicit love was 'indelicate and vulgar'. But Evelyn, the tiny twenty-three-year-old with little education, came back at him with such cool that the Times felt impelled to express its admiration: 'So clear in mind was the witness', so 'quick of wit', that she declared she knew 'instinctively that it was not right to marry Harry Thaw'.

Why had she not told the court of Harry's suicide attempt the first time round? Jerome quizzed. 'Because Mr Delmas said it would make Harry out to be too crazy.' And when Jerome queried her about Barrymore, Thaw's courtship, White's money, the Hummel affidavit, she answered it all with 'dauntless courage' and a straightforward veracity that turned Jerome's harshness to her favour.

This was Evelyn's finest performance. Perhaps the sheer crush of the public who had pushed or begged their way into the court – bearing personal letters to court officers or pleading varieties of personal reasons to be allowed admittance – had brought her star talents to the forefront. But then, as she admitted in her memoir, she had by this time learned how to be a witness – and Jerome no longer had the power to frighten her with his bullying tactics. During the recess, according to the *New York Times*, 'the corridors of the Criminal Court Building on the first floor were overrun by the curious, and many women and boys fought and scrambled for a chance to get a glimpse of the wife of the prisoner'.

42. Manic-depressive Insanity

Having had more time with Thaw, and perhaps more time to make good their earlier classificatory vagaries, the three defence expert witnesses, Drs Evans, Wagner and Jelliffe, had arrived at a uniform diagnosis for this second trial. They now determined that Thaw suffered from manic-depressive insanity. According to Dr Wagner, this entailed phases of both mania and melancholy in the patient. 'Suicidal attempts often mark these cases,' he stated, 'and such habits as the writing of incomplete letters, quick irregular habits of speech, nervousness and restlessness are all characteristic.'

With dark irony, Jerome stated that this 'manic-depressive insanity' was a new one for him. He had heard of other kinds, but hadn't had time to specialize in that branch, much as he would have liked to. His comment underlined how many different kinds of insanity had already been attributed to the defendant. The doctors were being inordinately inventive on behalf of their client.

In fact, manic-depressive psychosis had recently entered the psychiatric literature, and was soon to acquire a great deal of renown, since it seemed to make sense of a whole series of symptoms and solve certain puzzles. It was the famous German psychiatrist Emil Kraepelin, who in 1899 had taken the earlier classification of 'circular insanity', amplified the details, and called the new illness 'manic-depressive psychosis'. For the sixth and definitive edition of his *Textbook* – which served as an early model for the *Diagnostic and Statistical Manual of Mental Disorders*, the current bible of the American psychiatric profession – Kraepelin systemized its various characteristics in a copious depiction of what he considered to be an affective, or mood-based, illness.

Kraepelin was well known in the United States. The Swiss-born psychiatrist Adolf Meyer (1866–1950), for example, was influenced both by him and – oddly, since in Europe the two were deeply opposed – by Freud. Meyer introduced a Kraepelinian system of detailed history-keeping at the New York Psychiatric Institute, where he began working in 1902. He would become one of Thaw's doctors around 1909. Many other medics travelled to Heidelberg, where Kraepelin worked until 1904, and then to Munich to learn from the great classifier, whose punctiliously kept patient records provided the evidence for generalizing diagnoses.

In a volume that contained his writings on manic-depressive insanity and paranoia, Kraepelin listed many features that Harry K. Thaw shared with his own patients. Amongst these were 'tattered thoughts', 'so many thoughts in my head that I can't work', 'interpolated thoughts' which prevented consistent thinking as well as producing diffuseness in speech, heightened distractibility, rolling of the eyes and speedy, repetitive movement.

Kraepelin's patients were also subject to frequent delusions. In their manic state, like Harry's these might take on a paranoid flavour. They were surrounded by spies or being followed by detectives, despised by their neighbours, mocked, no longer greeted. They found allusions to themselves in the newspapers. They found poison in their coffee or in the washing water. They felt themselves hypnotized or magnetized by another. They spoke of the existence of a conspiracy against them. They experienced delusions of greatness, thought themselves of aristocratic origin and nurtured messianic projects. Some thought they were possessed, like Rockefeller, of vast sums of money, and spent it accordingly. In Harry's case, of course, he did more or less possess vast sums, so his spending didn't attract the police in the first instance. Bouts of fury as well as a marked sexual excitability were all symptomatic; and in the manic state, Kraepelin notes of these patients, they 'commit all possible acts of debauchery' and never show signs of fatigue. Evelyn's description of Harry in their remote Schloss comes to mind. In the depressive part of the cycle, when the patients are 'stuporous' and delusion is more difficult to determine, what Kraepelin calls 'delusional suicide' is often attempted.

It's hardly surprising that District Attorney Jerome had a little trouble with this latest of the defence's diagnostic moves. The pioneering George Robertson, Edinburgh's first professor of psychiatry and editor of the translation of Kraepelin's monograph on manic-depressive insanity, published in 1920, stated in his preface that 'as true Paranoia has also some affinities to some varieties of Mania, all these forms of insanity seem to merge into one another at their so-called boundaries or limits'. At the various hearings that followed upon Thaw's second trial, paranoia and manic-depressive insanity were often referred to as if they were more or less the same. Perhaps, in this second trial, the defence had agreed on 'manic-depressive insanity' because it was a diagnosis that could allow improvement. Given that Thaw was far less overtly agitated and visibly deranged at this trial, and indeed somewhat 'stuporous' or 'depressed', the current strategy could be said to fit more of the facts. But since the nature of manic-depressive insanity was that it was cyclical and would most probably recur, it also left the court free to make the judgement that it ultimately did.

Jerome didn't bother to call any of his own expert witnesses. Instead, in his summing-up he once more ridiculed the defence's attribution of insanity to Thaw. A good spanking in childhood would have done far more for his fits of temper than the best medical treatment: his teachers hadn't dreamt of thinking young Thaw insane until his mother had suggested it. Nor was there any report of insanity during the seventeen years between childhood and his meeting Evelyn Nesbit. Lawyers, bankers, drinking partners – none were called to testify to any madness on Thaw's part. As for the night of the murder, a man who knew how to grab his coat and go out with his wife, who knew enough to take his revolver with him, who dined and paid for dinner, who could tell a policeman that he had shot Stanford White and ask 'Is he dead?', who could discriminate between two brands of cigar at the police station . . . was not in Jerome's book an insane man.

Then, too, there was the time factor to consider: a period of three years had elapsed between Thaw hearing Evelyn's narrative about White, and the murder: time enough to go gallivanting around Europe and get married. There was certainly no ground here for the defence's initial 'brain storm' theory of insanity. Finally, what kind of honourable man is it who shoots the man who purportedly once dishonoured his wife, and then lets the story of his wife's shame be told in open court, lets it go into the records and be spread far and wide by the newspapers – all to save his own miserable life? Perhaps Thaw could have been forgiven if he had 'killed quick'.

In his directions to the jury, Justice Dowling reminded them of the strictures of the M'Naghten rules: 'The doctrine that a criminal act may be excused upon the notion of an irresistible impulse to commit it, when the offender has the ability to discover his moral and legal duty in respect to it, has no place in the law. But it is a defense if his mind is in such an unsound state that reason and judgment are overwhelmed, and he acted from an uncontrollable impulse and as an involuntary agent.' Justice Dowling was very careful to underline that 'Heat of passion and feeling produced by motives of anger, hatred or revenge, are not insanity. The law holds the doer of the act under such conditions responsible for the crime, because a large share of homicides committed are occasioned by just such motives as these.'

The jury retired at 11.45 on the morning of Friday 1 February and only reached their verdict on the Saturday afternoon. They determined that Harry K. Thaw was not guilty 'on the ground of his insanity at the time of the commission of the act'.

The broad smile that came over Thaw's face, probably because he assumed he had not only been saved from the electric chair, but also granted his freedom, was soon wiped. The judge read a memorandum he had evidently prepared in advance. Since, according to the testimony on manic-depressive insanity, there seemed to be no suggested possibility of cure; since it was reasonably certain that the illness recurred, and at unforeseen times; since there was 'danger of assaults or murders being committed by the person who is troubled or afflicted by this ailment'; and since, in the 'depressive state of this form of the malady, it appears from the testimony that there is danger that a person so afflicted will commit suicide', the defendant was dangerous to public safety.

The court therefore ordered that Harry K. Thaw be detained in safe custody and sent to the Matteawan State Hospital for the criminally insane in upstate New York.

Within minutes of his verdict being announced, Thaw asked his defence lawyer, Martin Littleton, to come and see him in the New York County sheriff's office, where he was being held until the journey upstate.

An exhausted Evelyn was lying on a sofa when Littleton arrived. Harry was smiling and impatient. Despite it being a Saturday afternoon, he ordered Littleton to proceed immediately to the Supreme Court to apply for a writ of habeas corpus. Littleton agreed, but he and his defence team second, Daniel O'Reilly, had already established that the court order had to be accepted for the time being.

It was O'Reilly who accompanied Thaw on the 4.39 train that would take them to Fishkill in upstate New York. Reporters teemed and the crowd cheered as Thaw got into the waiting car, where a journalist interviewed him and had him reminisce about the murder. Visibly happy at the attention, Thaw was at his joking best, though one of his jokes entailed taking back the cash fee he had paid O'Reilly while still in the sheriff's office.

Evelyn joined them on the train. At Fishkill more reporters were waiting, together with a crowd of local onlookers. Thaw's group ate and drank at the town hotel. Just after nine, the deputy sheriff indicated that it was already past lights-out time at the Matteawan Hospital. Reluctantly, but smiling for the photographers, Harry left to make the thirty-five-minute drive to what – despite his family's, and indeed at first Evelyn's, and certainly his own best efforts – would be his new home for years to come.

The Matteawan Hospital in Beacon had been established in 1892 to replace an earlier asylum at Auburn. This had housed criminals along with ordinary inmates, and had exceeded its capacity. Purpose-built, readily reachable by train, with 'an abundance of light and ventilation' and on a site that offered some 246 acres of 'good tillable land, pure water and pleasant scenery between the Hudson River and the Fishkill mountains', Matteawan was intended as a model correctional asylum, at first housing some 550 inmates. There was a work programme for those who could cook, farm or make clothing or rugs; twice-daily outdoor exercise, a variety of sporting activities, weekly movies, and special entertainments for holidays. By 1889, the hospital had grown beyond its bed space, and a new prison mental hospital was built for those who had gone mad while serving their sentences.

Lore has it that with his millions, Harry could afford his own room, special food, drink and cigars, as well as evening drives with warders along a road where he became well known – or so Evelyn recounted in her memoir. According to her, the private room meant that she and Harry also engaged in occasional marital activity. So she contended, to the accumulated Thaw family rage, when a son was born in October 1910.

43. *Fighting Lunacy*

In what became a precedent, replayed by many in the course of the century (including most recently in Britain in the shape of the moors murderer, Ian Brady), Harry K. Thaw battled for years with the courts against his 'insanity' ruling. He had no intention of extending his confinement beyond the bare minimum. But the superintendent at Matteawan and the State Board of Lunacy took a different view. They publicly opposed any notion that he was now cured of his insanity. His trial lawyers seemed to agree, while DA Jerome also made it known that he would oppose any application for a writ of habeas corpus. Only Evelyn, who took a room in Fishkill, publicly stated that her husband didn't belong 'with a group of hopelessly insane creatures'.

Three months after his institutionalization, Thaw with his mother's help had a new team of lawyers in place. Over the next seven years they would repeatedly file for habeas corpus in the hope that one of the various judges would deem Harry sane. Since his trial verdict had been 'not guilty on grounds of insanity', once he was determined sane his liberty would be returned to him. Failing that reversal, Thaw's only possibility of obtaining his freedom was somehow to make his way outside the state of New York: insanity was not an extraditable offence within American states.

Habeas corpus (or *habeas corpus ad subjiciendum* – literally, 'you hold the person or body subject') is an order or writ from a superior (in this case, federal) to an inferior court (state), requiring the person they are holding to be brought to the higher court in order to examine whether he or she is being legally detained. Some attribute its spirit, if not its exact fact, to Magna Carta: habeas corpus acts as a safeguard of individual liberty from dictatorial arrest without trial. The great English jurist William Blackstone states that the procedure was codified in 1679: it allowed the subject, a member of the family or an advocate to petition for a writ of habeas corpus to be issued by a superior court, commanding the addressee (often a lower court, or a sheriff) to produce the subject before a court of law. This 'most celebrated of English writs', as Blackstone called it, is effectively a civil action against a jailer. In America, it tests whether the confinement of the subject is a violation of his constitutional rights.

Appealing to the Supreme Court for writs of habeas corpus, followed by hearings, is an expensive business. But the Thaw family was as ever prepared to pay (or promise to pay) anyone and everyone's expenses – except Evelyn's.

Insane, and therefore legally incompetent, Harry was no longer in charge of his own finances. This left Evelyn, whose usefulness had by now greatly diminished, at the mercy of her mother-in-law, who had long wanted her son to divorce the 'chorus girl'. The dowager had had Evelyn followed by detectives, who kept a record of her late-night activities. Payments due to her as a wife arrived only erratically. She was ever short of funds; and her loyalty to Harry, more or less intact for the first period of his confinement, eventually reached breaking point. Not only were his moods increasingly sullen and violent, but there seemed to be diminishing hopes of any financial settlement. Following threats he had made on her life, Evelyn began to testify to his insanity and filed for an annulment of their marriage. Like so many other wives disapproved of by rich mothers-in-law, she had lost out to the family. Though rumours had it that her initial loyalty to Thaw had been bought at great expense, her own story, and indeed her return to her working career soon after Harry's incarceration, seem to prove otherwise. The Thaw family millions never made their way into Evelyn Nesbit's pockets.

At the first appeal hearing at the New York Supreme Court at White Plains in May 1908, the evidence of the Thaw trial was rehashed, and expert psychiatrists battled it out once more. The judge found Thaw was not sane, and refused to grant him his freedom. The form of insanity from which he suffered could recur, the experts agreed. 'The safety of the public is better insured by his remaining in custody and under observation,' the judge stated, 'until he has recovered or until such time as it shall be reasonably certain that there is no danger of a recurring attack of the delusion or whatever it may be.' Proving sanity in civil courts can be as difficult as proving insanity in criminal courts.

No longer the district attorney who had been elected by a landslide, William Travers Jerome, the man who had done more than anyone in New York to make the public appreciate the need 'of a fearless and incorruptible administration of the law', was now state prosecutor. He would not or could not let Thaw, the millionaire who had murdered the great and now rarely mentioned Stanford White, go. He was adamant that Thaw should not be allowed to buy his freedom: 'It has been said that in the end, the Thaw money would defeat the ends of justice,' he stated. 'But wherever this case has gone, and where it has rested, it has left a trail of ignominy, disgrace, filth and scandal behind it ... The state of New York will not permit justice to be defeated by the corrupt use of money if it can prevent it.'

Jerome's tactic was repeatedly to show not only that Harry was still insane, but that he was debauched and depraved and that the family as a whole was corrupt. In both the 1909 and the 1912 hearings the state called a Mrs Merrill, mentioned earlier, who in fear and trembling reported on Thaw's sadistic activities. She testified that he had kept rooms, first at 46th Street, then at 54th Street, under the name of 'Professor Reid'. Here came young girls he had falsely advertised for, who were subjected to terrible whippings. Some two hundred of them. One day, when she came running at their screams, Mrs Merrill had found two of them – one bleeding on the floor, the other at the mercy of his blows. She claimed that Thaw's eyes were protruding from his head and he looked like a madman. She got the girls out, but was terrified Thaw would kill her. This narrative of violence apart, Jerome made it equally clear that Mrs Merrill had been sought out by the Thaw family's agents prior to earlier trials, and had been subjected to threats and bribes and kept from court.

At the June 1909 hearing, it was also shown that Evelyn had received an extra five hundred dollars in her expenses envelope just before the trial, in order to keep her sweet and on Thaw's side. Many other, hostile, witnesses had been menaced and bought off. One Thaw lawyer turned prosecution witness, because he hadn't been paid all he had been promised. If Jerome didn't directly charge the expert psychiatric witnesses with foul practice and offering diagnoses for sale, he nonetheless had them confessing to lucrative links with Thaw family friends. From sometime in 1909, Adolf Meyer – soon to head the Johns Hopkins psychiatry department and the famously progressive Phipps Clinic – acted as one of Thaw's consulting psychiatrists. According to the *New York Times* of 27 July 1912, his performance in court did little to advance his reputation, since Jerome elicited from him the damning information that he was 'under engagement to take a position in an institution founded by friends of Harry K. Thaw'.

The Thaw millions seemed to insinuate their way into most minds. This was perhaps an unclassified madness all of its own.

Harry Thaw had to appear on the stand at all three of his habeas corpus hearings. He was plausible enough to begin with, though Jerome would eventually rattle him. Of the second hearing before Justice Mills in June 1909, the *New York Times* commented that many thought he would win his case, so 'cool and collected', 'quick and confident', was he for many hours when questioned by the former district attorney. Perhaps his demeanour was helped by the fact that at the local jail he was given a corridor of thirteen cells to himself; his suite was comfortably furnished and his meals sent in from the local hotel. Mother Thaw had evidently been at work for her dear son. Indeed, his treatment was so grand that the secretary of the State Prison Commission protested.

Defending himself against Jerome's attempt to prove him mad because he had gone to see a hypnotist in France, Harry explained to the court that he had done so because he thought White was hypnotizing his wife, and he wanted to learn more about how the procedure worked. To probe his grasp on sanity, the judge himself asked Thaw about the visible signs of his 'exaggerated ego' – part of the diagnoses both of manic-depressive insanity and of paranoia. Had he not sought repeatedly to correct his very expensive lawyers? Did he think he knew more than everyone? Harry struggled with the response.

Sanity is a very difficult thing to possess, even for those with a greater grip on it than Harry K. Thaw.

More grilling led Thaw to expose his own continuing sense of the justice of his killing Stanford White: whether this was a sign of on-going madness, or pointed to the fact that there had never been any, was something that it was too late to posit. On a long hot afternoon, and once more confronted by the rapid fire of Jerome's questions, Thaw finally lost his mask of composure, grew angry, tapped the floor nervously with his foot, and stumbled in his responses. His lips twitched so badly, he hid them behind a bunched handkerchief.

His mother's personal counsel, Clifford W. Hartridge, was appearing under subpoena. Notes and letters detailing his communication with the family had been lodged with the court. Hartridge revealed how he had been asked to pay off Mrs Merrill, the witness to Thaw's sadistic excess. Though the court was also told Hartridge was in the process of suing Mrs William Thaw for not having paid his full expenses, that did little to detract from the light he shed on Harry's violence.

Thaw was called back to the stand and interrogated by Jerome as to the veracity in his opinion of the fourteen psychiatrists who deemed him insane during his trial, and the fourteen who appeared at his first habeas corpus proceedings and swore that he had been crazy when he killed White. Thaw replied that he hadn't been insane in the way Jerome now meant: he had had a 'brain storm'. This was a temporary mental derangement, but not evidence of a diseased mind. He dis-agreed with all the 'bug doctors' who thought the latter. He nervously intimated that some of the doctors had been misinformed or indeed led astray by Jerome's office. The more Thaw talked, the more his paranoid delusions were again exposed.

Finally, the judge determined: 'He was a being who, in the eyes of several eminent alienists, was a paranoiac whose liberation from Matteawan would be a menace to the community.'

Thaw launched an appeal against the verdict, in the hope that a new jury trial to determine his sanity would be granted. It reached the Supreme Court, which in December 1909 ruled against him. Immediately, another appeal on grounds of habeas corpus was put in train. Meanwhile, Thaw's lawyers came up with another ruse: they declared him bankrupt in the state of Pennsylvania, and a writ of habeas corpus was issued for his appearance before the Pennsylvania State Court. But the sheriff of Westchester County, in whose custody Thaw was held, refused to obey the writ, and there was no authority to compel him.

Back at Matteawan, Thaw had long led a campaign against his treatment by the superintendent of the hospital, claiming he was no ordinary inmate to be locked up with others and forced into a bare cell from eight at night, only to be woken at six! He complained of abuses at the asylum, and eventually with the aid of the family wealth managed to force the hospital's existing heads out. He was probably right in complaining that inmates were not well treated, but this was hardly Harry's overriding intent. The replacement staff were all for pleading for his returned sanity. Bribes apart, it's not unlikely that they just wanted to get rid of him.

Thaw's third habeas corpus hearing didn't take place until June 1912. By this time Evelyn was a mother. Since Harry wouldn't recognize the paternity she claimed, she was in difficult financial straits. Luckily, she had at last made things up with her own mother, who offered to look after little Russell while she found work. It was impossible, given the scandal the murder had caused, for her yet to work at home, so she travelled to Britain where she played at the Hippodrome in London. In court, the estranged husband and wife rarely met each other's eyes.

Appearing before Justice Martin Keogh, Harry was even more nervous than at his prior trial and seemed lost, according to the *New York Times*, when Jerome questioned him about his decidedly strange letters to Evelyn. He eyed his own lawyer appealingly to come up with answers for him, and when he spoke his own, they were slow and faltering. The Matteawan assistant superintendent physician, Dr Roy D. Leak, however, testified that he thought Thaw was now a rational person. He claimed that he had complained about the previous superintendent and staff because they were mistreating him, guided as they were by Dr Flint, witness for the prosecution. They had placed Thaw in a dark room and heaped indignities on him. Dr Leak understood Thaw to be 'constitutionally inferior': this did not amount to insanity, though under the influence of alcohol, he might be provoked to violence.

Ever a liberal and worried about the effectiveness of disciplinary confinement, Dr William Alanson White, too, claimed that Thaw's insanity – which he himself had always thought temporary – had now gone: he was for all intents and purposes sane. He had examined Thaw back in 1907 and more recently several times at Matteawan. He had also read the Matteawan superintendent's 150-page report on Thaw, then spent three hours with him. Describing this examination, Dr White recounted how he had first gone through the standard mental tests: did Thaw remember him? what was the the date? who were the people around him? Then came some arithmetic and a few general-knowledge questions – the name of the president, the capital cities of European countries. Harry counted backwards, named the months, could describe the paintings and cathedrals he had seen on his travels. White also queried him about his alleged 'illusions': this probably refers to his certainty that he was being followed by Stanford White's agents. He saw Thaw again on 12 April and 3 June, and his opinion was that he was now a sane man.

In cross-examination, however, Jerome made it difficult for White to provide evidence supporting his opinion of Harry's present sanity. He quoted certain statements in a copy of his examination notes. These had Harry attributing conspiracy to others or labelling them paranoiac. For example, he was noted as claiming that Jerome had been bribed to keep him in Matteawan; that the judge's secretary in the earlier hearing had told him that Matteawan's Dr Baker – who had testified that he was still insane at the earlier trial – was a 'cold-blooded liar' and had been bribed into saying so. Like all longer-term inmates, Harry now had a good knowledge of the institutional language of asylum and court. He was well versed in the medical and psychiatric terms that had been attributed to him; and he now projected these outwards – claiming, for instance, that Dr Flint was paranoiac. Dr White didn't classify as insanity the fact that Thaw attributed all his own nefarious bribing acts, his own vision of the mental world, to others. It was true, though, White admitted to Jerome, that he had not talked to Thaw about certain of the women who figured in his writings. The implication was that his sadistic leanings could still present a danger.

This hearing also presented the testimony of the venerable Allan McLane Hamilton, who now took the stand for the first time since he had been hired by the Thaw family at the initial trial. He told the court that back then he had already reported to Mrs Thaw that her son suffered from chronic delirium, that he had all the signs of a person who had suffered a great shock, and that the best thing for the family and the public would be to have a commission of lunacy appointed to place him in an institution. In an altogether different tenor from some of Thaw's other alienists, Hamilton also confessed that he was an unwilling witness and had removed himself from the scene so as to escape Thaw's first trial; testifying, to him, meant breaching 'the sacred nature of the relations between a physician and his client'.

Given Hamilton's attitude to patient confidentiality, offering opinions in court, backed by evidence from the consulting room, was a tricky matter.

Of all the alienists, it was the ageing Dr Austin Flint – 'the popinjay', as he called him in his memoir – that Thaw most despised. Flint judged Thaw's newly discovered sanity laughable. In a 1910 article in the *American Journal of Insanity* he had referred to the Thaw appeals as a 'striking example of the misuse of the writ of habeas corpus'. Then, too, Evelyn and the elderly Flint had struck up a friendship, a fact that couldn't fail to send Thaw's ever rivalrous imagination into over-drive. At the last hearing, Evelyn had stated that he had threatened to kill her if he was released – and Flint was a firm believer in Thaw's potential danger. 'Under the influence of even a small amount of alcohol,' he stated, 'Thaw becomes quarrelsome and dangerous in the highest degree . . . These homicidal paranoiacs are especially dangerous to their supposed enemies, because they plot and scheme and murder, taking their victim unawares.'

More importantly, perhaps, Dr Flint – whom Thaw, imagining the world and the mental state of others in his own image, also labelled a 'paranoiac' – had on 10 January 1912 issued a statement in which he warned the public that a deep-laid plan for the release of Thaw was being hatched. If Dr Flint did not altogether state that the family millions were implicated in the fact that new officials favourably disposed to Thaw were now in place at Matteawan, the suggestion was there. Countering this claim in his summing-up, Thaw's advocate stated that his client's vociferous complaints about mistreatment at the hands of the facility's former chiefs had in fact led to considerable beneficial reforms for everyone. He may have been right, but this had little sway with the court.

Justice Keogh's decision came on 26 July, eighteen days after the hearing's start: 'Having listened to all the testimony and seriously considered it, I am of the opinion that Harry K. Thaw is still insane, and that his discharge would be dangerous to the public peace and safety.' Thaw's counsel, though expressing disappointment, stressed that Justice Keogh had also found Harry improved. There was hope to be had. A man who could hold his own in the horrible conditions of a place like Matteawan 'obviously cannot be very insane'.

A date for a further appeal, effectively a sanity review hearing, was fixed for 1913. Before that day came, certain officials of the asylum were charged with taking bribes to testify in favour of Thaw's sanity. It was decided to delay the appeal.

But Harry K. Thaw had had enough.

44. The Great Escape

Early on the morning of Sunday, 17 August 1913, Harry Thaw went out to the Matteawan exercise yard, where he was a familiar figure. That day he was earlier than usual, but the sole attendant thought nothing of it. When the milk cart arrived, Harry strolled along with him to open the gates so that the cart could come through. On the other side of the road, the attendant spied a dark limousine. Before he realized what was happening, Harry Thaw was inside the limo and being driven speedily away. By the time the police had been alerted and gave chase, Harry had been transferred to a Packard and was rushing towards the Connecticut state line at a speed witnesses said was an awesome seventy miles an hour.

Soon he was across the Canadian border. Five men had been hired, at a price rumoured to be twenty-five thousand dollars, to abet the escape. Before Thaw could join his mother at their country home in Pennsylvania, where according to her he was headed, he was picked up in the small Canadian border village of Coaticook and taken from there to the town of Sherbrooke. Here he was cheered at the station and welcomed as a man who had escaped American persecution. In his element, Harry rode through the streets in an open carriage waving his hat to those who shouted at him, 'Hurrah for British fair play.'

His stay in Sherbrooke was another of his wild adventures. He loved the attention of the press. In his interviews, he assured reporters he was a sane man, 'as sane as you or anyone else'. He had left Matteawan and come north because he knew he couldn't get a fair deal from the state of New York. He intimated that he was saddened by Evelyn's return to the stage, but stressed that neither she, nor Dr Flint, nor Jerome had anything to fear from him. He wanted to go back to his family and lead a quiet life.

The state of New York demanded extradition. Thaw's new Canadian team of lawyers refused. The federal government in Canada, however, bowed to American pressure, and on 10 September Thaw was extradited. Now a federal prisoner in the US, he nonetheless arrived in Concord, New Hampshire, to public cheers. Here he battled with the New York courts for over a year, trying to escape extradition to the state that wanted him back. In December 1914 he was finally ordered by the US Supreme Court to return to New York.

After a six-year absence, Harry Thaw was back in the Tombs. Temporarily at least, justice had triumphed over the millions.

In July 1915, Thaw was once more in the courts and pleading his sanity, this time before both judge and jury. Now, an expert on asylum life and on psychiatric as well as legal practice, when his entire history was again recapitulated by a new prosecutor he put up a credible performance of 'sanity'. There was no Jerome to make him nervous. Thaw still had no remorse over the killing of Stanford White. But the dead Stanford White seemed now to bear less of his irrational and jealous animus than did Dr Flint. During a moment that almost caused a mistrial, Thaw's advocate accused Flint of having a lip-reader with him in court, 'who interpreted whispered conversations Thaw had had with his counsel'. 'They have been watching some of Thaw's jocular remarks to me and are going to say it is evidence that he is insane,' he claimed.

It was clear that Thaw's lawyer had been taken in by his client's contagious paranoid discourse. Thaw enjoyed the fuss the lip-reading accusation caused. He was also buoyed by the nightly companionship of the sheriff who, report had it, took him out to dine sumptuously and to ride the overground. The half-hearted prosecution helped him as well.

Thaw's Toad of Toad Hall-like antics had endeared him to everyone along his route of escape from evil institutional forces. Now they continued to entertain the court. He openly called the psychiatrists 'bug doctors'. He stated, 'Dr Flint has no moral sense. He is a ridiculous person and just as prepared to say what is false as what is true. You can get any opinion from Dr Flint just as easy as a bartender gets beer from a spigot.'

Thaw was immensely pleased with this remark, and so was the crowded courtroom. Flint had made himself ridiculous in the public's eyes by stating that Thaw had attempted to hypnotize him, just as he had once set out to hypnotize young girls. No one seemed to worry too much about the murder, let alone Harry's track record of sadistic brutality. Like some presidential nominee, he seemed now to be on a winning ticket.

Playing to the gallery, Thaw won the jury over, and on 16 July they declared him a sane and thus a free man. He immediately filed for divorce from Evelyn, who, pleading illness in response to her sub-poena, hadn't appeared in court. In his divorce suit Thaw named as co-respondent a newspaperman, though Evelyn was now living with her dance partner, Jack Clifford. As soon as the divorce came through, she married him. The marriage didn't last.

Free, Harry went home to his mother and pontificated eagerly to the ranked Pittsburgh press on what a good, charitable and churchly citizen he was now going to be. He spoke of a campaign to rectify a legal system that had allowed a man to be committed to an asylum without a proper hearing on the question of his sanity. As that old hand Dr Hamilton had stated in court: people who aren't insane often have doubts about their sanity; the insane never do.

It didn't take all that long for the old brutal Harry to make a come-back. On 9 January 1917, the papers were full of a new sadistic scandal: this time Harry had kidnapped a Kansas youth, Frederick Gump Jr, whom he had met in an ice-cream bar in California. He had recruited the young man with the promise of work back east. Gump had been urged by his ailing father and impoverished family to accept, so good were Harry's rate of pay and his talk of a simultaneous technical edu-cation. There was even a letter confirming all this.

So Gump travelled east. Harry had asked him to come to New York, where he was staying at the McAlpin Hotel with his servant-bodyguard.

There, Harry Thaw, now a man of forty-six, held Gump against his will and proceeded to whip and abuse the boy to within an inch of his life. The next day, Gump somehow managed to escape and went to the police.

When the police finally tracked Thaw down, he was staying in a small Pittsburgh boarding house. Here he had tried to commit suicide by slashing his wrists. They also arrested his bodyguard, in whose pockets were letters from other young boys to whom Thaw had offered jobs. This time Mother Thaw decided to draw the line herself. She told reporters she could no longer resist the facts that demonstrated her son's insanity. She had applied to the court to have him declared insane. And although the New York State district attorney attempted to take the criminal, rather than the asylum, route to contain Harry within walls, Mrs Thaw won out. Harry was judged insane and committed to the Pennsylvania State Hospital in Philadelphia. The Gump family's attempt to sue for damages went on for years: the case was only finally settled out of court in 1924, when Thaw had determined to petition for his freedom once more.

Evelyn, on this occasion, decided to petition against Harry, claiming that he had not yet recovered his sanity: if he were freed, he would dissipate the estate in which their son had an interest. But Harry won his suit and was once more at liberty.

For a while, he displayed a little interest in an again divorced Evelyn and their, or her, son. He even helped her buy a new house in Atlantic City, and went to hear her sing at her run-down nightclub, the one that is said to have inspired Orson Welles in the making of *Citizen Kane*. But any hopes Evelyn might have held out of a reconciliation, or even a new marriage, were not to be. Even after his mother died in 1927, leaving him and his siblings one million each, it was too late for Harry to change his ways, as Evelyn had repeatedly hoped. She long held Mrs William Thaw responsible for at least a proportion of Harry's ways. But mother dead or alive, Harry carried on in the same way as ever, even managing to get himself barred from entering England, where in 1928 he was listed as an 'undesirable'.

It is not clear what triggered Harry's manic episodes or indeed the suicidal states that sometimes followed, but clearly, however implicated his mother might have been in his history, her death was no cure.

Poor Evelyn. Once the child star whose charismatic beauty seduced all and sundry, she grew into a despairing woman, addicted to morphine and alcohol, who several times attempted suicide. Right or wrong, as she said in her second autobiography, Stanford White was the only man she had ever loved. 'Stanny was lucky,' she purportedly added in a 1960s interview. 'He died. I lived.'

But the little girl who had saved her family from hunger with her modelling talents was a true independent spirit and a survivor. Stanford White had perhaps also spotted that, when he set out to educate her. She played in some ten silent films, sang and danced in a variety of clubs and cabarets around the country, even for short periods running her own. The clubs may have grown more down-at-heel over the years, but she carried on, her name appearing erratically in gossip columns – once, when her pet boa constrictor escaped into Lower Manhattan. 'He was an expert at keeping away the bill collectors,' she quipped. She also wrote her two autobiographies, and after the First World War ran a tea room in Manhattan. She lived to see the film made of her relationship with Stanford White. *The Girl in the Red Velvet Swing* (1955) earned her a Hollywood consulting credit, as well as needed funds and a revived interest in her life.

She died in 1967 in California, a grandmother of three, at the ripe age of eighty-two, though before she could witness her re-imagining in E. L. Doctorow's novel *Ragtime*. She had begun life as the object of painters' and photographers' gaze. She had inspired films and fiction. In the last part of her life, it was she herself who became the maker – of sculpture and ceramics, those very objects she had admired in Stanford White's houses. Her trajectory echoed women's possibilities through the course of the twentieth century. It also elaborated some of the many forms misogyny could take.

Harry K. Thaw, after more of the court cases he seemed to be as addicted to as the beatings he sadistically inflicted, died in Miami of a heart attack in 1947 at the age of seventy-six. He left Evelyn, the woman on whose behalf he had told himself he killed, a mere ten thousand dollars. It was the same amount he left a waitress he had had the briefest of contacts with in a Virginia coffee shop. But then the paranoid millionaire had never been accountable – and perhaps this waitress was now his idealized 'Boofuls'.

As for Stanford White, doubly forgotten as both man and architect for many years, in 1996 his great-granddaughter published *The Architect of Desire*. In retrieving his memory and his considerable achievements, his penchant for very young women aside, she discovered an autopsy report showing that at the end he had been suffering from Bright's Disease and incipient tuberculosis: he would probably have died of natural causes within a year of his murder.

45. *Assessing the Experts*

The Thaw case, which had preoccupied the courts for nine long years and cost the state over a hundred thousand dollars and the Thaw family ten times that, continued to cast a lurid light not only on its principal players but on the whole tricky subject of the role of the psychiatric witness in the courts. Could the contradictory opinions the experts provided ever be trusted in the hard evidential atmosphere of a forensic setting?

In January 1910, a Special Committee on the Commitment and Discharge of the Criminal Insane presented a report that damned the experts as 'unscrupulous'. They had, 'to the shame of the medical profession', both sworn Harry Thaw 'out of jail on an opinion of insanity', and attempted at another time 'to swear him out of the asylum by an opinion of sanity'. Their 'favourable opinions' could be bought by the family 'for cash'. The result would inevitably be that the murderer would be set free to 'direct his homicidal inclinations against some other citizen who has already fallen or may hereafter come under his displeasure'. And everything done according to the forms of law.

If those who feared murderous madmen on the streets were worried, the psychiatrists too were nonplussed by the Thaw trials. After his involvement, William A. White grew passionate about reforming the legal tests of insanity. 'Insanity' was a purely legal and sociological term that bore no relation to medicine, he noted. He didn't think the standard of 'responsibility' was an adequate marker for anyone. Nor did the sanity–insanity divide make any sense.

By 1916, White and Bernard Glueck's textbook, *Studies in Forensic Psychiatry*, put out by the American Institute of Criminal Law, was teaching that 'crime is a type of abnormal conduct which expresses a failure of proper adjustment at the psychological level'. This attitude was to prevail in professional circles until the physicalist and brain explanations – which the authors of this sentence had rejected – made a comeback in the 1970s.

In 1926 the young Karl A. Menninger, soon to become a leading player in the psychiatric and psychoanalytic field, asked White his opinion on 'The Credo of Psychiatrists' concerning crime which had just been pulled together by the American Psychiatric Association's Committee on the Legal Aspects of Psychiatry.

Some of the key points of the Credo read:

We believe
1. That the psychiatrist's chief concern is with the facilitation of human life adaptations, and with understanding and evaluating the social and individual factors entering into failure in this adaptation.
2. That crime is a designation for one kind of such adaptation failure, and hence falls definitely within the focus of psychiatry.
3. That crime as well as other behavior and characterologic aberrances can be scientifically studied, interpreted and controlled.
4. That this study includes a consideration of the hereditary, physical, chemical, social and psychological factors entering into the personality concerned throughout his life as well as (merely) in the specific 'criminal' situation. [All that remained for the twenty-first century to add to this buoyant list of scientific hopes was the term 'neurological'.]
5. That from the study of such data we are enabled in many cases to direct an attack upon one or more of the factors found to be active in a specific case to effect an alteration of the behavior in a propitious direction; or . . . make proper provision against subsequent . . . injuries to society. By the same experience and laws we are enabled in still other cases to detect and endeavor to prevent the development of potential criminality.

Part of this ambitious Credo (which came to inform aspects of the penal system in the US and was akin to eventual developments in Europe) specifically concerned the role of expert psychiatric witnesses. It is here that the malign experience of the Thaw trial is visible:

> We believe that psychiatrists should never be obliged to answer partisanly with 'yes' and 'no' to questions pertaining to such complex questions as commitability ('insanity'), responsibility, punishability and curability.
>
> We believe that psychiatrists testifying in legal cases should be employed by the court and report to the court after opportunity has been provided for a thorough psychiatric examination, with such aids as psychiatrists habitually use in clinics, offices and hospitals.
> . . .
> We believe the use of hypothetical questions in legal cases and the use of the words 'insane' and 'insanity' should be abandoned.

White wholly approved the Credo. Responding to the young Menninger, he underlined the psychiatrists' far-reaching designs:

> The idea of responsibility as related to the criminal is a fiction . . . [which] nowadays only serves to precipitate a metaphysical quarrel which is never decided every time anybody commits an anti-social act, whereas if all of them were considered psychotic they would all immediately be removed from the danger of further anti-social conduct by being properly segregated and then they would come to be let out only when there was a reasonable prospect that they had changed their method of reacting sufficiently to be a social asset instead of a social liability.

This statement has the aura of an echt Foucaldian warning: psychiatric power has a wish to control and police all behaviour; it thinks it can predict and prevent future danger, not to mention determine the boundaries of the normal.

In mitigation of the psychiatrists, it is worth underlining that where capital punishment exists, the psychiatric model at least doesn't equate deviance with an invitation to institutional murder – though the uses of psychiatry under a malign state in the old USSR were certainly both iniquitous and execrable. When Truman Capote, himself somewhat deviant according to the older psychiatric textbooks, wrote *In Cold Blood*, he was nonetheless adamantly on the side of the psychiatrists. The alternative to their assessment of the murderers Perry Smith and Dick Hickock was, after all, the electric chair.

To White, in the first more innocent decades of the twentieth century, the views of the Credo seem the only 'humane' way to tackle the crime problem: lock deviants up in psychiatric institutions rather than prisons, and make psychiatric rather than legal knowledge the dominant authority. All this in the hope that the prisoner/patient can be properly rehabilitated and become a useful member of society.

The problem in American law and with the 'not guilty by reason of insanity' verdict is that it is almost impossible, once having been deemed insane, to prove sanity and be released from a psychiatric institution. Harry K. Thaw's ultimate release owed a great deal to his persistence, his fame, and of course to his exceedingly deep pockets, not to mention his formidable mother. In the course of the last century and our own, the right to liberty of the 'institutionalized' would become a major feature within the politics of law and psychiatry.

Coda

'It is a well known phenomenon that the angel of medicine, if he has listened too long to lawyers' arguments, too often forgets his own mission. He then folds his wings with a clatter and conducts himself in court like a reserve angel of law.'

Robert Musil

The exemplary trials I have detailed in the preceding pages act as a prism through which the private emotions and public attitudes of High Victorian society, the *belle époque* and America's Gilded Age can be seen in the fullness of their inevitable contradictions. Like all cases, these are by their very nature unique. But the temptation to draw generalizations from them is nonetheless strong, and I would like to venture a very few.

It seems clear to me that where a 'criminal' woman can be understood as conforming to her time's ideas or ideals of femininity, juries are kinder to her and more prepared to think in terms of mitigation. In such cases, psychiatrists, too, are more likely to present arguments that allow passion to be conceived of by public and jury as a force that overwhelms reason and impinges on sanity, even legally conceived.

Putting Marie Bière side by side with Ruth Ellis – who shot dead her lover, David Blakely, in front of a Hampstead pub on Easter Sunday, 1955 – underscores the point. The fragile Bière and her defence lawyer managed to turn her shooting into a good woman's act of passionate justice against exploitative masculinity. In Ellis's case, the elements of such a defence never took hold. True, her crime was greater, but class and her way of inhabiting her gender played into the proceedings as well. A brassily blonde, working-class nightclub hostess, who had resorted to abortion when pregnant with Blakely's child, Ellis not only committed a crime, but sinned against the status quo. Never mind Blakely's violence and boozing, he was posh – upper-class and well connected. Ellis's class, her brazen looks and distinctly unladylike past undoubtedly played into her verdict in a Tory Britain more conventional in certain respects about women and hierarchy than their Edwardian forebears, who had accepted mitigation for Kitty Byron when the waif-like Kitty killed her upper-class lover.

Called in to assess Ellis, psychiatrists for both defence and Crown found no evidence of insanity, even though she was clearly confused in the way Marie Bière had initially been, and all but mute. When, after the trial, the judge Mr Justice Havers wrote to the Home Secretary stating that Ellis's was definitely a *crime passionnel* and recommended a reprieve, it was refused. Nor did a petition signed by some fifty thousand people help. The public outcry over Ruth Ellis's hanging – undoubtedly in part also a recognition of the extra-legal elements that had played into the trial – eventually contributed to the abolition of the death penalty in 1964.

Harry Thaw, it could be said, 'got away with murder' because of his wealth and because his crime, however mad, played into his time's ideals of heroic masculinity riding to the rescue of dishonoured child-maidens. His brutal perversions were largely ignored and inter-preted as such only by a few of the trial's psychiatrists. It took a second trial – and further testimony concerning his sadistic acts – to convince a jury of just how dangerous Thaw was. The American prostitute and so-called 'serial killer' Aileen Wuornos had none of Thaw's cultural or financial capital on her side: working-class, les-bian, her pleas that she had been defending herself against the violent aggression of (middle-class) men didn't sway the jury, while the press preferred to think of her as a transgressive monster. Her sentence was harsher than those meted out to far more sadistic male serial killers. Bar such extreme cases, however, 'criminal' women are still more routinely committed to psychiatric hospitals than men and verdicts of diminished responsibility more liberally given to women. This may be a reflection of the fact that women more rarely appear before the courts in homicide cases. The ratio in the UK is 9:1.

As for the mind doctors, many of the hopes of the 1926 'Credo' that William A. White so approved have largely been realized. Since the early shaping cases described in this book, the forensic psychiatrist has become a familiar and often indispensible figure in courts of law, in carrying out assessments of mental states both behind the scenes and, as an expert witness, on the public stage of the trial itself. Indeed, in our risk-averse present, so alert to 'dangerous individuals', forensic psychiatry is one of the growth areas in the mental health profession: with the closing of the asylums through the 1970s and 1980s in many Western countries, high-security psychiatric establishments or correctional facilities are now the largest 'asylums' left. Doubling as the policeman who patrols the borders of sanity as well as chief physician to the psychotic is an uneasy role, and one that has been open to criticism from too many sides to detail here. But in our anxious age, protecting society from potentially dangerous individuals has become one of the key disciplinary tasks of the forensic psychiatrist – even though cars kill far more people than do the mad.

On the more doctorly side, the mind medics now also engage with the courts in what has become known since 1996, particularly in the US, as therapeutic jurisprudence – a term coined by David Wexler and Bruce Winick to denote ways in which 'the knowledge, theories and insights of the mental health and related disciplines can help shape the development of the law'. In the European social democracies such a partnership has been in place longer: Holland, Sweden, Norway and Germany have strong traditions of therapeutic jurisprudence, though its effectiveness is ever related to the kinds of programmes (and finances) that are put in place.

Collaborative thinking between mental health and legal professionals grew out of the family courts, where antagonistic legal procedures made victims of the children of divorcing couples. Anna Freud was a pioneer in this area. Working 'in the best interests of the child', she joined forces in the last decade of her life with two Yale-based American lawyers, Albert Solnit and Joseph Goldstein, to develop ideas about child custody and protection which have since fed into jurisprudence. Now, in various jurisdictions, specialized courts which recognize therapeutic issues (for both perpetrators and victims) also exist for drug offences, domestic violence and sex crimes: judges can order (or offer) treatment as part of a community or custodial sentence. The recognition that many offenders need help beyond what any prison term can offer, if their crime is not to be repeated on release, is hardly new to the twenty-first century. But via the swings and round-abouts that mark the relationship between the law and the mental health professionals, we seem – now that prisons are full to bursting – to have entered a moment when therapeutic hopes for offenders are once again high. As this book goes to press, the UK government has announced a pilot scheme which will place mental health profession-als in police stations as well as courts – an attempt to cut reoffending rates by intervening early with those whose many 'crimes' are triggered by mental problems. Even psychoanalytically-informed therapeutic work, which demands more than short-term behavioural adjustments, is undertaken in centres such as London's Portman Clinic.

The Shapes of (Criminal) Passion

We think of passion as a powerful natural force. Like a volcano, it erupts. Like a flood, it washes away reason and language. It produces an irresistible impulse that can't be countered. The murderous pas-sions described in this book overwhelmed their subjects. They were powerless against them – or so it seemed to them. Christiana Edmunds propelled a poison chocolate into the mouth of the wife of 'Caro Mio'. In a Clytemnestra-style settling of scores, Marie Bière took aim at the man she blamed for killing her daughter. Like a heroic

Tosca bent on saving her loved one, Madame Caillaux riddled her husband's enemy with bullets in a newspaper office in full daylight.

In fact, as these cases illustrate, murderous passion is often also accompanied by a morbid obsessional quality. It is stealthy, practical and mimics rationality. It knows how to find poisons and weapons and opportunities. It has a strange Martian logic that parades as (self-)justification. Harry Thaw is convinced he's rescuing the woman he's enamoured of from the clutches of a Beast and avenging her despoliation. He pursues his rival indefatigably. Madame Caillaux is certain that killing Calmette will restore her husband's reputation and her own. The madness seems to lie in the certainty as much as in the deluded logic: the act will make the world better. Then, too, only if the act takes place will the obsession with the other, which fills the mind and intrudes on all other thoughts, go away. In that sense the murderer is possessed: hypnotized. The possession can stop only with the murderous act. In this respect, enacting the bloody deed does, at least momentarily, make the world better for the passionate killer.

The obsessional quality of *crime passionnel* was underlined by two crimes and their attendant courtroom and psychiatric dramas in the second half of the twentieth century. Each has a particular resonance in our own time. A troubled sexuality, a tension about masculine and feminine identities, suffuses these cases. The preoccupation they demonstrate with possessing a distant other, accompanied by vigilant surveillance, forefronts what has become one of this century's more characteristic love crimes: stalking.

In 1969 the Tarasoff case raised issues of dangerousness and medical confidentiality that still resonate. Prosenjit Poddar, a graduate student at the University of California, Berkeley, where he had arrived in 1967, met Tatiana Tarasoff at folk-dancing classes during the autumn of '68. From the caste of India's untouchables, Poddar had overcome a great many odds to arrive at Berkeley as an architecture student. When Tatiana Tarasoff kissed him at a New Year's Eve party, he was smitten. He was used to rather more circumspect behaviour in women. He interpreted her friendly kiss as a sign of love, marking the start of an intimate relationship.

Tatiana Tarasoff certainly hadn't intended that, and made it very plain to him. There were other men in her life. Poddar didn't, or couldn't, understand her 'no'. He began to follow her obsessionally. He grew depressed, felt humiliated and resentful, neglected his health and his studies. He failed exams. He told a friend he was going to blow up Tatiana's room. He wept and talked to himself. On the occasions when Tatiana agreed to meet with him, he taped their conversations, scouring them for explanations of why she didn't love him. He was a spurned lover whose thoughts had gone wild.

In the summer of 1969, while Tarasoff was in South America, a friend recommended Poddar get some help. He began to see a psychologist at Berkeley, Dr Lawrence Moore. In August, during the ninth session, he told Moore he intended to kill Tarasoff. Moore was convinced Poddar wasn't simply fantasizing or talking out his rage. He assessed his condition as acute and diagnosed a paranoid schizophrenia. He considered him so dangerous he asked the campus police to have him committed involuntarily. The police picked Poddar up, but like Moore's supervisor on examining Poddar a short while later, found him 'rational' and had him released. On 27 October, when Tatiana Tarasoff was back and Poddar had stopped seeing his psychologist, he stabbed and killed her with a kitchen knife.

Tried, Poddar was convicted of second-degree murder, served four years and was then released on appeal, on the condition that he return to India.

This tragic case, with its evident clash of values in the domains of sex, love and gender roles, contains some of the terrible cultural misunderstandings that have been implicated in 'honour killings' around the world, of which there are estimated to be some five thousand a year. In these, fathers or male relatives from traditional or tribal societies and now living in the West take vengeance on their daughters' independent choice of love object, which has impugned their 'honour' – though the brutality of the killings seems scarcely to impinge on that same honour.

The film *Banaz*, based on the murder, with parental approval, of a young Kurdish woman in London in 2006 by members of her extended family, makes vivid the plight of these girls. 'Why love should be so hated' as one of the women in the film exclaims, is a mystery, though it is also clear that the challenge to traditional masculinity is what brings this hatred in train. (In a hideous perversion of the romantic idea that two can make one, children here have no autonomous existence outside or inside the family unit. Since children are parental 'flesh', by some mental slippage they have no separate identity or individual will: masculine honour becomes more important than their lives.) One of the difficulties in preventing these honour killings bears a relation to the Tarasoff case: the police, even when alerted, don't know quite how to intervene in situations involving immigrants from traditional societies where 'domestic' problems, love or madness are in question.

When the Tarasoff family brought a case against the campus police, the health service employees and the regents of the University of California for failing to warn them that their daughter was in danger, the repercussions were felt throughout the Western therapeutic professions.

The trial and appeals courts at first dismissed the case: a doctor's first duty was to a patient, not to a third party – hence the protective privilege ceded to medical confidentiality. But then, in the California Supreme Court, that decision was reversed. Patient confidentiality had to be breached in situations of danger. The Supreme Court determined that a doctor or therapist has a duty to use reasonable care to give threatened persons such warnings as are essential to avert foreseeable danger arising from a patient's condition. After this ruling, the court was instructed to retry the Tarasoff parents' suit against the university.

Meanwhile, there was uproar in the profession and a second Supreme Court hearing ensued in 1976. Amici briefs through the American Psychiatric Association contended that psychiatrists were unable to predict violence accurately. But the court said that certainty wasn't required, only 'a reasonable degree of skilled care'. Only one judge out of three held out for the importance of confidentiality as a feature of treatment and refused what became the oft-quoted summing-up: 'The protective privilege ends where the public peril begins.'

The hegemony of the courts over medical treatment, including the psychotherapies, stirred indignation in the professions. But the private sphere would soon become even more porous to vigilance – not only that of the law and the state, but also of those cyber-networks that were still only dreams in the seventies.

Obsessional Pursuit

The Tarasoff case was a signpost to the love crimes to come, in one further way. It involved obsessional following, or what by the 1990s had become enshrined in law, first of all again in California, as the 'stalking' of the 'beloved'.

When the French psychiatrist G. G. de Clérambault in the 1920s wrote full clinical descriptions of the various arcs of erotomania in what have since become classic studies in the field, most of his cases were of women. He traced portraits of troubled characters, sometimes obsessional followers, in whom romantic illusions had toppled into delusions; proud women who were convinced that men of higher status were in love with them and sent them coded signs of their love in odd, secret ways, on occasion even sent imagined funds. Other erotic delusions were sparked by a vigilant jealousy after a (perhaps) imagined betrayal by a real or romantic lover or acquaintance, or a rejection that couldn't be accepted. Projected outwards, hostility and rage catapulted into delusions of persecution and an act of violence, which the patient deemed to be in self-defence and just.

We could speculate that the higher percentage of women in Clérambault's erotomanic cohort was due to the changing status of women at the time: there was a new class fluidity (downwards as well as upwards), particularly for servants, who felt 'entitled' to turn against upper-class lovers or masters – as the notorious maids, the Papin sisters, did in France in 1933. There was also a greater sexual openness as well as new opportunities. Change, of course, means uncertainty, a difficulty in reading social and sexual cues and that greater psychic strain which can sometimes result in breakdown. Signs of this were already present in the case of Christiana Edmunds, arguably a case of erotomania, certainly a woman who didn't recognize a 'no' and who wove a split-off, imaginary life around it in which her beloved maintained his perfections, as she did hers, and continued to adore her.

The impact of social factors can also be seen in the case of Marie Bière – an independent woman who over-invested in her child and in the idealized maternal image of the times and sought justice in the form of vengeance on an out-of-date lover who treated her as a disposable courtesan. As for Madame Caillaux, the new freedoms of the press, with their ability publicly to expose even the secrets one kept from oneself, thrust her into the role of a warlike Amazon bent on retrieving her reputation from slander and washing clean her own sexualized past. In Harry Thaw's case, Clérambault's love object of higher status migrated into the idealization of a whore he could rescue and transform into a Madonna.

Today, where psychiatrists do talk of erotomania in women, which generally accounts for only 1 to 4 per cent of psychiatric admissions, it tends to be in countries where change – in gender roles and sexuality – has been recent and very quick: Ireland is often cited. But the gender balance in passionate love crimes these days has shifted towards the male.

We live in times of anxious masculinity in which women's independence can destabilize fragile men. An aura of humiliation attends many love crimes and ignites them. Courtship codes misunderstood, as in the Tarasoff case; fantasies of total possession or of merger and union with the other, ruptured in reality but kept alive in fantasy, what some psychiatrists call a regressed confusion between self and other of the kind that made up the earliest mother-and-child love affair; delusional rescue scenarios in which the beloved will be grateful and shed all other courtiers – all these can play into the male love disorders characterized by stalking. Three out of four stalkers who engage in violence are male. Since men outnumber women ten to one in most other violent crimes, the 3:1 ratio means that women still commit more 'violence' in this intimately troubled domain than in others.

It was the case of John Hinckley Jr that cast stalking – and most emphatically celebrity-stalking – so prominently into the late twentieth century's imagination. The case also shifted the legal map in some states in America which had brought the 'irresistible impulse' rule into their jurisdictions and thus enlarged the scope of potential insanity rulings. After Hinckley, many returned to stricter M'Naghten definitions.

On 30 March 1981, John Hinckley Jr attempted to assassinate President Ronald Reagan, instead wounding him and three members of his entourage – all in an attempt to woo the celebrity he was in love with, Jodie Foster. Hinckley shares certain features with Thaw. Like the Pittsburgh millionaire, he came from money. His family were in oil in Texas, and generous supporters of the George Bush Sr presidential campaign. During Hinckley's trial, the papers talked of 'Dementia Suburbia', a direct reference back to Thaw's 'Dementia Americana'. Both men had an inflated sense of themselves, and unsteady boundaries, and were embroiled in fantasies of rescuing the 'soiled' innocent woman from her undeserved fate. Virginity was important to Hinckley: as in so many 'rescuers', good and bad, the pure and the impure can't be allowed to coexist in one person. Freud's conception of the oedipal infant's need to keep the mother unsullied by father seems uncomfortably close to hand here.

After repeatedly watching Jodie Foster in the film *Taxi Driver*, where she played a child prostitute under the sway of a pimp-assassin, Hinckley developed an obsession with the actress. He followed her to Yale, enrolled in a writing class, and began bombarding her with poems, messages and telephone calls. When she failed to respond, he decided that assassinating a president of the United States would impress her. He bought guns and tried to access President Carter. When he failed, he decided to target the new President, Ronald Reagan. He sent Foster a postcard of Reagan and his wife Nancy with the message: 'Dear Jodie, Don't they make a darling couple. Nancy is downright sexy. One day you and I will occupy the White House and the peasants will drool with envy. Until then, please do your best to remain a virgin. You are a virgin, aren't you? Love, John.'

According to the prosecution psychiatrist's 628-page report, which follows *DSM* classification and language, Hinckley suffered from three types of personality disorder: schizoid, narcissistic and mixed, with both borderline and passive-aggressive features – none of which, the lead doctor contended, amounted to legal irresponsibility. What the press seemed to understand as the 'suburban' part of his dementia were features he shared with many rich teenagers: resistance to parental demands, chronic feelings of emptiness or boredom, problems with his self-image, a desire for fame without any equivalent desire to work, and drugs. The opinion of Dr Park Dietz was that despite his mental disease or defect, '[Hinckley] did not lack substantial capacity to appreciate the wrongfulness of his conduct.' But Hinckley, like Thaw before him, viewed his assassination attempt as an accomplishment – one on a grand scale, which he had carried out on behalf of the woman he loved.

Dr David Bear and the defence psychiatrists painted a different picture – again one not dissimilar to Thaw's, though this time built around the category of schizophrenia (which began its psychiatric life only around 1911, after the Thaw trials, and was always linked to adolescent onset) alongside clinical depression. Hinckley, Dr Bear stated, was definitely psychotic on the day of the assassination attempt, suffering from the delusion that he had to 'rescue' Foster, who was 'a prisoner at Yale'. Bear wanted to introduce into court a CAT scan of Hinckley's brain as evidence: he testified that there was consensus amongst experts that the brains of one third of schizophrenics as well as those suffering from bipolar disorder had 'widened sulci' –

furrows or depressions on the surface of the brain. The judge first refused what was then a wholly novel form of expert testimony, but eventually agreed to allow it.

It may have been the very presence of the CAT scan – hard medical technology that translates psychological conditions into biological fact, rather than the less than convincing imagery it produces – that finally decided the jury. More recently, neuro-imaging, with its impressively bright pictures of the brain, has been used in a persuasive way in the courts, both to signal 'biological' disorder and to offer scope for therapy. Though neuro-images are as open to interpretation as any other kind, the newest breed of neuro-criminologists is adamant that neuro-evidence displays the link between certain kinds of brain formation (or deformation) and crime. Though they may concede that early environmental influences can reshape what nature has put in place, today's neuroscientists often enough contend, as the phrenologists did of yore, that certain brain deficiencies can predict crime: for example, poor functioning of the anterior cingulate, a small-volume amygdala, significant reduced development of the prefrontal cortex – all these may, it is asserted, be more evident in the brains of criminals.

But if crime is committed because of brain abnormalities, then responsibility is not within the individual's control and guilt is not an issue. As a defence in court, this argument can take the same shape as that relating to mental illness. Whether in Hinckley's case it was the early version of brain imaging, or the defence's description of his delusional state – which argued that his 'relationship to reality in the true meaningful sense has been severed', 'his inner world is all built upon false premises, false assumptions, false ideas' – that decided the jury is unclear. In any event, Hinckley was finally and unexpectedly pronounced 'not guilty by reason of insanity' on all thirteen counts against him.

Commentators pointed out that since the burden lay on the prosecution to prove beyond a reasonable doubt that Hinckley was sane, the jury had come to the only appropriate decision. Reagan himself quipped, 'if you start thinking about a lot of your friends, you would have to say, "Gee, if I had to prove they were sane, I would have a hard job."' Many thought the insanity defence should be abolished, since it provided a loophole in the law through which murderers escaped justice.

The Hinckley verdict caused thirty-nine states to rewrite their insanity legislation and put the burden of proof on the defence, others to narrow the range of expert witness, and still others to abolish the insanity defence altogether.

The old 'mens rea' test, however, could no longer altogether withstand the version of the human mind and emotions that psychiatry had put in place. Clearly, John Hinckley had an intention to assassinate the President and knew what he was doing and that it was wrong. Clearly, too, by any late-twentieth-century understanding, he was a deranged stalker, his obsession with Jodie Foster triggering a violent psychosis. Admitted to hospital, Hinckley's reports concluded that 'his defective reality testing and impaired judgement combined with his capacity for planned and impulsive behaviors make him an unpredictably dangerous person'.

Like Thaw's, Hinckley's lawyers filed repeatedly for conditional release and then more. Rejected at first, Hinckley did win permission by 1986 to spend time at the family home. But when twenty photos of Jodie Foster were found in his room along with evidence that he had been communicating with other killers, the pleas for release were scuppered and delayed. By the turn of the century, when he was permitted unsupervised furloughs to see his mother – to whom, like Thaw, he was deeply attached – there was still material related to Jodie Foster found in his hospital room. His obsession with her didn't cease. In 2012 his lawyers, reminiscent again of Thaw's, stated they had not been fully paid. Then in January 2013 there were rumours that Hinckley, on a visit home, had been involved in some unreported violence. Despite this, the fight to have him returned to his now eighty-six-year-old mother continued.

For all Hinckley's obsessional stalking of her, Jodie Foster never remembered meeting him.

By the 1990s, stalking – the 'willful, malicious and repeated following and harassing of another person that threatens his or her safety' – had become a statutorily defined criminal act in many American states. It now seemed that many people suffered from the unwanted pursuit by a sometimes jealous and always vigilant other. If stranger and celebrity stalking account for some 16 per cent of most samples, the rest know their stalker, while some 30 per cent have also once been their intimate.

This latter problem has grown with women's ability to step out of relationships, marriages or cohabitations that have become abusive or unhappy: husbands or partners refuse to accept that their partners have really gone, so pursue them mercilessly, sometimes to the point of extreme violence. Claire Waxman, whose case sparked the setting up of the British Paladin National Stalking Advocacy Service, was the victim of a ten-year campaign of harassment and relentless pursuit – what she calls 'mental rape'; she had a miscarriage and moved house five times before her pursuer was arrested, only to be released on probation to carry on his obsessive campaign.

The British Crime Survey estimates that 120,000 people are stalked every year; the US Bureau of Crime Statistics estimated 3.4 million victims between 2005–2006, while a source for 2011 puts the figure as high as 6.6 million. Exact numbers are difficult to come by, but their increase everywhere in the West points to a recalibration of what is acceptable and unacceptable behaviour in that broad domain of love – courtship, sex, marriage, separation. Women are now readier to go to the police and lodge complaints based on unwanted pursuit and menace, where once they might have suffered in silence. Since stalking often enough emerges out of a background of domestic violence, it is one more form of violence against women – one in which the stalker can carry on the semblance of a relationship while maintaining a predatory control.

Unquestionably, the cyber-world has made this form of malign and abusively possessive love far too easy. GPS tracking systems work for pursuers. Social media have blurred the line between private and public and make harassment simple for those so inclined. Email and texting have provided a ready and easy form of communication/pursuit; the love-deluded, like lovers themselves, have ever been prone to letter writing, an activity that engages the imagination as well as the other person's attention. The difference is that now there is no need to step into the reality of the street to pursue one's fantasies. Perhaps in a society increasingly based on surveillance, where we are watched and incessantly watch others – on screens inside the intimacy of our own homes, and out – this growing need to pursue and fully possess the desired other should come as no surprise. Nor, in a world where compliant porn images often serve as an early introduction to sex, is a 'No' always part of the emotional lexicon a rejected partner can understand or tolerate. Frustration is rarely understood as a step towards character building at a time when happiness is seen as an entitlement.

Women, of course, also stalk in the contemporary world. In his gripping memoir, *Give Me Everything You Have*, the writer and sometime teacher James Lasdun recounts the gruelling experience of being stalked both online and by email by a former student whose work he had encouraged. Lasdun's odyssey takes a well documented course. The young woman moves from infatuation with her teacher, to jealousy and perceived betrayal, to hatred and revenge. The form this latter takes is persecutory mail violently attacking Lasdun as a Jew; letters to his publishers, journals, places of work and on various websites 'exposing' Lasdun as a thief of others' ideas, a sexual predator on students, and so on. It's not clear whether publication of the memoir has stopped the stalking or not.

In 1999 Dr Paul E. Mullen, Professor of Forensic Psychiatry at Monash University in Australia, elaborated the most frequently used typology of stalking. It moves beyond an earlier American classification that had named three groups of stalkers – the erotomanic delusional type, the love obsessionals whose love delusions were part of a more extensive psychotic condition, and the simple obsessionals who had had prior involvement with their objects. Mullen's typology, instead, is based on motivational factors: it divides stalkers into the rejected, the intimacy seekers, the incompetent suitors, the resentful, and the predatory. He argues that this isn't a way of 'medicalizing deviancy', but of dealing with a persistent problem.

Recognized mental conditions – such as psychosis and personality disorder – can underlie the sustained harassment that stalking is. Although women make up only a small proportion of stalkers and, despite the portrayal in the film *Fatal Attraction*, less often engage in physical violence, they have a slightly higher incidence of mental illness than male stalkers – or perhaps, as has often been the case with women, it's simply that more illness is diagnosed. Deluded beliefs and uncorrectable assumptions about the thoughts and emotions of their object prevail in stalkers' minds. Evidence that their pursuit isn't welcome is discounted in the persistent hope of intimacy or reconciliation. Women tend to target former professional contacts, including doctors, colleagues or lovers, rather than strangers. They are motivated by 'intimacy seeking'.

Having had a prior relationship with the object of their pursuit significantly increases the risk of violence. For men who just can't let their former wives or lovers go, violence often ensues when the illusion that their love is *really* returned – a love which also armours their own sense of specialness – is threatened or shattered. Thus, the wrong kind of intervention from the police can actually trigger as yet unperformed violence.

Being the object of prolonged pursuit, even short of violence, can induce acute stress and leave psychological scars. Being spied on, being forced to move repeatedly, receiving thousands of emails, having to change mobile and other numbers and addresses, living in fear of violence every time you step out of the house or even when you stay in, being deprived of a social life or new relationships – are a form of intolerable harassment that too often leads to lasting psychological damage.

In Britain an Independent Parliamentary Inquiry into Stalking was set up in 2012 following the murder of Lorna Smith by her former boyfriend. The inquiry set out recommendations for change to the inadequate 1997 protection-from-harassment laws. These came to fruition in the Protection of Freedoms Act 2012, which named a specific offence of stalking. This was a signal for police to take mounting levels of complaint seriously and understand that even when victims of stalkers don't suffer physical abuse or assault, they undergo psychic damage – or psychological GBH. In March 2013, protection from harassment or gender-based violence granted in one EU country was extended to cover the entire European Union.

In north London, a National Stalking Clinic led by the forensic psychiatrist Dr Frank Farnham has been established. Working hand in hand with the courts, the clinic assesses perpetrators and the risk they pose as well as offering treatment programmes, often as part of the offender's probation. Farnham thinks of stalking as a behavioural problem – not a mental illness. It can be modified and changed with an appropriate treatment plan. The short prison terms meted out to stalkers by the courts often lead only to a repeat of the criminal activity as soon as release comes. Farnham would like to see the criminal justice system, from the police to judges and to probation officers, re-engage with psychological concepts so that stalkers, sexual offenders, angry and violent men, can be 'cured' of reoffending. Though he doesn't use the term, he is talking about therapeutic jurisprudence: crime, viewed like this, is as much an issue for the health services as it is for the courts.

On the ground, the victims of stalking, like the newsreader Alexis Bowater, head of the Network for Surviving Stalking, talk of making treatment mandatory for offenders. We may be 'socialised through romantic films to think that the guy will always eventually get the girl, but stalking is not a romcom gone wrong – it is serious and pathological . . . Stalkers will repeat-offend until they are treated. So there needs to be mandatory treatment, and there needs to be better support for victims.'

Mandatory treatment for offenders may be a good in many instances. However, if like Harry Thaw the offender fails to recognize the wrong in his criminal act, or experiences no despondency or shame – the very sign of his understanding that he is a member of a larger social group – then it is unlikely that therapeutic procedures will have any lasting effect.

Passionate Transgressions

In one of the very few essays in which he tackles the idea of criminality, Freud engages with Shakespeare's murderous, megalomaniacal 'crookback', Richard III. He notes that, like Richard, those who have experienced some illness in earliest childhood, or some form of suffering for which they bear no guilt, often determine that they live at an unjust disadvantage. This can be the case even when they don't altogether know or can't recall the cause of their ills. Such individuals may later claim specialness or seek compensation in reparation for their wrongs. Some may turn to crime. Others may be loath to give up forbidden pleasures and gratifications. The search for reparation can also take a rebellious social or political form, such as revolution or the feminist movement. (Writing in 1916, Freud notes laconically that women, because of their secondary status, all nurture a grievance.) Like Richard III, such individuals claim a confident exceptionality:

> . . . since I cannot prove a lover,
> To entertain these fair well-spoken days,
> I am determined to prove a villain . . .

Perhaps our interest in criminals, in crime and detective stories has something to do with the imaginative recognition that criminals and revolutionaries mirror each other in their search for justice. The legal scholar Donald Black argues that the most common motives for homicides are moralistic. Citing him, Steven Pinker in his book on violence, *The Better Angels of Our Nature*, names as instances: retaliation after an insult, escalation of a domestic quarrel, punishing an unfaithful romantic lover . . . From the point of view of the killer, such murders are 'really instances of capital punishment with a private citizen as the judge, jury and executioner'.

With far less dramatic self-awareness than Richard III, a Christiana Edmunds, a Marie Bière, a Madame Caillaux, a Harry Thaw, share their sense of 'specialness' with Shakespeare's villain. Massed across a population, their inner grievance might have become of the kind that leads to revolution. Instead, their passionate crimes were a contorted attempt to seek what they saw as justice or honour. In the case of Bière and Caillaux, their sense of specialness and outrage evoked a kindred emotion in the jury, and they were acquitted. Nor did they ever commit fresh crimes.

Somewhere in the early hidden history of these criminals, the love of those nearest to them may have failed. Freud conjectures that it is through such early childhood love – which he calls the great educator – that 'the incomplete human being is induced to respect the decrees of necessity and to spare himself the punishment that follows any infringement of them'. The relatively law-abiding, we might say, have good early attachments. If they don't, if they become 'criminal', it is sometimes possible for the doctor to engage in what Freud here calls an 'after-education' and guide the patient to 'make the advance from the pleasure principle to the reality principle by which the mature human being is distinguished from the child'. Freud's language is no longer popular in the profession, but his idea of therapy as an 'after-education' is a resonant one in the forensic setting. Ever pessimistic about the powers of analysis, however, he worried that perverse gratifications might be difficult to give up. Contemporary therapists are more bullish in their confidence.

Looking back, it's clear that over the course of the last two centuries, the mind doctors have grown their power arm in arm with the state, while also tempering the law. Where possible, they have prevented the state from carrying out too many judicial murders. Their own 'correctional' methods were certainly sometimes punitive, but on the whole their Hippocratic pledge mediated some of their ability to harm. By recognizing the disordered emotions and confused reason to which the law in its disciplinary strictness can be blind, they did a little to humanize their times and ours.

That said, there are no easy solutions to the terrible difficulties posed by love gone awry. It is a good that the legal system, this entity that carries great symbolic weight, sends us signals of the behaviour it expects of us – even in 'love' and its many malign semblances. It is right that our courts of justice carry on the tug of war between what constitutes madness and what badness. It might be better still if the law were more modest in its view of the human ability to control acts by reason alone, or to transform the punishment of prison into a functioning 'reasonable' morality. If our prisons initiated programmes that led, at least for some, to an ability to live without delusional structures, that would certainly be a boon.

However, it is hardly likely that the whole messy, mad and rapturous terrain of humans engaged in (criminal) passion will suddenly transform itself into a tranquil, bucolic and reasonable landscape – one that both the law and psychiatry approve and in which trials of the metaphorical or legal kind never take place. What we would hope from our mind doctors is that, given how far their forensic reach now stretches, they remember that their profession is also an art – an art of understanding the human, which goes beyond the classificatory schema of their ever expanding diagnostic manuals. Maintaining a sense of their patients' inner experience – not only as a wild landscape to be contained by controlling agents (such as antipsychotics) or tamed through a course of mental workouts – will keep them distinct from the law enforcers. The latter must inevitably implement the rigours of the law – though, one hopes, with a better understanding of gender and with a penal system that prevents reoffending by offering treatment and emotional education where that is palpably necessary.

If, as our media and literature make manifest, we continue to be fascinated by trials of passion, it may well be because we recognize how akin we are to those whom passion drives into transgression, whether it's the transgression of reason which is madness or the transgression of ethics which is crime. And like the juries who deliberated on the fates of the subjects of these pages – Christiana Edmunds, Marie Bière, Gabrielle Bompard, Madame Caillaux, Harry K. Thaw and Evelyn Nesbit – we want to be part of the process that distinguishes guilt from innocence.

Notes

PASSION GOES TO COURT

p. 2   *the norm today*: On some of the important general ideas at play here, see Michel Foucault, trans. Alain Baudot and Jane Couchman, 'About the Concept of the "Dangerous Individual" in 19th-Century Legal Psychiatry', *International Journal of Law and Psychiatry*, vol. 1 (1978), pp. 1–18

p. 4   *be their due*: Robert Henly, *A Memoir of the Life of Robert Heneley, Earl of Northington* (London: John Murray, 1821), p. 42. Available at http://books.google.co.uk/books

p. 5   *attack themselves*: Anna Motz in *The Psychology of Female Violence* (London: Routledge, 2008) and Estela Welldon in *Mother, Madonna, Whore* (London: Karnac, 2004) have written brilliantly about female perversion and the babies that become its object

PART ONE

p. 14   *diseased animals*: Anthony S. Wohl, *Endangered Lives: Public Health in Victorian Britain* (Cambridge: Harvard University Press, 1983)

p. 14   *arsenic-tinted paper*: For widespread use of arsenic, see George Robb, 'Circe in Crinoline: Domestic Poisonings in Victorian England', *Journal of Family History*, vol. 2, no. 2 (April 1997), p. 182

p. 16   *find it out*: *Daily News*, 26 August 1871

p. 19   *Obscene Publications Act*: See Kate Summerscale, *Mrs Robinson's Disgrace* (London: Bloomsbury, 2012), pp. 186–7

p. 22   *either of them*: *Brighton Gazette*, 24 August 1871

p. 22   *poisoned myself*: *Manchester Times*, 26 August 1871

p. 24   *Christmas*: *Brighton Gazette*, 8 June 1871

p. 25   *monstrous*: Robb, 'Circe in Crinoline', p. 177, citing the judge in the trial of Anne Merritt in 1850; *The Times*, 9 March 1850

p. 28   *in the scene*: *Daily News*, 25 August 1871

p. 28   *the poisons*: *The Times*, 1 September 1871

p. 28   *stalkers*: See, for example, *Give Me Everything You Have* (New York: Farrar, Straus & Giroux, 2013), James Lasdun's memoir of his years as the subject of a stalker who sends him cascades of emails

p. 32   *identified*: *The Times*, 9 September 1871

p. 35   *tampering with sweets*: *The Times*, 8 September 1871

p. 35   *frequently wept*: *The Times*, 9 September 1871

p. 35   *between them*: Ibid.

p. 38   *the Muse*: I am grateful to Andrew O'Hagan for this elaboration of Burns's passage

p. 39   *your wife*: *The Times*, 6 July 1857

p. 40   *witness box*: 'Science in the Witness Box', *The Times*, 23 January 1856

p. 40   *1829*: *The Times*, 1 September 1829

p. 41   *fashionable visitors*: Anthony Lee, 'The Sad Tale of the Margate Architect and the Brighton Poisoner', http://www.margatelocalhistory.co.uk/Articles/Edmunds%20tale. Lee provides fascinating material on William Edmunds and his architectural projects, as well as on his sister Mary, tried on a charge of libel in 1815

p. 41   *unacquainted*: Memorial of Sydney Cornish Harrington to Secretary of State for the Home Department, January 1972, National Archives HO 45 9297/9472 C477970

p. 43   *sent there*: From the petition sent by Ann Christiana Edmunds to the Home Secretary, January 1972, National Archives HO 45 9297/9472 C477970

p. 43   *affidavit*: Ibid.

p. 45   *supervision*: Report of the Metropolitan Commissioners on Lunacy, 1844 (London: Bradbury & Evans, 1844), pp. 44–5. Available at http://www.archive.org/stream/reportofmetropol00lond#page/n3/mode/2up

p. 46   *to the head*: *The Times*, 17 January 1872

p. 46   *sleep*: National Archives HO 45 9297/9472 C477970

p. 48   *Sussex*: *Morning Post*, 22 September 1856

p. 49   *apparatus*: J. Crichton-Browne, MD, FRSE, 'Clinical Lectures on Mental and Cerebral Diseases', *British Medical Journal*, 29 July 1871, pp. 113–14

p. 50   *roused at all*: William Acton, *The Functions and Disorders of the Reproductive Organs* (London: J. & A. Churchill, 6th edn, 1875), p. 212. Available at http://archive.org/details/functionsdisorde00actorich

p. 51   *century*: See, for instance, Edward John Tilt (who had also written a key book on the menopause), 'On Hysteria and Its Interpreters', *British Medical Journal*, 16 December 1871, pp. 690–2

p. 52   *self-control*: Julius Althaus, MD, MRCP, 'A Lecture on the Pathology and Treatment of Hysteria', *British Medical Journal*, 10 March 1866, pp. 245–8

p. 53   *large a one*: George Drysdale, *The Elements of Social Science* (London: E. Truelove, 1861), pp. 179–85; above quote, p. 180. Available at http://archive.org/stream/elementssocials01drysgoog#page/n4/mode/2up

p. 54   *eleven languages*: Mary S. Hartman, *Victorian Murderesses* (New York: Schocken Books, 1977), p. 158

p. 55   *clitoridectomy*: In the 1860s Isaac Baker Brown thought female masturbation occasioned everything from hysteria to epilepsy to death. See his *The Curability of Certain Forms of Insanity, Epilepsy, Catalepsy, and Hysteria in Females* (1866); available at http://archive.org/stream/oncurabilitycer00browgoog#page/n5/mode/2up. He was notorious for his clitoridectomies. But in 1867 he was expelled from the Obstetrical Society of London for carrying out the operations without consent, while the Lunacy Commission investigated him for carrying out unlicensed operations on 'lunatics'. See also J. B. Fleming, 'Clitoridectomy: The Disastrous Downfall of Isaac Baker Brown, FRCS', *Journal of Obstetrics and Gynaecology of the British Empire*, 67(6) (December 1960), pp. 1017–34

p. 56   *marvelous results*: Ibid., p. 248

p. 56   *functional disorders*: *Brighton Gazette*, on front page of various issues during 1869

p. 56   *orgasm*: Rachel P. Maines, *The Technology of Orgasm* (Baltimore: Johns Hopkins University Press, 1999)

p. 57   *could not breathe*: *The Times*, 17 January 1872

p. 59   *speak of desire*: This is true even of passions between women, as that between Emily Faithfull and Helen Codrington suggests. See Emma Donoghue's retelling of that relationship in *The Sealed Letter* (London: Picador, 2011)

p. 60   *so well*: Summerscale, *Mrs Robinson's Disgrace*

p. 61   *too strong*: Ibid., pp. 204–7

p. 61   *had it*: 'The Robinson Divorce Case', *Lloyd's Weekly Newspaper*, 27 June 1858

p. 63   *middle life*: *The Times*, 12 June 1876, as cited by Hartman, *Victorian Murderesses*, p. 165, but not found in *The Times* of that date

p. 64   *melancholy*: J.-E. D. Esquirol, *Des Maladies Mentales*, 3 vols (Paris: Baillière, 1838). Available at Gallica.fr. Vol. 2, pp. 32–7

p. 67   *the prison*: *The Times*, 30 December 1871

p. 67   *correction*: *The Times*, 1 January 1872

p. 69   *accused sister*: *Daily News*, 16 January 1872. As below in description of Christiana

p. 69   *committed*: 'Household Crime', *Household Words*, 1852, p. 277, cited by Robb, 'Circe in Crinoline'

p. 71   *the second*: See, for example, the images in *Vaught's Practical Character Reader* (1902) in *Public Domain Review*, http://publicdomainreview.org/2013/03/19/phrenology-diagrams-from-vaughts-practical-character-reader-1902/, accessed 5 April 2013

p. 73   *shop in them*: John Ruskin, *Fors Clavigera*, letter 30. Available at Archive.org

p. 76   *gesticulation*: *Daily News*, 16 January 1872

p. 77   *prosecutorial behaviour*: Thomas Seccombe, 'Ballantine, William (1812–1887)', rev. H. C. G. Matthew, *Oxford Dictionary of National Biography* (Oxford: Oxford University Press, 2004); online edn January 2009, http://www.oxforddnb.com/view/article/1227, accessed 5 April 2012

p. 77   *twice he lost*: John Andrew Hamilton, 'Parry, John Humffreys (1816–80)', *Oxford Dictionary of National Biography*

p. 79   *court of justice*: *Daily News*, 16 January 1872

p. 84   *vicious impulses*: From Henry Maudsley, *The Pathology of Mind* (London: Macmillan, 1895), cited in my *Mad, Bad and Sad* (London: Virago, 2008), p. 111. Also, see T. H. Turner, 'Henry Maudsley', *Oxford Dictionary of National Biography*

p. 86   *insane neurosis*: Henry Maudsley, *Responsibility in Mental Disease* (London: C. Kegan Paul, 3rd edn, 1876), p. 40

p. 88   *complexity*: See my *Mad, Bad and Sad* for a fuller history of this movement

p. 89   *be spared*: Matthew Hale, *The History of the Pleas of the Crown* (1736), pp. 34–5, cited in http://www.deathpenaltyinfo.org/Legal%20Historians%20Brief.pdf, accessed 1 May 2012. United States Supreme Court, no. 06-6407, Brief of Amici Curiae of Legal Historians in support of petitioner Scott Lewis Panetti v Nathaniel Quarterman

p. 90   *his affairs*: Maudsley, *Responsibility in Mental Disease*, pp. 90–1

p. 90   *punishment*: The full case from which other quotations are taken is available in *A Complete Collection of State Trials and Proceedings for High Treason and Other Crimes and Misdemeanours, from the earliest period to the year 1783*, compiled by T. B. Howell (London: Longmans, 1816), vol. 16, pp. 696–766. Available at http://books.google.co.uk/books

p. 92   *character of insanity*: *The Speeches of the Hon. Thomas Erskine (now Lord Erskine) when at the Bar* (London: James Ridgway, 1813), vol. 1. Available at http://books.google.co.uk. Also quoted in Maudsley, *Responsibility in Mental Disease*, pp. 90ff

p. 92   *case of 1812*: See R v Bellingham, Session Papers, Justice Hall, Old Bailey, 1811–13, Fifth Session 1812, pp. 263–74, cited in Kathleen S. Goddard, 'A Case of Injustice? The Trial of John Bellingham', *American Journal of Legal History*, vol. 46, no. 1 (January 2004)

p. 93   *justice myself*: Ibid., p. 8

p. 94   *right from wrong*: Ibid., p. 12, and R v Bellingham, p. 273

p. 95   *adopted*: OBSP R v Bellingham, 1812, case 433, at http://www.oldbaileyonline.org/browse.jsp?id=t18120513-5&div=t18120513-5&terms=john|bellingham#highlight

p. 96   *day and night*: Much of Cockburn's opening and closing statements can be found in G. W. Keeton, *Guilty but Insane* (London: Macdonald, 1961), pp. 62–105, 94

p. 96   *have to say*: Ibid., p. 98

p. 98   *reasoning self*: C. C. H. Marc, *De la folie: considérée dans ses rapports avec les questions médico-legales* (Paris: Baillière, 1840), p. 6. Available at http://books.google.co.uk/books?id=-hPaV1T29awC&printsec=front-cover#v=onepage&q&f=false

p. 99   *prevented*: Hansard, 13 March 1843, 'Insanity and Crime', House of Lords debate, 13 March 1843, vol. 67, cc. 714–44

p. 100   *later noted*: Maudsley, *Responsibility in Mental Disease*, citing Judge Ladd in the case of State v Jones in New Hampshire, p. 99

p. 101   *liable to punishment*: Cited in Keeton, *Guilty but Insane*, p. 104

p. 102   *cunning*: See *The Times*, 16 January 1872, for the various quotations from the case

p. 104   *two years later*: J. M. Rigg, 'Martin, Sir Samuel (1801–1883)', rev. Hugh Mooney, *Oxford Dictionary of National Biography*, http://www.oxforddnb.com/view/article/18210, accessed 5 April 2012

p. 108   *fortitude*: *The Times*, 16 January 1872

p. 109   *medical men*: *Reynold's News*, 20 January 1872; *The Times*, 20 January 1872

p. 109   *Christiana Edmunds*: Ibid.

p. 110   *reprieve*: Ibid.

p. 112   *execution*: Letter of 18 January 1872 from Baron Martin to Home Secretary, National Archives HO 45 9297/9472 C477970

p. 113   *diminished radically*: Martin J. Wiener, *Men of Blood: Violence, Manliness and Criminal Justice in Victorian England* (Cambridge: Cambridge University Press, 2004), pp. 19–23

p. 114   *other means*: Robb, 'Circe in Crinoline', p. 186: 'Women tried for poisoning their husbands between 1830 and 1900 were convicted 60% of the time – a much higher conviction rate than ... in general, in which only 40% of the accused were found guilty'

p. 114 *prison population*: Lucia Zedner, *Women, Crime and Custody in Victorian England* (Oxford: Clarendon Press, 1991), passim. For current statistics on percentages of female to male prisoners, see http://news.bbc.co.uk/1/shared/spl/hi/ik/06/prisons/html/nn2page1.stm

p. 114 *guilty of murder*: Wiener, *Men of Blood*, pp. 128–30

p. 114 *1890s*: Ibid., p. 148

p. 115 *manslaughter*: Ibid., p. 149

p. 115 *was the same*: Ibid., p. 133

p. 116 *consideration*: National Archives HO45/9297/9742 C477970

p. 117 *insane than Christiana*: Memorial of Sydney Cornish Harrington, National Archives HO45/9297/9742 C477970

p. 117 *outrage or injustice*: *Daily Telegraph*, 22 January 1872

p. 118 *symptoms*: Nick Hervey, 'Gull, Sir William Withey, 1st baronet (1816–1890)', *Oxford Dictionary of National Biography*; online edn, May 2006, http://www.oxford dnb.com/view/article/11730, accessed 4 May 2012. See also my *Mad, Bad and Sad*

p. 118 *his house*: Mark Stevens, *Broadmoor Revealed, Victorian Crime and the Lunatic Asylum* (online); M. P. Park, R. H. R. Park, 'The fine art of patient–doctor relationships', *British Medical Journal*, 329 (2004), pp. 1475–80, http://www.bmj.com/ content/329/7480/1475?variant=short, accessed 6 May 2012

p. 119 *accordingly*: Sir William Gull to Secretary of State, Home Department, 23 January 1872, National Archives HO45/9297/9472 C477970

p. 121 *acquitted as insane*: Forbes Winslow, 'Insanity and Homicide', *British Journal of Psychiatry*, April 1872, pp. 64ff

p. 121 *next century*: Anon., 'The Legal and Medical Tests of Insanity', *British Medical Journal*, 27 January 1872, p. 104

p. 122 *brain disaster*: Anon., 'The Legal Test of Insanity', *British Medical Journal*, 3 February 1872, pp. 129–30

p. 127 *presence*: Broadmoor Hospital Case Notes for Christiana Edmunds, pp. 206f, 208, 2011; D/H14/D2/1/2/1, courtesy Berkshire Record Office

p. 129 *kind to her*: Broadmoor Hospital Case Notes, letter and notes of 1874, D/H14/D2/2/2/204/4

p. 130 *occasion for it*: Ibid., p. 208, 8 July 1876

PART TWO

p. 137   *shoot*: Much of the material on Marie Bière comes from Judicial Dossier D2 U8 96 of the Archives de la Seine, now housed in the Archives de Paris. The dossier contains all the materials prepared by the *juge d'instruction* for the trial and includes police reports and witness statements, supplemented by newspaper reports of the trial proceedings. The most famous of these are from the pen of Le *Figaro*'s Albert Bataille, the assiduous court reporter who from his arrival in Paris in 1875 at the age of just twenty had made a reputation as the best and most accurate of the court journalists. Marie Bière's case also features in his *Causes Criminelles et Mondaines de 1880* (Paris: É. Dentu, Éditeur, 1881)

p. 140   *follow her*: Émile Zola, *Carnets d'Enquêtes* (Research Notebooks), p. 312, quoted in Frederick Brown, *Zola: A Life* (London: Macmillan, 1995), p. 418

p. 142   *open heart*: Judicial Dossier D2 U8 96, pp. 6–8 of the *juge d'instruction*'s papers

p. 160   *evidence*: Presse Judiciaire Parisienne, *Le Palais de Justice: Son monde et ses moeurs*, prefaced by Alexandre Dumas *fils* (Paris, 1892), pp. 340ff. I am indebted here as with so much else of this juridical matter to Ruth Harris, *Murders and Madness* (Oxford: Clarendon Press, 1989)

p. 161   *criminal woman*: Cesare Lombroso and Guglielmo Ferrero, *Criminal Woman, the Prostitute, and the Normal Woman* (*La donna delinquente*,1893), trans. Mary Gibson and Nicole Hahn Rafter (Durham, NC: Duke University Press, 2004), p. 183 and passim.

p. 161   *fin de siècle*: Ruth Harris in *Murder and Madness* (Oxford: Oxford University Press, 1989) does far greater justice to this subject than I have space for here

p. 162   *prior crime*: Eliza Earle Ferguson in *Gender and Justice: Violence, Intimacy and Community in Fin-de-Siècle Paris* (Baltimore: Johns Hopkins University Press, 2010) provides interesting insight into this phenomenon and the mores of the working-class areas of Paris

p. 169   *legal arena*: For a full exploration of this case, see my *Mad, Bad and Sad*

p. 170   *circulation*: Hélie Courtis, *Étude médico-légale des crimes passionnels* (Toulouse: C. Dirion, 1910), pp. 10–11, 104–5. Cited in Edward Berenson, *The Trial of Madame Caillaux* (Berkeley: University of California Press, 1992), pp. 30–2

p. 171   *abortion*: Jack D. Ellis, *The Physician-Legislators of France: Medicine and Politics in the Early Third Republic 1870–1914* (Cambridge: Cambridge University Press, 1990), p. 208 and passim

p. 174   *drove to crime*: Bataille, *Causes Criminelles et Mondaines de 1880*, pp. 13, 14, 20 and 37 passim below

p. 178   *juries*: *Le Figaro*, 16 December 1882; *New York Times*, 11 June 1882

p. 178   *the name*: Presse Judiciaire Parisienne, *Le Palais de Justice*, p. 288

p. 182   *asylum*: Laure Murat, *La Maison du Docteur Blanche, Histoire d'un asile et de ses pensionnaires* (Paris: J. C. Lattès, 2001), p. 200

p. 183   *offence*: Auguste Motet, 'Accès de somnambulisme spontané et provoqué', *Annales d'hygiène publique et de médecine légale*, 3rd series, 5 (1881), pp. 214–25 at http://www2.biusante.parisdescartes.fr/livanc/?p=216&cote=90141x1881x 05&do=page, accessed 30 August 2012

p. 184   *maternity*: Medical report dated 16 March 1880 in Marie Bière's Judicial Dossier D2 U8 96

p. 186   *ten francs*: Harris, *Murders and Madness*, p. 138

p. 186   *reporting*: Notes found in Judicial Dossier D2 U8 156, 18 February 1884

p. 192   *procedure*: 'Maître Lachaud', *Le Figaro*, 16 December 1882

p. 194   *lighter than men's*: Harris, *Murders and Madness*, p. 210. See also Ferguson, *Gender and Justice*

p. 196   *difficult tasks*: 'Échos de Paris', *Le Petit Journal*, 13 April 1880, p. 3

p. 197   *happy*: *Le Figaro*, 8 February 1881, p. 4

p. 201   *from above*: Alexandre Dumas *fils*, *Les Femmes qui tuent et les femmes qui votent*, ebook #29937 at Project Gutenberg (pp. 94–5 of the original text)

p. 201   *failed to*: Ibid., pp. 25–6

p. 204   *nature*: Judicial Dossier D2 U8 156

p. 207   *crowd*: See, for example, Paul Aubry, *La Contagion du meurtre: Étude d'anthropologie criminelle* (Paris, 1896), cited also by Harris, *Murders and Madness*, p. 235

p. 209   *Hamming It Up*: *Le Figaro*, 18 April 1883

p. 211   *unreliable*: See Jean-Martin Charcot's lecture of 1890, 'Hypnotism and Crime', reproduced at http://baillement.com/lettres/charcot_forum.html; and Gilles de la Tourette, *L'hypnotisme et les états analogues au point de vue médico-légal* (Paris: Plon, 1887), pp. 328–82; Jacqueline Carroy and Marc Renneville, 'Une cause passionnelle passionnante: Tarde et l'affaire Chambige (1889)', in Champ Pénal, Penal Field, 34th French Congress of Criminology, 15 September 2005, http://champpenal.revues.org/260; and Ruth Harris, 'Murder under Hypnosis', in *The Anatomy of Madness*, vol. 2, ed. W. F. Bynum, Roy Porter and Michael Shepherd (London: Tavistock Publications, 1983), pp. 197–241

p. 215   *proud*: *Le Temps*, 11 November 1888

p. 217   *criminelle*: G. Tarde, 'L'affaire Chambige', *Archives d'anthropologie criminelle*, vol. IV (1889), pp. 92–108

p. 218   *alters*: See my *Mad, Bad and Sad*, chapter 6

p. 221   *closer look*: Archives for this case are in box D2 U8 267 at the Archives de
          la Seine, from which my trial information comes. *Le Figaro* followed
          the case, and though Albert Bataille didn't take to its protagonists, it
          is collected in his *Causes Criminelles et Mondaines* for 1890. The illustrated
          papers loved the story and invented images for the main players. Jules
          de Grandpré Beaujoint in the serialized feuilleton *La Malle Sanglante*
          (Fayard, 1890) devoted over a thousand pages to it, with illustrations,
          songs, extracts from the press and not a little padding about the
          vagaries of hypnosis, plus the kind of speculation that in Britain
          would fall under contempt of court

p. 226   *consciousness of man*: Sigmund Freud, quoted in Ernest Jones, *The Life and
          Work of Sigmund Freud* (Harmondsworth: Penguin, 1964), p. 211

p. 227   *flesh*: Reproduced at length, though perhaps not altogether accurately,
          in Grandpré Beaujoint, *La Malle Sanglante*, a distinctly sensationalist and
          popular rendition of the case

p. 230   *epileptics*: Grandpré Beaujoint, *La Malle Sanglante*, pp. 56—60

p. 238   *Germany*: Sophie Humann, 'Henriette Caillaux tira six fois', *Valeurs
          Actuelles*, 26 April 2012, http://www.valeursactuelles.com/histoire/
          actualit%C3%A9s/henriette-caillaux-tira-six-fois20120425.html,
          accessed 14 November 2012

p. 239   *campaign*: Le Matin, 1914, pp. 3, 17

p. 239   *Saint-Lazare*: Newspaper coverage apart, there are few remaining
          official archive sources for the trial of Madame Caillaux: a fire in
          the fort of Montlignon in 1974 put an end to the investigating mag-
          istrate's dossier. The police records, whether by intent or accident,
          have also disappeared. The papers, however, gave extensive cover-
          age both of the murder and of the July trial. Most of my rendition
          of the facts of the case comes from *Le Matin*, *Le Figaro* and *Le Petit
          Journal* for March and July 1914, as well as Edward Berenson's fine
          The Trial of Madame Caillaux (Berkeley: University of California Press,
          1992)

p. 239   *emotion*: Le Petit Parisien, 21 July 1914

p. 244   *drove me on*: Le Matin, 29 July 1914, carries the full text of the final day of
          the trial, which contains both advocates' summary statements, reca-
          pitulating the evidence as well as their pleas

p. 246   *respect*: Le Figaro, 30 July 1914; Le Matin, 29 July 1914

p. 249   *[her] offence*: For the full materials on the R v Emma [Kitty] Byron case,
          see National Archives CRIM/1/80/3, C479803; also Ginger Frost, '"She Is

But a Woman": Kitty Byron and Edwardian Criminal Justice', *Gender and History*, vol. 16, no. 3 (November 2004), pp. 456, 538–60

p. 250 *own sex*: Ibid., p. 552

p. 250 *impossible*: R. Krafft-Ebing, *Psychopathia Sexualis*, sometimes translated as *The Psychology of Sex* (New York: Rebman Company, 1899), pp. 1–2, 14

p. 251 *Courtis*: Joelle Guillas, *Crimes of Passion* (Cambridge: Polity Press, 1990), p. 196

PART THREE

p. 255 *tenderloin*: For a history of New York, see Edwin G. Burrows and Mike Wallace, *Gotham: A History of New York City to 1898* (Oxford: Oxford University Press, 1999) and Kenneth T. Jackson (ed.), *The Encyclopedia of New York City* (New Haven: Yale University Press, 1995)

p. 256 *million*: http://www.measuringworth.com/calculators/uscompare/relativevalue.php

p. 257 *skylight world*: Paula Uruburu, *American Eve* (Riverhead Books: New York, 2008), p. 72

p. 258 *States*: Charles C. Baldwin, *Stanford White* (New York: Springer, 1971), pp. 208–9; also Gerald Langford, *The Murder of Stanford White* (New York: Bobbs Merrill, 1962)

p. 258 *Monroe's*: Uruburu, *American Eve*, passim

p. 261 *romance*: From *Mamzelle Champagne*, cited in Uruburu, *American Eve*, p. 281

p. 261 *indiscretion*: Uruburu, *American Eve*, p. 270, quotes the *New York Tribune* description of the new look as 'a little short of revolutionary in its application of such searching sculptural indiscretion to the female form'

p. 264 *ennercent*: Harry K. Thaw, *The Traitor* (Philadelphia: Dorrance & Co., 1926), p. 147

p. 265 *pleasure house*: *New York Times*, 26 June 1906

p. 267 *Caillaux's*: *New York Times*, 25 January 1916

p. 269 *community*: *New York Times*, 29 January 1906

p. 273 *fourteen years*: Cited by Uruburu, *American Eve*, p. 48 and below, p. 49

p. 280 *one failing*: Evelyn Nesbit, *The Story of My Life* (London: John Long, 1914), p. 53 and also above, pp. 49–57

p. 283 *agreed with me*: Thaw, *The Traitor*, p. 101

p. 284 *annoyed*: Nesbit, *The Story of My Life*, p. 80

p. 287 *put up with*: Freud, S. (1894). Draft H. 'Paranoia,' in *The Complete Letters of Sigmund Freud to Wilhelm Fliess, 1887–1904*, ed. J. M. Masson (Cambridge,

MA and London: The Belknap Press of Harvard University Press, 1985), p. 108

p. 288   *done to us*: Ibid., pp. 109–10

p. 291   *future husband*: Nesbit, *The Story of My Life*, p. 85

p. 296   *girls' lives*: Thaw, *The Traitor*, pp. 112–13

p. 298   *identical terms*: Nesbit, *The Story of My Life*, p. 94

p. 300   *apparent cause*: Cited in *New York Times*, 18 August 1913

p. 300   *harm Harry*: Langford, *The Murder of Stanford White*, p. 35

p. 302   *disgusting particulars*: Jean Marie Lutes, *Front-Page Girls: Women Journalists in American Culture and Fiction, 1880–1930* (Ithaca: Cornell University Press, 2006), p. 76

p. 302   *decent men*: Quoted in Langford, *The Murder of Stanford White*, p. 65

p. 303   *whatever*: Thaw, *The Traitor*, pp. 149–51

p. 305   *at the time*: F. A. Mackenzie (ed.), *The Trial of Harry Thaw* (London: Geoffrey Bles, 1928) contains the most verbatim material of all the books on the trial

p. 305   *reasonable doubt*: Quoted in ibid., p. 42

p. 307   *photographer*: Arthur P. Shimamura, 'Muybridge in Motion: Travels in Art, Psychology and Neurology', *History of Photography*, 26, part 4 (2002), pp. 341–50

p. 307   *insane*: W. A. White, *Insanity and the Criminal Law* (New York: Macmillan, 1923), p. 91. Quoted in Emil R. Pinta, *Paranoia of the Millionaire* (New York: Nova Science Publishers, 2010), p. 9

p. 310   *objective*: Allan McLane Hamilton, *Recollections of an Alienist* (New York: George H. Doran, 1916), pp. 284ff. Available at http://books.google.co.uk/books

p. 310   *because insane*: *New York Times*, 14 January 1917. Although the words 'guilty but insane' were used about Christiana Edmunds after her trial, the actual use of this as a courtroom verdict came in 1883 with the Trial of Lunatics Act

p. 311   *at this time*: William A. White, letter of 4 November 1916 to Arthur P. Herring; and below, letter to Dr Fisher, November 1919, quoted in Gerald N. Grob, *The Inner World of American Psychiatry 1890–1940* (New Jersey: Rutgers University Press, 1985), pp. 171–4

p. 312   *arrest*: See Thaw, *The Traitor*, pp. 153–5, for a description by Thaw of this early examination, in which nothing seemed to him to have been examined

p. 313   *continental literature*: http://en.wikisource.org/wiki/'Epidemics of Hysteria', *Popular Science Monthly*, vol. 49 (August 1896)

p. 315   *therefor*: Quoted in Mackenzie, *The Trial of Harry Thaw*, pp. 45–6. The current relevant part of the New York State Code reads: 'S 40.15 Mental disease or defect. In any prosecution for an offense, it is an affirmative defense that: when the defendant engaged in the proscribed conduct, he lacked criminal responsibility by reason of mental disease or defect. Such lack of criminal responsibility means that at the time of such conduct, as a result of mental disease or defect, he lacked substantial capacity to know or appreciate either: 1. The nature and consequence of such conduct; or 2. That such conduct was wrong'

p. 316   *queen*: Langford, *The Murder of Stanford White*, p. 91

p. 318   *about them*: Quoted in Mackenzie, *The Trial of Harry Thaw*, pp. 63–4, and Langford, *The Murder of Stanford White*, pp. 111–12. There are very slight differences in the versions

p. 324   *sane man*: Mackenzie, *The Trial of Harry Thaw*, pp. 109–16 passim

p. 326   *helpless child*: Cited in Langford, *The Murder of Stanford White*, p. 147

p. 326   *a fool*: Nesbit, *The Story of My Life* (London: John Long, 1914), frontispiece

p. 327   *self-protection*: Langford, *The Murder of Stanford White*, p. 172

p. 327   *self-possessed*: Nesbit, *The Story of My Life*, p. 193

p. 330   *question*: New York Times, 15 March 1907

p. 330   *1904*: Pinta, *Paranoia of the Millionaire*, p. 17

p. 331   *in the wind*: New York Times, 13 February 1907

p. 331   *brought to bear*: William James, 'Are We Automata?'. Available at http://psychclassics.yorku.ca/James/automata.htm

p. 333   *is wrong*: Mackenzie, *The Trial of Harry Thaw*, pp. 170–5

p. 334   *dragon*: New York Times, 22 March 1907

p. 334   *community*: Mackenzie, *The Trial of Harry Thaw*, p. 182

p. 335   *every way*: Langford, *The Murder of Stanford White*, p. 202

p. 336   *human laws*: Mackenzie, *The Trial of Harry Thaw*, pp. 191–2

p. 336   *allowed him*: Quoted in ibid., p. 192

p. 340   *sob sisters*: Jean Marie Lutes, 'Sob Sisterhood Revisited', *American Literary History*, vol. 15, no. 3 (fall 2003), pp. 504–32, 504

p. 340   *honor*: Quoted from the *New York Evening Journal* in the *Pittsburgh Gazette*, 25 January 1907

p. 341   *did then*: Helena Kennedy, *Eve Was Framed* (London: Vintage, 2005), pp. 96ff

p. 342   *heard it*: See Jean Marie Lutes, *Front-Page Girls*, for an in-depth account of the women reporters' points of view on the case, pp. 60ff

p. 344   *Thaw trial*: Cited by Pinta, *Paranoia of the Millionaire*, p. 24

p. 345   *the question*: Britton D. Evans, 'Court Testimony of Alienists', *American Journal of Insanity*, vol. 66, New York State Lunatic Asylum, July 1910 (at Harvard University, digitized 3 April 2007), pp. 83–109, 92

p. 346   *humanity*: Ibid., pp. 90–1

p. 350   *affections*: See Estela V. Welldon, passim, for the mother–child relations that can feed into criminality

p. 353   *prisoner*: New York Times, 21 January 1908

p. 354   *insanity*: New York Times, 29 January 1908; also Mackenzie, *The Trial of Harry Thaw*, p. 235, and Pinta, *Paranoia of the Millionaire*, p. 26

p. 355   *delusional suicide*: Emil Kraepelin, *Manic-Depressive Insanity*, trans. R. Mary Barclay, (Edinburgh: E. & S. Livingstone, 1921), pp. 19–24 passim, 220–9, 267, 275. Available at http://www.archive.org/details/manicdepressivei00kraeuoft

p. 357   *motives as these*: Mackenzie, *The Trial of Harry Thaw*, pp. 243–4

p. 359   *mountains*: New York State Archive

p. 360   *creatures*: Langford, *The Murder of Stanford White*, p. 240

p. 362   *may be*: Mackenzie, *The Trial of Harry Thaw*, p. 249

p. 362   *of the law*: Outlook Magazine, cited in Langford, *The Murder of Stanford White*, p. 58

p. 362   *prevent it*: Mackenzie, *The Trial of Harry Thaw*, p. 254

p. 362   *kill her*: New York Times, 21 June 1912

p. 363   *confident*: New York Times, 19 June 1912; also 30 June 1909

p. 364   *violence*: New York Times, 30 July 1909

p. 365   *community*: New York Times, 19 June 1912

p. 367   *his client*: New York Times, 20 June 1912

p. 367   *habeas corpus*: Cited by Pinta, *Paranoia of the Millionaire*, p. 49

p. 368   *unawares*: New York Times, 18 August 1913

p. 368   *very insane*: Mackenzie, *The Trial of Harry Thaw*, p. 275

p. 370   *is insane*: New York Times, 10 July 1915

p. 373   *I lived*: Pinta, *Paranoia of the Millionaire*, p. 56

p. 373   *bill collectors*: Uruburu, *American Eve*, p. 269

p. 375   *displeasure*: Quoted by Mackenzie, *The Trial of Harry Thaw*, p. 299

p. 375   *any sense*: See William A. White, *Outlines of Psychiatry* (New York: Nervous and Mental Disease Publishing Company, 1915), chapter 1 and passim; and White, *Insanity and the Criminal Law* (New York: Macmillan, 1923), chapter 9

p. 376   *psychological level*: Bernard Glueck and William A. White, *Studies in Forensic Psychiatry* (Boston: Little Brown, 1916), p. 1

p. 377   *social liability*: Grob, *Inner World of American Psychiatry, 1890–1940*, pp. 284 and below 285

p. 378   *electric chair*: In an interesting note on psychiatric history, Dr Jones, who had examined Capote's cold-blooded murderers and was an expert witness at their trial, consulted with the veteran psychiatrist Dr Satten. The latter concurred with his assessment of the two murderers – paranoid, with low self-esteem and an inability to contain impulses. He co-authored a 1960 article with the very same Karl Menninger who sent White the psychiatrists' Credo. By then, Menninger was the doyen of the premier clinic and training centre that bore his name in Topeka, Kansas. In 'Murder without Apparent Motive', *American Journal of Psychiatry* (1960), pp. 48–53, the authors write: 'In attempting to assess the criminal responsibility of murderers, the law tries to divide them (as it does all offenders) into two groups, the "sane" and the "insane". The "sane" murderer is thought of as acting upon rational motives that can be understood, though condemned, and the "insane" one as being driven by irrational senseless motives. When rational motives are conspicuous (for example, when a man kills for personal gain) or when the irrational motives are accompanied by delusions or hallucinations (for example, a paranoid patient who kills his fancied persecutor), the situation presents little problem to the psychiatrist. But murderers who seem rational, coherent, and controlled, and yet whose homicidal acts have a bizarre, apparently senseless quality, pose a difficult problem'

CODA

p. 379   *angel of law*: Rober Musil, *The Man without Qualities*, trans. Burton Pike (London: Pan Macmillan, 1995), p. 263

p. 382   *sentence*: See David Wexler and Bruce Winick, *Law in a Therapeutic Key: Developments in Therapeutic Jurisprudence* (Durham: Carolina Academic Press, 1996); Dawn Moore, 'Translating Justice and Therapy', *British Journal of Criminology*, 47 (2007), pp. 42–60

p. 384   *a year*: HBVA Honour Based Violence Awareness Network at HBV-awareness.com provides data on honour killings worldwide

p. 385   *so hated*: *Banaz – A Love Story*, directed by Deeyah, Fuuse Films

p. 386   *peril begins*: http://www.adoctorm.com/docs/tarasoff.htm, accessed 23 April 2013

p. 387   *1933*: See my *Mad, Bad and Sad* (London: Virago, 2008), pp. 305–8

p. 387   *Ireland*: Brendan D. Kelly, 'Erotomania: Epidemiology and Management', *Therapy in Practice*, vol. 19, no. 8 (2005), pp. 657, 668, 660

p. 389 *conduct*: http://www.trutv.com/library/crime/terrorists_spies/assassins/ john_hinckley/9.html, accessed 23 March 2013

p. 390 *brains*: 'How to Spot a Murderer's Brain', *Observer*, 12 May 2013. See also Adrian Raine, *The Anatomy of Violence: The Biological Roots of Crime* (London: Allen Lane, 2013)

p. 390 *hard job*: http://www.trutv.com/library/crime/terrorists_spies/assassins/ john_hinckley/11.html, accessed 23 March 2013

p. 392 *campaign*: Sophie Goodchild, 'Stalking Victim Backs First Advice Service', *Evening Standard*, 9 May 2013

p. 392 *estimated*: http://www.victimsofcrime.org/library/crime-information-and-statistics/stalking#ftn1, accessed 14 October 2013

p. 394 *reconciliation*: Paul E. Mullen and Michele Pathé, 'Stalking', *Crime and Justice*, vol. 29 (2002), pp. 273–318; and Mullen, Pathé and Rosemary Purcell, 'The Management of Stalkers', *Advances in Psychiatric Treatment*, 7 (2001), pp. 335–42

p.394 *seeking*: S. Strand and T. E. McEwan, 'Violence among Female Stalkers', in *Psychological Medicine* (Cambridge: Cambridge University Press, 2011); DOI: 10.1017/S0033291711001498; J. Reid Meloy, Kris Mohandie and Mila Green, 'The Female Stalker', first published online 23 February 2011, DOI: 10.1002/bsl.976

p. 395 *victims*: Quoted in 'Do the New Stalking Laws Show We Are Taking This Crime Seriously?', *Guardian* blog post by Homa Khaleeli, 26 November 2012

p. 395 *social group*: Estela V. Welldon, *Playing with Dynamite* (London: Karnac Books, 2011) pp. 171–190

p. 396 *Richard III*: Freud, 'Some Character-Types Met with in Psycho-Analytic Work', in *Standard Edition of the Complete Psychological Works of Sigmund Freud*, vol. xiv (1916, 1925), pp. 311–14

p. 396 *gratifications*: I am grateful to the Australian psychiatrist Edwin Harari for his lucid exposition of this material in a lecture on personality disorders

p. 396 *executioner*: Steven Pinker, *Better Angels of Our Nature* (London: Allen Lane, 2011) p. 83

Select Bibliography

Bataille, Albert, *Causes Criminelles et Mondaines de 1880* (Paris: É. Dentu, Éditeur, 1881)

Berenson, Edward, *The Trial of Madame Caillaux* (Berkeley: University of California Press, 1992)

Berrios, G. E. and Roy Porter (eds), *A History of Clinical Psychiatry: The Origin and History of Psychiatric Disorders* (London: Athlone Press, 1995)

Bornstein, Brian H. and Richard L. Wiener, *Emotion and the Law: Psychological Perspectives* (New York: Springer, 2010)

Bynum, W. F., Roy Porter and Michael Shepherd (eds), *The Anatomy of Madness: Essays in the History of Psychiatry*, 2 vols (London and New York: Tavistock Publications, 1983)

Cherki-Nicklès, Claude and Michel Dubec, *Crimes et Sentiments* (Paris: Seuil, 1992)

De Clérambault, Gaëtan Gatian, *L'Érotomanie* (Paris: Les empêcheurs de penser en rond, 2002)

Downing, Lisa, *The Subject of Murder: Gender, Exceptionality and the Modern Killer* (Chicago and London: University of Chicago Press, 2013)

Dumas, Mireille, and Yann Queffélec, *Passions Criminelles* (Paris: Fayard, 2008)

Eigen, Joel Peter, *Witnessing Insanity: Madness and Mad-Doctors in the English Court* (New Haven and London: Yale University Press, 1995)

Foucault, Michel, *Madness and Civilization*, trans. Richard Howard (London: Random House, 1965)

— 'About the Concept of the "Dangerous Individual" in 19th-Century Legal Psychiatry', trans. Alain Baudot and Jane Couchman, *International Journal of Law and Psychiatry*, vol. 1 (1978), pp. 1–18

Freud, Sigmund, 'Psycho-Analytic Notes on an Autobiographical Account of a Case of Paranoia (Dementia Paranoides)' *SE*, 14, vol. 12 (1958), pp. 1–82

— 'Some Character Types Met with in Psycho-Analytic Work', *SE*, 14, vol. 14 (1957), pp. 309–32

Glueck, Bernard and William A. White, *Studies in Forensic Psychiatry* (Boston: Little, Brown & Co., 1916). Also available online at Project Gutenberg

Grob, Gerald N., *The Inner World of American Psychiatry 1890–1940: Selected Correspondence* (New Brunswick: Rutgers University Press, 1985)

— *From Asylum to Community: Mental Health Policy in Modern America* (Princeton: Princeton University Press, 1991)

— *The Mad Among Us: A History of the Care of America's Mentally Ill* (New York and London: Free Press, 1994)

Harris, Ruth, *Murders and Madness: Medicine, Law and Society in the Fin de Siècle* (Oxford: Clarendon Press, 1989)

Hartman, Mary S., *Victorian Murderesses: A True History of Thirteen Respectable French & English Women Accused of Unspeakable Crimes* (New York: Schocken Books, 1977)

Keeton, C. W., *Guilty but Insane* (London: Macdonald, 1961)

Kennedy, Helena, *Eve Was Framed: Women and British Justice* (London: Vintage, 2005)

Krafft-Ebing, Dr R. von, *Psychopathia Sexualis* (New York: Rebman Company, 1906)

— *Text Book of Insanity Based on Clinical Observations* (Philadelphia: n.p., 1905)

Langford, Gerald, *The Murder of Stanford White* (New York: Bobbs Merrill, 1962)

Leader, Darian, *What Is Madness?* (London: Hamish Hamilton, 2011)

Mercader, Patricia, Annick Houel and Helga Sobota, *À la vie, à la mort: psychologie du crime passionnel* (Paris: Presses Universitaires de France, 2008)

Mohr, James C., *Doctors and the Law: Medical Jurisprudence in Nineteenth-century America* (Oxford and New York: Oxford University Press, 1993)

Motz, Anna, *The Psychology of Female Violence: Crimes Against the Body* (Hove: Brunner-Routledge, 2001)

Nesbit, Evelyn, *The Story of My Life* (London: John Long, 1914)

— *The Untold Story* (London: John Long, 1934)

Norrie, Alan W., *Crime, Reason and History: A Critical Introduction to Criminal Law* (London: Weidenfeld & Nicolson, 1993)

Pinta, Emil R., *Paranoia of the Millionaire: Harry K. Thaw's 1907 Insanity Defence* (New York: Nova Science Publishers, 2010)

Schopp, Robert F., Richard L. Wiener, Brian H. Bornstein and Steven L. Willborn (eds), *Mental Disorder and Criminal Law: Responsibility, Punishment and Competence* (New York: Springer, 2009)

Seal, Lizzie, *Women, Murder and Femininity: Gender Representations of Women Who Kill* (Oxford: Palgrave Macmillan, 2010)

Shapiro, Ann-Louise, *Breaking the Codes: Female Criminality in Fin-de-siècle Paris*, (Stanford: Stanford University Press, 1996)

Smith, Roger, *Trial by Medicine: Insanity and Responsibility in Victorian Trials*, (Edinburgh: Edinburgh University Press, 1981)

Thaw, Harry K., *The Traitor: Being the Untampered with, Unrevised Account of the Trial and All That Led to It* (Philadelphia: Dorrance, 1926)

Unsworth, Clive, *The Politics of Mental Health Legislation* (Oxford: Clarendon Press, 1987)

Uruburu, Paula, *American Eve: Evelyn Nesbit, Stanford White, the Birth of the 'It' Girl, and the Crime of the Century* (New York: Riverhead Books, 2008)

Ward, Tony, 'Psychiatry and Criminal Responsibility in England 1843–1939', thesis, De Montfort University, Leicester, 1996

Welldon, Estela V., *Mother, Madonna, Whore: The Idealization and Denigration of Motherhood* (London: Karnac, 2004)

— and Cleo Van Velsen, *A Practical Guide to Forensic Psychotherapy* (London: Jessica Kingsley, 1997)

Wiener, Martin J., *Men of Blood: Violence, Manliness and Criminal Justice in Victorian England* (Cambridge: Cambridge University Press, 2004)

Index